Social Security

Social Security

The System That Works

MERTON C. BERNSTEIN

JOAN BRODSHAUG BERNSTEIN

Basic Books, Inc., Publishers
New York

Library of Congress Cataloging-in-Publication Data

Bernstein, Merton C.
  Social Security.

  Bibliographic references: p. 295.
  Includes index.
  1. Social security—United States.   2. Pension trusts
—United States.   3. Medicare—United States.
I. Bernstein, Joan Brodshaug, 1933–   .   II. Title.
HD7125.B48   1988   368.4'3'00973   86–47762
ISBN   0–465–07916–4

TO
Alpha and Melvin Brodshaug
and
Johanna Karin, Inga Saterlie,
Matthew Curtis, and Rachel Libby
Bernstein

Contents

Contents

Foreword

This book has a thesis: If people knew more about Social Security, they would be less anxious about its future; if they knew more about private retirement and state and local plans, they would be less complacent about their yield and reliability. More than that, we believe that the public and opinion makers should know more about Social Security, our most important and most pervasive domestic program, which touches everybody's economic lives, if not directly then indirectly.

The book is not an encyclopedia. Rather, it sticks to basics. That requires considerable selectivity and simplification. We are aware of the dangers of over-simplification and have endeavored to avoid them. We have sought to present arguments and evidence fairly, but we have emphasized arguments and data that have had little currency, particularly in the popular media.

Our principal effort is to present information pertinent to the overriding issue of Social Security—its reliability over the long haul. Second, we address the roles of other income maintenance systems to demonstrate the difficulties they present. That leads to a discussion of the major income maintenance choices, which should take account of the strengths and weaknesses of the several systems. The book concludes with a similar overview of Medicare. Of necessity, that last chapter must be more tentative because so much is changing and should change in the area of medical care. We hope to remedy some misconceptions and direct fresh attention to critical issues.

—MERTON C. BERNSTEIN

JOAN BRODSHAUG BERNSTEIN

St. Louis, Missouri

Acknowledgments

At the end of a movie, we always stay to read the credits. It is astounding how many minds and hands it takes to make a film. Books are lower budget and involve fewer people. Still, we hope that the audience reads book credits also, because we owe much to many.

First, the idea for this book originated with Martin Kessler, president of Basic Books. He kept urging that it stick to essentials and remain intelligible for the nonexpert reader.

Our indebtedness—and yours if the book succeeds to any degree—extends especially to those experts who read major portions of the manuscript. Chief among them is Robert M. Ball, Commissioner of Social Security under Presidents Kennedy, Johnson, and Nixon, America's most important architect, analyst, and defender of the Social Security system, and its endlessly patient exponent. Alicia Munnell, Senior Vice President and Director of Research of the Boston Federal Reserve Bank, and Joseph Grolnic, Senior Researcher there, also critiqued most of the manuscript. Footnote readers will see our great debt to Dr. Munnell's extensive writing on Social Security and on private, state, and local pensions. To all three, we offer our warmest thanks.

Other experts who generously shared their knowledge and provided welcome criticism included MCB's* colleague, Gary Boren, probably the nation's leading expert on legal aspects of deferred compensation; Edward Greenberg, Professor of Economics, Washington University; James Schulz, Professor of Economics at Brandeis University; Ray Schmitt, Social Legislation Specialist of the Congressional Research Service; and Professor Rashi Fein of the Harvard Medical School, all of whom devoted sizeable chunks of their summer vacations to the task. They are not only smart, but obviously very nice people.

* Merton C. Bernstein, one of the authors of this volume.

Acknowledgments

Virginia Reno of the Social Security Administration's Office of Research and Statistics repeatedly provided data and explanations of many excellent studies done in her shop, as did her associate Susan Grad, an expert on income of the elderly. Lawrence Atkins and Laura Erbs, professional staff members of the U.S. Senate Committee on Aging, repeatedly and rapidly supplied requested documents and information. Several members of the SSA Office of the Actuary rendered assistance when asked, including Harry Ballantyne, Chief Actuary, Francisco Bayo, Long Term Actuary, Stephen Goss, John Wilkin, and Bruce Schobel, the last of whom gave extensive help. Former Chief Actuary Robert Myers, who also served as Executive Director of the National Commission on Social Security Reform, repeatedly responded to inquiries, mostly by return mail, as seems his custom. These many individuals unselfishly shared their expertise and generously gave their time. They helped improve this effort. Naturally, we alone remain responsible for any errors.

Paul Nelson, Staff Director and Chief Economist of the U.S. House Committee on Banking, Housing and Urban Affairs constantly supplied a great array of documents pertinent to this undertaking.

We cite numerous authors of books and studies. Those citations should be read to include our great appreciation for the painstaking work done by their authors. We especially wish to mention two great sources of information: the Office of Research and Statistics of the Social Security Administration, whose *Social Security Bulletin* and many studies constitute the main body of statistical information about Social Security; and the Employee Benefit Research Institute, led by Dallas Salisbury, which has generated a great deal of valuable supplementary information about private retirement and deferred income programs.

The School of Law of Washington University provided inestimable help. Former Dean Hodge O'Neal and Dean Philip Shelton reduced MCB's non-teaching duties to a minimum so as to maximize book work time. Maria D'Agrosa-Sweney and Alice Gill, Washington University School Administrators, are the great facilitators of myriad support services. Librarian Bernard Reams, Reader Service Librarian Margaret McDermott, and Government Documents Specialist Carol Gray provided assistance beyond what mere words can describe.

Barbara Aumer, Bruce Ching, Ilse Arndt, and Mary Schelling performed miracles with their word processors, churning out and keeping track of innumerable drafts. They were fabulous. John Russo reproduced many versions of many chapters and, finally, the entire text—with speed and a smile. MCB's Secretary and coworker, Joanne Margherita, generated endless drafts, filed many cubic yards of documents, and coordinated the manuscript at several different difficult stages. Without her generous help this book would not have been ready until 1990! "Thank you" simply does not suffice. Research Assistant Robert Kerr ran down all sorts of information and produced the graphs.

Acknowledgments

Our children have listened to and joined in many discussions about various parts of the book. They were most patient with us and certainly understanding. Joan's parents, Alpha and Melvin Brodshaug, also lent their moral support, going back to their invaluable help more than twenty years ago when they made it possible for us to collaborate on *The Future of Private Pensions*.

We also received a great deal of help from many authors, most prominently Jane Austen, Anthony Trollope, and Mark Twain, who kept us reasonably sane during the many months of sometimes painful conception and delivery. They also helped replenish our stock of words; without them, we might have run dry.

We do not lay claim to being the second coming of Beatrice and Sidney Webb. But, working together has produced not only a book but great pleasure. We seldom complimented each other (although we sometimes did), but we always complemented each other—testing, strengthening, refining, and discarding ideas and contentions. We had some great arguments but also lots of fun and helped each other get through some boring and even trying times. Working together was a partial answer to the emptying of the nest.

Finally, we wish to thank Helen Kelley, the best of all neighbors, and our other neighbors for their patience. With the book done, the yard and lawn should start to look respectable again.

—J.B.B.

M.C.B.

Prologue: The Bad News and the Good News

Sooner or later, most of us will need retirement income. The good news is that we can depend on Social Security benefits to be there when we need them. Social Security benefits alone, however, will not enable most to maintain their accustomed living standards after retirement. So, supplementation is needed, either from private plans, savings, or a more generous Social Security program; otherwise many will face declining living standards throughout their older years. The bad news is that other retirement income plans are surprisingly less dependable. Many participants won't get benefits; for those who do, benefits will probably be degraded by inflation.

Medicare—the medical care portion of Social Security—faces two major problems: bringing program income into balance with program expenditures, and meeting the unsatisfied medical-care needs of an aging population. Chief among these unmet needs are methods to enable older people—and the disabled—to live independently and to avoid institutionalization as long as possible in the interests of human dignity and lower cost. That is no small order, but we must start to fill it.

While the great majority of Americans register their support for Social Security, many express doubt that the system will be able to meet its obligations in the next century. Some also express concern that, even if Social Security does make good on its promises, future beneficiaries will not get as good a deal as their parents and grandparents did. Some, especially the affluent, believe that they could do better on their own, that, unencumbered by mandatory Social Security payroll taxes, they could invest like amounts more advantageously.

1

Prologue: The Bad News and the Good News

In what follows, we show that the Social Security cash programs are in good financial health, that over the next few decades they will build up large reserves that will enable the Social Security cash trust funds to make good on the system's promises over the long term.

Given the commonly accepted view that Social Security is at best rickety and perhaps fatally flawed, all of this may seem too good to be true. Our first purpose is to provide fuller and more accurate information than most people now have. Part I describes what Social Security does and why, explains the "crisis" that Social Security passed through at the beginning of the 1980s, and analyzes what Congress did to restore it to both short- and long-term health. We find its problems less daunting than commonly supposed and conclude that Social Security's prospects are far more secure than most people expect. A chief goal is to demonstrate that the idea that a demographic trap awaits us in the next century is misconceived and—baldly put—mistaken.

In the 1970s, population projections for the next century prophesied that the older population, defined as age sixty-five and over, would expand in comparison with the working age population, defined as those age eighteen through sixty-four. From this simple "fact" many deduced that there would be too few young people to support too many old people, the "adverse dependency ratio." With the discouraging long-range future that so many accepted as inevitable, it was but a short step to deduce that in the early 1980s the sky was already falling.

This apparently compelling syllogism omits many relevant factors. Chapters 2 and 3 explain why the future of Social Security is as solid and assured as any human institution can be. The demographic death blow that some believed had already struck Social Security in the 1970s and early 1980s not only did not occur, but within the next few years, the less rapid growth of the elderly population and the relatively greater growth of the population in their middle years will produce fabulous and unprecedented surpluses in the Social Security cash program trust funds, surpluses that will balance the shortfall projected to begin in the third decade of the next century. Reserves would have accumulated even without the 1983 rescue package, fashioned in 1982–1983 by the National Commission on Social Security Reform, and enacted soon afterward by Congress. Those measures assured that the funds would weather the 1980s and created "close actuarial balance" between expected income and projected outlays for the remainder of the seventy-five-year term for which the Social Security actuaries make projections. More than that, we demonstrate that estimates of some key program factors have been unduly pessimistic. One in particular, the expected detrimental effect of greater use of fringe benefits, can be readily overcome by legislation we propose. This, and more realistic assumptions on immigration, should readily balance other factors that might be overly optimistic. Taking

2

account of these factors, future program income should be solid, reliable, and adequate.

A proper appreciation of Social Security's role also requires understanding the basic arrangements and limitations of other retirement income programs and several programs that masquerade as retirement programs. Part II describes group employment-based pension programs and unfrocks the programs that are nothing more than tax-favored deferred income schemes in pension clothes. Many are not in truth retirement plans but, more accurately, simply tax shelters for income of the financially most fortunate. The resulting tax losses increase deficits, limit needed programs, and impose larger tax burdens on the rest of us. Even real pension plans are in reality less extensive, less substantial, and less reliable than generally believed.

Social Security decision making is essentially democratic, subject to extensive study and debate with checks and balances of an economic as well as a political nature. In contrast, much private plan decision making is largely unseen and undemocratic. Those who make decisions frequently have interests at odds with the majority of beneficiaries. Attempts at congressional control often resemble the fitful efforts of "revenuers" whom moonshiners outwit with new dodges and hideouts. Problems and prospects for private plans are analyzed in part II.

Part III considers our major Social Security and private plan choices. It starts with a consideration of the context—the income and resources of the elderly. Contrary to a widely held impression, most of the elderly live on modest incomes, certainly less than what they themselves received when they were younger and employed. They may not have certain expenses of their younger days, but other expenses common to the elderly rise, while they lose advantages widely enjoyed by younger people. The small group of well-to-do beneficiaries pay taxes on half of their Social Security benefits, and so are not unduly enriched, as some complain. Part III demonstrates the indispensable retirement income role played by Social Security, and analyzes how it provides participants with their money's worth and deals fairly with both present and future generations.

The age at which the older worker retires is often not a matter of his or her choice. Health, employment policies, and the economy determine, to a considerable extent, the age at which a person retires. That age, in turn, affects the size of the benefit and the lifetime income derived from it. Congress, along with the press and general public, panicked in 1983 and made a serious mistake in raising normal retirement age in the next century. That mistake can be repaired—and should be.

Part III also considers whether private arrangements can, in some measure or combination, supplant Social Security in part or entirely. We conclude that such private arrangements are unreliable, and that they could not possibly displace

MANKOFF

Drawing by Mankoff; © 1985 The New Yorker Magazine, Inc.

or replace Social Security. Analysis of state and local government retirement programs leads to equally stark conclusions; several programs are accidents waiting to happen. The financial elite can and do stack private pension plans, IRAs, salary reduction plans, and Keogh plans for the self-employed one upon the other—sheltering income from taxes at the expense of those who cannot participate so extensively in such arrangements. That is not fair, nor is it good tax policy, and may even yield negligible additional savings. On top of that, conventional pension plans may discourage employment of older people while for employers Social Security is age neutral.

Not everything about Social Security is just right. Women have some proper concerns about how effectively their needs are met. Answers to some of those needs are in the making, but more money will be required to make them happen.

Part IV explores the theory and practice of Medicare and the special problems it faces—a burgeoning older population and exploding medical costs. We describe what is being done, and what more can be done, to provide adequate and affordable health care, independent living, and, when necessary, long-term institutional care for the elderly and the disabled.

Most people do not know—do not want to know—how fragile their family's economic health is. Given the low savings rate of Americans, few families have substantial personal reserves for periods of financial adversity. Adversity arises either from loss of current income or from unavoidably increased expenditures, frequently both. Income can drop through job loss, disability, or death of a

working family member, often a parent. Disablement often produces both reduced income and increased expenditures for medical care and other services
for the stricken person. Indeed, tending a disabled or dying family member
often reduces the income of others in the family who curtail their work to help
care for the victim. The death of a parent often means not only the loss of that
individual's earnings but also of his or her services, which other family members
must provide or purchase or do without. Retirement almost always means a
substantial drop in income.

We all live on the slopes of Mt. Vesuvius. Today we harvest grapes, but
at any moment the great volcano can erupt and destroy our fields, health, and
prosperity. Occasionally the mountain rumbles, but only rarely does it spew
death and destruction. Each day, however, lava seeps down, encroaching on
those nearest the edge of the crater. Most of us ignore that havoc and continue
to till our own acres. Most of us believe, along with the population of Hercu-
laneum, that Vesuvius won't erupt, that is until we see the lava and feel the
heat. Then we begin to understand what Social Security provides and why.

PART I

SOCIAL
SECURITY

1 Social Security: What and Why

Social Security is a program for all seasons. It provides a protective mantle not just for the elderly but for all generations, not just for the retired, but for almost everyone at work and for most of their family members as well, either directly or indirectly. It provides protection all of us need against income loss—when we work, when work is over, or when we depend upon the work of others. The benefit to all generations, and much else about Social Security, is not well or widely understood.

In early life, Social Security protects us against the economic calamity that accompanies the personal tragedy of a parent's death or severe disablement. Social Security benefits replace a portion of former earnings to sustain us and our family. When age compels our parents to cease working, Social Security provides them with income and Medicare provides a major portion of medical care. When one older parent dies, the survivor continues to draw Social Security benefits and obtain medical care under Medicare. And, when we ourselves reach retirement age, Social Security provides at least a basic income to sustain us and Medicare assures that medical care, hospitalization, surgery, or convalescent care will be forthcoming.

Many people, anxious about the decades ahead, however, are afraid that Social Security will not come through as it has in the past. Indeed, distrust and disbelief that Social Security will "be there when my time comes" pervade the press and public.

Social Security and Its Setting: 1935–1980

Enacted in 1935, Social Security was meant to alleviate the cruel poverty and despair in which so many elderly found themselves when no longer able to work. Heavy unemployment among the elderly and growing distaste for the county poor-house led to state legislation for old age pensions. State action was spotty, however, and the law generally required personal penury and a showing of inability of children to support their aged parents. Most importantly, many states had no such laws and those that did paid meager benefits.[1] With most states unable to pay even that, state resources were no match for the financial needs of the elderly.

Even before the program first made monthly benefit payments in 1940, Congress made some basic changes. In its original version, Old-Age Insurance Benefits were to provide only retirement benefits. But a 1937 advisory council, led by J. Douglas Brown of Princeton and Reinhard Hohaus of the Metropolitan Life Insurance Company endorsed the recommendations of the Social Security Board's Arthur Altmeyer and counseled that Social Security should provide social insurance protection for other family members—wives and children who also bear the brunt of income loss caused by retirement and death. Congress quickly agreed, thereby creating Old-Age and Survivors Insurance (OASI).

Moreover, the council agreed with those economists who urged that Social Security operate on a pay-as-you-go basis rather than building up large reserves. Such a change met the fear that substantial reserves would dampen the economy and avoided the problem of how the federal government should invest huge sums. It also enabled the system to start paying adequate benefits soon after its inception. Pay-as-you-go was adopted in practice but the law continued provisions to build reserves at later dates; Congress repeatedly postponed those increases.

Under pay-as-you-go, current employee contributions and employer payroll taxes roughly equal benefits paid and administrative expenses. A relatively small reserve tides the program over brief periods when collections temporarily fall short of payout. That small amount goes into a trust fund managed by the secretary of the Treasury (the managing trustee), the secretary of Health and Human Services (in that trustee's current incarnation), and the secretary of Labor; the 1983 amendments provided for two public members in addition. The managing trustee pays out benefits at the beginning of each month and issues special obligation bonds to the trust fund equal to any amounts unused for benefit or administrative purposes. Those bonds can be cashed in without

10

penalty whenever needed; hence the "special obligation." The reserve, though small, does not remain idle: the trust lends funds to the U.S. government for its operations and collects interest on the money lent.

For most of its first three decades, Social Security financing caused much discussion but few operational problems. Many had difficulty accepting the pay-as-you-go concept and felt uneasy about the lack of a "mammoth fund" to secure promised payments. Through 1949 the payroll tax remained low—1 percent of taxable income. Benefits were also modest and, because of the small number of persons eligible for benefits, total payout was small. Tax collections annually exceeded outgo and the trust fund grew modestly.

Following World War II, the economy experienced the beginning of an economic revolution. Employment remained high, incomes rose, production boomed, millions bought homes and appliances and cars, many children from formerly poor families finished high school, went on to college, and some entered the professions. Despite anxiety and recurrent recessions, the bulk of the population experienced their first taste of economic comfort. Although affluence still lay ahead, new economic aspirations and even expectations stirred. Organized labor gained political and collective bargaining power. Employers, revived by war production and the postwar Niagara of consumer purchasing, concentrated on making products and money, granted high wages, and established and expanded paid vacations, sick pay, and health insurance not only to executives and managers but also to rank-and-file working people. America's foreign trade flourished. Ours was the only major economy intact—we generously aided the reestablishment of Europe's economy, at least up to the Iron Curtain, and we quickly became the world's largest producer and merchant.

In the late 1940s, some of these developments led to union demands for private employer-financed group pension plans for workers to augment modest Social Security benefits. Then, acting on the blueprint provided by a Social Security advisory council in the late 1940s, Congress in the early 1950s revised Social Security, seeking to make up for a decade in the doldrums. Coverage expanded during the 1950s to include all of industry, the armed forces, the self-employed on a mandatory basis, and—on an optional basis—state and local government and nonprofit institution employees. The taxable earnings base moved from $3,000 to $3,600 in 1951 and $4,200 by 1955. The employee contribution rate and the employer payroll tax went to 1.5 percent in 1950 and 2 percent by 1955. Minimum and average benefits increased rapidly. The trust funds continued to run annual surpluses and to build reserves.

The 1950s, despite the Korean War and recessions, saw the beginnings of general affluence. Not all participated equally and some were left behind, but wages, earnings, incomes, consumption, aspirations, and expectations all rose. The nation launched the interstate highway system, the largest public works project in the history of humankind. A powerful economy supported unprecedented levels of living.

Private employment-based health insurance expanded, usually paid by employer contributions with some employee contributions as well. Social insurance also grew. Unemployment insurance increased coverage and the duration and level of benefits. State workers' compensation laws, designed for work-connected injury, became universal by the end of the 1940s, when a few stragglers finally adopted them; but many states limited benefits and their duration and provided sparse coverage for illness.

In the mid-1950s, Congress resolved a continuing debate by establishing the Social Security Disability Insurance (DI) program. First limited to those fifty and over when originated in 1956, by 1960 it insured all those who worked under Social Security for extensive periods. The new program added a trust fund for DI with its own modest and separate payroll tax of .25 percent (one-fourth of 1 percent), collected along with the OASI tax. OASI became OASDI. The maximum amount of earnings subject to tax grew to $4,800 and, as the 1950s closed, the payroll tax rose to 3 percent. Benefits for women as workers and wives also improved, as did minimum benefits.

By 1960, OASDI had grown into a major program with widespread support in the populace and among politicians—at least Democratic politicians. Most Republicans remained opposed or wary;[2] the business community was concerned about the bite of the payroll tax and the growth of so large a public program. Benefits for all in this period remained modest.

Since then, benefits have improved and become inflation-proof. They now provide the major source of income for the retired and for survivors. To meet the costs of increased benefits and the introduction of Medicare in 1966, Congress raised payroll taxes and the amount subject to such taxes. Most people did not mind.

In the 1980s, with the postwar boom past and productivity fluctuating, Americans, having weathered two oil crises and endured several recessions, are not as optimistic as they used to be. While Social Security retains massive public support, there exists considerable concern over whether we can continue to afford it, whether future generations of retirees can depend on it, and whether it gives us our money's worth.

Social Security—the Grand Design

The design of Social Security responds to pervasive practical problems and embodies a clearly defined philosophy. Every member of society depends upon current money income; the great majority live upon earnings derived from current work, either one's own or another family member's. But common risks—injury, illness, unemployment, death, or retirement—threaten that income stream. When a parent dies, income provided by that parent ends. So it is with injury and illness of any substantial duration. Retirement (whether by choice or necessity) stops or reduces income derived from work. Social Security benefits provide a partial substitute for lost income when these common hazards of life occur.

Social Insurance

Social Security is a social insurance system. Employees pay contributions, matched by equal amounts from employers. These amounts earn eligibility, much as insurance premiums do. But, as *social* insurance, the recipients and amounts of benefits are determined in part by family relationships and common needs, factors that private insurance usually ignores.

Social Security provides a partial income substitute as a return for past work and contributions rather than "demonstrated need." Demonstrated need means, in effect, turning one's purse inside out and spreading out personal papers (bank accounts, insurance) for some official to measure against a yardstick by which a legislature defines "need." That is how the "needs-tested" (or "welfare") programs proceed—by ascertaining the income and assets of the elderly, the disabled, and families with dependent children.

Social Security avoids needs or means testing for several very good reasons. Administering such needs-test procedures increases program costs prodigiously. While the Social Security cash programs (for retirees, survivors, the disabled and their families) incur slightly more than 1 percent of payments for administrative expenses, Supplemental Security Income (SSI), which pays benefits to a comparable population but on a needs-tested basis, costs 7.05 percent to operate.[3] Additionally, designers and defenders of the Social Security program argue that the program does not require needs testing because most recipients do in fact need a substitute for lost earnings in order to maintain living standards.

The system can dispense with a needs test because, among other reasons,

Social Security pays its own way from funds provided primarily by contributions by employers, employees, and the self-employed; not everyone knows that Social Security is self-sustaining. Having paid contributions throughout their working life, recipients regard benefits as earned. Benefits derive from deferred pay earned quite as much as our cash pay. In a sense, all of us who work maintain and build the economy from which benefits are ultimately derived. Further, the absence of a needs test encourages savings to supplement program benefits. Were a needs test used, many would not save and some would even "spend down" in order to qualify.

The absence of a means test and the view by most people that they earn their benefits are factors that undoubtedly account for the enormous popularity of the system.

Universality

Social insurance programs operate most efficiently when they apply to the entire population at risk. Originally, the Social Security system covered about 60 percent of the working population, but subsequent changes extended coverage. By 1986, it covered 95 percent of the working population. The only significant groups remaining outside of Social Security coverage are some public employees: the minority of employees of state and local governments that have not chosen such coverage and those employed by the federal government prior to 1984. Inasmuch as those newly employed in the federal civil service after 1983 are covered, the federal government category constitutes a slowly shrinking area of noncoverage. Members of the armed forces are covered.

As an employment-based system that meets employment-associated risks, Social Security does its job best when it applies to all work. People do not stay put in their jobs and jobs do not stay put either. Hence, when Social Security applies to all employment, employees build their eligibility and credits wherever they work. Universal coverage also enables the benefit formula to operate according to its design, because the weighting of the benefit formula works properly only if all work counts in computing benefits. Throughout our working lives, we have little certainty of where we will find work and how long any job will last. Inasmuch as we do not know when we will move from one risk category to the next, we all share in the advantages of universal coverage. The economy works best when working people can be readily redeployed according to their inclinations and the need for their skills. This adaptability is one of the great strengths of the U.S. economy. Social Security frees employees to move as opportunity offers; it presents none of the disincentives to move and adapt that private and government employee plans often involve. Social Security lubricates where many other plans put sand in the gears.

Universality also protects against "adverse selection," the process by which private plans selectively cover those, such as the young, who cost least to insure for health care and to cover for a retirement program, leaving the high-risk, high-cost people to some other plan whose cost will necessarily be higher.

Since older age tends to increase costs of health care insurance (owing to greater susceptibility to disease, longer exposure to accidents and hazards of the workplace and life) and cause progressively higher cost for pension coverage, a system that spares us discrimination based upon age-associated costs of insurance coverage works to everyone's advantage. Age discrimination in employment, by reducing the productive potential of older workers and increasing their unemployment, raises the cost of supporting the unemployed elderly for the community. The country loses production while experiencing higher costs to provide sustenance and care.

Near-universal coverage constitutes one of Social Security's great strengths. This contrasts with the partial and uneven coverage of private plans and of state and local government employee programs for retirement income.

Where Social Security Money Comes From

Some 95 percent of the work force pays into and is "covered" by Social Security, and this group is growing progressively larger as more federal employees join the Social Security system.

Payroll Taxes and Other Sources

The employee and employer in covered employment must each pay equal amounts of payroll tax on taxable earnings. The employee then gains credit toward eligibility for a variety of benefits. Back in the 1940s, taxable pay was $3,000 annually per employee; by 1987, that amount had risen to $43,800. Each year the taxable (and so creditable) amount is adjusted automatically by the percentage by which the national average wage increases. Each individual pays FICA (Federal Insurance Contributions Act) taxes of 7.15 percent on his or her creditable/taxable earnings; the employer pays an equal amount.

Under SECA (the Self-Employed Contributions Act) self-employed persons, in effect, pay the combined employer/employee rates, or 14.30 percent of earnings, including HI (Hospital Insurance under Medicare) with the proceeds credited in like shares to the three trust funds. For the remainder of the 1980s, the self-employed will receive a tax credit for a portion of their remittance.

15

Starting in 1990, half of the total will be treated like the employer's share and so will be deductible as a business expense for tax purposes.

Almost all of the revenue of the OASDI fund comes from payroll taxes and interest earned by the trust funds. Further, the 1983 amendments channel into the trust funds the income tax derived from taxing up to half the benefits of high-income beneficiaries.

Revenue for Medicare Part A (HI) comes from a portion of the payroll tax. Medicare Part B, Supplementary Medical Insurance (SMI), derives from premiums paid by those over sixty-five who choose coverage (25 percent) and general revenue (75 percent).

The trust funds earn revenue through the investment of trust funds in special obligation bonds, interest-bearing loans to the U.S. Treasury.

The Contributory Principle

A key element of the program is that employee contributions help fund program benefits. Those contributions serve several major purposes. In the first place, employees contribute roughly half the revenue of the cash programs and HI, providing essential fuel to make the programs run. Earmarking those and employer contributions assures a flow of revenue to pay benefits. Very importantly, employee contributions give participants the knowledge that they have helped finance their benefits. Such contributions also help to resist a needs test as the basis for benefit eligibility. These elements give beneficiaries a sense of dignity that may be the most important feature of the program. The subtraction of employee contributions every payday, listed weekly on their pay stubs and annually on their W–2 tax forms, induces a sense of restraint produced by the realization that benefits cost them money and that higher benefits would require higher contributions and so reduce pay. However, earmarked taxes that produce known benefits also seem to be more generally acceptable than other taxes. Some middle- and upper-income earners resent the increases in the amount of their pay subject to tax. They possibly regard these as tax increases though the adjustments do no more than keep taxable payroll in step with average pay. Also, many such taxpayers do not know how valuable their benefits are and that higher taxable pay results in higher benefits (more on the relationship of contributions to benefits shortly).

Equal contributions by employers probably tend to have a quite similar effect, perhaps engendering more resistance because the employers do not benefit directly. Employers do benefit, indirectly, from the entire program, because Social Security benefits facilitate retirement and put vast purchasing power in the hands of millions. Most economists regard employer contributions as employment costs that otherwise would go to employees as cash pay or other benefits.

Most current beneficiaries, of course, do not make current contributions and so are not subject to the same restraint in their demands upon the programs. However, as former contributors to the program, their earlier FICA pay deductions and SECA contributions should sensitize them to the costs of Social Security.

At any one time, working contributors outnumber beneficiaries and will continue to do so. Politicians find this fact sobering: the antipathy to raising contributions balances beneficiary interests in improving benefits. In the 1980s, Congress has exhibited great reluctance to boost rates. So, earmarked contributory taxes work in two ways: they make taxation for the program more acceptable than other taxes, but they also restrain demands for program improvements.

The contributory principle lives—and works.

Earned Income Credit Makes Payroll Tax More Progressive

For some reason, the earned income credit seldom figures directly in discussions of Social Security, although it plays a major role for low earners. Its main purpose is to ease the impact of the payroll tax. Low-paid married people or household heads with children receive a credit against their taxes; the credit is greatest for those with low taxable income and decreases as earnings get higher.

The Tax Reform Act of 1986 relieved millions of low-income earners from the federal income tax by increasing personal exemptions which will move in concert with inflation. In addition, it expanded the Earned Income Credit to 14 percent of earnings up to earnings of $5,714, lifting the maximum credit from $550 to $800. And, at lower percentages, starting in 1988, it will reach up to $17,000 (up from the 1985 level of $10,999). On top of that, these amounts will adjust with inflation. Taxpayers with children and earnings whose tax liability falls below the amount of the credit receive the difference between the credit and their tax liability as a "refund." In sum, the Earned Income Credit does what it is supposed to do—cushion the impact of the FICA tax on millions of families with low and modest income.

Those amounts often more than offset the employee's FICA contribution. Indeed, for some, they offset part of the employer's contribution as well. If, as many believe, the employer's contribution would be spent for compensation, these employees recapture a portion of that otherwise foregone pay.

The earned income credit recognizes the FICA tax burden on low-paid parents and so spares those with income of $6,500 or less, an amount of income tax roughly equivalent to the FICA tax (and sometimes more). Indeed, many who pay little or no income tax receive refunds. This arrangement serves several purposes. As income tax policy, it reduces the total tax burden of low-paid people with children. By preserving the FICA contribution in full, however, the device maintains restraints associated with the Social Security contributory principle. In addition, it makes the FICA tax more progressive for families with children, a group with greater need for current income than others of their age. And the device rewards paid work.

The earned income credit explains why many pay larger FICA taxes than income taxes. Not infrequently, this fact is described as if it were a dreadful, unintended outcome as in: "Why, many people pay more in Social Security tax than income tax!" But it's not just some dumb mistake; it's the way it is meant to be. When the purposes of the earned income credit are seen and understood, both Social Security and the income tax look more sensible.

And Where the Money Goes—Cash Benefits

Benefits are earnings-related but not directly proportional to credited earnings. Two major principles—"equity" and "adequacy"—underlie the benefit formula so as to reward higher earnings and contributions with larger benefits but also to replace a larger portion of low earnings. These principles derive from two fundamental ideas. First is that one's own effort should be rewarded; this supports equity. Second, low-paid people need benefits to replace a high proportion of former earnings; they require all or most of their earnings to pay for necessities and are least likely to accumulate other retirement benefits or significant savings. To promote benefit adequacy, the benefit formula is weighted in favor of the less well paid. In addition, because family composition results in differing income needs, OASDI provides both "primary benefits" to the insured worker and "auxiliary benefits" to other family members who presumably depend to some degree on the insured's earned income.

Primary Benefits for the Retired and Disabled

Social Security bases benefits on the average of covered lifetime earnings. Until the 1970s, a retiree's career earnings divided by the number of months he or she had worked (since 1950 or since turning twenty-one less the five poorest years) produced that person's Average Monthly Wage. A benefit formula was applied to that average monthly wage to determine what portion would be replaced by the benefit. For those with low average wages or salary, the benefit replacement was high. As one moved up the earnings scale, the benefit also went up, but replacement rate went down.

In 1977, Congress made a major change in figuring the average wage. In the post-war period, wages, salaries, and earnings had risen steadily, reflecting both inflation and, even more important, greater productivity and a general rise in living standards. Counting the amount of dollars from many earlier years produced average credited earnings well below the retiree's earnings just prior to retirement.

The remedy provided was brilliant, although complex. Past earnings are translated into their current equivalent which, when averaged (after dropping out the five poorest years), produces the Average Indexed Monthly Earnings (known as AIME). Then the Social Security Administration (SSA) applies the benefit formula (which also is adjusted to parallel the movements of average wages) to the AIME to ascertain the Primary Insurance Amount (PIA), that is, the insured person's basic benefit. For a person who always earned the average wage, and retires at sixty-five, the PIA replaces about 42 percent of former average earnings. People with lower than average former earnings get a benefit replacing a higher percentage of former earnings; people with above-average earnings get a smaller portion of prior earnings. (To see in more detail how this works out, consult appendix A which follows this chapter.) The differences between lower- and upper-income participants are smaller than the benefit formula might appear to provide. Working out the actual numbers shows that the insured persons in the middle and upper bands of the benefit formula do better than the marginal rates might initially lead one to believe. In fact, middle- and upper-income earners often fare better than the benefit formula suggests because of "auxiliary benefits" and the more generous family maximums for middle- and high-income earners. In addition, most people start benefit receipt before age sixty-five with actuarially reduced benefits, and so obtain rates of replacement below those indicated by the formula. Many higher earners do not retire early, however, and so obtain unreduced benefits. These factors can narrow the difference between the percentage of former average pay provided by benefits for the low-paid and the middle-income and higher earners, somewhat offsetting the weighting in favor of the low-paid.

Auxiliary Benefits

When an insured worker retires, a spouse aged sixty-five or more becomes eligible on the insured worker's record for a benefit of 50 percent of the insured worker's PIA. The spouse qualifies for this benefit at age sixty-two (if the insured has retired), but with a 25 percent reduction below what it would be if first drawn at age sixty-five. The spouse's benefit begun at ages *between* sixty-two and sixty-five is reduced proportionally. No showing of dependency is required. Rather, the law assumes the mutual dependence of husband and wife. The low savings rates of Americans demonstrate that most families spend all or most of currently earned income for housing, food, and other essential and shared purposes. If one parent stays home in order to care for home and children, not only do all family members share current income, they also depend upon the services of the partner who ceases or curtails paid employment. For all or most of their minority, children depend upon the earnings of parents. Assumed dependence of members of nuclear families seems realistic.

At the specified age, a married person gets the PIA generated by his or her own earnings record and, if the spouse's benefit would produce more, an additional amount to equal that higher amount. One-fourth of wives retiring in 1982 found that benefits under their own records exceeded their spouses' benefits. (That group should grow as more women spend more years working for pay and differences between pay to men and women narrow.) Another 13 percent whose husbands had not retired received benefits based on their own account. Among married new beneficiaries in 1982, 35 percent received only the spouse's benefit.

When widowed, the survivor becomes eligible at age sixty for a benefit equal to the deceased partner's PIA, and, at sixty-two, a supplement if that benefit exceeds the benefit provided by his or her own earnings record. In 1982, one-fourth of the new beneficiaries were widows. Thirty percent of the widows first receiving benefits in 1982 drew only on their own accounts rather than on their deceased spouses'. With men, it is usually, but not always, the reverse— they do better by drawing solely on their own work records. One advantage of each partner drawing on his or her own account is that if one's spouse's earnings produce a benefit reduction under the earnings test, that reduction does not reach the benefit based on one's own earnings.

A "young widow," one below the age of sixty, qualifies for a survivor's benefit if she has minor or disabled children in her charge. Each child seventeen years or younger is eligible for a child survivor's benefit of 50 percent of the dead parent's PIA. Widowers get the same benefits as widows.

Auxiliary benefits push the replacement rate above that provided by the PIA alone. Two principles interplay. Low-income earners obtain higher replacement rates and so their basic benefits start closer to former earnings and their auxiliary benefits approach the family limit more rapidly than those with higher earnings. The PIA replaces a smaller portion of the former earnings of middle- and high-income earners; the more generous family maximums for middle- and high-income earners and the greater use and frequency of eligibility for the spouse's benefit moderate the weighting in favor of low-income earners in the benefit formula for PIA.

"Weighting" and "family maximums" are important ingredients of the benefit formula, and their principles and how they work in practice should be kept in mind; the precise formulas need not be.

The Disability Insurance (DI) program pays like benefits to eligible insured and family members.

Minimum Benefits

Formerly, OASDI paid one of two minimum benefits to new retirees. The notion underlying these minimums was that a person who worked long enough to qualify should obtain at least a moderate benefit. (See "Eligibility for Benefits" in the next section.) In the early 1980s, the minimum applicable to most primary beneficiaries and surviving elderly widows was $122. Many will regard $122 as a pittance; but on a relative basis, it was a substantial pittance. That minimum was "frozen" in 1977 and would have become unavailable to new retirees in a few decades.

Some opponents argued that most who qualified for that minimum had spent very little time working under Social Security. It was theoretically possible for a person in his or her early fifties who had not worked or had worked outside Social Security previously to work part-time for a relatively short time and ac-cumulate the necessary quarters. It was argued that those who qualified for the minimum did so by satisfying the formality but not the spirit and the purpose of the minimum provision. Arguably, then, that minimum was being misused. In 1981, in response to President Reagan's proposal, Congress voted to abolish it outright, ending the minimum to those receiving it and denying it to those who subsequently would have qualified.

Some congressional Democrats, however, launched a counter-offensive, aided by organized labor and groups representing the elderly. Their figures showed that women were the most usual recipients of the minimum and that many were on the margins of poverty. The upshot was a restoration of the minimum to those who had been receiving it or would become eligible that year; those who reached sixty-two after 1981 do not qualify for it.

But another "special minimum," about which many people are not in-formed, designed for *long service* but low-earning Social Security participants, survived. Under this provision coverage for eleven years yields an extremely small minimum benefit—$19.40 in 1987. But for those with sixteen or more years of service with minimum covered earnings, the "special minimum" produces more substantial benefits: a PIA of $115.80 for the sixteen-year participant; a

PIA of $385.80 (with a family maximum of $579) for the thirty-year participant and who retires after 1986. While below the average benefit, these special minimums do reward low earners with *long*-term program participation.

Cost-of-Living Adjustment (COLA)

Constructing the PIA by translating past wages into their current equivalent and making similar adjustments in the benefit formula insures that the value of credits reflects movements in earnings close to the time of retirement, disability, or death. In that fashion, when benefits begin, they reflect recent earnings and help achieve the replacement rate sought.

Why a COLA for Benefits? After retirement, cost-of-living adjustments maintain the purchasing power of benefits. Without COLA the purchasing power of benefits would erode and the replacement rate decline.

Maintaining the purchasing power of benefits becomes crucial to benefit adequacy in an economy where price inflation has been unremitting for almost two generations. If benefit amounts remain the same from the time they begin, their value dwindles as prices increase. Since 1940, the Consumer Price Index (CPI) frequently increased more than 5 percent a year. (A useful rule of thumb to calculate the impact of inflation is: a 4 percent annual price increase for fifteen years cuts benefit value almost in half.) Without COLA, beneficiaries would suffer constant financial demotion.

When we work, most of us have a fighting chance to keep pace with inflation through better pay, promotions, overtime, moonlighting, and other family members going to work. As age reduces strength, stamina, or the marketability of our skills, those options diminish or disappear. The disabled and their spouses seldom have such options. Surviving children usually must concentrate on schooling. Surviving spouses with children usually must limit work activity because of family obligations, obligations greatly increased by the loss of a partner. Moreover, second pensions—for those lucky enough to have them—seldom protect their benefits against inflation.

Prior to 1975, to avoid attrition in the value of benefits, Congress periodically increased benefits by specified across-the-board percentage increases (often accompanied by a somewhat more generous boost in the minimum). For the most part, such improvements initially exceeded the preceding CPI increases, but in the succeeding period, prices often overtook benefits again. Higher prices and increased benefits did not move hand-in-hand; they played leap frog.

In the period 1952–72, Congress voted eight such increases. All raised benefits somewhat more than prices except for the 1959 and 1965 increases, which never did overtake inflation. As poverty rates among the elderly were disturbingly higher than among other population groups, several increases were meant to improve the purchasing power of benefits. A 12.5 percent net increase in 1954 and a 14.1 percent net increase in 1972 were dramatic and substantial increases, but each of those was followed by two-year periods during which the price increases again outdistanced benefits.

The history of irregular and unpredictable cost-of-living adjustments set the stage for "automatic" benefit increases. Leading Republicans viewed provisions to "index" benefits to the CPI as a measure to protect against irregular but overly generous improvements by Congress.

How COLA Works.   In 1972, Congress provided that, starting in 1975, cash benefits would rise with the CPI whenever it rose by at least 3 percent. In 1986, Congress legislated full COLA regardless of the amount of CPI change.

Ordinarily, COLA's additional cost to the trust funds is offset by larger increases in payroll taxes because wages tend to rise more rapidly than prices do. Hence COLAs do not weaken system reserves except under rare and extraordinary income conditions. Moreover, increases from COLA are figured into financing of the program so they need not be the unexpected, additional costs many apparently believe them to be.

Eligibility for Benefits

Eligibility for Social Security benefits requires long and substantial service in Social Security–covered work. Meeting the prescribed criteria demonstrates the individual's reliance on earnings. Such reliance warrants providing an income substitute to the earner and close family members who, it is reasonably presumed, share and rely upon that income, at least to some degree.

"Fully Insured," "Currently Insured," and "Disability Insured" Status

Long substantial work is demonstrated by achieving "fully insured" status. That means, in the main, one quarter of covered employment for each year elapsed since 1950 or when a person reaches age twenty-one (whichever comes later) until an insurable event—death, disablement, or reaching age sixty-two—occurs. Starting with those retiring after 1990, forty quarters will suffice.

For each $460 in covered earnings in 1987, a worker receives one quarter of credit, up to a maximum of four quarters. Prior to 1978, earnings in covered employment of $50 a quarter sufficed. The amount has moved up to reflect increases in creditable/taxable earnings. And it will continue to move in concert with average wages. The SSA actuary's "best guess" forecast predicts that in 1990 the amount required to earn a quarter of credit will be $520. Fully insured status qualifies the worker for all retirement and survivor benefits.

"Currently insured" status, which requires six quarters of coverage out of the most recent thirteen, is an alternative test that makes available survivor benefits to an insured person's children under eighteen years of age and to a spouse with a child under sixteen in his or her charge. The notion is that such concentrated recent earnings bespeak strong recent attachment to work and a contribution to the support of children and spouse. This kind of protection is akin to life insurance under which survivor benefits become payable as soon as the insured is accepted for coverage and pays the first premium. This status— achieved with relatively short service—is of special value to women, who often leave work for childbearing and rearing. Upon a woman's reentry into work for pay this rather quickly entitles her child to a survivor's benefit of 75 percent of her PIA at her death.

A fully insured person becomes "disability insured" after working in covered employment for twenty out of the preceding forty quarters. If younger than age thirty-one, one qualifies after having worked for at least six quarters and one half the quarters elapsed after age twenty-one.

Normal Retirement Age

"Normal retirement age" means the first age at which a person may retire and receive a full unadjusted benefit. From the outset of the program, that age has been set at sixty-five. Starting in 1956 Congress added early retirement for women at a lower age with a lower benefit; in 1961, men received comparable treatment. An insured person electing to start benefits at age sixty-two receives a benefit 20 percent lower than the benefit otherwise payable at age sixty-five. Theoretically at least, the OASI fund is unaffected by the age at which retirement begins for those sixty-two to sixty-five because the average *total* payouts begun at any one age equal the average started at any other age.

The Earnings/Retirement Test and the Delayed Retirement Credit

Few aspects of Social Security involve more misunderstanding than the "earnings test," also known as the "retirement test." The first name roughly describes what it does; the second name indicates why.

The most basic purpose of Social Security is to provide a substitute for earnings no longer received. Early in the program Congress specified the amount of employment earnings beyond which a person would not be considered retired. In response to popular demand, Congress repeatedly liberalized the figure. The earnings threshold used to demarcate employment from retirement now moves in parallel with the average wage of the general population.

As 1987 opened, the average retiree received $489 a month, or $5,844 for a year. For retirees sixty-five and older, no benefit reduction occurs until the individual earns more than $8,160. The benefit itself does not count as earnings.

For every $2 of earnings *above* the designated amounts, the benefit is trimmed $1. So, before earnings would wipe out benefits, earnings must exceed the threshold amount plus double the benefit. In 1987, a sixty-five-year-old retiree receiving average benefits lost no benefit at all until his or her income from earnings exceeded $8,160. A retiree receiving the maximum 1986 benefit of $789 a month ($9,468 for a year) could receive $17,628 from the combined benefit and earnings before losing any benefits because of earned income. All benefits would not disappear until earnings exceeded $27,096—a very substantial sum. Beyond that, however, a year without benefits earns a delayed retirement credit of 3 percent; in 1990 that credit will begin to increase, gradually reaching 8 percent by 2009. (The SSA actuary regards 8 percent as the full actuarial equivalent of benefits that start a year earlier.) Also starting in 1990, benefits for those retiring after the normal retirement age will be reduced by $1 for each $3 earned in excess of the test amount, thereby increasing the amount that can be earned and decreasing the amount of the benefit reduction. At age seventy the retirement test no longer applies. At that point, most people do not have earnings. Regulations governing substantial employment provide comparable results for the self employed.

The applications of the earnings test are somewhat complex and so may obscure OASDI's basic purpose—to provide a substitute for the earnings lost through retirement, death, or disablement. In the case of those drawing auxiliary benefits, earnings rebut the presumption, based upon the individual's relationship with the insured worker, that the person continues to be dependent. Some find fault with the earnings test without realizing how it works. As can be seen, it is extremely generous and will become more so.

These principles do not apply with absolute rigor. The age seventy cutoff for the application of the earnings test resulted from a political compromise to meet, at least in part, the objections of those who can and do continue to work, earn, and pay into the system.

Those with the greatest earnings potential also may feel disadvantaged by the retirement test because they see it as reducing their lifetime drawings from the system.

However, starting in 2009, when the 8 percent annual benefit improvement for delayed retirement reaches full effect, this will clearly not be the case. Each year without drawing benefits up to age seventy will increase benefits by the full actuarial value of the delay.

For the disabled, the earnings test is not meant to measure retirement but the capacity for substantial gainful employment. Passing that limit disqualifies the recipient except for trial work periods when the disabled person attempts to return to work.

Different Treatment of Investment Income

The earnings test takes no account of income derived from investments. Some complain that this differing treatment discriminates unfairly and unjustifiably against low-paid people who tend to have little or no investment income. However, the earnings test adversely affects few low-paid people because they seldom reach the limits on earnings. Moreover, investment income has no relevance to the purpose of the earnings/retirement test—it provides no indication of whether the individual is retired. By not taking account of unearned income, the Social Security retirement test encourages savings, a desirable objective. Finally, the partial taxation of benefits of those with high income takes account of investment income, and diminishes the disparity between the treatment of earned and unearned income.

Disability Insurance Eligibility

Congress added the Disability Insurance (DI) program in 1956. Many expressed concern that it might be expensive and overly generous because disability programs for the military and state and local governments' protective services frequently had not been stringent in conferring disabled status and benefits. In the 1920s, private insurers had sold such coverage at a loss to induce people to purchase life insurance. Hence their benefits outstripped premiums paid. Opponents of DI used that bad experience to argue against the program, and it proved a caution. As a result, Congress prescribed stringent eligibility requirements. It also provided for a separate trust fund to facilitate keeping tabs on the new program and to insulate OASI if DI turned out to cost more than contributions.

To qualify as disabled, one needs to demonstrate a physical or mental incapacity for "any substantial gainful employment." The theoretical ability to perform any kind of job that exists in the national economy in substantial numbers is the benchmark. Such jobs need not exist in the locality or, in fact, be open anywhere if they exist in substantial numbers around the nation. Nor does a denial of benefits require showing that if there were an opening for such a job the disabled applicant would be hired. It is a tough test designed to limit eligibility to those who lack the mental or physical ability to perform jobs that exist quite apart from the individual's actual employability, employment potential, or job openings. The statute calls for taking into account the individual's age, education, and experience in considering his or her residual capacity, and regulations prescribe less stringent criteria for applicants aged sixty or over. The residual capacity test is particularly hard on people with substantial education. The more schooling or training one has acquired, the greater the list of jobs that he or she theoretically might perform.

To qualify for disability benefits, one must be fully insured and have worked in covered employment for twenty of the last forty quarters before disability commences. Younger people, however, can become disability insured with fewer covered quarters commensurate with their more limited opportunities to work. The applicant must wait for five months after the disability begins before benefits start, a provision justified as a practical means of limiting benefits to the long-term disabled. At age sixty-five, DI retirees revert to OASI retirement, and they receive an unreduced retirement benefit; the years before sixty-five are not treated as early retirement.

Limited Taxation of Benefits

Prior to the 1983 amendments, no part of Social Security benefits was subject to federal income tax. As most states base their taxable income arrangements upon the federal law and computations, they, too, did not tax benefits as income.

The 1983 amendments made a limited change starting in 1984. If total income—from all sources—exceeds specified amounts—$25,000 for an individual and $32,000 for couples filing jointly—then up to one half of the Social Security cash benefit is subject to federal income tax. The tax applies only to income (counting half the benefit) that exceeds the threshold. The Treasury credits the proceeds of that tax to the OASDI trust funds, a unique arrangement that recaptures a portion of benefit dollars from high-income recipients and recycles them into the trust funds. The arrangement taps no existing source of tax revenue and subtracts from no other program. Only half the benefit is subject to tax because, as employees, beneficiaries paid their FICA contribution from taxed income; the employer's half of the FICA contribution is paid from pre-tax income.

In computing the $25,000 and $32,000 threshold amounts, *all* income counts. Individuals with substantial amounts of *earned* income tend not to be affected by the new tax arrangements because the earnings test reduces or elim-

27

inates their benefit in any event. The new arrangement bites for the first time at "unearned" income. For couples with one person retired and one at work, the latter's earnings, if substantial, can bring the tax into play.

Several policies underlie this new arrangement. The most basic is that all income should bear its appropriate tax burden. What is appropriate is determined by one's level of income; the ideal is that all persons with equal income, regardless of source, should bear equal tax burdens.

This notion justifies not continuing to exempt all Social Security benefits from income tax. It also justifies taking account of all other income in determining whether and how much of the Social Security benefit to tax. In consequence, the new arrangement requires that even otherwise tax-exempt income, such as interest payments on state and local bonds, be counted. This led to the false accusation that the Social Security Act subjects state and local bond income to taxation. In fact, no part of such income is subject to tax. For example, compare two couples both with combined income of $40,000 from all sources. One couple obtains $5,000 of that amount from tax-exempt bonds. Both couples would pay federal income tax on one-half their Social Security benefit to the extent that all income exceeds $32,000. But the couple with $5,000 of tax-exempt income would pay their federal income tax on $5,000 less than the couple without such exempt income. Because the threshold amounts of $25,000 and $32,000 are not indexed for inflation, the benefits of more and more beneficiaries will become subject to tax. This development moves Social Security toward parity with other retirement program benefits.

Some decry this change as improperly subjecting the needy to taxation. The simple answer is that this new element does not affect the needy any more than income taxation already does. Congress draws lines for imposing taxes and sets rates as matters of general tax policy. In line with general policy, Congress in 1986 excluded *all* low-income recipients from income taxation.

Others claim, however, that subjecting half the Social Security benefit to tax when total adjusted income exceeds specified amounts is, in effect, a needs test. The claim seems ill-founded for several reasons. In the first place, a needs test applies not only to income but to assets, an essential element in determining whether one is needy. The change in regard to Social Security benefits takes no account of assets. Second, none of the prying that accompanies need-testing programs comes into play.

Congress's speedy enactment of this new tax arrangement never took notice of its impact upon state taxation. As most states base their income tax on the federal returns, subjecting half the benefit to federal taxation resulted in making it taxable for state income tax purposes as well. Senior citizens protested, usually with success. As a result, most states continue to exempt Social Security benefits from their income tax.

Social Security Taxes and Trust Funds: Collection and Disbursements

Although deducted in one piece totaling 7.15 percent, the FICA tax really contains three separate contributions: the largest, 5.2 percent, goes to the OASI trust fund; another much smaller segment, 0.5 percent, is funneled into the DI trust fund; and the third, 1.45 percent, is earmarked for the HI trust fund (Medicare Part A). SECA, the tax for the self-employed, doubles these percentages.

In 1988 tax rates go up a notch to 5.53 percent (OASI) and 0.53 percent (DI); the HI tax remains at 1.45 percent. They will total 7.51 percent applied to creditable/taxable earnings. Present law provides for one more boost of OASDI tax rates in 1990, to 5.6 percent (OASI) and 0.6 percent (DI), for a final total of 7.65 percent. No further tax increases are scheduled and present estimates indicate the likelihood that no further increases in OASDI taxes will be needed for sixty-five years (discussed in chapter 3). The situation with HI gets more touch and go toward the end of this century (see chapter 11).

One more fund rounds out the picture: Supplementary Medical Insurance (SMI), or Medicare Part B, from which noninstitutional providers like doctors are paid. If current beneficiaries are sixty-five and older or disabled, they pay monthly premiums if they desire SMI coverage. Currently, in the late 1980s, the beneficiary monthly premiums are set to generate 25 percent of the cost of the program for old-age beneficiaries. In 1987, that amount was pegged at $17.90. The federal government contributes the remainder of the funds needed by SMI—some 75 percent of its cost—from general revenues.

Congress chose a separate trust fund for each program to enable monitoring of each kind of eligibility; separate funds make visible each program's income, outlays, and trends. However, OASI and DI have the same trustees: the secretaries of Treasury (the managing trustee), Labor, and Health and Human Services and two persons from outside government. The commissioner of Social Security acts as each board's secretary. Social Security's Office of the Actuary, after consultation with experts in the departments headed by government trustees, provides the OASDI and DI boards with actuarial data and analysis. The same cabinet officials function as trustees for the HI and SMI trust funds except that their secretary is the administrator of the Health Care Financing Administration (HCFA). HCFA's actuary keeps tabs on program elements peculiar to HI and SMI, using OASDI estimates for all elements common to the programs.

The Social Security Administration (SSA) maintains participants' records at its Baltimore headquarters. Working through its many local offices and traveling representatives, who appear regularly at various accessible places throughout the country, SSA processes applicants' claims for benefits. Verifying eligibility for retirement and survivorship benefits is relatively simple in most cases, because it depends primarily on the age of the participant, credited work (extracted from annual employer reports and entered on each participant's own record), and, for survivorship, the death of the insured worker, the relationship of the claimants, and their ages. Due to the objective nature of eligibility determinations, OASDI administrative costs only come to about 1.2 percent of benefit payments—a record unmatched in the private insurance industry. All of the programs pay their own administrative expenses from their respective trust funds.

Establishing DI eligibility is more complicated because of the need to make medical diagnoses which may themselves establish disablement and sometimes to ascertain the applicant's residual work capacity based on nonmedical factors such as training. State agencies make the initial determination which is subject to review and appeal.

Initial eligibility for HI benefits presents no difficulties once an applicant establishes eligibility for cash benefits and reaches age sixty-five or is approved for DI. The latter also requires a wait of twenty-four months before HI benefits become payable. SMI participation is available at age sixty-five even without HI eligibility. Determining the amounts due for services rendered by providers to Medicare participants, however, is another, much more complicated story (see chapter 11).

That is how Social Security is designed and works. The next step is to describe how it got into trouble and then out of it.

Appendix A: The Benefit Formula*

The benefit formula in 1987 was the total derived by separating an individual's Average Indexed Monthly Earnings (AIME) into three segments or bands and taking percentages from each band as follows:

* The source for both appendices A and B is 1987 *Trustees Report*, OASDI Trust Funds (Washington, D.C.: U.S. Government Printing Office, 1987), p. 115.

90 percent of the first $310 of AIME

plus 32 percent of AIME between $311 and $1,866

plus 15 percent of AIME above $1,867

(PIA) Primary Insurance Amount

So, *every* insured, not just the low paid, receives 90 percent of his first $310 of average monthly earnings, 32 percent of the next band, and 15 percent of any AIME amount above $1,866. Thus, replacement rates of AIME vary according to one's average former earnings. As can be seen, this formula is weighted in favor of lower earners, but all beneficiaries get the same amount of replacement for the same band of former earnings.

The relatively few people with average monthly earnings of $310, which produces an annual income of $3,720, probably work only part-time or part-year. So, the 90 percent weighting for this band of income—which goes to *all* earners—is a way of replacing a portion of very low income for people with somewhat higher earnings. As one goes up the income ladder, the replacement rate drops. A person with an AIME of $1,866 would obtain a PIA of $776 (90 percent of $310 plus 32 percent of $1,556—the amount in excess of $310), which replaces 42 percent of $1,866. Someone in the upper band obtains a benefit of $518, which replaces a lower percentage.

The amounts at which the "bands" change are known as the "bend points." The amounts and bend points change so as to keep them proportional with average wages.

Some proposals to cut benefits advocated reducing the size of one or both of the lower bands, that is, moving the "bend points." Most people had no idea what that meant. Those attempts did not succeed.

Appendix B: Formula for Family Maximums

Family maxima vary with the amount of PIA. The maximums for the second band are more generous than for the lowest because the lowest component of PIA is so heavily weighted for the lowest earners. Hence, the lowest earners' PIA takes them closer to former pay than the PIA of higher earners.

These abstractions take on more meanings if one looks at the formula for figuring the family maxima:

150 percent of the first $396 of PIA

plus 272 percent of PIA from $397 through $571

plus 134 percent of PIA from $572 through $745

plus 175 percent of PIA of $746 and above

2 What Went Wrong and How It Was Fixed

What people thought went wrong with Social Security in the early 1980s and what actually threatened differ appreciably. Talk of imminent bankruptcy and an increasingly unfavorable "aged dependency ratio" led to cries of "crisis" and "crash"; many believed that Social Security would sink under impossible burdens of an aging population. In fact, the danger was temporary and not systemic. And the financial problems faced by Social Security proved manageable with relatively slight adjustments and no basic redesign, except for raising the retirement age.

Most people don't know how the program was fixed, and many people doubt that it really was. This chapter describes the main reasons that Social Security cash programs got into financial trouble in the 1980s, why people thought Social Security was in more trouble than it was, what the bipartisan National Commission on Social Security Reform proposed, and what Congress did to fix it.

How Social Security Looks Ahead

To test how effectively the System will meet its obligations far into the future, the Social Security Administration's Office of the Actuary makes forecasts of the ensuing seventy-five years. Just as professional photographers bracket their best guess aperture with openings one stop above and one stop below, the actuaries make three sets of estimates and two versions of their central estimate. In all, the actuaries construct four sets of predictions: I—Optimistic; II-A—Central Optimistic; II-B—Central Pessimistic; and III—Pessimistic. II-B is widely regarded as "the best guess."

"Optimistic" and "pessimistic" in this context require explanation. Optimistic means developments that reduce program costs (and so increase trust-fund reserves), while pessimistic applies to factors that increase costs (and so reduce trust-fund reserves). If people generally live longer, good news to most of us, that is bad news for the fund, a pessimistic factor because long life means more benefit outlays. Conversely, if retirees and their survivors die at comparatively young ages, that's good news for the trust funds and gets classified as optimistic. Most of the other factors, such as employment, wage rates, and inflation have actuarial implications that correspond to their other real-life consequences.

Program income depends heavily upon the number of people at work. That naturally varies with unemployment, the ages at which people start and stop work, and how many jobs remain outside Social Security coverage. Old-Age, Survivors, and Disability Insurance income also varies according to what people get paid (because FICA taxes a percentage of pay), and, of course, the FICA tax rates.

On the payout side, the major variables are the number of people who qualify for benefits and retire, die, or become disabled, the size of their benefits, and the movement of the consumer price index (CPI), which determines the amount of cost-of-living adjustment (COLA).

Officials estimate the long-run cost of OASDI in terms of the "percentage of taxable payroll," which overcomes the difficulties of describing program costs for fluctuating levels of pay and prices. This method normally provides a ready comparison in very summary terms of what it costs to provide benefits.

The Social Security Administration actuaries, after consultation with many experts including the staffs of the cabinet officers who function as trustees, make estimates about each of these elements for each of the sets of projections—I, II-A, II-B, and III. The trustees' annual report announces these forecasts in summary form. In the mid-1970s, the reports caused consternation by predicting the possible inability of the funds to make timely payments later in the long-run 1980s. Another short-term crisis developed in the early 1980s. How did those situations arise?

How Social Security Got into "Trouble"

In 1950, program coverage expanded and benefits began to improve. In 1956, Congress began the Disability Insurance (DI) program and in 1965 enacted Medicare. These changes, all designed to provide a reasonable substitute for lost income and to preserve living standards, were financially manageable. In 1968, 1970, 1971, and 1972, Congress enacted benefit increases purposely exceeding increases in the CPI in order to improve benefits so that they at least kept pace with improvements in the earnings of the working population. That led in turn to the 1972 legislation providing for COLA, a formula for automatic adjustments to match increases in the CPI. COLA increases started in 1975.

Two problems emerged, one long-term and the other brief and transitory. The economy slowed after the oil shock of 1973, helping to produce higher-than-expected inflation and lower-than-expected productivity and real earnings. Throughout the post–World War II period, wage rates had advanced more rapidly than prices. Changes in wages directly affect trust-fund income. As wages increase, the payroll tax base increases and program income grows. Beginning in 1975, benefits were to rise in tandem with increases in prices as measured by the CPI. The program projections assumed that wage increases would continue to exceed price increases. Since that relationship did not hold in the late 1970s and early 1980s, wage improvements lagged behind the CPI increases. When assumptions were changed to reflect that development, the forecasts showed the trust funds getting into trouble. Growing unemployment increased the number of beneficiaries and reduced the work force paying FICA. These developments increased payout and reduced trust fund income beyond what had been predicted only a short time before.

In 1977, to meet the long-run problem, Congress changed the benefit formula, phasing in a less generous method that still achieved the intended goal of maintaining benefit purchasing power in the face of inflation. It took effect in 1979. Congress also boosted FICA rates and started a FICA increase in 1990 that was originally scheduled for 2010, bringing projected income into balance with projected payout over the ensuing fifty years.

The program's planners knew that the 1977 changes provided little margin for error over the short term but they did meet funding requirements for fifty years into the future. The economic assumptions on which those forecasts depended did not materialize, however, largely owing to the second oil price shock and an economic slowdown that baffled economists.

What Went Wrong and How It Was Fixed

Experts in the field fully expected the usual relation of wage improvements to prices to reassert itself. In addition, the anticipated slowed retirement rate, mirroring the low birth rate of the Depression and war years, the growth of the work force, reflecting the baby boom, and the increased tax rates in 1985 and 1990 (enacted in 1977) were expected to restore the trust funds to surplus by 1990 at the latest. In consequence when the Old-Age and Survivors Insurance trust fund dwindled, Congress in 1981 permitted borrowing among the several trust funds so that those funds with a surplus could tide over those that ran dry. In 1980, Congress enacted disability benefit reductions in response to criticism that more people qualified for benefits than had been intended and that benefits for young disabled persons were unduly generous even though, as the 1980s began, the DI trust fund had built up moderate reserves. Starting with 1981, a year before required by law, the Reagan administration carried on a review of DI with unexpected rigor. Many beneficiaries, especially those with mental illness who had special difficulty coping with the review process, lost eligibility and benefits. Applicants met the same zeal to trim the benefit rolls. As a result, the DI trust fund prospered while the disabled suffered. Although hospital and medical care costs were increasing faster than the general cost of living, the Hospital Insurance (HI) trust fund ran at a surplus. Hence, OASI could and did borrow from DI and HI surpluses without tapping general government revenues.

In advocating the 1977 amendments, the Carter administration gave assurances that they would keep the cash programs solvent well into the next century. When, soon after, the SSA actuary forecast a long-term deficit, many took this as proof of the utter unreliability of the program's actuarial studies.[1] Few nonexperts realized that the new long-term projection covered seventy-five years, a quarter of a century longer than those underlying the 1977 amendments. No knowledgeable person should have been surprised that those last twenty-five years would be deficit years when no attempt had been made to *plan* (as distinguished from look) that far ahead.

This forecast of a deficit, despite its modest dimensions, caused many to conclude that Social Security was moribund, struck down with a fatal case of "adverse aged dependency ratio" (a supposedly newly discovered economic disease more fully explored in the next chapter). The press and public heard and repeated that in the next century disaster awaited Social Security because the older population would grow as the baby boomers retired and the succeeding generation of workers to support them would shrink owing to low baby boomer birth rates. To top it off we all were going to live "too long"—not too long for our desires but too long for the trust funds. Indeed, many believed that actuarial Armageddon had already arrived.

The National Commission on Social Security Reform

In May 1981, the Reagan administration unveiled its proposals to trim Social Security benefits drastically and rapidly. It proposed raising normal retirement age and reducing benefits. Originally advertised as a means of bringing Social Security revenues into balance with its outlays, it quickly became apparent that the benefit cuts exceeded that announced goal by many billions. Within a week of the Reagan administration proposals, both houses of Congress rejected many of the major proposals with near unanimity.

As 1982 opened, a major recession was in full cry. Unemployment reached rates that caused people to start talking about the Great Depression. The economy appeared to be stuck in the doldrums with no sign of an economic breeze. The second oil price shock continued to raise prices and reduce real wages. Many in Congress and in the editorial columns counseled that the elderly should contribute to deficit reduction by making "sacrifices" and "sharing the pain" to meet looming deficits. The chief candidates for sacrifice were Social Security benefits in general and COLAs in particular. In addition, many advocated raising retirement age, although most only dimly understood what that meant in practice. Having been scorched in 1981, the Reagan administration did not dare again propose specific cuts.

In September 1981, President Reagan proposed a bipartisan commission to study Social Security's problems. House Speaker Thomas P. O'Neill indicated that he might agree. The president in December 1981 issued an executive order to set up the National Commission on Social Security Reform (a name clearly implying the need for basic change). He structured the commission so that the president appointed five members, the Republican congressional leadership five, and the Democratic congressional leadership another five. In sum, those appointed by Republicans totaled ten, while Democratic appointees numbered only five. Many feared that this two-to-one majority meant that the Republicans could work their will after the 1982 elections. It did not work out that way at all because each side needed the other and both needed a solution, even though they defined the problem differently and sought different remedies.

The commission held its first public meeting in February 1982.[2] Many read the tea leaves and found differing portents. Its composition, broadly representative of diverse views, foretold both problems and possibilities. It could easily deadlock, but if it somehow achieved a compromise package, it could command broad support. Many thought that the White House designed the commission only as a holding action to defer meaningful consideration until after the 1982 election, when the commission would become irrelevant and the political process would resume. Few in or out of the commission were optimistic.

Who Was Who

First, the cast of characters.

Chair Alan Greenspan had headed President Ford's Council of Economic Advisers. Admittedly not an expert in Social Security, he had a good reputation as a competent conservative economist with some political savvy. Rather low-voiced, he was articulate but not a colorful or commanding speaker. At the first commission meeting, many thought him too mild to lead so diverse a group into agreement.

Diversity marked the Republican appointees. The most important other Republican, Robert Dole, was in his second year as chair of the powerful Senate Finance Committee. Given his rumored presidential ambitions, many thought it unlikely that he would cede any of his committee's primary role in shaping Social Security legislation to the White House, let alone to a bipartisan group outside of Congress. Senator William Armstrong, an energetic, outspoken critic of Social Security "generosity," chaired the Finance Committee's Subcommittee on Social Security. That position, some thought, might enable him to block proposals not just from the Democrats but from more liberal Republicans on the commission. John Heinz of Pennsylvania, chair of the Senate Special Committee on Aging, up for reelection in 1982 in a state with a large elderly population, was just such a liberal Republican. The House Republican contingent included a correspondingly discordant pair. Barber Conable wielded much influence as the ranking Republican on the Ways and Means Committee. Conable had a reputation as a thoughtful, nondemagogic supporter of a limited Social Security program. Representative William Archer of Texas, ranking Republican on the House Ways and Means Subcommittee on Social Security, was a vigorous critic of Social Security, seeking to trim what he outspokenly regarded as its excessive generosity.

Noncongressional Republican appointees also presented considerable diversity. Robert A. Beck, chairman of the board of the Prudential Insurance Company, frequently enunciated the view that Social Security had gone too far and was inadequately funded. He was clearly inclined to trim it. Alexander Trowbridge, president of the National Association of Manufacturers (NAM), also carried some seemingly built-in contradictions. Appointed to the commission by a conservative Republican, President Reagan, he had been President Carter's secretary of Commerce. Rounding out the Republican team were former Representative Joe Waggonner of Louisiana and Mary Falvey Fuller. Though a

37

Democrat, Waggonner, a small-town banker, was so conservative that he hardly qualified as a mainline member of that party. Fuller, an energetic West Coast businesswoman, had served on the 1979 Social Security Advisory Council. Looking at this extremely diverse group of Republican appointees, one could only wonder whether they could forge a common position among themselves.

The five Democratic appointees shared a common core of dedication to the Social Security program. They did not seem to be a group that would yield enough ground to lure the Republicans into a compromise.

The doughtiest die-hard Democratic supporter of Social Security surely was—and is—Claude Pepper, a representative from Florida, in particular the Miami area, a bastion of elderly Americans. If his presence on the commission was not remarkable, the absence of two Democratic House members—chairman of Ways and Means Dan Rostenkowski and Social Security Subcommittee chairman Jake Pickle, who would have to process any commission proposals—was; but they had chosen not to participate as members. Their nonplayer status added to the expectation that the commission would prove fruitless.

Daniel Patrick Moynihan, ranking Democratic member of the Senate Finance Committee's Social Security Subcommittee, completed the congressional contingent. Up for reelection in New York in 1982, his life was complicated by the combination of strong grassroots and organized labor support in New York for the Social Security program and the counterpoint of a series of editorials in the influential *New York Times* that advocated paring down benefits, trimming COLA, and raising retirement age, all anathema to Social Security supporters. Despite the *Times*, Senator Moynihan remained an unyielding supporter of an undiminished program throughout the years of growing "crisis." The other Senate designee was Lane Kirkland, president of the AFL-CIO, and staunch supporter of the program. He had not one reason in the world to agree to any reduction in Social Security—except to preserve as much of it as possible.

Former representative Martha Keys, who had served on the House Ways and Means Committee, was selected by the Speaker. Keys had also served as an assistant secretary of Health and Human Services under President Carter. A strong supporter of the program, she had a special interest in improving the lot of women.

It is no denigration of any other commission member to say that the most remarkable and important was former Social Security Commissioner Robert M. Ball. Starting in 1939 a few years out of college, he spent most of his professional life in the Social Security Administration. As executive director of the 1949 Advisory Council, he had presided over shaping the 1950 "new start." Tall, smiling, affable, and, according to one reporter, "courtly," Bob Ball, as so many know him, combines several other crucial qualities: total mastery of the history and provisions of the Social Security system; a reputation for absolute integrity;

a nonconfrontational style; and, not least, the ability to subordinate his own role to that of others. Although he took the lead among the five Democrats, it was always with their consent and good will. He kept in touch with other leading figures who played major roles in the Social Security battle, such as Speaker O'Neill, Representatives Rostenkowski and Pickle, Cy Brickfield, executive director of the American Association of Retired Persons, Bill Hutton, director, and Jake Clayman, president of the National Council of Senior Citizens. Key among them was Wilbur Cohen, who had been secretary of Health, Education, and Welfare when Ball was commissioner. They maintained an easy relationship of cooperation and trust, not a common Washington commodity. Cohen, a leading figure in the program since 1935, chaired Save Our Security, the leadership council for about one hundred groups supporting Social Security.

The cast is not complete without some other key players. Heading the commission staff as executive director was Robert J. Myers. The longtime chief actuary and also deputy commissioner of the Social Security Administration, Myers had developed complete mastery of the mathematics of the system. Indeed, he had been their principal author. A deep believer in the basic design of Social Security, he is nevertheless an austere person who regards the system as appropriate only for modest financial support. A man with no taste for frills, he's averse to financing frills for anyone else. Myers had his own agenda: keep the system intact, but make it leaner. He assembled a very competent staff, including some who had worked for him at the Social Security Administration. Although unsung, they did impressive work.

Chairman Greenspan chose as his personal assistant a fine lawyer, Nancy Altman, who had served as Republican Senator John Danforth's legislative assistant. She was involved in day-to-day commission activities and kept Greenspan apprised of pertinent developments—jobs she performed impressively.

Senator Dole chose an extremely conservative Finance Committee staff person, Carolyn Weaver, an outspoken critic of the program, to serve as his part-time staffer at the commission, which some took as a hint that Senator Dole would opt for cuts wherever possible.

The Democratic staff (not so identified) included Merton C. Bernstein, coauthor of this book, Betty Duskin, former legislative director of the National Council of Senior Citizens, and Eric Kingson, then a professor of social policy at the University of Maryland (and now at Boston College).

Commission members Conable, Archer, Armstrong, and Moynihan designated staff assistants, and they all played important roles. Bert Seidman, Director of the AFL-CIO's Social Security Department, played a major role on the Democratic side. Bob Ball's own staff consisted of a part-time executive secretary, Betty Dillon (a person who could accomplish wonders in brief periods), Howard Young, a widely respected actuary with the United Auto Workers, and Lori

Hansen, who capably followed Hill activities for the invaluable Social Security Study Group headed by Elizabeth Wickenden.

With all that diversity, observers thought that it would take a miracle for the commission to accomplish its announced goal: a consensus package to bring Social Security into what they would agree constituted financial balance. Some also tended to believe that Social Security was in such dreadful condition that only major surgery could save it, surgery that the Democrats were sure to reject.

Nonetheless, the miracle happened.

Basic Strategic Decisions

At the outset, the Democrats had to make a crucial decision. Some program supporters advocated forcing commission decisions before the 1982 elections so as to compel Republicans to advocate program cuts as their agenda for Social Security. Proponents of this strategy argued that if Social Security could be made a central campaign issue, popular opposition to reductions would strengthen the hands of the program's supporters in Congress. Senators Armstrong and Heinz were up for reelection that fall, and some believed that they would have to act to support the program or, if they advocated cuts, as Armstrong well might, suffer the political consequences. For some that was a tempting scenario.

However, given the pervasive belief that Social Security was in deep trouble deriving from systemic difficulties, no one could fashion a Democratic package that could assuredly gain ready understanding and support. None of the Democrats advocated reducing benefits. They supported revenue increases, to be achieved in part by expanding coverage. But a formula limited to those features was unsalable. The Democrats hoped to persuade commission members, many of whom did not have intimate knowledge of the program, that it was basically sound and that a package of specific measures, none radical in themselves, could be fashioned that would meet the program's short-term and long-term needs. In addition, Democrats hoped that the White House, so badly burned by its 1981 proposals to cut benefits, would seek to avoid another such escapade.

Commission Meetings—Boring But Beneficial

The first commission meeting in February 1982 was well attended by media and interest group representatives. The press found this and the subsequent monthly meetings dull and lacking in newsworthy developments. Only once were there any fireworks, when Senator Moynihan attacked the president for endorsing a proposal that Social Security contribute $40 billion to reducing deficits, a clear call for cuts, although it did not so specify. That led to an angry public clash with Senator Armstrong. Otherwise the monthly meetings before the 1982 election seemed to be exercises in marking time. But things were going on, even if not obviously or dramatically.

Each of the monthly meetings explored a subject. One session, for example, focused on private pension plans. Quintin I. Smith, Jr., the president of Towers, Perrin, Forster & Crosby, a leading pension consulting firm, and Alicia H. Munnell, senior vice president of the Boston Federal Reserve Bank, who had written on the economics of private pension plans, made presentations. The former made no attempt to suggest that private plans could or should enlarge their scope so as to displace Social Security in some fashion. Some on the commission were struck by the omission. A later proposal to displace Social Security to some degree with individual accounts fizzled when Michael Boskin presented such a proposal in another monthly session but mustered no support. Munnell firmly made the point that private plan coverage seemed stuck in a rut, with about half the private work force covered but half left out: coverage extended primarily to upper-pay and unionized employees, with only sparse coverage for low-pay, nonunion employees, minorities, and women. Further, she pointed out that while Social Security protects benefits from erosion by inflation, private plans rarely do so and then not fully. Munnell cast doubt on the claim that Social Security depresses private savings, a line of analysis launched and given prestige by Martin Feldstein. Her report that Feldstein had used a faulty computer program left his argument in shambles. At a subsequent meeting, Henry Aaron of the Brookings Institution and former Health, Education and Welfare assistant secretary for research and policy, reenforced the point that Feldstein's position lacked supporting proof.

No one connected with the commission thereafter seriously argued that private plans could take over some portion of the job assigned to Social Security cash programs. The private-substitute door shut, but because it did not slam, no one seemed to notice. Meanwhile, commission members and staff probed problems and explored proposals. Doors kept closing and fewer choices remained.

Bob Ball drew up lists of modifications that would bolster the system's financing. For example, few knew or know that all members of the armed forces participate in Social Security. But, unlike most other employers, the armed services provide housing and food. Whatever their quality, those items have great value and would ordinarily be regarded as current income on which income tax and FICA would be payable. As most service people who receive these benefits also get low pay, the federal government pays the FICA equivalent on those benefits. However, the United States had not made those payments for the value of housing and food on a current basis. Rather, it made contributions to the Social Security trust funds only when armed forces personnel went on the rolls, then paying its estimated proportional share. If the United States were to pay up its arrears on that account, an estimated $18 billion would be pumped into the trust funds immediately. Not a dramatic act, but it would help in the short run where needs were most urgent; that seemed fair and possible.

At Ball's request, the staff assembled a shopping list of the cost impact of proposals for both benefit reductions and raising income. Items were put on the shopping list without identifying who had proposed them. In that way, Ball made it possible to get cost estimates for cuts that the Republicans would not themselves put forward, certainly not at that juncture. The idea was to see just how much revenue or savings different kinds of proposals would generate. It meant that packages could be assembled, discussed, and modified. It meant that there could be bargaining about numbers without concentrating primarily on ideological arguments. Almost any idea that had been mentioned seriously made the list. Without that catalogue there could have been no bargaining.

The Impact of the 1982 Elections

During 1982, various groups had polled the nation on Social Security issues. The polls consistently demonstrated majority support to maintain benefits and opposition to radical changes such as phasing out Social Security. A *Los Angeles Times* survey even showed public preference for a tax increase over cutting benefits. Polls showed some conflict over attitudes toward COLA: a Harris poll indicated support for basing COLA on the lesser of wage or price increases (68 percent in favor; 26 percent opposed), but the *Los Angeles Times* poll showed majority opposition to reducing or delaying COLA (54 percent opposed; 40 percent in favor).[3] The polls and the election indicated that the public wished to preserve Social Security and had little taste for radical change or substantial reductions.

During the 1982 campaign, Representative Pepper toured the country at the invitation of Democratic congressmen, congresswomen, and candidates, some of them quite conservative. At each stop, Pepper would appear with the Democratic incumbent or hopeful before an assemblage of "senior citizens," people Pepper could muster and who identified him as their champion. Pepper would put his arm around the candidate and warn that Social Security was on the chopping block, that the Republicans had already proposed deep cuts, that they had been temporarily thwarted, but that 1983 would be the year of reckoning. "Send this candidate back to Congress to help protect Social Security," he intoned. "I need his (her) help."

In the election, the Republicans had some scares; they barely held their Senate majority and lost a net of twenty-six seats in the House. The Social Security issue and especially Pepper's campaign received major credit for the unfavorable Republican showing. Most Republican survivors had little stomach for another knock-down, drag-out fight on Social Security in which they were seen as the bad guys intent on reducing retiree benefits.

The Commission Meetings: November 1982 to January 1983

Originally the post-election commission meeting was planned for only three days in mid-November. A thoroughly unpretentious motel in Alexandria, Virginia, just across the Potomac from Washington, D.C., was selected. Cautioned that one round of meetings probably could not achieve a settlement and that initial meetings would produce positions that the parties would have to mull over and discuss with principals and constituent groups, an additional day, December 10, was reserved.

Just prior to the commission's November 1982 meeting, Greenspan, Myers, and Ball agreed that they had to identify the size of the deficits to be met, whether by benefit reductions or income increases. The chairman and Myers insisted that for the short term, throughout the 1980s, the actuary's pessimistic assumptions (III) be used while Ball urged using the more pessimistic of the intermediate assumptions (II-B or "best guess") for the long term. In conceding the use of the pessimistic assumptions for the short term, Ball acted realistically. The press and critics repeatedly charged that during the 1970s the best guess had proved wrong. To placate the common view that Social Security was in deep trouble, Ball and the Democrats agreed to use the pessimistic assumptions for the short term; however, they repeatedly pointed out that they did so only to provide an ample margin for error, although they believed that the assumptions overstated the problem faced. This qualification never did register in the press.

For the long haul, using the II-B assumptions made sense because over time the multitude of fluctuations among those assumptions tend to offset one another. Moreover, Greenspan, used to forecasting, understood, as many others do not, that the assumptions are used as a guide, not as a precise measure of what will occur. Ball readily persuaded the Democrats to accept this formulation of the deficit problem. Greenspan also obtained acquiescence from the Republican-appointed members.

The November meeting began with both the short-term and the long-term deficits defined. The press reported that the Democrats conceded that the short-term (1983–89) deficit could be as high as $200 billion but omitted to mention that the Democrats did not concede that they expected the deficit to be so large. The agreed-upon long-term deficit was set at 1.8 percent of payroll, the figure used by the Social Security Administration actuary and trustees in their 1982 annual report. The size of that figure did not get much media attention either.

But it surely was far more modest than the popular press and public believed the long-term deficit to be.

At that juncture, few in the press or public realized that starting in the 1990s the trust funds would almost surely start to run substantial surpluses. Indeed, the "bankruptcy" talk had caught on so thoroughly that imminent and total collapse was widely regarded as likely, a view not shared by most of those who followed the programs closely.

November: Negotiations Begin. A commission breakfast meeting on Thursday produced no headway, and the first public session opened in a ballroom packed with commissioners, staff, SSA people, a couple of White House observers, a battery of television cameras, lots of press, and an assortment of interested spectators. Soft-spoken Alan Greenspan got things off to a slow and quiet start. The significance of his announcement that the commission agreed about the size of the short- and long-term deficits dribbled away like a poorly told joke. Not much happened in public view and by lunch break many in the press grumbled that nothing was happening. But they were wrong.

After a quick lunch, the Democrats caucused. Ball reviewed the package the group had already adopted. It consisted of bits and pieces: (1) requiring federal government catch-up payments on military-service wage credits; (2) crediting the trust funds for benefit checks that remain uncashed for more than six months; (3) banning withdrawals by state and local employee and nonprofit employee groups; (4) moving the next payroll tax increase to an earlier date; and (5) covering federal government new hires. All these actions enhanced income, but none was really radical; they were reasonable and hard to argue against, except for accelerating the payroll tax. All of that was readily acceptable to Democratic supporters, except that Kirkland declared unacceptable the coverage for federal employees unless conditions laid down by the AFL-CIO executive council were satisfied.

The next day, Ball also proposed that the Democrats make a concession— a one-time, three-month delay on the COLA and a small decrease in benefits. According to the shopping list of alternatives, such a delay would reduce outgo by about $20 billion during the 1980s, a very substantial amount that would cancel about an eighth of the short-term shortfall. Claude Pepper looked stunned. In his soft, gracious way, Pepper asked Ball to repeat the COLA item. Ball did, explaining that the Republicans had to obtain some benefit payments reduction and that this was the least painful for beneficiaries because it would not change the basic benefit formula, the other major alternative for reducing outlays. If the Democrats refused to budge, the Republicans could accuse them of planting themselves in concrete and destroying any possibility of agreement. Furthermore, it appeared the Republicans did not want to be identified with any proposals for benefit reductions—at least any that could not be accepted without political finger pointing. The group discussed the matter and all reluctantly agreed. Pepper in particular was upset.

Ball's moves proved absolutely correct. The Republicans now had a daring Democratic proposal that included retreat on a Democratic, or at least liberal Democratic, holy of holies—the COLA. That put the next move up to the Republicans. Some progress was made on a few of the smaller items such as banning withdrawal of state and local government groups (good for $3 billion) and the U.S. payments for the military, and crediting uncashed checks (a relatively small amount). For the first time, discussion began on removing the bargain enjoyed by the self-employed, who got the same benefits as employees but paid SECA that was only roughly three-fourths the combined employee/employer FICA tax rate. If they paid amounts equal to those contributed by employers, another $18 billion would be gained during the short term.

Nothing jelled despite two and a half days of meeting. While private talk grew among knots of commissioners and some key staff, the public sessions ground on and finally concluded, apparently without event.

The decision to meet again in December was reconfirmed. At that time Greenspan reported that the White House people had not yet given their attention to the subject and he needed time to get them to focus. His perception was that no one, especially Dole, was willing to agree to a package unless the White House also agreed to support it.

December: "The Sky Is Falling."   Meanwhile, in December 1982, the *New York Review of Books* published two articles by former secretary of commerce Peter Peterson that resembled other articles that had appeared in the early 1980s. But Peterson's eminence commanded considerable attention. He argued that, unless curbed, Social Security would run a $51 billion annual deficit by the year 2050 and employers and employees would need to pay 44 percent of taxable wages "just to break even" by 2035. His opinion, based on the pessimistic projections he found more plausible than the best guess set,[4] was, naturally, a shocker from someone long regarded as a moderate who presumably had statistical sophistication. The *New York Review of Books*, a slightly left of center journal, hardly seemed the place for a know-nothing right-wing attack.

The Peterson analysis was based on an overly simple assumption: all the bad things then going wrong with Social Security and Medicare would continue to go wrong, and at the same rate. But this was a totally unrealistic assumption. Medicare accounted for 60 percent of Peterson's projected 2050 deficit. Increases in medical care costs had been substantially outpacing the general rate of inflation. Peterson's analysis assumed unchecked Medicare costs until 2050, while in fact both Congress and the administration contemplated rather radical cost containment action. Moreover, he projected Medicare seventy-five years ahead while the trustees of the Hospital Insurance Fund did not make projections beyond twenty-five years, because they regarded key elements of the program far more subject to unpredictable change than the major elements affecting OASDI.*

Peterson asserted that "when the baby boom generation retires early in the next century, the system will disintegrate," even though he acknowledged in a footnote that the projections he used understated immigration, a powerful factor in the demographics of Social Security.[5] Most of the press didn't question that hyperbolic forecast. But a detailed memorandum by Robert Myers blunted the Peterson attack. He informed Greenspan and the commission members that the Peterson analysis lacked credibility. Only in March 1983, when the then current debate was largely over, did the *New York Review of Books* publish a lengthy, detailed, and withering rebuttal by Alicia Munnell and yoked it with a reply by Peterson.[6] Although his articles did not persuade the commission, for some their melody lingers on.

Finessing Medicare. Peter Peterson was not the first to discover the threat to Social Security solvency posed by the rapid growth of Medicare costs. Data appearing in the Senate Finance Committee's 1981 "blue book," analyzing Social Security costs and trends, made it abundantly clear that unless Medicare costs moderated in the late 1980s, the Medicare Hospital Insurance trust fund, although robust in the early 1980s, faced trouble.

The commission Democrats had decided that tackling Medicare would be premature. Concerned over the predictions and the peril to the program, they concluded that before the financing needs of Medicare were addressed, efforts to curb provider costs must be pressed vigorously. Only when those efforts reached their full potential could the dimensions of the financing problem be defined. They decided that the commission should not address Medicare's finances. Greenspan, Myers, and the Republican appointees had no heart for a Medicare struggle either. In retrospect the decision seems correct. Had Medicare been included, the commission's task would have been absolutely impossible. Without it, prospects for achieving an agreed solution were only improbable.

Back to the Drawing Board. The early December scheduled commission meeting produced no change. Greenspan asked the Democrats for more time. They agreed. No progress resulted. Then, in mid-December, an article by Senator Dole appeared on the Op-Ed page of the *New York Times*. Senator Moynihan went out of his way to compliment him on it. Dole responded by

---

* In 1985, the trustees began to make seventy-five-year projections for Medicare. Their earlier practice, using twenty-five years, makes much more sense.

46

asking if something might not be done to break the commission deadlock. They called other commissioners.

Of course, a great deal more happened. At one point after the November meeting, Trowbridge, the president of the National Association of Manufacturers, floated a series of proposals featuring cuts. As he was a Democrat, the proposal could not be attributed to the Republicans, or so some people thought.

One of the proposals did catch the eye of upper echelon White House staff who thought that Democrats were interested in it. That led Richard Darman, assistant to President Reagan, to discuss it with Ball. While the proposal was not acceptable, or even close, the exchange enabled Ball to explain the Democrats' position and probably helped to pave the way for later bargaining.

Meanwhile, the Office of Management and Budget started to pay attention as did presidential Chief of Staff James Baker and Darman. They were working on the budget and the figures did not look good. They needed to find offsetting money, and Social Security once again looked like a candidate. The Democrats' offer of the COLA delay would help. So would accelerating the payroll tax; that would pump in funds sooner than 1990 and make the budget "outyears," the late 1980s, look better than they were looking on the Office of Management and Budget's forecasts. And, as later comments by White House staff indicated, the administration did not want to get into another shouting match over Social Security in which Reagan and the Republicans looked like the bad guys intent on cutting the program. They repeatedly said—and continue to say—that that was a bad rap. However, they apparently recognized that it was a charge that stuck. Indeed, at that juncture Reagan's public approval ratings fell below those of Jimmy Carter at a comparable point. The White House was looking for a success or, at least, to avert a failure. Most important, Social Security funds stood on the brink of exhaustion and each party sought to avoid blame for failing to provide a solution.

Negotiations resumed, this time with White House people, including David Stockman, and a handful of commissioners. Claude Pepper, Lane Kirkland, and Martha Keys did not participate in the face-to-face meetings. That suited them and Ball, the Democrats' chief negotiator along with Moynihan. Ball and Moynihan could ask for breathers to consult and return saying that an absent Democratic member would not agree or had put forward some condition or proposal. Ball kept in close touch with the office of House Speaker Thomas O'Neill because it was crucial that he and the White House agree on a package. Concurrence by Rostenkowski and Pickle also was essential and Ball kept them informed as well.

Meanwhile, Ball cast about for a means that would satisfy the Republicans that benefits had been cut but would not drive off the Democrats and program supporters. It was reasonably clear in negotiations that what were labeled benefit cuts had to equal what were labeled tax increases in order to reach agreement. The two sides were able to agree on $40 billion for each category. The remaining $70 billion to $120 billion had to be sought elsewhere. The principal answer turned out to be taxation of benefits for high-income recipients. Something of a precedent existed in Unemployment Compensation. For Ball and the Democrats, and according to tax policy analysis, taxing benefits would not be a benefit reduction any more than any tax reduces pay rates although it reduces net income. But the Republicans apparently could regard it as a benefit cut. It reportedly appealed to the president, who expressed the view that his rich friends could afford it. In all likelihood, many of them would have such high earned income as to disqualify them for benefits, at least until age seventy, when the earnings test no longer applies. Such a tax appeared in the growing tentative package; it was worth an estimated $30 billion during the 1980s all by itself. The taxes collected would be funneled to the Social Security trust funds. That made it the functional equivalent of either a $30 billion cut, at least in some eyes, or an equal revenue increase. Progress was being made.

Agreement over some temporary income tax relief to cushion the blow of increased rates under SECA, the Social Security tax for the self-employed, came early. Much harder—and indispensable—was Republican agreement to Kirkland's demand for somewhat similar treatment for the proposal to speed up employee tax contribution rates. That did make it, but only after hard and complex bargaining.

By mid-January the chief negotiators had concluded agreement on a package. The three-month COLA delay became a six-month pause, with the additional three months traded for cancelling an earlier concession to lower benefits; so the benefit formula remained intact. The Democrats accepted it (Kirkland dissenting only about coverage of federal employees). It remained to recruit the support of a majority of the Republican-appointed members. Initially, Archer, Armstrong, Beck, Fuller, and Waggonner would not touch the package. But White House efforts and a concession by the Democrats making it easier to trigger the stabilizer, a device to prevent trust fund depletion by COLA outpacing increases in wage rates, assuaged Beck and Fuller, and so a majority of Republican appointees joined. The "consensus package" was announced late in the evening of January 15, 1983, in the overcrowded offices of the commission in an old row house facing Lafayette Park.

Many on the commission played important roles in the eventual success. Special credit must go to Alan Greenspan. Despite his deceptively mild manner, as chairman he repeatedly nudged the process along, created an environment of civility, and kept the lines of communication open. Most importantly, he never seemed to draw ideological lines, never bad-mouthed an idea or person, and, finally, he wakened the White House and got it to enter active negotiations.

Ball gently led the united Democrats and had high credibility with most, possibly all, of the Republican appointees. He was firm but adaptable, adroit at maneuver but not devious. Greenspan and Ball created and nurtured a feeling of mutual respect and considerable trust. Greenspan had chosen able associates. Myers, the most important, commanded universal respect for his technical mastery. No one could get a time bomb wrapped in a baby blanket past him. His steadfast opposition to Social Security "expansionists" gave him credibility with conservatives. He was indispensable to achieving the consensus. To lesser degrees so were many others.

Against all odds, the commission process, which came to include negotiations between the White House staff and the Democratic members on behalf of Speaker O'Neill, had produced a consensus package.

The Consensus Package: What and Why[7]

For the short term, 1983–89, the package added up to an estimated $168 billion in combined additional income and reduced outgo. That met the short-term goal. The package also met about two-thirds of the long-term goal of 1.80 percent of payroll. For that last third, the Democrats and Republicans agreed to disagree and to propose alternative ways of meeting that shortfall. Here is what they *did* agree upon.

Reaffirming Social Security Design

Usually overlooked, the first and *unanimous* recommendation of the commission was that the essential design of the cash programs be maintained without change:

> The members of the National Commission believe that the Congress . . . should not alter the fundamental structure of the Social Security program or undermine its fundamental principles. The National Commission considered, but rejected, proposals to make the Social Security program a voluntary one, or to transform it into a program under which benefits are a product exclusively of the contributions paid, or to convert it into a fully-funded program, or to change it to a program under which benefits are conditioned on the showing of financial need.[8]

That says a lot.

The Financial Package and Some Real Reform

About half the changes the commission did propose (and Congress adopted) fell into two major categories: benefit reductions or accelerated tax collections. Had the full cost of meeting short-run needs been met only by such measures, the increased taxes would have been too much for the Republicans and the benefit cuts too large for the Democrats. Other measures were needed.

Several of the changes enhanced income by making a program change that arguably rectified mistaken policy (such as a gap in coverage for employees of nonprofit organizations) or an unduly favorable arrangement (such as the lower taxes paid by the self-employed than for employees with comparable earnings). These measures—arguably neither tax increases nor benefit cuts—produced the revenue needed to round out the package. Another change provided that if trust fund reserves fell dangerously low, benefit adjustments would be based on the rate of change of wages if it were lower than the increase in prices, a substitute for COLA. A set of four amendments remedied some provisions that bore harshly on women. Most curious, and hardly noticed, was a change that makes the program more costly by increasing benefits for those who, starting in 1990, delay retirement past age sixty-five. This provision met the president's desire to make some long-term change. It also was music to Pepper's ears.

COLA Delayed. At Chairman Greenspan's request at the February meeting, a "sensitivity study" was made to isolate the factors that had adversely affected trust-fund income in the latter part of the 1970s and early 1980s. The study confirmed that the unexpected reversal in the usual and expected relationship of wages and prices had been the principal culprit.

Several had proposed that the COLA should be the *lesser* of either wage rate increases or CPI increases. Were that done, the trust funds would not fall behind, but, opponents of the proposal noted, beneficiaries would lag behind either progress made by wage earners or increases in the cost of living. On top of that, proponents of the new formula argued, the changes in CPI exaggerate real life changes in the cost of living. The CPI elements for housing overstate costs for beneficiaries, because the CPI registers *new* mortgage rates, which had increased rapidly under the impact of inflation. As most people, including beneficiaries, do not buy new houses, that mortgage interest rate overstates the real cost of housing. The rejoinder that climbing mortgage rates on new housing lead to boosts in the price of other housing was not widely heard. Even after the Bureau of Labor Statistics changed the CPI formula to reduce the impact of mortgage interest, the mortgage-interest-overstatement argument continued. In human affairs, conclusions once drawn often outlive their causes.

With this background and the public mood and attitude, the Democratic commission members concluded that they had to make some limited concessions on COLA or possibly suffer yet greater reductions if the matter were later decided by Congress without a compromise package.

The main method agreed upon for reducing outgo was a one-time, six-month delay in COLA from July to January. That would "save" the Social Security trust funds an estimated $40 billion over the ensuing seven-year period, but not all at a time as one might think. Obviously, it would eliminate six months of adjustment. In addition, the delay reduces such payments for every year thereafter, because the COLA is based upon the benefit payable when the adjustment is made. Hence an increment, once skipped, is never fully made up; COLA remains one step behind where it would have been without the one-half-year delay. As a result, based upon the II-B assumptions, the House Ways and Means Committee report estimated that the change would decrease benefit outlays throughout the 1980s, as seen in table 2.1. Over the long haul the COLA delay constituted a benefit reduction of about 2 percent and accounted for almost one-quarter of the estimated short-term savings in the package.

TABLE 2.1
Projected Benefit Decrease Effect of Delaying COLA Six Months (in Billions)

Year	1983	1984	1985	1986	1987	1988	1989	*Total*
Amount	$3.2	$5.2	$5.4	$5.5	$6.2	$6.7	$7.3	$39.4

SOURCE: *Report to accompany S.1., Social Security Amendments of 1983*, S. Rept. 98–23 (1983), p. 15.

The COLA delay bought preservation of the benefit formula and the assurance that replacement rates would remain the same for all future beneficiaries as they were in 1982 for those with comparable earnings.

The concession also bought ratification of the principle that the value of benefits, once awarded, would not be eroded by increases in the cost of living. But that did not end the COLA debate.

COLA and the "Stabilizer." The concern that COLA might once again outpace wages and deplete the trust funds argued for a stabilizing device to forestall such an undesirable development. The commission agreed that if the trust fund reserves fall below 15 percent of annual outgo expected to be paid the following year, COLA would be the *lesser* of the percentage of wage increases or CPI increases. Beck insisted on the 15 percent trigger through 1988. When the Democrats agreed, he signed on, bringing Fuller with him. For the years thereafter, Congress set the trigger level at 20 percent of the next year's expected total benefit payments. But the consequent reduction from normal COLAs need not be a permanent reduction for those who receive lowered benefits under the "stabilizer," as it came to be called. Once the trust funds regain a level equal to 32 percent of the next year's expected outgo, those who actually had their benefits reduced would be repaid to the extent possible from funds in excess of that level.

Of course, when Congress adopted the stabilizer in 1983, no one could be certain that it would not go into operation. That likelihood was small, however, and was expected to diminish throughout the 1980s. Although some risk was involved, it seemed greatly outweighed by the reassurance that if price increases again outstrip wage improvement COLA will not imperil trust fund solvency. Adopting the stabilizer caused groups representing the elderly considerable concern, but it helped stave off further cuts in COLA while simultaneously improving the grounds for congressional and public confidence in program solvency.

Extending Coverage

Extending program coverage improves program revenues, especially in the short term. It also improves *net* long-range finances. Obviously, the more people covered, the larger the revenues will be. Although outlays must eventually increase, advantage shows up immediately—before most of the newly covered qualify for benefits.

In addition, many of those newly covered would have qualified for "windfall" benefits by working short-term at covered employment, but would have gotten a better cost/benefit result than those who work under Social Security all the time. Making coverage mandatory for newly-hired federal civil service employees and those of almost all nonprofit groups produced $20 billion in the short run (1983–89) and reduced the long-term projected deficit by about one-sixth. Preventing the withdrawal from Social Security of state and local government employee groups produced a short-run addition of $3 billion.

Several commission members favored mandatory coverage for all state and local government employees. The commission report overstates the objections and understates the support for such a move, the merits and constitutionality of which are discussed in some detail in part III of this book. At the time of the commission's deliberations, it did not seem prudent to have any significant part of the package subject to serious constitutional question, and thus potentially unavailable to finance a portion of the projected shortfall. Supreme Court action since 1982 has significantly reduced the seriousness of the constitutional question.

Most non-profit organizations, the bulk of which had elected coverage anyhow, did not fuss about the proposal for mandatory coverage. But organized groups of federal civil service employees vigorously opposed covering new hires, arguing that the future adequacy of civil service retirement funding depends somewhat upon their contributions. This argument did not persuade Congress and the provisions for mandatory coverage survived. The change contemplated restructuring the civil service retirement system so that it provides a second layer of coverage on top of Social Security, like that provided by many state and local government plans and private group employee plans. Efforts to enact that new structure succeeded in 1986.

Reducing "Windfall" Benefits

Those who draw a pension from noncovered employment necessarily spend very substantial periods outside of the Social Security system. Receipt of a pension from noncovered work, typically from a state or local government or a nonprofit organization not participating in Social Security, identifies a person whose apparently low wages were not meant to qualify him or her for the weighting in favor of the low paid. The commission recommended and Congress crafted a complicated set of provisions designed to pay lower Social Security benefits to some with pensions from noncovered work. The change produces only slight savings to the trust funds. However, it reduces some of the advantage of staying out of the Social Security system, although the provisions are too complicated to be well understood by most participants in state and local pension plans.

A somewhat similar situation arises with couples in which one spouse qualifies for Social Security, thus earning a benefit for the spouse, while that spouse draws a pension of his or her own from another public program. In 1977, Congress provided that in such circumstances the Social Security "auxiliary" benefit would be reduced one dollar for every dollar that the spouse drew from the other public pension. In 1982, Congress relaxed those requirements and exempted auxiliary benefits where the spouse was dependent on the Social Security earner for one-half of his or her support. The 1983 benefit package scrapped that 1982 amendment and provided once again for the dollar-for-dollar offset but only up to two-thirds of the amount of the public plan benefit.

These provisions salvage or recapture some small amount for OASDI and, just as important, eliminate an unjustifiably sweet deal for those who earn pensions in public programs outside of Social Security.

Taxation of Benefits for Higher-Income Persons

Originally, Social Security benefits were exempt from income tax as a result of the design of the Social Security Act, which separated the benefit provisions from the tax provisions.*

The commission recommended that half the benefit be subject to income tax for those with specified amounts of income well above the average for older persons and that the taxes so derived be recycled into the trust funds. That accomplishes several desirable goals. The OASDI fund obtains additional revenues without a commensurate payroll tax rate increase. The measure taxes away some of the benefits obtained by upper-income recipients, thereby partially meeting a complaint of some critics that the program provides benefits to rich people who do not need them. When Congress acted, it made subject to tax up to half the benefit of those whose entire income, including the as-yet-untaxed half of the Social Security benefit, exceeds $32,000 for married couples and $25,000 for a single person. The income used to measure whether the threshold is met includes asset income, thereby meeting another criticism—that the Social Security earnings test reduces benefits for people with work income but ignores income from investments, no matter how substantial. The recommendation yielded an estimated $30 billion in the short run and reduced the long-term deficit by one-third.

Because the income level for determining when the tax kicks in does not adjust for inflation, the tax becomes applicable to more and more taxpayers as inflation and real earnings growth raise income. Eventually, tax policy applicable to all income will determine what amounts are simply too low to be taxed; the fact that some comes from Social Security will make no difference.

Full Payroll Taxes for the Self-Employed

The recommendation to raise SECA taxes to equal the combined total of employee contribution and employer payroll taxes netted $18 billion in the short run and about one-fifth of 1 percent of payroll over the long run. Half of the total contribution is treated as a tax-deductible business expense, beginning in 1990, making it the functional equivalent of the employer's payroll tax. This recommendation was not so much a tax boost as the end of a specially favorable arrangement.

* A staff member of the 1935 Committee on Economic Security, Tom Eliot, suggested that such a structure would improve chances for the act to pass constitutional muster, because of Congress's undoubted power to tax wages and to confer benefits. Then the Treasury ruled that for tax purposes benefits were not earned income but a gratuity and so not taxable.

What Went Wrong and How It Was Fixed

Accelerating Payroll Tax Increases

Roughly one-quarter of the short-term financing derived from accelerating the FICA tax rate schedule. As the law stood in 1982, employees and employers each paid 5.4 percent of taxable payroll for OASDI and another 1.3 percent for HI; slightly higher rates were scheduled for 1985, 1986 and 1990. The package provided for moving to these new rates more quickly, with one small boost in 1984 and another in 1988. The additional $40 billion these changes yield during the 1980s matches amounts saved through delaying COLA.

In total, equal amounts come from revenue improvements and benefit reductions, supplemented by other revisions, such as improved coverage that increased program income. As it turned out, benefit reductions did not bear as heavily on beneficiaries as some feared and most expected when the commission began work.

Debate over Retirement Age:
One Agreement and Agreeing to Disagree

The commission agreed upon one change concerning retirement age—the Delayed Retirement Credit—and agreed to disagree about another—whether to raise "normal retirement age."

The Deferred Retirement Credit (DRC). Prior to 1983, the law provided a DRC of 3 percent for each year retirement (the start of benefits) was postponed past age sixty-five. However, 3 percent is less than the actuarial equivalent of benefits begun at age sixty-five. As a result, people who delayed benefit receipt until any age up to seventy-two (at which time the retirement test no longer applied) would receive, on average, lower lifetime benefits than those who start receiving benefits at age sixty-five. Some considered the DRC arrangement unfair. Others considered it a low priority for change, because the OASI system is designed to replace earnings lost or diminished by retirement.

Nonetheless, the president wanted to give those who defer benefit receipt past normal retirement-age a higher DRC even though to do so increases the benefit payout and does so in favor of the nonretired with substantial earnings. The negotiators agreed to changing the DRC from 3 percent to 8 percent a year (up through age sixty-nine); the 8 percent increment provides the actuarial equivalent of the delayed benefits. This fit the Republican view that an 8 percent DRC would be age neutral and would encourage people to work longer. Despite the added cost to the system, the Democratic-appointed members agreed.

Under the agreement, starting in 1990, about 0.5 percent will be added to the DRC every other year, and will reach the full 8 percent DRC in 2009.

Thereafter, the 8 percent DRC will apply to each year of benefit deferral past normal retirement age. The net effect is to make a better and fairer deal for those who can delay retirement—those with the most substantial earnings and best health. The change was estimated to cost 0.10 percent (one-tenth of 1 percent) of payroll.

Raising Retirement Age—Not in the Package.   The consensus package agreed upon by all of the Democratic-appointed members and a majority of the Republican-appointed members added up to additional revenues or savings to the trust funds of $168 billion during the 1980s. That came within the bounds, $150 to $200 billion, set for meeting the short-term projected deficit. For the long term, the package totted up to 1.22 percent of payroll, or 0.58 percent short of the assumed long-term deficit. The commission majority agreed to recommend as a package all of the items upon which they did agree and to put competing proposals before Congress for the remaining 0.58 percent. Each knew roughly what the other would propose.

All of the Republican-appointed commissioners, except Armstrong, proposed raising retirement age gradually in the next century. They argued that people will live longer, that older workers will be in greater demand, that the change would reduce the payroll tax burden on younger workers in the future, and that, with the long lead time, people could adjust to the new higher age. They also declared that, before the change began, Congress could adapt the DI program to meet increased needs for those who could not continue to work for "reasons of health."

The commissioners appointed by Democrats proposed enactment of a small payroll tax increase—less than one-half of 1 percent on employees and an equal amount on employers—to begin in 2010 if, at that time, the trust funds indicated the need of those additional revenues. They argued that raising retirement age was an unfair and ineffective method of attempting to lengthen working life and that existing law met the varying needs of working people through the options available: "early" retirement, "normal" retirement, and "delayed" retirement. Furthermore, they argued, raising retirement age to sixty-seven constituted a lifelong benefit cut of 12.5 percent for some beneficiaries and the cut would fall in the future upon those who would bear the brunt of the payroll tax increases in the package. (Part III of this book explores both sets of arguments.) The Democrats' proposal included a refundable tax credit for employees for the additional amount. In effect, the credit would make the tax increase into a general revenue contribution.

Such was the package and recommendations submitted to Congress. To ease the pain of higher rates, a one-year tax credit for the amount added to

1984 FICA taxes was allowed. In effect, then, a small contribution came from general revenues. In any event, the negotiators felt that they had balanced benefit reductions and revenue increases as well as argument and political power permitted. In a thoroughly democratic outcome, no group got its way entirely; all gave up something. All who agreed to the consensus package got what they wanted most—a settlement. How these recommendations added up is summarized in table 2.2.

What Congress Did

The consensus package was sent to Congress in early 1983. Federal employee unions laid down a barrage of objections and criticism to covering newly-hired federal government employees. Their testimony dominated the hearings and the lobbying but to no avail. Congress needed the Social Security consensus package. Some flirted with proposing amendments, particularly for their friends the federal employee unions, but members of Congress soon realized that the package would unravel if any significant part were removed.

Congress accepted the commission recommendations and played its major role where the commission had not agreed: what to do about the last one-third of the long-term deficit. Here the brief debate concentrated on two major alternatives: a refinement of the Republican-appointed commission members' proposal to raise normal retirement age or the Democratic-appointed members' proposal to raise the payroll tax sometime in the next century.

The major actors in the House agreed that the only amendments the House would consider were the proposal to raise the normal retirement age in two steps in the next century, and the Pepper substitute, to make a small payroll tax increase starting in 2010, should it prove necessary, in lieu of increasing retirement age.

Despite a rousing ovation when "Senator" Pepper rose to speak in the House, a *Time* magazine cover story on his long service to seniors, and the accolades by many who lauded his role in shaping the consensus package, a group of Democrats joined most Republicans in rejecting the Pepper substitute. A similar kind of coalition in the Senate favored raising retirement age. As a result, Congress decided to meet the one-third of the long-term projected deficit for which the commission did not make an agreed-upon recommendation by raising retirement age in two steps in the next century, as provided in the House bill.

TABLE 2.2

Summary of Commission Recommendations to Congress

	Savings and Additional Financing Generated	
	Short-Range Yield (in Billions)	Long-Range Deficit Reduction (as % of Payroll)
Recommendations		
1. Cover nonprofit and new federal employees	$ 20.0	.30%
2. Prohibit withdrawal of state/local government employees	3.0	—
3. Tax benefits of high-income earners	30.0	.60
4. One-time six-month COLA delay	40.0	.27
5. Eliminate "windfall benefits"	.2	.01
6. Accelerate tax-rate schedule	40.0	.02
7. Revise SECA taxes	18.0	.19
8. Credit by lump-sum U.S. Government FICA liability	18.0	—
TOTAL SAVINGS of Recommendations	$169.2	1.39%

	Costs Generated	
	Short-Range	Long-Range
Recommendations		
1. Increase DRC to 8% per year by 2010	—	0.10%
2. Continue benefits on remarriage for disabled widow(er)s/divorced widow(er)s	$ .1	—
3. Index deferred widow(er)'s benefits based on the greater of wages (or CPI)	.2	.05
4. Permit divorced spouse 62 or over to receive benefits when husband is eligible	.1	.01
5. Increase benefit rate for disabled widow(er)s aged 50–59 to 71.5% of primary benefit	1.0	.01
TOTAL COSTS of Recommendations	1.4	.17
NET SAVINGS of Recommendations	$167.8	1.22%

Competing Proposals to Meet Remaining Long-term Needs
- Republicans: Raise Retirement Age.   0.65 percent deficit reduction
- Democrats Raise Payroll Tax 0.45 percent   0.58 percent deficit reduction starting in 2010.

Cost-free Commission Recommendations
- Reallocate OASD1 tax rate between OSAD1 and DI.
- Allow interfund borrowing from H1 by OASDI.
- Base automatic benefit increases on lower of CP1 or wage increases after 1987 if fund ratio is under 20 percent or with catch-up if fund ratio exceeds 32 percent.

NOTE: The commission sought to meet a short-range shortfall estimated at between $150 billion and $200 billion; it also needed to meet a long-range deficit of 1.80 percent of payroll.
SOURCE: *Report of the National Commission on Social Security Reform*, January 1983, table A, chap. 2, p. 5.

Summing Up: The Foundation for the Future

The commission consensus package, plus the provisions to raise retirement age in two stages in the next century, became law. In early 1983 a relieved President Reagan signed the bill in the company of equally relieved members of Congress and the commission.

The consensus package for Social Security "reform," as enacted by Congress, did several major things:

- It preserved the major characteristics of the program;
- It provided for cash program solvency in the 1980s, even under adverse economic circumstances;
- It provided for cash program solvency in the long term under the "best guess" projections;
- It preserved the benefit formula, thereby assuring for the future the same levels of replacement for people with comparable incomes;
- It delayed COLA, but assured it in most circumstances;
- It introduced taxation of some benefits, limited at first to those with high incomes.

Two major changes did occur that almost went unnoticed:

- Normal retirement age will rise twice in the next century, cutting benefits significantly for all;
- The larger delayed retirement credit will improve the position of those who delay retirement.

Other changes, especially those with the most impact on the short-run situation, included:

- Putting already-scheduled payroll tax increases into effect sooner;
- Extending mandatory coverage to newly-hired federal employees and to almost all nonprofit employees (most of whom already participated);
- Requiring catch up payment from the federal government of its payroll tax obligations for military service wage credits;
- Crediting uncashed benefit checks to the trust funds against which they had been charged;
- Ending the preferential treatment for the self-employed so that they pay payroll taxes equal to the total paid for employees.

For defenders of the faith, the changes agreed upon were mostly minor, and many strengthened the program and made it fairer. For those who saw the crisis as an opportunity to perform major surgery on Social Security, "real reform"

59

had not been achieved. For those, persuaded that there had been a mammoth crisis, the resolution seemed so mild that they doubted that reform had been achieved or that the system really had been fixed. But many members of the press and public continued to feel that Social Security, though very desirable, would not continue to work as it should, starting in thirty to forty years.

We will see about that.

3   The Outlook
for Social Security

Social Security's Future Is Secure

"When my time comes, Social Security won't be there." Sometimes put as a question, this view still commands considerable support. Many persist in the belief that in the next century Social Security will falter or fail. That conclusion is not so much a diagnosis as an impression, left over from the hectic and confusing public debate in 1981 and 1982 about how to assure Social Security's solvency. It ignores the remedies provided by the 1983 amendments recommended by the Greenspan commission and adopted by Congress. Those who had become persuaded that Social Security required radical change did not believe enough had been done when less than radical measures sufficed.

The cries of crisis greatly exaggerated the underlying reality. Incomplete demographic and economic analysis led many to assume not only imminent crisis but eventual catastrophe for Social Security. Contrary to the commonly accepted view, however, the dependency ratio—the ratio of those employed to those not employed—in the next century is more favorable than it has been in the recent past, when account is taken of all dependent groups. A tight labor market may well induce and enable older people, especially women, to work longer than they do now. Immigration can increase the size of the younger work force. The extreme pessimism about productivity, so common as this decade opened, seems unwarranted. And the depressing effect on Social Security revenues that fringe benefit growth is projected to have appears unrealistically pessimistic and can be avoided by a simple change in the FICA tax structure without increasing burdens beyond those already scheduled for 1990.

Not least, the future of Social Security is secure because it serves all generations and so enjoys widespread public support.

For many, the central issue is whether Social Security can meet its obligations now and in the future. Most surprising to many is that Social Security has in fact reduced federal deficits and that very large Social Security trust-fund reserves impend. That prospect requires important choices to be made from several major scenarios, decisions that have yet to be widely addressed.

The trustees of the Social Security cash programs led off their 1987 report with this declaration:

> The actuarial estimates . . . indicate that the assets of the Old-Age and Survivors Insurance (OASI) and Disability Insurance (DI) Trust Funds are expected to be sufficient to permit the timely payment of OASDI benefits for many years into the future. The long-range 75-year estimates indicate that, under the intermediate assumptions, the OASDI program will experience about three decades of positive actuarial balances, with continuing actuarial deficits thereafter. The positive actuarial balances in the first part of the 75-year projection period nearly offset the later deficits, so that the program, as a whole, is said to be in close actuarial balance.

While the prose is dull, this statement from the secretaries of Health and Human Services, Labor, and Treasury, came as welcome reaffirmation of all such reports since the 1983 amendments. What underlies these reassurances merits exploration.

Why Doubts Arose

As we have seen, two major factors combined in the 1980s to undermine public confidence in the soundness of the Social Security system: warnings that in the short run bankruptcy impended and that in the long run the elderly population was increasing more rapidly than the working population. The ensuing cries of peril drowned out the trustees' forecasts that predicted a long period of growing reserves starting in the 1990s and lasting well into the third decade of the next century, possibly beyond. Even the pessimistic forecast predicted that once the trust funds weathered the 1980s, their reserves would increase as the post–World War II generation flooded the employment market and scheduled payroll tax rate increases went into effect in 1990. On the benefit payment side, the low birth rates of the 1930s and early 1940s would slow the rate of growth of the elderly population in the 1990s.

Forecasts projecting a deficit beginning in the 2020s caused agitation. What people heard was "deficit," and few stopped to inquire about its expected size. A number of commentators, among them the *New York Times* editorial page, expressed dismay that one method of estimating the long-term OASDI deficit put it at $4.2 trillion.[1] That obviously daunting figure derived from a congressional requirement that the Social Security actuary periodically report the condition of the Social Security funds according to the actuarial practice used for estimating the costs and funding of private plans. For such plans, actuaries consider a closed group consisting of the initial participants for a period ending with the death of the last of that group. However, actuaries, almost all of them in private practice, when surveyed by the U.S. General Accounting Office, registered their view that Social Security, with a constant influx of new participants, should *not* use a closed group to measure the status of the OASI and DI trust funds. Only 11 of the 389 actuaries surveyed regarded the closed-group analysis as an appropriate method.[2] In contrast, the open group projections for seventy-five years, the usual actuarial practice of the Social Security Administration, produces estimates of program income and outlays that now are in close actuarial balance.

The Major Factors Affecting Social Security Solvency

To sort out fact from fear, the projections of the major variables affecting the labor force and the number and longevity of beneficiaries—birth rates, immigration, and longevity—require examination. Next, the aged dependency ratio (which, above all else, causes such a crisis of confidence in the system), productivity, and the size of the covered payroll enter into the equation. Some of these factors can be affected by policy decisions.

To arrive at forecasts, the office of the actuary works with pertinent data for a factor from the past and applies adjustments that appear relevant for various periods in the future. An "ultimate rate" for 2000–2060 is a rate that expresses the average for that period with the lean years balancing prosperous years and the assumptions themselves interacting. (Ultimate rates start for different factors at different times; a few, like GNP, vary throughout the forecast period.)

The Size of the Work Force

How many people work and pay FICA taxes is a key element in determining trust fund incomes. Ninety-five percent of the work force is covered by Social Security, so we must see what portion of the population works.

Labor-Force Participation. The labor-force participation rate describes the percentage of a group who work or actively seek work. Such rates vary by sex and age. The lengthening period of employment preparation for the young, the lessening work participation of older men, and—in the other direction— the growing proportion of women who work for pay, have been the major labor-force developments since World War II.

In 1952, 87 percent of men aged sixteen and over worked; by 1982 that figure had dropped to 77 percent, owing to the steadily lower participation rates of men over fifty.[3] Just which factors contribute to that clearly observable trend is open to debate. Some ascribe the availability of early retirement under Social Security since 1961 for men as a major factor. Others attribute it to the availability of supplementary pensions at progressively lower ages. Private plans liberalized early retirement provisions, enabling participants with substantial plan service to retire and draw benefits that were not actuarially reduced fully or at all. Indeed, many companies, for example Dupont, Eastman Kodak, and Xerox, have offered special inducements for early retirement so as to pare their work forces, from executives to plant production line workers.

While studies do not wholly agree, the best evidence indicates that the combined availability of *both* Social Security and private plan benefits enable most of those who retire voluntarily to do so. Many "retire" involuntarily (see chapter 8, "Retirement Age").

For the future, the Social Security actuary assumes that labor participation rates for each age group will not decline further but will rise slightly and then level off early in the next century. Hence, the principal variation for determining *overall* labor-force participation becomes age. Due to the expected larger pro- portions of older men in the population, overall male participation rates will decline as the older groups, with lower participation rates, grow in proportion to the younger groups, with higher rates.[4]

For women, the changes in the recent past have been dramatic. During the period 1952–83, work-force participation by women rose from 35 percent to 53 percent, which boosted the combined male-female rates from 60 percent to 65 percent despite the drop in male work-force participation. The actuary recognizes that certain powerful social and economic forces will continue to encourage women to work: the growing pattern of two-earner households, the greater status and independence women obtain through paid work, and the comparative shrinkage of the labor force will contribute to greater labor-force participation by women of all ages. The actuary projects that women's total rates will continue to increase from about 54 percent in 1984 to almost 60 percent by 2000. For the next century, the actuary projects trends similar to those for men, a diminishing rate for women overall, dropping from about 55 percent in 2020 to about 50 percent by 2060, owing to the aging of the women's work force, increased numbers of older women, and the assumed continued low labor-force participation of older women.[5]

Overall, taking into account the projected aging of the work force, the Social Security actuary's II-B assumptions project total labor-force participation will drop from 64.9 percent in 1982 to about 60 percent in 2060. These projections are possibly too pessimistic, given other forces that will create incentives and opportunities for both men and women to remain at work. During that period, normal retirement age will rise twice, effectively reducing Social Security replacement rates at any given age. The delayed retirement credit will rise to 8 percent a year by 2009 and so, arguably, encourage some people to work longer. And, over the next seventy years, the younger segment of the labor force will shrink compared to the overall population, possibly creating more market demand for older workers.

Furthermore, the actuary's assumption that the future participation rate of older women will mirror current low participation patterns may prove unduly pessimistic. For many women in their fifties and sixties in the years after 2000, paid employment will have become a way of life. The common expectation is growing that adult women *will* work, both from the need for two incomes in a family and the need for financial independence for single living and in the event of ever-more-common divorce. By the third decade of the next century, almost all women will have been actively in the work force in their early adult years, and the pattern of resuming work after childbirth or rearing may well become common. Nonetheless, the actuary assumes no such continuation in greater work activity by these "new" older women but assumes instead that the lure of leisure and the factors that now keep male labor-force participation appreciably higher than female rates will continue. (Built into the actuary's forecast are increased rates of disablement for both men and women.)

Some analysts anticipate that as supplementary pension plans mature, they will yield larger benefits to more people. This factor could encourage retirement and offset the factors that otherwise may spur greater labor force participation. On the other hand, pressures may build to curtail generous early retirement options under private and government plans, thereby luring fewer people out of the labor market at ages below sixty-two.

Participation in the labor force does not assure paid employment, the significant factor for Social Security payroll taxes. Hence, to project Social Security's future income realistically, a factor for unemployment must be applied.

Since the 1982 unemployment rate averaged 9.7 percent, the skeptical considered the ultimate rate of 5 percent to be suspiciously low. Given the fact that the actuary and others forecast a labor shortage in the next century, higher then current labor force participation rates and lower unemployment rates seem a likely result.

A tight labor market would offer improved opportunities and boost compensation for women, minorities, and older people. Increased compensation and employment opportunities could lure back into the job market disabled and elderly people for whom opportunities currently do not exist at all or for whom compensation is too low to compete with Social Security benefits (that themselves are not princely) and supplementary plan benefits (that, on average, are lower). Such people will thus join the ranks of those paying Social Security payroll taxes and strengthen Social Security financing. However, actuarial forecasts for the next century assume that the proportion of older men and women actively in the labor market will follow past patterns. The consequence of the Social Security actuary's assumptions is to project a shrinking work force after the year 2000, paying fewer FICA and SECA tax dollars to the trust funds while at the same time assuming increasing payout from early retirement.

Of course, unemployment rates may stay high. On the other hand, if employment proves less than forecast because of improved productivity, the net effect should be to increase real earnings, a factor that improves program revenue.

Mortality and Longevity. The conquest of common killers, such as tuberculosis, infectious disease, and polio, by antibiotics and vaccines has transformed the patterns of death and life in this century. Deaths caused by heart attack, other coronary diseases, and stroke have dropped dramatically. Medication and technology continue their advance. In consequence, fewer adults die in their 50s and 60s, and older people live longer than their predecessors did.

The Social Security actuary foresees continued improvements in life expectancy through 2060 but at slower rates than in the period 1900–1980. Even that may overstate the outlook. Only in the recent past have scientists identified new killers such as Legionnaires' Disease and AIDS; and they keep making fresh discoveries about the environmental dangers in new agricultural, manufacturing, and household chemicals.

Nonetheless, we must proceed prudently on the assumption that death rates will continue to decline. Even assuming higher labor-force participation by older people, greater longevity means more extended periods for the payment of Social Security retirement and survivor benefits. Most of us want that for ourselves, yet some fear that it will impose unbearable costs to the system.

Birth Rates. The birth rate is one variable that determines how many new Americans will be available for the future labor force. Changes in birth control technology and attitudes toward work and children have produced a dramatic drop in the U.S. birth rate (as measured by how many children the average woman will bear through her lifetime). The steady downward trend in modern times reached a rate of 2.1 during the 1930s depression. But with the post–World War II baby boom it rose, peaking at 3.7 in 1957. By 1976, the rate slowed to 1.7 and has been hovering just above 1.8 (1.86 in 1985) since then.

The birth rate may rise in response to immigration. Since a large portion of the recent legal immigrants are Hispanics, who have higher birth rates than the native-born population, some rethinking of the rate may be in order. However, Asian immigrants, once here, tend to maintain small families. In any event, immigrants usually are younger than the resident population and thereby increase the proportion of people in the child-bearing years. Naturally that affects the outlook for the size of the working-age population in the next century.

The Social Security actuary projects a long-term birth rate of 2.0 starting in 2011, for the II-B assumptions. Even that rate falls below the level at which the population perpetuates itself. In part that rate has been chosen because the U.S. has never experienced a lower rate for any extended period. The Bureau of the Census has adopted 1.9 as its forecast.[6]

If the rate continues below 2.0, pressure to augment immigration could increase. Former Chief Actuary Robert J. Myers (in a manuscript he is readying for publication) forecasts just such an interaction.

Immigration.   One specialist observes that after four decades of insignificant immigration (between the mid-1920s and mid-1960s) "many scholars and policy makers have been slow to recognize that since the mid-1960s, immigration—in all its diverse forms—has again become a major feature of the U.S. economy. During 1980, for example, it is probable that more foreign-born people came to the United States for permanent settlement than in any previous year in the nation's history. . . ." Noting the emerging trends, the demographer Leon Bouvier observed in 1981 that "immigration now appears to be almost as important as fertility" for population growth.[7]

Studies show that immigrants tend to be substantially younger than the resident population, and recent analysis shows that a high percentage are children. In short, immigration means more young bodies, and, as it always has, a fresh stock of people with vitality and determination—characteristics people need to uproot themselves and their families and go to alien soil. Cuban American enterprise already is legend: Vietnamese valedictorians and spelling bee champions abound. Asian Americans constituted more than 10 percent of the classes entering Harvard College in 1984 and 1985—compared with their 1.5 percent share of the general population.

Immigration plays a key role in determining how many people are available to work and pay FICA taxes (one need not be a citizen to participate as either an employee or a beneficiary). The significance of this factor is readily apparent when studying the projections of the long-term Social Security deficit used by the 1982 Greenspan commission. The Social Security Administration's II-B estimate of the seventy-five year deficit was 1.8 percent of payroll. At that time, the Social Security actuaries assumed an annual immigration rate of 400,000. When the actuary's office later investigated the effect of alternative assumptions, it found that each additional 100,000 immigrants produce a long-term deficit reduction of about 0.13* percent of payroll.[8] If the immigration rate assumed in 1982 had been double, almost one-third of the projected deficit would have been eliminated. If the immigration rate were to triple, two-thirds of the entire deficit projected in 1982 would have been cancelled.

In the early 1980s, Social Security actuaries then used the 400,000 figure for II-A and II-B because it corresponded to the legal rate of immigration in the early 1970s. But the figure excluded legal refugees and illegal immigrants, the latter because their numbers cannot be ascertained. The 1985 trustees' report adjusted immigration figures upward to 500,000, taking account of legal refugees. However, the 1987 trustees' report II-A and II-B estimates assume *net* legal annual immigration of 400,000; the reduction results from also assuming annual emigration of 100,000. Little hard information about emigration exists; it seems as conjectural as that about illegal immigration. Information about the age profile of emigrants is crucial to drawing some conclusions about the impact of this phenomenon on population growth and the work force. We would argue that illegal immigration should probably be regarded as, at the least, counterbalancing emigration. Realism requires making some conservative assumptions about the size and composition of illegal immigration.

The Economic Policy Council of the United Nations Association of the United States of America has estimated that total net immigration (legal and illegal) exceeds one million per year.[9] The major influx consists of Mexicans driven to cross the border because of rampant Mexican population growth and unemployment. Mexico will have a surplus working population of at least 11 to 13 million for the remainder of this century and well into the next even under more favorable economic circumstances.

The Mexican border is not the sole leak in U.S. immigration control. The coast of Florida and the Canadian border also afford opportunities. Furthermore, an indeterminate number of persons enter the country legally, as visitors or students, and then overstay, simply disappearing into the urban millions. For example, an Indian taxi driver blithely told this story: He worked as an engineer for a ship-breaking crew in one of the Persian Gulf states. When his job ended there, his employer obligingly certified that he would return to that job; the certificate enabled him to obtain a visitor's visa to the United States. It cost him a round-trip ticket, with the return portion going unused. By the time he told

---

* The 1987 *Trustees Report* modifies this figure to 0.10 percent for each 100,000 immigrants over the currently assumed 400,000.

this story, he had been in the United States long enough to marry and have a child. He planned within the week to meet his brother and sister-in-law at Kennedy Airport to repeat the formula. The United States does not possess a more pleasant, ebullient, or energetic resident.

Some believe that, in the long run, illegal immigrants cost Social Security more than they contribute. Assuming that most illegal immigrants will work for low wages, those who qualify for benefits will tend to be high cost to the Social Security system because of the weighting of benefits in favor of those with low average lifetime earnings. However, some studies show that those who stay move up the income scale. Therefore, classifying all illegals as lifetime low earners seems unwarranted.

Immigration experts know little about actual illegal immigrant patterns. Experts differ as to the length of time Mexican illegals stay in the United States and how many would qualify for benefits. Even so, most believe that employers regularly pay Social Security taxes for illegals because to do otherwise would prove that the employer knew they were illegal entrants. *Time* magazine's July 1985 special issue on immigration settled on 70 percent as the portion for whom Social Security taxes are paid, though it did not indicate how it derived that figure. If the majority of employers do pay Social Security taxes on their illegals but many of those will not qualify for benefits, illegals become money makers for the program. Moreover, nonresident aliens pay income tax on half their benefits without a threshold.

Immigration legislation enacted in October 1986 designed to regain control of our borders (as the proponents put the proposition) depends heavily upon making employers liable for knowingly employing illegals. It remains to be seen whether this device will discourage illegal immigration and employment. A 1982 General Accounting Office study reports that laws in Canada, West Germany, France, Switzerland, Greece, Hong Kong, and Sweden imposing penalties on employers for hiring illegal aliens had little effect. Employer evasion, difficulties in coordinating governmental agency enforcement activities, limited personnel, and light penalties all contributed to reported lack of success.[10] While the report does not demonstrate the impossibility of effective control of employment of illegal aliens through sanctions directed at employers, the widespread lack of success strongly suggests the difficulty of such undertakings, especially in periods of budget-imposed stringency. The Mexican whip of necessity and the U.S. lure of employment and better pay will continue to drive and draw millions of hopefuls across our permeable borders.

At the height of debate over legislation to curb illegal immigration, the Immigration and Naturalization Service employed 7,600 people—fewer than one-third the number of people on the New York City police force—of whom about 3,000 were deployed along the Mexican border. Short of an offensive and expensive Berlin-style "wall," the United States will not and cannot physically seal its 2,000-mile border with Mexico.

High U.S. unemployment might discourage immigration. However, given the low standards of living throughout most of the world and the sad contrast between widespread repression or stratification elsewhere and freedom and opportunity here we can expect the United States to remain irresistibly attractive. Many will continue to have the urge, the energy, and the determination to enter the promised land.

The major point to keep in mind is this: when and if labor shortages threaten owing to the increase in the older population and the relative decrease in the numbers of labor market entrants due to lower birth rates, our economy can gain eager workers by increasing legal immigration. Such a step would become acceptable if the U.S. economy needed more people to work.

Too Many People, Too Few Jobs.   Confronted by the argument that illegal immigration probably counteracts the threat of the dread aged dependency ratio or, if it does not, that we could expand legal immigration to obtain whatever numbers of people we wish, many ask: Where will we find jobs for all of those people? This is the reverse of the question posed by the aged dependency ratio, but a legitimate one.

A scarcity of jobs could result from either great growth in productivity, shrinking of overseas markets for U.S. manufactured and agricultural goods, increased imports, or an unforeseen long-term decline in effective demand.

If productivity produces job scarcity, fewer people would be required to support a larger dependent population. Expanded leisure, longer vacations, shorter work weeks, and earlier retirement would be desirable ways of sharing work and the products of work should that occur. Higher productivity combined with reduced work hours have been the pattern for most of this century. Thus far, the economy has been able to absorb such changes.

The Dread Aged-Dependency Ratio

Few ideas have captured the public mind so completely as the notion that in the next century a combination of low birth rates and increasingly long life will produce too few young people to support too many old people who draw Social Security benefits. Since the early 1980s, everyone has heard this litany: in the 1940s, 30 people at work supported 1 Social Security beneficiary; by 1950, that ratio fell to 16 to 1. That was only to be expected for a new program with few people eligible in its early years. At the beginning of the 1980s, the worker/beneficiary ratio dropped to 3.5 to 1; and in the second or third decade of the next century, the actuary's projections show a ratio of only 2 people at work to each 1 drawing benefits.*

The ratio is calculated by dividing the older population (sixty-five and over) by the younger population (eighteen to sixty-four; sometimes twenty to sixty-four), sometimes denominated the working-age population. However, for starters, this division by age group is faulty because many in the eighteen to sixty-four group do not work and some sixty-five and older do work. (While many do not take account of this distinction between age and working status, the SSA actuary does.)

The aged-dependency-ratio analysis persuaded many that a fundamental, chronic, and worsening imbalance between old and young threatened Social Security solvency immediately and constituted a fatal flaw for the future. It appeared to follow that in such a situation those fewer workers would have to bear much larger burdens unless benefits were reduced. However, the focus of the aged-dependency-ratio analysis is faulty. More pertinent to the ability of the economy to support an older population is the total dependency ratio—the relationship of all dependent groups to the working population.

Taking that approach, we find that the ratio of persons in supposedly non-producing age groups in the 1960s and 1970s was less favorable than the projections for that ratio throughout the next fifty years (see table 3.1 and figure 3.1).

The President's Commission on Pension Policy working paper described the implications of the data contained in table 3.1: "When *both* the young and the old are counted as dependents, the *net* effect of the shifts in both of their populations tends to be small."[11] Note especially that the level of total dependency in the 1960s and 1970s will not be reached again at least through 2040. A similar 1983 Census Bureau comparison projects that the "total support ratio" (its terminology) will not be as unfavorable as it was in 1960 through the next ninety years.[12]

The aged-dependency-ratio approach totally ignores the costs of the dependent young. Though the amount expended to support a young person generally is less than that required for a retired person, national total expenditures for young people constitute a major segment of gross national product. Taking account of the costs of education and training, roughly $100 billion annually in the mid-1970s, the largest nondefense, nontransfer governmental costs in our society, the dollar amounts dedicated to the young are formidable.

If the dependent young become a smaller portion of the population as projected, some of society's wealth now directed to their support, education,

---

* Program planners fully anticipated these developments which derive, so far, in large measure from maturation of the system. Both maturation and demographic changes have been taken into account in preparing long-range financial projections.

TABLE 3.1

Potential Dependent Population
as a Percentage of the Potential Working Population
(100 = Equal Numbers of Dependent and Nondependent)

	Aged Dependency (Population 65 Yrs. and over Divided by Population 18–64) × 100		Total Dependency (Population 65 Yrs. and over and 0–17 Yrs. Divided by Population 18–64) × 100	
Actual				
1930	9.1%		67.8%	
1940	10.9		59.7	
1950	13.4		64.4	
1960	16.8		81.6	
1970	17.5		78.0	
	Series II	Series III	Series II	Series III
Projected				
1980	18.4%	18.4%	64.3%	63.2%
1990	20.0	20.0	63.5	58.7
2000	19.9	20.2	53.2	56.5
2010	20.2	21.2	59.4	52.8
2020	31.8	37.6	73.8	70.3
2040	30.6	39.0	71.8	71.5

NOTE: While the commission report refers to the "*Potential* Dependent Population" and the "*Potential* Working Population," public discussions drop the "potential" and treat the age groups as if they truly equal dependents and supporters.
SOURCE: Bureau of the Census, *Current Population Reports*, ser. P-25, no. 704, July 1977; and President's Commission on Pension Policy, "Demographic Shifts and Projections: The Implications for Pension Systems," 1979, p. 28. Series II and III indicate two different sets of assumptions about birth and mortality rates.

and training might be redirected to the retired population. The United States may not want to reduce educational efforts in proportion to the shrinkage in the young population, nor do we advocate such a contraction; quite the contrary. We only seek to show how the oversimplified aged-dependency-ratio approach takes a complex set of factors and reduces them to a formula that eliminates important variables.

Immigration and greater employment opportunities for older people, women, minorities, and the disabled can produce a larger working population if the economy requires it. Or, increased productivity could reduce the need for workers. Ignoring these variables, some discussions of the ratio improperly assume that if there are fewer people aged eighteen through sixty-four vis-à-vis older people, then the financial burden on working people becomes unbearable.

FIGURE 3.1

Dependency Ratios of Older and Younger Persons
to Working-Age Population, 1965–2055

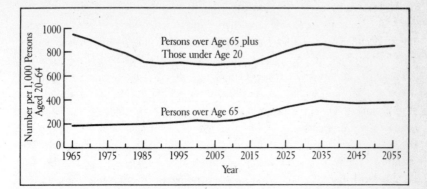

SOURCE: Reprinted with permission, from Wilbur Cohen, "Reappraising Social Security Fifty Years Later," *Economic Outlook, U.S.A.* (Third Quarter 1985): 65. Derived from the 1984 Report of the Board of Trustees of the Federal Old-Age and Survivors and Disability Insurance Trust Funds, 98th Cong., 2d sess., 5 April 1984, H. Doc. 98–200, 85. Former Secretary Cohen noted: "Three different sets of assumptions are made [about the total dependency ratio]. In 1960 the ratio was 91.5 percent of the working age population, twenty to sixty-four. It is never estimated to be this high under alternatives one or two and not to reach 92 percent under alternative three until the year 2050."

While the SSA actuary also finds a worsening of the aged-dependency ratio, it projects other offsetting factors sufficient to maintain the program in "close actuarial balance" under the II-B assumptions.

Improved Productivity: Increasing How Much There Is to Share[13]

Even assuming that the projected demographic crunch materializes in the extreme form currently predicted, the Social Security cash program should have adequate resources to meet current law commitments. Proportionally fewer people at work can generate sufficient goods and services to support a proportionally larger group of older persons because of steady, even if modest, improvements in productivity. The amount of goods and services an economy produces is the result of four basic ingredients of an economy: the size of the labor force, capital, knowledge and technology, and natural resources. As in any equation, if one element, say labor, declines, it can be offset by an increase in any one or a combination of the other elements.

Since the beginning of the industrial revolution people have been working less but producing and consuming more. Agriculture demonstrates improved productivity most strikingly. At the turn of the century, approximately 40 percent of the U.S. population engaged in farming. Today, about 3 percent do, a greater than thirteenfold reduction.[14] By the logic of the aged-dependency ratio, we should be starving, because not enough people work at producing food. These data demonstrate dramatically that the number of bodies at work does not necessarily determine the level of sustenance possible for growing numbers of elderly or the burden borne by the remainder.

Since the close of World War II, the United States, the western democracies, Japan, South Korea, Taiwan, and several "third world" countries have experienced unprecedented improvements in their general standard of living. Today we take for granted the luxuries of a half-century ago—telephones, refrigerators, automatic washing machines, more than one set of clothing, meat and chicken several times a week, restaurant meals, completing high school and college, and one, two, or more cars (in collaboration with our banks, to be sure). Meanwhile, the six-day work week, the standard in the 1930s, has shrunk to five days. Paid vacations, a luxury of the few a half-century ago, are now standard. Most of us do not work harder than our forebears; probably the opposite. Science and technology have generated more and cheaper goods while our real incomes have grown. Productivity improvement—more output with less time worked— is the key to this new era of affluence and, for some, even opulence. Even with fewer people at work, living standards can rise. There is nothing theoretical about it.

Why then the panic about the projected demographic crunch? In part, although the SSA actuary takes full account of it, the productivity factor is often overlooked in public discussions. Furthermore, concern over the prospective aged-dependency ratio coincided with a slowdown in the growth of productivity.

Despair over U.S. productivity deepened in the early 1980s just when Congress and the 1982 commission considered the design of a rescue package. People talked about the demise of the era of cheap energy as if that alone underlay the remarkable economic expansion of the post–World War II period. Certainly from 1973 onward, leaping petroleum costs and a faltering nuclear power industry gave cause for concern. As Japanese cars and cameras, Korean shoes and steel, and Taiwanese and Thai textiles gobbled up an ever-larger share of the U.S. market, the future of the domestic economy appeared shaky. Some suggested that the United States had lost its touch, that it must learn to do with less and to share a shrinking pie. That mood of dejection dominated the Social Security debate.

Starting in the mid-1970s, real earnings fell as prices outpaced average compensation. Production faltered. A decline in the rate of new U.S. patents indicated to some that even our inventiveness was drying up. Many complained about the decline of the work ethic and disparaged the "new worker," the hedonistic youth who purportedly pours more energy into Saturday night fever than Monday-through-Friday work. The business community bemoaned the deadening hand of bureaucracy, contending that environmental health and safety controls increase production costs and prevent U.S. industry from competing successfully with producers in less environmentally conscientious areas.* As a larger proportion of the work force became employed in the service industries and manufacturing employment shrank, the view began to take hold that U.S. productivity was doomed to slow down.

Despite actual improvements in productivity in the recent past, many maintain that economic productivity will not improve. The *New York Times* financial page headline, reporting the conclusions of two eminent economists in 1983, blared, "Productivity Study Implies Dim Future."[15] William Baumol of Princeton and Edward Wolff of New York University predicted that "the quality of life thirty years from now could deteriorate because many of the services we associate with quality of life will become relatively more expensive while mass-produced things become cheaper and cheaper." An example, taken from Baumol's earlier study of the arts, pointed out that it takes the same number of "musician hours" to play a Mozart quartet now as it did when Amadeus minted it, yet live concert tickets recently had become more expensive. In Mozart's time, however, one had to be of the nobility or haute bourgeoisie to enjoy live concerts. Larger halls, recordings, radio, and television make such performances available today to millions of people. In terms of hours of musical consumption provided, current musical production sates many more appetites for the same number of musician hours worked. Unfortunately some writers extrapolated from Baumol and Wolff's atypical example and sadly observed that poor productivity in the services dooms us to a poorer life.

Indeed it is the commonly expressed view that growth of the service sector relative to manufacturing inevitably means less or no growth because, as with the quartet, productivity cannot be improved in the service sector. One must be skeptical. First, service production is especially hard to measure. Second, some improvements have been dramatic. Take telephone service. In 1950, some 565,000 employees served 39 million phones. But, by 1980, less than double the number of people (938,000) served four times the number of instruments (157 million).[16] Similarly, over the decade 1975–84, the number of checks processed by Federal Reserve Banks increased almost 50 percent while the number of employees dropped about 10 percent.[17] Ian Ross, former president of Bell Laboratories, reported in the early 1980s that for about twenty years the number of components on a silicon chip doubled *every year*. A few years ago,

---

* That comparison may be unduly self-congratulatory. For example, Engineering Professor Seymour Melman reports that pollution controls in the Japanese steel industry "are at least as rigorous as those in the United States." Seymour Melman, *Profits Without Production* (New York: A. A. Knopf, 1983), p. 234*n*48.

the rate of doubling capacity became eighteen months, arguably a slowdown but still a fantastic rate of progress. At the same time, he said, the cost per transistor decreased one thousandfold.[18]

Despite such developments, many in the press and public seemed to hear only the bad news. Opinion polls in the 1970s showed that a majority expected their children to be worse off economically than the respondents were. (A possible hidden factor here is the chronic parental worry as to whether their children ever will be self-supporting.)

In 1979, a masterly review of the literature on productivity by Professor Mark Perlman concluded that:

> fluctuations in productivity growth rates are inherent, and the poorer performance of the recent [five years], which was preceded by the unusually high performance of the early and mid-1960s, is in the usual course of such things likely to be followed by somewhat better, although not record-breaking, figures.[19]

Similarly, a 1987 Congressional Budget Office review of the literature on productivity concluded that "many of the factors that are believed to have contributed to the slowdown in productivity have reversed in recent years.[20] However, CBO cautions against undue optimism because of several factors, such as overcapacity in office building space and continued problems in energy production. Even so, for the short run on which its forecasts concentrate, it assumes real GNP growth in the vicinity of 2.7 to 2.8 percent through 1992.[21]

A major factor in the recent productivity slowdown, some believe, was the unprecedented growth of the labor force. MIT Professor Lester Thurow observes that when the baby boom generation hit the labor market in the 1970s, no commensurate amounts of new capital were introduced. The ratio of capital to labor (the amount of equipment available to the average worker) decreased. This pattern, says Thurow, was the rational response of entrepreneurs to a rapidly swelling labor supply and consequently lower labor costs. The process was accelerated by the growth in the service sector and the Reagan administration's policies of reducing the amount and duration of unemployment compensation while pressing for economic policies that increased unemployment. Employers found it feasible, indeed desirable, to use more labor and less capital in their endeavors.[22]

If, as predicted, the labor supply shrinks, employers will behave in a similar (but opposite) fashion. As labor becomes scarce, and so higher priced, company strategists will infuse greater amounts of capital, thereby increasing productivity. In consequence, fewer workers will produce more goods and services than their counterparts do today.

Even in the booming 1950s, GNP declined in the recession years of 1954 and 1958.[23] Despite slowed productivity growth, and except for the recessions in the mid-1970s and the early 1980s, the accepted data show productivity advances—albeit at a slower pace than in the 1950s and 1960s—since the close of World War II.

Two basic economic developments do cause concern about the future of productivity: the allocation of resources and the pursuit of paper profits. For decades, Seymour Melman, a Columbia University professor of engineering, has argued that the heavy U.S. emphasis on armaments beggars the civilian economy, diverting the talents of engineers and scientists. Comparing the German and Japanese experiences he notes:

> In the United States in 1977, for every $100 of new producers' fixed capital formation, the military spent $46. In West Germany in 1977, the figure was $18.90 and in Japan it was $3.70. On an average, from 1960 to 1978 the United States used for military purposes $52 of capital resources for every hundred dollars [for] civilian productive purposes.[24]

Meanwhile, in the decade 1965–75, average annual productivity in Japan grew 10 percent, in Germany, 5 percent, and in the United States, 2 percent.[25] Similarly, he points out that federal government expenditures for research and development exceeded those for all private enterprises, but that in 1981, 71 percent of U.S. government research and development went to military programs.[26]

Second, the pursuit of paper profits and the quest for quick results on the bottom line that impel the takeover movement also arguably introduce economic distortions and diversions of talent. CEOs who mount takeovers or defend against them do not have the time or attention to give to the long-term investments and innovations upon which future improvements in productivity depend.

These elements can limit our economic future. Unless we turn our attention to more productive endeavors, we will all be poorer and have less to share. Growing concern over these trends suggests that remedies may be undertaken.

We do not argue that productivity growth has not slowed but that pessimism generated by the slowed growth of the 1970s and 1980s should not be taken to mean that economic development in the United States has reached the end of the line. The country has real problems. We also have good prospects.

Sar Levitan and Diane Werneke provide a useful discussion of policy decisions that can feed productivity growth.[27] They advocate improved schooling and greater training and retraining programs, measures advocated in 1987 by President Reagan, Secretary of Labor Brock, many in Congress, and presidential candidates in and out of Congress. Thus, we may be on the verge of major efforts that can improve productivity.

Long-Range Actuarial Forecasts for GNP

The 1983 II-B best guess projections for GNP showed a revival of growth in the 1980s followed by slower growth in the 1990s, leveling off to a long-term annual increase of 2.6 percent.* Although below the post–World War II average, the rate nonetheless struck many as unduly optimistic. Similar skepticism greeted the interest rate assumptions. Rates that had ranged as high as 22 percent in the late 1970s were forecast to level off at 6.1 percent starting in 1990. Some regarded these predictions as a sham manufactured to enable a paper rescue of Social Security.

Well, interest rates did indeed moderate and come within the predicted range. And GNP improvements postulated for the early 1980s erred on the side of caution as the following data show:

TABLE 3.2
Movements of GNP 1983–85

	Trustees 1983 Forecast II-B (in percentages)	Actual (in percentages)
1983	+2.4	+3.4
1984	+4.1	+6.6
1985	+3.7	+2.3

SOURCES: First column: 1983 Annual Report—Federal Old-Age and Survivors Insurance and Disability Insurance Trust Funds, table 10, p. 37. Second column: U.S. Congressional Budget Office, "The Economic and Budget Outlook: Fiscal years 1987–1991," (February 1986), part I, table I-15, p. 55, based on U.S. Department of Commerce data.

In assessing the 1985 comparison, account must be taken of the fact that the actual 1985 GNP change was based on a higher floor than the 1983 II-B forecasts.

The question naturally arises as to whether we can rely on the forecasts made by the actuaries and adopted by the trustees. We can, provided that the nature of those projections is understood. They are *not* predictions. Rather they

* The *1987 Trustees Report* forecasts lower improvements in GNP (table 10, p. 33). A note to that table makes it clear that the projected "size and age-sex distribution of the population" is the key factor. In our judgment, the assumptions reflect the unduly low projections for immigration. Even so, the report continues, other factors offset these more pessimistic GNP assumptions and so overall "close actuarial balance" is projected.

are estimates of the most likely sets of conditions that can reasonably be expected. The "best guess" is the one regarded as most likely to occur, but shaded on the side of caution and pessimism.

The actuaries constantly monitor the assumptions, taking account of their own new studies and those of other experts, and modify assumptions to reflect changes that seem to constitute a trend. Even so, the estimates can err. Indeed, they must. It would be uncanny if any set of human beings, no matter how smart and zealous, could foretell the future. Miscalculations of one sort are offset by the reciprocal action of other factors. So, for example, low birth rates (an area of special concern), which produce a labor shortage, would stimulate both legal and illegal immigration. Some labor market experts opine that there is no such thing as a labor shortage because the demand for labor will lure such people as retirees and the disabled into the labor market and employers will enlarge their capital investments.

The frequent criticism that the actuarial estimates have been mistaken in the past and have led to incorrect congressional action mistakes what the forecasts do. They give us guidance about the likely range of outcomes of present decisions and provide benchmarks to gauge how well we are doing in achieving those goals. While the economic future is not assuredly rosy, neither is it forbidding. We have a powerful free economy. The trustees repeatedly report that the cash programs are in close actuarial balance over the next seventy-five years and most experts agree.

How Much People Pay: Solving the Covered Payroll Puzzle

Social Security trust fund income depends on how many people work, how much they earn, and how much of earnings comes in cash and how much in fringe benefits. Employees and employers pay FICA taxes on cash compensation but *not* on most fringes. Assumptions about the percentage of total income in the form of fringe benefits were a significant factor in the pre-1982 Social Security actuary's predictions of a long-range funding crisis. Yet this variable never figured in the public discussion. These assumptions still constitute a projected drag on program income, a drag that can be ameliorated and even eliminated.

The Social Security actuary still projects that noncash compensation will continue to grow more rapidly than total compensation. Though total compensation will grow larger, the projections anticipate that the taxable portion of compensation will diminish. In 1981, Professor Yung-Ping Chen of the American College and McCahan Institute (institutions funded by the insurance industry) noted that between 1953 and 1980 the portion of compensation received in cash declined. But, he wrote, if fringes were to grow only at the same pace as cash earnings, the long-term deficit would be 1.26 percent rather than the 1.58 percent then predicted under II-B.[28]

Two questions arise: Will fringe benefits continue to grow as a proportion of total compensation as projected? If they do, can that erosion of taxable payroll be reduced or avoided?

Fringe Growth Slowing. Fueled by a burgeoning economy, the two highest-cost fringe benefits—pensions and health insurance—grew phenomenally in the 1950s, 1960s, and 1970s. In the 1980s, as their costs have increased, employer resistance has grown. The Employee Benefit Research Institute (EBRI) reports that employer contributions to pension plans as a percentage of total compensation *declined* between 1980 and 1983.[29] Furthermore, coverage for the principal kinds of benefits (retirement, health, and life insurance) is now so extensive that future benefit cost increases represent an ever smaller percentage of total coverage. And, in the 1980s, many employers succeeded in requiring employees to bear a larger portion of medical-care premiums. Most segments of the economy and government have mobilized against rising health-insurance costs. Limitations on deferred income plans imposed by the 1986 Tax Reform Act also should reduce the use earlier projected. Therefore, in the future, it seems reasonable to expect less rapid growth in fringe benefits.[30] The 1984 trustees' report scaled down fringe-benefit growth assumptions 25 percent from the previous year's prognostication. This adjustment produced a long-range projected improvement in the trust fund of about 0.125 percent of payroll. The 1987 report further reduced the estimate of shrinkage in cash wages.

In the 1970s, employers and insurers combined to improve workers' compensation benefits as part of their fight to resist proposed mandatory federal standards. Although occupational disease coverage remains scandalously scant, prospects are dim for further substantial improvement in workers' compensation. Fringe-benefit growth seems to be slowing.

Fixing the Fringe Benefit Problem. A relatively simple and eminently feasible legislative change can reduce the impact of fringe-benefit growth upon FICA collections. If the employer payroll tax were applied to total compensation (wages and fringes) and the employer tax rate lowered so that its yield would equal employer payroll taxes when the rates reach their 1990 level (the year of the last scheduled rate boost), the total employer contribution and burden would remain steady regardless of the source of compensation. The FICA rate reduction might make such a change more acceptable to employers in general and especially attractive to employers who offer few or no fringes. The projected loss of revenue from projected contraction in cash pay would be cut in half.

If a similar arrangement were made for employee contributions, the problem caused by the projected shrinkage in the taxable payroll base would disappear. Such a shift for employees may be more difficult to implement and more questionable as a matter of policy. For example, employer contributions to private pension plans produce only deferred income, and then only to those plan participants who qualify for benefits. To treat the employer pension contributions as current taxable income to all employees in the plan would tax them for income they do not possess and have no assurance of possessing. Nonetheless, all contributions constitute employee compensation on the employer's part.

As a practical matter, the application of payroll tax to all employer compensation payments would be relatively easy, because employer records register outlays for such payments (even for self-insurers). Application to employee fringes that confer current benefits and protection would be more complex but manageable with computerized payroll records.

This proposed change would enhance the outlook for Social Security financing without increasing employer or employee burdens. The change would simply avoid an unintended and unjustifiable contraction of contributions. The benefit formula would require adjustment so as to produce benefits equal to those now based on cash earnings alone.

Some argue that removing the Social Security tax advantage now accorded fringes would discourage uses that are socially desirable. However, the income-tax advantages of fringes create a far greater incentive for their use. By comparison, the incentive to offer or withdraw fringe benefits created by their Social Security tax treatment is insignificant. The 1983 amendments made 401(k) contributions subject to FICA (but not income tax). No reports of slackened interest in the device resulted: on the contrary, their use increased.

In sum, fringe benefits probably will not grow as projected. If they do, the problem can be cut in half by making all employer compensation payments subject to FICA, but at lower rates. Similarly, making fringes of current benefit subject to FICA even at a reduced rate for employees would further reduce the problem. If fringes become taxable as a part of total compensation for Social Security purposes, the actuarial balance is estimated to improve markedly. Legislation can put the issue to rest.

Social Security, the Budget, the Deficit, and the National Debt

Few subjects cause more confusion than the relationship of the Social Security trust funds to the deficit, the budget, and the national debt.

Three of the four trust funds, OASI, DI, and HI, are self-sustaining. Their income from employer and employee contributions, taxes on benefits, and interest on the reserves invested in government bonds, and miscellaneous minor other income, pays for both the benefits and the administrative expenses of the program. The fourth trust fund differs. Supplementary Medical Insurance (SMI) derives part of its income from premiums paid by participants—roughly a quarter. General Treasury funds obtained from federal taxes supply the remainder of that trust fund's income.

In most years, the current income of the OASI, DI, and HI funds in combination have exceeded their payout, leaving modest multibillion dollar balances. Alicia Munnell, senior vice president of the Federal Reserve Bank of Boston, reports that Social Security trust fund income (counting the federal government's payments along with all other employer payments) exceeded payout in thirty-nine of the forty-nine years through 1986. During that same period, the remainder of the federal budget showed deficits in forty-three years; in thirty-one of those years, Munnell found, Social Security surpluses offset the deficit in the remainder of the budget, putting it into surplus in two years, 1949 and 1969. As Munnell reports, during its first forty-nine years of financial operations, that is, from 1937 through 1986, Social Security trust funds including Medicare (HI) collected $2.235 trillion and paid out $2.180 trillion, producing a $58 billion surplus. Even if the modest indirect general revenue contribution made by the tax credits given for some FICA and SECA contributions for a short time in the 1980s are taken out of account, the trust funds produced reserves of more than $50 billion in their first half-century.[31]

For a few years in the early 1980s, the OASI fund borrowed from DI and HI reserves to keep going, but did not tap general Treasury funds for the purpose; instead, the reserves performed their function of carrying one or another trust fund over periods of low cash flow.

Since enactment of the 1983 amendments, OASDI reserves have been rebuilding and have repaid the HI fund with interest. The only Social Security program that contributes to the federal budget deficit is the general-revenue-funded portion of SMI, which amounted to about $18 billion in fiscal year 1985.

Originally, Social Security trust fund revenues and outlays appeared in a separate statement of governmental accounts apart from the Administrative Budget of the United States. Beginning in fiscal year 1969, a new unified budget consolidated all accounts with their own earmarked revenues into the administrative budget. Hence, all income and outlays from all programs, those like Social Security with earmarked income, and those dependent upon general revenues, were reported together. In consequence, when OASDI and HI trust funds run a positive balance, the total U.S. deficit appears lower. This provides a powerful inducement to budget makers to reduce Social Security benefits. Such a reduction, without a commensurate reduction in Social Security taxes, diminishes total outlays and so produces a greater surplus, thereby reducing the overall budget deficit or even producing a surplus.

The 1983 amendments provided for separating Social Security's financial operations from the budget by 1993. In 1985, Congress accelerated that process except for the purpose of counting Social Security toward Gramm-Rudman deficit reduction targets. However, Gramm-Rudman exempted Social Security benefits from its mandatory cuts.

OASDI Reserves and How They May Be Used[32] *

After just scraping by during the 1970s and the first half of the 1980s, Social Security OASDI trust funds face a markedly different future. Surplus will pile on top of surplus. The process has already begun. By the end of fiscal year 1986, the OASDI reserve totaled some $45.8 billion. Those reserves should build dramatically over the next thirty years, totaling roughly $9.6 trillion by 2020,† possibly more. This results from a combination of factors: lower rates of retirement owing to the low Great Depression and World War II birth rates; greater numbers in the work force as a result of the baby boom generation; the modest 1988 and 1990 increases in FICA and SECA rates; and real growth in

---

* This entire discussion draws largely upon Alicia H. Munnell and Lynn E. Blais, "Do We Want Large Social Security Surpluses?" *New England Economic Review* (September–October, 1984): 5. This splendid article lays out with great clarity the arguments for and against accumulating large reserves. Non-economists can handle this discussion. It kindly segregates a mathematical section which is not central to understanding the main points.

† Chief Actuary Harry C. Ballantyne, "Long Range Estimates of Social Security Trust Fund Operations in Dollars," Social Security Administration, Actuarial Note 127 (April 1986), table 1, p. 2.

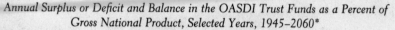

FIGURE 3.2

Annual Surplus or Deficit and Balance in the OASDI Trust Funds as a Percent of Gross National Product, Selected Years, 1945–2060*

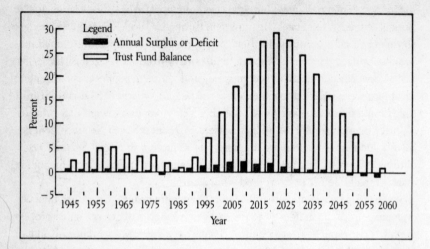

* Figures for 1945–1980 represent the average of the annual surplus or deficit and balance in the OASDI trust funds over the preceding five years. Figures for 1985–2060 are annual figures projected under the alternative assumption II-B. 1984 OASDI Trustees Report.
NOTE: From Alicia Munnell and Lynn Blais, "Do We Want Large Social Security Surpluses?" *New England Economic Review* (September–October 1984):7.
SOURCES: Social Security Administration, *Annual Report of Trustees of the Federal Old-Age and Survivors Insurance and Disability Insurance Trust Funds* (GPO, 1984), table 33, p. 78; *Social Security Bulletin, Annual Statistical Supplement 1982* (GPO, n.d.), tables 14 and 18, pp. 70 and 72; Harry C. Ballantyne, A.S.A., *Long-Range Projections of Social Security Trust Fund Operations in Dollars.* Office of the Actuary, Actuarial Note 120 (May 1984); and *Economic Report of the President* (GPO, 1984). table B-1, p. 220.

wages. On the basis of the best guess actuarial forecast, beginning in about 2030 the OASDI trust funds will begin to run annual deficits that will grow steadily larger. Figure 3.2, developed by Alicia Munnell, depicts the past, present, and future surpluses and deficits using the 1984 II-B estimates. In the 2030s, when trust fund payout begins to exceed income, the period of decumulation will begin.

Under current law, the total surplus and total deficit will be roughly equal through 2060 (the point at which current projections stop).

What happens with the surplus funds in the interim will determine how the annual shortfalls that start around 2030 will be met.

Three scenarios seem possible.

First: Enhancing Private Investment

To enhance private investment, the reserves would continue to be used to purchase bonds issued by the Treasury and other government agencies. For the foreseeable future, the vast deficits run by the federal government require borrowing, which, in the main, takes the form of government bonds issued to private investors and is generally known as publicly-held debt. Private funds used to purchase government bonds and notes become unavailable for private investment. The ensuing scarcity of private funds for private investments, known as "crowding out,"[33] pushes up interest rates and discourages private investment in new enterprises.

OASDI reserves reduce the amount Treasury must borrow from the public. As a result, private savings that, but for the OASDI surpluses, would be required to finance federal spending, must move into private investment. The new funds will become available for new enterprises and will drive down interest rates. Both developments should facilitate borrowing by private enterprise, as well as by state and local governments, increasing the wealth-producing capacity and infrastructure of the nation. In subsequent years enlarged production would help generate additional federal revenues with which to pay off the special obligation bonds when the OASDI trust funds decumulate.

In other words, using Social Security surpluses to purchase government bonds, making them unavailable to private investors, would produce the equivalent of true savings and spur economic growth.[34]

Second: Masking Deficits Elsewhere in the Budget

Alternatively, the reserves can be used to continue masking government deficits by combining the income and payout accounts of Social Security with those of all other government programs, in effect, continuing the "unified budget." If the OASDI reserves are used to make the government books look better and thereby encourage continued or enlarged expenditures, unmatched by adequate general taxes (as has been the case throughout the 1980s), federal borrowing will remain high. Furthermore, investment in the private sector will not be encouraged to the same extent as in scenario one because a larger portion of the surpluses will go into the larger debt.

The salutary purpose of separating OASDI accounts from those in the general budget is to make sure that the consequences of other major programs can be identified. If the OASDI surplus is not used to reduce the public debt, then when the period of decumulation begins in the 2030s and OASDI cashes in its special obligation bonds, the Treasury will have to borrow to refinance the expanded debt or Congress will have to increase general taxes, or possibly both. The population at that time would be taxed to redeem the special obligation bonds out of an economy less productive than under the first scenario; general revenues would be smaller, or FICA and/or general tax rates would have to be higher.

Third: Reducing FICA or Improving Benefits

The growing reserves may encourge cancellation of the payroll-tax increases scheduled for 1988 and 1990. In addition, or instead, the payroll tax may be redistributed so as to increase revenues for HI and decrease those for OASI. That would ameliorate the funding difficulties many foretell for HI. Further, the increasing costs of SMI might also lead Congress to divert some payroll-tax revenues into that trust fund, which might lessen the incentive for HI and SMI cost control. Such diversion should be undertaken only if and when further Medicare cost control becomes impossible.

It might be argued that if FICA and SECA were lowered, the larger amount of funds in private hands would become available for investment. However, consumers spend most of every dollar received on current consumption. In that case, it does not get saved.

Some fear that large reserves may lead Congress to improve benefits, lessening or eliminating chances for the first scenario. Some, Paul Light reports, deny the significance of the impending surpluses for future solvency, alleging that any surpluses will be used simply to sweeten benefits without providing assured financing. However, given the intense concern over funding adequacy, such a development seems unlikely.

Indeed, it may be especially desirable to improve benefits and services to the older elderly. Within the limits of human ability to look ahead, however, program improvements should be financed fully over a long period of time so as to minimize the cost burdens in any given period. That argues against tapping the reserves to enhance benefits.

The Arguments Against Large Reserves

Attractive as the first scenario is, some Social Security experts argue against permitting such huge reserves to build. Even with the separation of Social Security accounts from the unified budget, those making federal budget decisions will look to the net amounts resulting from government taxation and spending. If an OASDI-produced surplus cancels deficits in other programs, some will find higher expenditures in non–Social Security expenditures more acceptable. Indeed, it has been argued that it will be impossible to tell whether an OASDI surplus is reducing debt or expenditures. The numbers can be totalled separately, however, and Congress may well insist that the non–Social Security budget be required to be justified by itself.[35]

Munnell and Blais point out that the projected Social Security reserves are created by those who pay into the funds until 2030. The question becomes: should we maintain the 1990 rates and build the large reserves throughout the work life of this group, when those at work after 2030 are expected to have higher real income and would be better able to bear the burden of a higher tax rate? The payroll tax, it is argued, makes a questionable instrument for forced savings. Rather, the more progressive income tax is the preferable vehicle for mandatory savings because it bears less heavily on the low-paid. However, it is income tax revenues that will be used to repay the bonds in the large reserves as they come due. So, the more progressive income tax plays a role in the large reserves scenario.

As things stand, after the last payroll tax increase in 1990, all participants will pay the same FICA/SECA tax rates on comparable income. If a surplus were not desired, those at work until 2030 could pay lower FICA/SECA tax rates. Then, starting in 2030 or so, the annual shortfalls would require raising those rates to match the payout.

Munnell and Blais also point out that massive accumulations of funds for investment by the federal government may exceed the supply of government bonds and so raise questions about investment by the federal government in private undertakings, a problem avoided by continuing on the essentially pay-as-you-go financing arrangement pursued up to the present by OASDHI. Furthermore, the monopolization of government obligations by the federal government would alter, and might impair, the means by which the Federal Reserve Board affects the money supply so as to dampen or stimulate the economy. However, the Fed might advantageously use other financial instruments for this purpose.

Of course, if the full 1988 and 1990 increases do not go into effect and the projected reserves do not materialize, higher rates than now scheduled will be necessary, starting in the 2020s, to offset the deficits that would start soon thereafter under current projections. The required increase would be on the order of 1 percent for employees and another 1 percent for employers (a combined 2 percent for the self-employed). Those increases seem modest, especially because they should come out of yet higher real earnings and so would not impair living standards.

These are powerful arguments that must be weighed against the desirability of building confidence in the future of Social Security, a confidence that probably would be enhanced by the prospect of large reserves to fuel economic growth.

In any event, OASDI will need the 1988 and 1990 FICA/SECA rate increases in order to produce a reasonable reserve, at least until the mid-1990s, when reserves should reach the neighborhood of 150 percent of a year's benefits, a higher level than advisory councils and others have advocated in the past. Such an amount would tide the system over temporary shocks and give Congress, the trustees and the executive branch, and the most interested groups time to consider whether remedial action is needed and what form it should take.

As the 1990s unfold, all concerned will possess more adequate information about the size of impending reserves, the condition and outlook of Medicare, how the economy is faring, and the other major variables pertinent to a decision about future tax rates.

The Outlook for Social Security

As the system now stands, under the actuary's best guess, the OASDI programs are in "close actuarial balance" until the sixth decade of the next century (as far ahead as anyone looks), even *with* essentially the same demographic projections many have found so daunting. If some actuarial assumptions have been overly optimistic (e.g., fertility or productivity growth), other unduly pessimistic factors (for example, immigration and growth of fringe benefits) offset them. The adjusted II-B projections used by the trustees remain conservative forecasts of the future actuarial balance of the OASDI funds. Beyond that, the enormous reserves now expected can help fuel an expanded and more productive economy on which the living standard of future generations depends.

The very demographic developments that make the young fearful over the financial future of Social Security should reassure them. Undoubtedly, in the next century, those over fifty-five will constitute a larger proportion of the population than today. Polls repeatedly show that support for a strong Social Security system is found among all age groups. Even in 1982, a period when the public and Congress felt enormous concern over the federal government's finances and additional taxes were unthinkable, the National Commission recommended and Congress imposed taxes earlier than scheduled and increased the payroll tax on the self-employed, an action impossible without deep underlying popular support. At the same time Social Security proved largely invulnerable to major reductions, except for the change in retirement age, the implications of which most people do not yet understand. Some 11 to 12 percent of the population is now over sixty. In the next century, when the older population becomes proportionally larger, Social Security should be that much more invulnerable if, as some believe, Social Security support is especially intense among older age groups. The young of today, who will be the old of tomorrow, ought to see that their political strength, combined with that of their children, will enable them to repel any proposals to dishonor program commitments to them.

Of course, some deplore such interest-group politics. One might just as well deplore the wind and the sea. They exist. Interest groups exercise power in our democratic system. In a pluralistic society, the interests of some groups tend to moderate the power of other groups. At bottom, Social Security prospers with the electorate because support for it pervades all age groups. As younger people come to believe in the future reliability of Social Security, support will grow still stronger. This crucial political dimension may well provide Social Security's greatest future strength.

PART II

PRIVATE
PROGRAMS

Social Security, though the largest source of retirement and disability income replacement for most people, is not the sole provider. The question repeatedly arises as to what role should be performed by private plans. The answer depends upon the goals assigned to each system and how well—and for how many—each fulfills these goals.

Conventional wisdom holds that retirement income depends on a three-legged stool composed of Social Security, private employment-based group plans, and individual savings. Some add a fourth leg to provide for those without sufficient income from the other three, needs-tested programs, such as Supplemental Security Income for those sixty-five and over, the blind, and the completely disabled, who fall below income and asset levels set by a parsimonious statutory formula. In addition, programs like food stamps, public and subsidized housing, and Medicaid (medical care provided under a federal-state program) may provide supplementary needs-tested aid.

Chapter 4 describes the development and essential features of the second leg of the stool, private employment-based group pension plans. Chapter 5 considers the deficiencies discovered in those plans and how the Employee Retirement Income Security Act (ERISA) and supplementary legislation sought to ameliorate their shortcomings and stem their abuses. Chapter 6 analyzes the role that private pensions can reasonably be expected to play for retired American workers and their survivors, and also describes some types of plans that masquerade as retirement income programs.

4   Private Pensions before ERISA: What and Why

Private retirement income programs constitute a patchwork quilt—a patch here, a bit of padding there, some beautiful plush velvet squares beside a threadbare spot—that covers, at best, half the bed. They can be explained only by reviewing decades of history and happenstance.

Private Plans and How They Grew

Beginning in the 1870s, a handful of U.S. companies instituted programs to pay periodic sums to long-time employees who retired. By the early 1930s, over three hundred companies provided such benefits to no more than 140,000 individuals, including about 50,000 former railroad employees.[1]

These early arrangements did not provide systematic, actuarially-based advance funding to assure plan ability to pay their promises. Indeed, most plans made no promises and even those that appeared to do so retained the right to modify or even discontinue benefit payments. The Great Depression wrecked many such programs, notably in the railroad industry. After that debacle, an industry-union-government agreement established the Railroad Retirement Act, which assumed some of the obligations of that industry's derailed private plans.

During World War II, employment-based private group pension plans began to "take off," but for reasons unrelated to retirement income security. Rather, employers used pension plans to lure employees. During the war, em-

94

ployers could sell almost anything they could produce. The trick was to obtain the materials and people to produce it. The draft reduced the labor supply, and government controls constrained employer ability to attract employees with wages. Regulations, however, exempted group health insurance and pension plans from those limits. Moreover, the government contracted for its vast new needs on a cost-plus basis. Other features of pension plans made them attractive to employers. Pension plan contributions enjoy tax deductibility to the corporate employer, and earnings on plan reserves (amounts not needed currently to pay plan benefits) incur no tax until distributed years later to beneficiaries, who could include corporate owner-employees and managers.* Under such hothouse conditions, union interest in employment-based private group pension plans flowered and employer opposition withered.

By the end of World War II, some courts had begun to treat corporate pension promises as binding, at least once payment of benefits had begun.[2] Courts strictly enforced any eligibility conditions, however, denying benefits to employees who missed the specified service period by as little as a few weeks, even if due to plant closing.[3]

Employers could hedge pension promises as they desired. They could reserve the right to discontinue a plan,[4] and set benefit eligibility conditions that only a minority—even a small minority—of employees could meet. Employers typically appoint their own officers as trustees for company plans.

Several industries, usually those offering short periods of episodic employment and characterized by numerous and usually small employers (as in the coal, construction, garment, maritime, textile, and trucking industries), utilize multi-employer plans. All employers contribute according to amount of payroll, number of hours worked, or output, as in the mineworkers' plans. Multi-employer plans credit almost all employment with any participating employers, but also imposed stringent service requirements to qualify for benefits, typically twenty or twenty-five years, with employment continuing to retirement. Unions and employers jointly administer multi-employer plans.

The 1942 tax code prescribed specific conditions to "qualify" corporate employment-based group plans for deductibility of contributions and exemption of plan earnings from taxation. They continue in force and require that the plan (1) operate for the "exclusive benefit of . . . employees and beneficiaries"; (2) apply contributions and earnings to employee benefits; (3) satisfy valid employee claims before the employer may recapture any plan funds; and (4) be nondiscriminatory, that is, not favor officer, stockholder, or highly-compensated employees over other employees.

---

* We use the past tense in referring to features that existed before ERISA (1974) but that have changed. We use the present tense in referring to characteristics that existed before ERISA and continued thereafter.

Nevertheless, the nondiscrimination rules permit decidedly advantageous treatment for employees with substantial earnings. The tax law specifies minimum coverage.[5] Even the prescribed percentage, however, overstates the requirements, because those who do not meet participation requirements, primarily part-timers and the irregularly employed, may be excluded from the measuring group.

In addition, Congress simultaneously declared that excluding employee earnings below the maximum Social Security taxable amount, then $3,000, did not constitute discrimination,[6] although the obvious effect was to confer private plan benefits solely, primarily, or disproportionately upon high earners.

The rationale for this seemingly inconsistent provision was that the Social Security *benefit* formula favors the low paid. Thus, the argument went, employer *contributions* to *both* Social Security and the private plan and their combined benefits should be compared in determining whether the employer's retirement benefit arrangements discriminate. So far, so good.

However, in making this comparison, the IRS credited the employer as paying for half the Social Security benefit. This does not square with reality because a particular employer makes Social Security contributions for an employee only as long as he or she is employed there, while other employers make contributions for that employee throughout the rest of his or her working lifetime. Nonetheless, the IRS concluded that the particular employer's contribution accounted for half the Social Security benefit. As that theoretical contribution at the time produced a Social Security primary insurance amount that replaced 37.5 percent of the lowest-paid employees' earnings, employers could make contributions to a private plan that did the same for the highest-paid employees. This claimed equality also ignores the several ways in which Social Security in practice produces proportionally larger benefits for upper-income earners than the primary insurance formula suggests (see chapter 1). Further, the private plan benefits and contributions of higher-paid employees often exceed those of Social Security. Nonetheless, the IRS regulations regarded the much larger employer contribution on behalf of high-paid employees as "proportional" to those for low-paid employees, and thus nondiscriminatory.

The process by which a plan takes formal account of Social Security in regard to either contributions or benefits is called integration. The IRS has lengthy and intricate regulations governing integration. These basic conditions survive in the mid-1980s, but have been refined and tightened by later legislation.

In the 1940s, the wartime demand for older workers led many to work rather than retire and draw Social Security. After the war, workers and unions paid fresh attention to retirement income and found Social Security benefits to be extremely modest. The average worker-only benefit paid $24.50 a month.[7] In contrast, manufacturing monthly wages averaged $177.59 at that time.[8]

Employers resisted union demands for employment-based pension plans fueled by employer contributions, arguing that Social Security should meet retirement needs. Although ideologically in agreement, unions found that Social Security benefits were too low for retiree needs and that pension demands had greater acceptibility than demands for higher wages.* In addition, 1949 federal court decisions held that the National Labor Relations Act requires employers to bargain about pensions. By the beginning of the 1950s, employers in major industries acceded.

The Korean War reproduced many of the World War II conditions that encouraged employment-based private pensions. In the 1950s, funding private pension plans appeared easy. Comparatively low plan contributions grew in value and provided spectacular dividends when invested in stocks.

However, a blueprint of the social and economic functions of plans, their income replacement goals, and their role in complementing Social Security did not exist. Rather, fragmentary arguments—such as encouraging employee loyalty—were used to justify plans, and employers were permitted to set any eligibility criteria. Like Topsy, private plans just "growed."

By the mid-1960s, critics began to question the adequacy and fairness of plan design and outcomes.[9] A description of common plan features will assist in appraising those criticisms, the "reforms" ERISA contained, and the current and future role of private pensions.

The Basics of Pension Plan Design

Defined-Benefit Plans

The classic form, the "defined-benefit" pension plan, promises a described benefit, specifying either an amount or a formula for determining the amount payable. "Pattern plans," as those negotiated with major unions in industry became known, typically provide a specified dollar amount every month for each year of credited service under the plan. White-collar plans usually provide monthly benefits based upon a formula linked to salary, such as 1 percent of average pay (over the best five or ten years or last few years of employment) times the number of years of service. Final pay plans now predominate for white-collar workers. In both such plans, the employer undertakes to provide the defined benefits by making periodic contributions to the plan sufficient to

* For example, President Truman's 1949 Steel Industry Fact Finding Board rejected the union case for increasing steelworker wages but found merit in union demands for a pension program financed by employer contributions. *Labor Arbitration Reports* 13 (1949):46.

fund the promised benefits. With "advance funding" the employer contributes more than the benefits currently payable each year of the plan, producing "reserves" which, invested, yield tax-free earnings. In some mature private plans these earnings pay a sizable portion of the benefits. How much depends upon the age of plan participants, how early in the program they retire, their longevity in retirement, the timing of contributions that build reserves, and earnings on reserves.

Many employers regard a defined-benefit plan as risky because the amounts required to fund such a program depend upon variables that cannot be known beforehand. The number of employees who achieve benefits at retirement depends upon employee turnover and death rates prior to reaching retirement age. As these factors cannot be known, the actuary estimates them, taking into account the age and sex of the covered employee group. Young employees are assumed to have higher rates of turnover, older employees lower. Women are assumed to have higher rates of turnover than men, but they tend to live longer. Assumptions about these variables are based upon standard tables adapted to the observed or assumed peculiarities of the covered group.

The plan actuary also makes assumptions about projected earnings on fund reserves. Contributions that exceed current benefit payment requirements generate tax-free income for the trust to pay future benefits. Low initial contributions require that a greater portion of the total benefits be paid from that source rather than earnings. Higher contributions early in the life of the plan enable payment of a larger portion of benefits from earnings on reserves. Amounts not contributed will be available to the employer for other business purposes, but the favorable tax treatment of plan reserve earnings often makes it attractive to the employer to pay higher contributions and to borrow money for other business purposes, deducting interest payments on the loan paid from otherwise taxable income.

Defined-Contribution Plans

Many employers prefer "defined-contribution" plans. Despite the connotation of the name, such plans often leave to the discretion of the employer when and how much to contribute. Contributions are sometimes keyed to profits or stock bonuses.

The benefits paid by defined-contribution plans are whatever the credited contributions and earnings on them will buy when the employee reaches benefit status. Thus, the employee bears that risk. Widely regarded as retirement income programs, defined-contribution plans often operate as deferred income plans that can be cashed out when leaving a covered job or sometimes borrowed against prior to retirement. (A major exception is TIAA-CREF which serves the university community. It offers immediate vesting and prohibits cash outs.)

Private Pensions before ERISA: What and Why

Discussions of pension plans often are primarily about defined-benefit plans. While less numerous than defined-contribution plans, they remain common with very large employers and so cover more employees. Frequently the same employer will use both forms and, indeed, other tax-favored plans for the same group of employees.

Employer Control over Participation and Eligibility

Prior to 1974, the Internal Revenue Code left plan designers and sponsors free to prescribe the conditions of plan participation, the amount of hours or earnings that earned service credits, what periods of absence caused a break in credited service, and most important, what accumulation of credited service earned eligibility for benefits. Each condition constitutes a hurdle to attaining benefits.

Many plans did not provide for participation until an employee reached a specified age, such as twenty-five or thirty, and also had worked for some stipulated period, often several years. Eligibility for benefits frequently required at least ten years and often as much as fifteen, twenty, or twenty-five years of unbroken service. However, innumerable factors, such as plant closings, layoffs, ill health, and family obligations, lead to interruptions in employment, especially for women and gray- (manual service) and blue-collar workers. These common interruptions, however brief, often made it impossible to meet the continuous service requirements. Many plans even made retirement benefits contingent upon active service with the company at the time of reaching the specified retirement age, a requirement readily defeated by ill health.

Although the opportunity to cumulate credits under multi-employer plans improves chances to achieve eligibility, these plans tended to have the most demanding eligibility requirements and less frequently offered protective provisions for vesting, disability, or early retirement than large single-employer plans.

Length of Credited Service—the Key to Benefits

Single-employer plans count only service with that employer when determining eligibility and benefits. Most blue-collar plans use benefit formulas that provide a specified dollar amount every month of retirement for each year of credited service. Not all years necessarily count for the same amount because improvements in the benefit formula need not apply to earlier periods.

White-collar plans usually peg benefits to earnings, using some percentage of average pay for a selected period multiplied by years of service. Similarly, amounts of defined contributions vary with earnings and length of service.

Clearly, the number of years of credited service an employee earns is a crucial factor both in achieving eligibility and determining the size of plan benefits paid to individual participants.

Past Service Credits

Designers and sponsors of any plan basing benefits on length of service face a dilemma. If the plan gives credits only for work after inception of the plan, those who retire during its early years will obtain paltry benefits. If work predating the plan earns credits, the plan starts with an unfunded liability, which must be retired while the plan also funds currently earned credits. Almost all plans in the defined-benefit category credit some past (also called "prior") service, that is, past or prior to the start of the plan. If at the outset a plan covers many long-service employees, it begins with a sizable chunk of past-service liability. Similarly, when a plan improvement applies to years of service prior to the inception of that improvement, this also creates past-service liability.

Retirement Age/Early and Disability Retirement

Plans specify the age, called "normal retirement age," at which a participant may retire and receive a full benefit calculated on the plan formula. Most plans set sixty-five as the normal retirement age, but pre-ERISA requirements ranged widely.

Numerous plans (mostly single-employer plans) also permit retirement before the normal retirement age for those with extensive service, sometimes with reduced benefits to take account of the longer period of benefit payment. As the 1960s progressed, many plans lowered the early retirement age but did not reduce early retirement benefits proportionally.

A few unions, notably in the automobile industry, achieved rank-and-file demands for "30 [years of service] and out." Some older employees desired such arrangements because they were tired of work, while younger employees sought them to enhance their own job opportunities. Such plans often pay a special additional bridging benefit until a person becomes eligible for Social Security payments.

Vesting

The great majority of employees separate from pension-covered jobs before reaching normal retirement age. They do so both voluntarily and, quite often, involuntarily. Vesting confers upon a separating employee who meets specified length-of-service criteria a claim to benefits upon reaching normal retirement age, and sometimes early retirement age.

The pension claim is based upon the benefit formula as it exists when the employee separates. Such "frozen" credits do not participate in later plan improvements. A very large number of plans provided for vesting for those separating after specified periods of *unbroken* service. Pre-ERISA vesting typically required fifteen or twenty years of service and, often, a specified age as well, such as forty-five or fifty. The age element often transformed the length-of-service condition into a longer service requirement in practice.

Moreover, because employers usually observe seniority, even in some non-union operations, they tend to lay off shorter-service employees when work slackens. Since employees with service long enough to qualify for vesting were more likely to remain until retirement (given the chance), vesting salvaged benefits for only a small proportion of employees.

Vesting's greatest value occurs in total shutdowns or when everyone's job is lost. But then the plan's ability to pay becomes an issue. Benefits for vested claims were generally subject to the sufficiency of plan funds. Rarely did employers guarantee that benefits would be paid from general company assets if plan reserves did not suffice to meet obligations.

Plan Funding

Starting in the 1940s, advance funding according to actuarial principles became a key feature of defined-benefit plans. Advance funding requires that contributions to a plan, plus the earnings on contributions not required to pay current benefits, which constitute a plan's reserves, suffice to pay benefits as they come due. Such a description, however, suggests more adequate funding than the law required and practice provided. Actuarial principles assume funding over the life of a plan, considered to extend until the last original plan participant retires or dies. Funding according to approved actuarial principles does not assure a plan's ability to meet its accrued liabilities if it should terminate prior to running its full projected course.

Prior to ERISA, the Treasury and IRS did not concern themselves with the adequacy of funding or the security of employee expectations. Rather, they sought to prevent employers from exceeding permissible tax-deductible amounts and to enforce the nondiscrimination requirements. Thus, regulatory requirements for funding did little more than attempt to assure that employers made periodic payments, perhaps no more than interest on the unfunded past-service liability. Indeed, "interest only" funding was permissible and occurred.[10]

Plan Purposes

The assumed purpose of plans is to supplement Social Security retirement benefits. That supplementation arguably becomes more urgent as one moves up the income scale because Social Security's benefit formula replaces a smaller percentage of higher pay. Women, low-paid, part-time, seasonal, minority, and nonunion workers (often overlapping categories) tend to be sparsely covered.

Employee interests may vary. Conventional wisdom holds that older employees are more concerned about retiring and retirement income than younger employees, but younger employees frequently care about job security and advancement. Many consider an attractive retirement program a means of making retirement feasible and desirable for older employees, thereby opening jobs and opportunities. In many communities, especially small ones, those older workers may be relatives whose financial security may be a concern of younger co-workers.

Employers have a variety of interests to serve with a plan covering rank-and-file employees. A plan may attract employees and hold them. This latter function is a prime justification for imposing length-of-service conditions. Yet when employees are separated involuntarily in shutdowns, those conditions may defeat pension eligibility even though the employee wants to stay and it is the employer who no longer desires his or her services.

The availability of benefits may enable an employer to ease out "surplus" people when jobs must be trimmed or, similarly, to ease out high-paid older people and replace them with lower-paid, younger personnel.

It is commonly believed that tax advantages constitute a major inducement to employers to install a plan. A plan enables corporate owner-employees, family-member employees, and other highly-compensated executive and managerial employees to shelter income from taxation. The recipient eventually pays taxes when drawing plan benefits, frequently at lower rates because a retiree often falls into a lower tax bracket. Between the time the corporation makes the contribution until benefits start, plan amounts not needed for current benefit payments can be invested, produce tax-free earnings, and be reinvested—a very advantageous way to save.

To qualify for such favorable tax treatment, an employer must offer plan coverage to employees on a nondiscriminatory basis. As already explained, however, many employees can be excluded and portions of wages and salaries subject to Social Security can be left out of account, thereby concentrating the plan contributions and benefits on high-paid personnel. For some plan advisers and designers, the name of the game is to maximize the insiders' share and minimize the benefits and costs of rank-and-file employees without running afoul of the law and so losing plan "qualification" for advantageous tax treatment.

It is arguable which of these purposes deserve the preferential tax treatment accorded plans. Eligibility conditions often create "horizontal inequities" between people otherwise equally situated. Those who work side by side at equal jobs for ostensibly equal pay may end up with very different total compensation; the pension winners (those who obtain benefits at retirement) get paid more than the pension losers (those who do not qualify and even those separated with vested benefits) for the very same periods of work. Since most economists agree that pension costs come out of some other form of employee compensation that the employer otherwise would pay, that differential comes out of the losers' pockets.

Unions seek pension plans and their improvement as a means of expanding compensation. Economists would dispute that any net gain results unless the tax advantages of plans amplify the total amounts made available to them as compared with equal amounts of currently taxable pay. Benefits tend to redound largely to long-service employees, who also are the people who stay in the union; separated employees tend to drift away. Further, funds in plans jointly administered by unions and employers give union officials power positions with financial institutions and purveyors of services. For example, some union lawyers get substantial fees for servicing plans, enabling them to provide other services at lower rates.

In addition, many private pension advocates claim that private plans constitute our largest single source of savings and provide the wherewithal for economic growth. That is not so much a purpose as a claimed by-product.

Plan Performance Criticized

During the 1950s and 1960s, plans proliferated, estimated plan coverage grew, pension divisions of banks and insurance companies expanded, pension consultants prospered, and pension reserves swelled by the tens of billions of dollars. Questions arose, though, as to whether the resplendent pension quilt provided adequate cover. An early major effort to question plan adequacy came with the publication in April 1964 of *The Future of Private Pensions*,[11] which argued that the majority of employees simply did not, indeed could not, work for employers long enough to meet the length-of-service conditions of most

103

plans. Median employee tenure, typically five, six, or seven years, fell way below service requirements of fifteen and twenty years. Participants in multi-employer plans, many with even longer service requirements, often had no pension to show for twenty or more years of labor.

The book documented situations in which employees failed to achieve pension eligibility. For instance:

- Acquisition of a firm, followed shortly by large-scale dismissal of former employees, which enabled the acquiring company to recapture years of pension contributions, because few former employees qualified for benefits;
- Plant and unit shutdowns preventing employees from continuing work and thereby attaining the required length of service;
- Plant shutdowns after a few years of operation making it impossible for employees to meet length-of-service conditions;
- Job loss just before retirement age, preventing employees from satisfying plan conditions for employment up to retirement.

In August 1964, *New York Times* financial writer Robert Metz reported on the book and simultaneously publicized the frustrated pension expectations caused by the 1963 shutdown of the Studebaker automobile plant in South Bend, Indiana.[12] Their plan reserves proved inadequate to cover the valid claims made by thousands of separated employees.

Employees and the public were amazed to discover that when private plans terminate they were required to pay valid claims only to the extent of plan reserves. Employees had no recourse to the employer's assets. It was a shock. But not the first or the last. A study of a similar occurrence with Packard showed not only massive loss of pension benefit expectations, but, in addition, discharged employees, many in their forties and fifties, had difficulty in getting decent jobs or any jobs. Most of the participating employees were over forty. Interviews with former Packard employees more than two years later found that 58 percent had obtained manufacturing jobs—but of these, all over age fifty had thereafter lost those jobs. As for the others, 22 percent still had no job at all[13] and 20 percent had service jobs, in which pension coverage is rare.

A similar fate befell the more than 13,000 employees "released" by Republic Aviation in 1963 and 1964. A Disarmament Agency study showed that "production workers, who constituted the bulk of the work force, tended to move down the occupational ladder."[14] At each lower rung, the chances of pension coverage diminish.

These were not isolated cases.

As the 1960s closed, almost half (45 percent) of those employees in plans with vesting needed ten years of service to qualify, another 36 percent could qualify with fifteen years of service, while 19 percent required twenty years or

TABLE 4.1
Median Job Tenure—1968 (in Years)

	Men			Women		
	40–44	*45–49*	*55–59*	*40–45*	*45–49*	*55–59*
Whites	<10*	10.4	14.9	<10	4.4	8.3
Nonwhites	<10	8.8	11.9	<10	4.1	7.4

* < = less than.
SOURCE: Edmund O'Boyle, "Job Tenure," *Monthly Labor Review* 92 (September 1969): 18, table 1.

more. Compare these requirements to the tenure that people actually achieved on the job.

As table 4.1 shows, the only group with median job tenure above ten years was white males over forty-five years of age and nonwhite males over fifty-five years. Even in those groups, large numbers would not qualify for ten-year vesting. Job tenure in the sectors where pension coverage was most common, such as manufacturing, was somewhat longer, but not much. Especially notable was the comparatively short job tenure of women of all ages in most industries.

Furthermore, critics of plan performance noted that claims for plan coverage seemed greatly overstated, varying between 28 and 33 million participants, as compared to the Department of Labor's count of only 19.5 million. Apparently fewer employees entered the pension sweepstakes than was commonly thought.

In early 1965, the President's Committee on Corporate Pension Funds (often referred to as the Cabinet Committee) originally appointed by President Kennedy, filed its report after months of delay and wrangling within the Johnson administration. The report summarized the major shortcomings of private plans. Its recommendations were modest. It proposed vesting "after a reasonable period of service," by which it appeared to have meant 50 percent after ten years, with increasing degrees of vesting for each year of additional service. It urged less exclusionary plan participation requirements.[15] And it advocated that plans fully fund current service as earned and retire unfunded past service liability over thirty years.

The report constituted a major development but its publication did not stir much public interest.

U.S. Senate Pension Study: Few Winners

A Senate labor subcommittee pension study launched in the late 1960s found that only a tiny minority of participants qualified for benefits. Its 1970 report stated:

> in the sample of plans studied, which had lengthy service requirements, only 5 percent of the millions of employees covered since 1950 had ever received benefits, only 8 percent had qualified for benefits, and while most of these employees had only worked a very short period of time (less than 5 years), there were substantial numbers of workers who had longer periods of service and failed to qualify for benefits.[16]

Private pension enthusiasts asserted that the Senate study misrepresented the true potential of private plans. They claimed that as plans proliferated, their coverage would increase, and, as plans and employees "matured," ever more employees would achieve eligibility with the requisite long service. Yet the Senate survey limited itself to plans at least twenty years old, the most venerable and stable programs.

Plan defenders also contended that employee turnover occurs primarily among the young and that as employees age they become steadier, less flighty, and achieve long service. Indeed, actuarial tables build on this assumption. While the assumption sometimes corresponds to reality, it does not answer the pension problems precipitated when jobs leave employees. Massive layoffs had very little to do with employee age or restlessness.

Self-Dealing and Conflict of Interest

The Senate subcommittee also found instances of improper use of pension funds. For example, it reported that

> one financially ailing company tried to borrow over a million dollars from a subsidiary's pension pool for use as operating capital. Another had a policy of investing more than half its pension funds' assets in the company's own common stock and in the real estate of a company subsidiary. Still another company routinely dipped into its pension funds for cash to make acquisitions.[17]

Despite national newspaper publicity and lively debate among professionals and critics, the bulk of the populace seemed unconcerned or uninformed about questionable pension plan performance. That changed radically in 1971 when "60 Minutes," stimulated by the Senate labor subcommittee staff, devoted a segment to private pension problems. Although it noted the corruption issue, the presentation highlighted the difficulty of meeting plan eligibility conditions. Consciousness had been raised. Pension problems started to become a national issue.

Robert MacNeil and Jim Lehrer followed with an hour-long special focusing on the Studebaker-like fate of a group of Pennsylvania bakery employees. The multi-employer plan to which the company had belonged refused to pay off valid claims because the bankrupt bakery's contributions did not meet the liabilities to its former employees. Some long-time employees were stranded—in part because of the absence of effective funding.

NBC opened its fall 1973 season with an hour-long documentary special, "Pensions—The Broken Promise." That program made pension reform a live national issue that the pension industry could no longer simply ignore or oppose.

Pension professionals began to propose "reforms." Usually they urged minimal standards for participation, vesting, and funding but maximum flexibility for employers and unions to continue to make key decisions about pension design and administration, enabling them to preserve extensive "self-dealing," or transactions between plan sponsors (mostly employers but frequently unions as well) and the plans. Employers, banks, insurance companies, and unions joined, for the most part, to urge minimal protections for employee interests, although some in organized labor parted company to urge a pension benefit guarantee mechanism, invoking the precedent of the Federal Deposit Insurance Corporation.

Industry and union representatives, opposed by only a handful of pension reformers, dominated the debate that ensued. Plan sponsors and their financial allies succeeded in trimming back several proposals by Senator Jacob Javits to enhance employee interests. Senator Javits and key Senate staff people, notably Frank Cummings and Michael Gordon, nonetheless persevered in pursuit of a bill to reduce opportunities for the most blatant abuses. Considering their lack of interest-group allies, they accomplished wonders. Yet it remains to be considered whether the outcome, the Employee Retirement Income Security Act (ERISA) and its supplements, have proven equal to the need.

5 Pension Reform: Shadow and Substance

The Employee Retirement Income Security Act of 1974 (ERISA),[1] had a single announced purpose—to improve the chances of people employed by companies with retirement income plans to receive benefits. A statute of epic complexity, it addressed two major impediments to that goal: the difficulty of qualifying for benefits and the questionable ability of many plans to make good on their promises. But it made far less than an all-out attack, and did not attempt to rout the underlying problems besetting plans. It neither mandated coverage nor assured all, or even most, plan participants that they would enter the winner's circle. It did, however, impose some new basic rules providing minimum standards to ameliorate the most blatant plan shortcomings and abuses.

ERISA: Enhancing Eligibility

ERISA prescribed which employees most retirement plans must allow to participate: employees aged twenty-five and over (later changed to age twenty-one[2]) who complete one year of service. And it defined a year of service for participation and vesting requirements as not less than one thousand hours in any twelve-month period (along with some special arrangements for particular employments with peculiarities such as seasonality).

108

Pension Reform: Shadow and Substance

Getting into the Game—Plan Participation

By permitting exclusion of those who do not work at least one thousand hours in a year (equivalent to one-half the normal full-time of forty hours a week for fifty weeks), a large part of part-time or seasonal "women's work" can be ignored. Once an employee becomes a participant, a plan may suspend that status if he or she does not work at least five hundred hours in a subsequent twelve-month period.*

ERISA limited the conditions that constitute "breaks in service" which deprive an employee of service already credited. ERISA permits a break to cancel prior service credits only when the break exceeds the length of such service.[3] Clearly, such a provision does more for unionized employees, who have recall rights, than for nonunionized employees, who do not.

The 1984 Retirement Equity Act added that an interruption must last more than five years before a break may cancel prebreak credited service. However, even unionized employees seldom have reemployment rights after extended absence. Several commentators have cheered these 1984 reforms as especially valuable to women who leave the labor force for maternity and childrearing. But, in the absence of a right to return to a former employer after such an extended period, these limits help only those few with special talents for whom the employer will always make a place. Greeted with great fanfare as a boost for women's pension expectations, these provisions afford less help than they appear to.

Vesting

One hundred percent (full) vesting means a legal right to claim at retirement age benefits earned by the employee's credited service. ERISA required plans to offer one of three vesting formulas: 100 percent vesting after ten years of credited service; two alternatives conferring partial vesting beginning after either five years or when age and service add up to forty-five years. Both formulas culminate in 100 percent vesting after fifteen years.

Plan sponsors (employers, or both unions and employers in bargained plans) may select from the three options. Sponsors could minimize vesting by choosing the "rule of forty-five" for a group of young employees or one of the other formulas for a group in which older employees predominate.

---

* The statute also provides for special rules for particular kinds of workers with special work patterns, such as maritime employees who must get a year's credit if they work at least 125 days.

Under the ten-year rule,* the one most commonly used, an employee separated *before* ten years of service need be granted no pension benefits. An employee separated from the job *after* ten years of service becomes entitled to whatever benefit ten or more years of service earn at the time he or she leaves the job. Payment begins at retirement age, or sometimes early retirement age.

Amounts of benefits turn out to be rather disappointing, yielding less than many expect from vesting. A plan that confers a monthly benefit of $15 for each year of service (a fairly good blue-collar plan) would vest a benefit of $150 a month ($1,800 a year) for the separated employee with ten years of credited service. Some white-collar plans generate decidedly larger benefits. But, perhaps surprisingly, private-plan benefits tend to be modest.

The 1974 act conferred some limited rights on certain survivors of participants who qualified for vesting when they die prior to reaching retirement age. It also required plans to pay the surviving spouse of a retiree 50 percent of the retiree's benefit; that survivor's option, however, could be declined by a participant without the spouse's agreement. Subsequent legislation requires the spouse to approve the retiree's rejection of the survivor option.

Disablement

ERISA did not directly address the problem of disablement, which can defeat pension eligibility by disrupting the work needed to qualify for pension benefits. The 1974 break-in-service rules and somewhat more stringent rules subsequently enacted afford a measure of protection for those with nonpermanent disabilities, provided that the injury or illness does not result in loss of the pension-covered job and the individual actually returns to the same employer. No federal statute of general applicability outlaws employment discrimination based on disability, but the rehabilitation statute bans discrimination against the handicapped in federally-assisted activities.[4]

In sectors not covered by the rehabilitation act, about half of the states appear to have comprehensive statutes prohibiting discrimination because of a disability. Among the remainder of the states, a miscellany of statutes attempts to protect job rights of employees injured on the job, but an analysis of some such statutes found them sketchy and of dubious efficacy.[5] Moreover, no federal statute and few state laws require adaptation of jobs or equipment to enable impaired persons to perform a job.

The statutory vesting provisions afford some protection against income loss from a temporary or permanent disability that causes job separation. If death

---

* Changed to mandatory vesting after five years of service by 1986 legislation summarized at the close of this chapter. The impact of both is considered in the next chapter.

occurs, the act's survivor protection may help the widows or widowers of some older employees.

Some employers' plans do provide disability benefits for long-service employees either under pension plans or separate insurance. Both usually deduct Social Security Disability Insurance (DI) benefits and any other payments, such as workers' compensation, receivable by virtue of the same condition. Such benefits tend to add modest supplements to DI benefits for the disabled.

Enhancing Plan Ability to Pay Benefits

The other major goal of ERISA was to enhance the ability of pension plans to pay the benefits for which employees qualify by imposing explicit fiduciary responsibilities for plan officials, more stringent funding requirements backed by a new federal insurance agency, the Pension Benefit Guaranty Corporation (PBGC) created by the act, and by making some employer assets available to satisfy claims when plan funds fall short.

Minimum Funding Requirements

The cost of a plan equals what it will pay out to all beneficiaries over its lifetime. The two major components of cost and benefits are "current costs" (for credits earned during the current year even though payable in the future) and "past-service costs" (benefits earned by employment predating the plan and specified plan improvements). Each time a plan confers a new higher benefit amount for years already worked, a fairly common occurrence, the plan adds a new layer of past-service liability.

ERISA requires that current costs be met as incurred. In addition, ERISA prescribes minimum schedules for funding past-service liability. Sponsors of new plans must fund such liability over thirty years, starting when the new plan makes the promise. It gave existing plans forty years.

Limiting Misuse of Funds and Conflicts of Interest

Hundreds of billions of dollars pass through the hands of pension officials and the employees and outsiders they hire for plan activities. Obviously, every dollar should reach the intended beneficiaries and not stick to the palms or bank accounts of the employer, union, trustee, bank, insurer, administrator, or other plan functionaries except as fitting payment for proper services rendered.

111

Quite apart from any directly dishonest use, control over such funds confers power and opportunity. For example, whoever decides what bank or insurance company will handle plan funds has superior access to that institution for unrelated transactions. A bank that receives tens of millions of dollars in plan deposits or provides investment services will be attentive to the credit needs of those who make deposit decisions.

The most obvious conflict of interest arises in direct dealings between the plan and those who make plan decisions. Investment of plan funds in the employer's securities or loans to insiders or friends of insiders, plan purchases of employer assets, the lease of plant or equipment from the plan by the employer or union, the payment of rent by the plan to either, or the payment by the plan for services rendered by employer or union officials—all present opportunities to exploit the plan and divert its resources to nonbeneficiaries.

Investment of plan funds in the employer's business by stock purchase or loan seems especially questionable. Folk wisdom soundly counsels against putting all of one's eggs in one basket. It is imprudent to have both current pay and future retirement, disability, survivor income, and retirement health benefits depend on the economic health of the same enterprise. Terms may be set that unduly favor the enterprise at the expense of the plan—a discrepancy that can be hard to discover, hard to prove, and thus hard to prevent and even harder to remedy.

Plan sponsors and unions obviously cherished the power conferred by their control over these vast funds. When Congress considered ERISA, no effective counter-lobby took the field, despite twenty years of congressional concern over possible misuse of trust funds. Congress responded by limiting investment of defined-benefit plan funds in the employer's enterprise to 10 percent of plan assets; it did not place like limits on defined-contribution plans. Though the limit may sound modest, estimates of plan holdings put them at over a trillion dollars. Such a kitty enables management, through its appointed plan trustees, to use plan funds for such purposes as fending off unfriendly takeovers through plan purchase of stock shares—which may or may not be in the beneficiaries' interest. (For a further discussion of plan sponsor conflicts of interest, see chapter 6.)

The Pension Benefit Guaranty Corporation (PBGC)

To avoid more Studebaker-like tragedies, the United Auto Workers (UAW) persuaded Congress to enact a system of insuring a large portion of promised benefits. The UAW compared its proposal to the Federal Deposit Insurance Corporation (FDIC), then an untroubled paragon among federal government entities. Opponents, however, pointed out a major difference—FDIC guarantees

112

deposits actually made, while the proposed program guarantees payment of promises.

Opponents also objected that the insurance requires solid, well-funded plans to pay the freight for the shaky ones, thereby increasing plan costs. The alternative, risk-rated contributions (assuming such an arrangement could be constructed), would place the heaviest burdens on the plans least able to pay, further weakening their funding. Congress chose to use a flat-rate per capita premium to fund the program but continues to puzzle over the dilemma.

Critics also pointed to the possibility that unscrupulous or careless sponsors could repeatedly increase plan benefits and thus saddle the insurance program with promises that the sponsors never meant to redeem or never could. To mitigate this problem, Congress provided that a benefit improvement does not become completely insured until it has been in operation for five years; after the first year, only 20 percent of a newly added benefit is insured, 40 percent after the second year, and so on.

ERISA also made a major change in the liability of sponsors to make good on their pension promises. Before ERISA, an employer could limit its pension liability to whatever assets the plan had when it was terminated, provided it made contributions when due. At that time, the law had no minimum contribution requirements. Hence, employers could walk away from a pension plan collapse without further obligation. ERISA established a guarantee for vested rights (up to certain limits that rise with inflation), which the insuring agency, PBGC, pays. PBGC, in turn, may sue the employer for up to one-third of the employer's assets (in the case of single-employer plans) to make good plan fund deficiencies. Some sophisticated employers, however, have taken troubled divisions and set them adrift as separate entities with separate plans. When they sink, they leave PBGC with a substantial burden and insufficient sponsor assets from which to collect.

PBGC is mired in lawsuits over such ploys. There is concern that PBGC cannot prevent some of the games corporations have learned to play. Although PBGC administers this program and acts as insurer, Congress sets the premiums. There is great doubt that premiums are adequate or can be made adequate to their potential liability, especially for multi-employer plans. Indeed, PBGC's 1981 request for a premium increase languished until 1986 before Congress finally enacted it. Curiously, in projecting its funding needs, PBGC does not include any assumptions about major plan failures of the kind that made the program necessary. It has justified this omission with the explanation that it has had no experience with a large plan failure. However, it and the pension community held their breath when the Chrysler Corporation and several farm implement manufacturers hovered on the brink of bankruptcy. The bankruptcy of the Wheeling Steel-Pittsburgh Steel Corporation and of LTV in 1986 dumped billions of dollars of unfunded liability onto PBGC. (Now PBGC has experience with large plan failures.) These developments rendered the 1986 PBGC premium increase inadequate before the year was out. The insurer's own financial reliability is in serious doubt.

Reporting Requirements

ERISA requires extensive record keeping and detailed reports for the approximately 900,000 employee benefit plans in operation. Many employers and plan professionals bemoan the detail, time, and money that these reports demand.

In contrast, Social Security-covered employers use simple formulas to compute FICA taxes and remit the taxes periodically. This requires little bother or outlay.

Both employers and unions fought against a total ban on self-dealing. They won. Once self-dealing is permissible, but with limits of amount and kind, records must be kept in great detail. Those records must be translated into reports to give participants and beneficiaries and administering public officials some chance to keep the handlers true to their duties. This is not to say that most or even many would abuse their trust, but, as the good guys cannot be readily distinguished from the bad guys, all must report.

The solution to burdensome reporting requirements is not less reporting. The solution is to remove the opportunities for self-dealing, for peculation, petty or grand, and for diversions to purposes other than serving participants and beneficiaries. Even so, trusts require intricate record keeping.

Largely Untouched by ERISA: Pseudo "Retirement Savings"

In addition to traditional pension plans, the retirement income industry has invented ESOPs, PASOPs, TRASOPs, 401(k)s, H.R. 10s (Keoghs), and IRAs.* They, too, provide tax-advantageous ways of putting aside funds and property, ostensibly to provide retirement income. Even before these were cre-

---

* These are: ESOP (Employee Stock Ownership Plan); PASOP (Payroll Stock Ownership Plan); TRASOP (Tax Refund Stock Ownership Plan). The various SOPs receive favorable tax treatment: 401(k) is a tax provision permitting employees to defer income and so defer income tax on pay credited to their account; 403(b) plans provide similar arrangements for non-profit organization employees; H.R. 10 (Keogh) is a tax provision by which self-employed persons may contribute earnings to an account in their own name, payable in the future. The contributions are tax deductible; these contributions and the earnings on the account are not taxed until drawn as benefits.

ated, profit-sharing plans and stock bonus plans existed, also providing tax shelter, ostensibly for retirement. We say ostensibly because they can be tapped and used before reaching retirement and for nonretirement purposes.

Profit-sharing plans, ESOPs, TRASOPs, and so on, are considered defined-contribution plans; they receive the same kind of tax advantages—deductibility by the employer for contributions and tax-free earnings for recipients on plan funds until paid out as benefits. ERISA does not require any particular minimum funding of such plans.

These forms of tax shelters do not assure that money contributed will be used for retirement income. A 1986 study shows that few employees use distributions from pension or deferred-income plans for either retirement or savings.[6]

Profit-Sharing Plans

In profit-sharing plans, the sponsor need make contributions only if there are profits. Some bargained plans obligate the employer to make specified contributions derived from profits, but in the absence of bargaining, the employer may retain discretion to contribute or not as long as it does so often enough to satisfy the IRS requirement that a plan is "permanent." But "permanent," doesn't mean permanent; it only means of indefinite duration.

Contributions must be allocated to individual accounts according to the plan's formula, which must not discriminate in favor of the highly paid. Enjoyment of the contribution must be deferred at least two years, except in case of "hardship." Otherwise, the employee may draw his or her share under statutorily limited plan-specified conditions, most commonly layoff or job separation. On separation and withdrawal it may be "rolled over" (meaning it will not be taxed if moved into another tax-sheltered investment), but need not be. In the event the employee uses the funds, they become taxable as income.

Stock-Bonus Plans

These resemble profit-sharing plans in that they may limit the obligation to make contributions only out of profits. But some may also provide for contributions whether or not there are profits. Although the name implies that contributions are made in stock, they can be made in cash. The contributions are allocated to individual employee accounts. For closely held corporations (those with few stockholders and no public trading of shares), the employee must be able to require the corporation to purchase the employee's shares of stock in order to qualify for favorable tax treatment. However, most employees who lack union protection would not be able to force a reluctant employer to do so and keep their jobs. As a practical matter, only an exiting employee is assured the right to the cash value of his or her stock holdings. Even then, lacking a regular market, valuation of shares for this purpose is a tricky and unpredictable process.

The employee-participant also has certain voting rights, which often will not be significant, especially in a closely held corporation dominated by the owners. One participant of our acquaintance reported that in a takeover battle, employee shareholders were told to vote with current management or lose their jobs—a rather limited voting right.

ESOPs, TRASOPs, and PASOPs

Employee Stock Ownership Plans (ESOPs) have not accounted for much coverage but get much publicity, not least because Senator Russell Long, former chairman of the Senate Finance Committee and, through 1986, ranking minority member, held them in high esteem. They are coming into more widespread use, however.

ESOPs (and their variants TRASOPs and PASOPs) are subject to a web of regulations we need not enter. They share this attribute: the employer's contribution consists of its own stock. Theoretically, this gives employees an ownership interest in the enterprise and, eventually, effective control. Eventually may take a long time.

Suffice it to say that ESOPs are regarded by some as subject to employer abuse. Among the major problems they present are: both current and future income are in one basket—the current employer; shares contributed may be overvalued, an abuse not readily discovered and whose attempted rectification may come too late; there is no assurance that a valuation placed on stock when it is contributed, even if fair and proper, will stay the same until it is cashed out. Employees without union representation have little opportunity to challenge the administration of such plans, the valuation of contributions, and other arrangements between plan sponsors and administrators who would, in other plans, be disqualified persons because their interests obviously conflict with those of plan participants.

ESOPs' tax-favored status depends even less on dedicating earnings to retirement income purposes than other tax deferral arrangements do. The employer receives tax deductions for contributions to ESOPs. Under certain circumstances, it may even receive a tax credit—that is, a dollar credited against its tax liability for each dollar of contribution. When that happens, the U.S. Treasury, in effect, makes the entire contribution.

ESOPs give employers great leeway to serve their own interests. Under one form, the leveraged ESOP, the plan trust takes a loan to purchase company

116

stock. The stock is then "contributed" to the ESOP and the purchase price of the stock goes to the employer. The loan (usually guaranteed by the employer) is secured by the stock. So far, the employer has used the arrangement to generate corporate funds and the ESOP trust starts with a debt equal to the valuation put on the shares. The trust does not have any funds of its own at the outset; its only possible source of income is dividends (the declaration of which is often within the employer's control) and employer contributions. In closely held corporations, dividends are rare. Retiring the loan depends primarily on contributions from the employer corporation. As those contributions come in and the plan's debt is retired, proportional parts of the pledged stock become allocated to the ESOP. If contributions dry up, the lender is stuck with the assets of the guarantor, which, under such unpromising circumstances, may not be worth much.

The ESOP carries the additional advantage to employers that it is subject to more permissive limits on the amounts that may be allocated to insiders, that is, individuals who own more than 10 percent of the company's shares, officers, and employees receiving more than $60,000 in annual pay.

One would think that the main safeguard in such arrangements would be the reluctance of lenders to advance money on shares of questionable value both when the loan is made and during the pay-out period. But interest payments received by the lender on such loans are taxed at lower than regular rates, an inducement for a lender to enter into a deal it otherwise might not consider. If the business is credit-worthy, the favorable tax treatment to the lender can result in lower interest rates charged to the borrower on the loan.

A sound business would not have to go through such a rigamarole. Rather, ESOPs provide a route for a marginal company to obtain capital or for a retiring employer to "sell" his or her business to employees. In the absence of a union, the seller sets the terms.

ESOPS and their variants constitute very unpromising vehicles for generating a reliable flow of retirement income.

As compared with defined-benefit plans, defined-contribution plans, profit-sharing, stock bonus, and ESOPs have both advantages and disadvantages.

They are simpler to administer; while records must be kept, of course, actuarial evaluations need not be made. Under profit-sharing plans, the beauty is that the employer need not make any contribution if there are no profits. However, the employer may not reduce its bargained contributions, as it can to defined-benefit plans if fund earnings prove more favorable than expected; good fund earnings often produce pressure to improve benefits. Defined-contribution plans, to which ERISA vesting requirements apply, typically provide earlier employee vesting than defined-benefit plans. If and when the plan terminates, the employer has no lingering duty for further contributions, and faces no possible claim against company assets, as might be the case with a defined-benefit plan whose assets do not meet valid claims.

From the employee's point of view, earlier vesting provides a clear advantage. Once the employee is entitled to vesting in a defined-contribution plan, whatever the employer contributes goes to the employee's particular account. The employee has no assurance, however, of an employer contribution. From the employer's point of view, such an arrangement gives the employee a stake in the enterprise's success and an incentive to work effectively; but if the employer mismanages or manipulates profits, the employee, no matter how hardworking, obtains no profits. Where the bulk of the plan assets consist of stock in a closely held corporation, which typically has no ready market, the employee has a hunk of ownership of dubious value not readily convertible into predictable income. Even when the employee owns something that is in fact marketable, just what that amount will be cannot be known until retirement. In retirement, the former employee bears the risk of what income his share will produce whereas in a defined-benefit plan, the plan must pay specified benefits.

Once regarded as offbeat and not taken seriously, ESOPs receive such enormously favorable tax treatment that they threaten to develop into a serious leak of taxable revenue. Their use has proliferated, not least because they often fit into takeover strategies. ESOPs have moved to center stage, not for their utility in providing retirement income, but rather for their alluring nonretirement uses.

H.R. 10 (Keogh) Plans

Originally only corporations could operate "qualified" plans; partnerships and sole proprietorships could not. Lawyers and doctors in particular sought comparable tax breaks but were reluctant to incorporate because, it was thought, professional standards requiring personal liability to clients and patients prevented them from incorporation (a status which confers liability limited to corporate assets).

Representative Eugene Keogh led the successful fight for such legislation with the introduction year after year of a bill for that purpose, H.R. 10. Hence, the plans are known as "Keoghs" or "H.R. 10s." The 1962 legislation made available the same kind of deductibility for employer contributions and the deferral of taxation of plan earnings as with corporate plans, but Congress limited Keoghs to specified annual amounts and percentages of earnings. In addition to requiring nondiscriminatory plan treatment for employees of partnerships and the self-

118

employed, the original legislation also required vesting after three years, in recognition of the high employee turnover in small firms.

H.R. 10 plans no longer operate under special limitations on contributions and vesting. Rather, they must observe the participation, nondiscrimination, contribution, and vesting requirements applicable to corporate plans. However, statutory protection against "top-heavy plans" (those unduly favoring insiders) often require these and other plans to provide quicker vesting than ERISA normally requires so as to avoid undue concentration of benefits among the best paid.

Originally designed to provide opportunities for retirement savings for those who could not establish corporate plans, H.R. 10s now are available to corporate employees who also have self-employment income. So, for example, corporate officers who serve on the boards of directors of other enterprises can establish a Keogh plan for their director's fees even if, as is likely, they participate in a corporate plan or plans.

H.R. 10s have not been as widely used as might be expected, probably because of the invention of the professional corporation for the purpose of making the favorable tax treatment of corporate pension plans available to lawyers and doctors.

Salary Reduction Plans—401(k)s

Employees may shelter income from current taxation through salary reduction plans. They elect to take less pay and the amount foregone goes into their own individual accounts. Formerly the tax law imposed an upper limit of $30,000 in such annual reductions for an individual. The 1986 Tax Reform Act lowered that limit to $7,000. Both amounts suggest that this device is especially useful to upper-income earners. Frequently, employers match some or, occasionally, all of the employee's "contribution." Any funds drawn from such an account are taxed as income. However, control over the timing enables one to delay tax payments and meanwhile invest the accumulation; any earnings are not taxed until drawn. The participant must start drawing down the account by age seventy. Any withdrawal prior to age fifty-nine and a half is subject to a 10 percent tax.

Participants may use the money by borrowing it for statutorily-specified purposes. While they must pay interest, it goes to their own account. Under such an arrangement employees save taxes on the salary not drawn; they save taxes on the earnings; and they pay no tax on the money that they lend themselves until they draw it as income when they choose.

Of course, this tax device can only be used by people who earn more money than they currently need (plus what they borrow).* If the sums were truly surplus to their needs, they would save much or most of it anyway.

IRAs—A Flash in the Pan

ERISA established Individual Retirement Accounts (IRAs) to make available to employees not covered by a plan advantages similar to those enjoyed by employees covered by corporate plans and by the self-employed with Keoghs. Certainly equality of treatment made an appealing argument. The 1974 act provided that a corporate employee *without* plan coverage could establish his or her own IRA. An annual contribution up to $1,500 (but no more than the individual's actual earnings) were tax deductible and earnings on the account were not subject to income tax until withdrawn. Withdrawals made prior to age fifty-nine and a half were subject to a small tax penalty.

Not many employees used the new device, probably because most employees without corporate plan coverage fall in the categories of low-paid or part-time employment and therefore lack disposable funds for the purpose. Oddly enough, the higher one's tax bracket, the less discouraging is the penalty for cashing out because the taxes saved will sometimes offset the penalty imposed. So, for example, a person paying an effective rate of 30 percent or more (as is possible under the 1986 act) comes out ahead, despite the penalty, if he or she cashes out after only five and a half years. But those in lower tax brackets must wait longer before the penalty ceases to bite. Because of this feature, IRA contributors may advantageously withdraw contributions and earnings well before reaching retirement age. Hence, despite the "Retirement" in its name, IRAs need not be limited to retirement purposes—although many people probably use them for that or start out thinking that they will.

The 1981 tax act sweetened IRAs—indeed, transformed them. The tax advantages were no longer limited to employees without plan coverage. Rather, employees with plan coverage could have the tax advantages in addition to those conferred by his or her corporate plan and the contribution amount was raised to $2,000 ($2,250 for a couple with only one working spouse). The justification offered for this transformation was that it would encourage savings and, incidentally, give a boost to thrift institutions that were then ailing.

IRAs are not subject to the antidiscrimination provisions ordinarily applicable to pension and many other deferred-income arrangements to which employers contribute. So employers and executives can set them up for themselves without

---

* Tax regulations require that a substantial portion of the lowest-paid two-thirds of an employee group elect to participate.

making comparable arrangements for rank-and-file employees. Nor do they carry any obligations to surviving spouses. Even so, the employer may set up such a plan for employees, pay administrative fees and perform payroll deduction functions.

These new arrangements proved very attractive, especially for high tax bracket employees. By 1986, IRA accounts exceeded $200 billion at a cost of deferred tax, for contributions alone, of about $60 billion. In addition, another $3 billion of taxes on plan earnings were deferred annually. 1986 legislation curtailed IRAs.

The 1986 Tax Reform Package

Private plan pension reform surged unexpectedly in 1986. In October 1985, Senator John Heinz and Representative William Clay introduced a pension reform proposal crafted by Senate Aging Committee staffers Steve McConnell and Lawrence Atkins and House Labor Committee Pension Counsel Phyllis Borzi in consultation with some private plan experts. Although supported by important groups, most notably the American Association of Retired Persons (AARP), no one expected much early attention to the measure, let alone action. Potential opponents paid it little mind. But, when the Tax Reform Act gathered steam in the Senate, those pension proposals, scaled down somewhat to improve acceptability to the business community, became a part of the package. That move happened so quickly that industry opponents did not have time to muster an effective countercampaign while endorsement by supporters such as AARP, the Pension Rights Center, The National Organization of Women (NOW), and the Older Women's League (OWL), helped win Senate Finance Committee support. Their adoption also enabled senators to say that, although the package eliminated deductibility for many IRA contributions, the pension proposals would enhance the retirement income prospects of future retirees.

The package improved protection for employee interests, probably much more than ordinary, deliberate legislative procedures would have. It is likely that the package reaches the high-water mark for pension reform, the best that can be expected for a very long time.

It requires earlier vesting for single-employer plans (full vesting after five years of service or 20 percent vesting starting after three years, increasing by 20 percent with each year of additional service, reaching 100 percent after seven years); sets more comprehensive minimum participation standards; puts a top limit of 50 percent of Social Security retirement benefits that can be used to reduce integrated private plan benefits; imposes a 10 percent nondeductible tax on the employer-recipient of funds from a terminated plan; adds a 10 percent income tax on plan withdrawals (but with numerous exceptions); and sets an upper limit on the interest assumptions (125 percent of the rate used by PBGC) a plan may apply when computing the present value of vested benefits; imposes a $7,000 limit on the annual amount of contributions to 401(k) and comparable nonprofit organization plans; eliminates the deductibility for IRA contributions for those participating in employer plans (but preserves tax deferment for earnings on both past and future IRA contributions). As the ads so often say, it does "much, much more," but these provisions are the most pertinent to improving employee interests.

Despite reforms, questions remain whether the ERISA and subsequent protections suffice, whether plan reserves amounting to a trillion dollars (and far more in the future) are sufficiently safeguarded from unscrupulous or inept use, whether the tens of millions of families with a stake in those plans can rely upon them, and whether, even for those who achieve benefits, those benefits can be relied upon to supply the supplementation expected.

6   Private Pensions: Chronic Problems

> I question whether we can be content to rely for retirement income on a system that leaves so much to chance and that stacks the odds against particular career patterns and types of employment. I wonder how our retirement income programs, structured the way they are today, will be able to keep pace with the changes now going on in the work force and deliver the benefits this nation will need in the future.*

Was Senator Heinz talking about Social Security? Not at all. He was talking about employment-based group pension plans when introducing a bill to reform private plans. Most of his proposal was later embodied in the Tax Reform Act of 1986.

The private sector has been ingenious in devising new, and ever newer, deferred-benefit programs, which also defer tax liability and reduce tax collections. As a result, although all taxpayers bear extra burdens, plan benefits go disproportionally to those with the best-paying, steadiest jobs—those for whom plan coverage is the most common and plan arrangements the most generous. But even members of that fortunate group cannot be certain of making it into the winner's circle. Those who participate in plans but receive no or low benefits still pay for the benefits because their cash compensation is lower than it would be in the absence of a plan. Only about half the private work force, very probably less, enjoy plan coverage to begin with. While many believe that eventually a majority of working people will achieve plan eligibility in one job or another, such an outcome is far from certain. Though vesting provisions are universal

---

* Senator John Heinz, (R-Pa.), then Chair of the U.S. Senate Special Committee on Aging, *Congressional Record*, S13799 (October 22, 1985, daily ed.).

now in the private sector, average tenure on most jobs is too short to produce eligibility for a substantial benefit. Many who achieve some benefits will find them small, so small, indeed, that the plan administrator may pay them off in cash or the recipient may cash them out. Among the most serious of all plan defects is the lack of inflation proofing and the poor prospects of achieving it. Post-retirement improvements do occur but in no dependable fashion, and the record shows that such improvements lag behind inflation. Because an employer has no duty to bargain about the benefits of retirees, the prospects of even these improvements are probably reduced.

The Structural Problems of Private Plans

Pension plans labor under some inherent limitations. Most important, only a portion of the work force participates because not all employers have plans and not all their employees participate. Furthermore, a plan's existence depends upon the continuation of the particular firm or the firms that participate in a multi-employer plan. For employee participants, eligibility and benefits depend upon the length of their employment, which in turn often depends not only on the continuation of the employer, but of the particular unit of the employer for which that employee works. The design and financing of defined-benefit plans assume that the enterprise will operate for thirty or forty years; indeed, to meet commitments to pay plan improvements, adequate financing requires continued company existence for thirty years after the adoption of each improvement. This continuity does not often occur in today's dynamic economy; even the giants that account for the bulk of plan coverage continually open, expand, contract, and close operations.

For most who achieve eligibility, benefits begin at a modest level and do not keep pace with increases in the cost of living. The ability of plans to make good on their benefit promises continues to be questionable, not least because the Pension Benefit Guaranty Corporation (PBGC), the guarantor, itself remains overcommitted and underfunded. It will almost surely remain so because the dominant interest group, large plan sponsors, resists higher premiums.

Private plans cost the Treasury tens of billions in tax expenditures.* The claim that pension accumulations constitute the most important pool of capital for investment and expansion remains unproven and, indeed, possibly overstates the case (see chapter 9).

---

* A "tax expenditure" consists of taxes that ordinarily would be collected but are not because of some special treatment provided by law.

Private Pensions: Chronic Problems

Private plan administrative costs are high and cadres of money managers attempt to make investments that "beat the market," frequently in vain. Conflict of interest is built into a system that is too vast to be policed effectively; efforts to do so, exemplified by ERISA, are costly and provoke complaints of overly detailed government regulation.

These deficiencies add up to a vast system of balkanized plans whose ultimate effect in terms of retirement income remains problematical and unpredictable. Few people know what, if anything, plans will provide them because the future uncertainties of their work and inflation condemn them to ignorance of their pension fate.

Who will be the winners and losers can be guessed roughly. Likely winners are in the group of those who have the best jobs for most of their working lives, or at least for long periods just preceding retirement (the period that one can least foresee), who are employed in stable companies or stable industries, whose personal health holds up, whose own skills remain in demand, who command good pay, and who make or influence their enterprise's decisions about pensions. Likely losers are those with the least control over their economic fate, the less well paid, nonunion employees, large groups of minority workers and women, part-time workers (again with overrepresentation of women and minorities), and those with jobs in unstable or rapidly changing industries, companies, and regions.

What *kind* of a plan covers employees may make an enormous difference to individuals and society. Pension professionals caution that defined-benefit plans provide greater future certainty than defined-contribution plans because the benefit value of the latter becomes known only at retirement. They express concern over the shift from defined-benefit to defined-contribution plans.

Both kinds of plan, however, are beset, almost equally, with variable factors. A defined-benefit plan formula enables participants to translate their work and earnings records into specific amounts. Even so, their eventual benefit outcome requires forecasts about length of credited service, the formula in use at various stages of future working life, and the continuation of their plan, company, or job, all unknowable variables, to say nothing of inflation.

Defined-contribution plans present these and other variables.* Despite the name, contributions may depend on profits and, at times, discretionary employer decisions. Only when one's accumulation becomes known and payable at retirement age does the participant learn what retirement benefits it will purchase. That depends on economic circumstances and other assumptions, such as interest and mortality rates, at that particular time. On the other hand, defined-contribution plans tend to offer somewhat earlier vesting so that a greater portion

* Teachers Insurance and Annuity Association-College Retirement Equities Fund (TIAA-CREF), nonprofit programs for university and college teachers and personnel, provide protective features that are not frequently found in other defined-contribution programs.

of participants can expect to qualify for some benefits. While vesting in a defined-benefit plan gives the participant a claim, vesting in a defined-contribution plan gives one an accumulation of investments.

From the point of view of meeting societal goals for *retirement* income, however, defined-contribution plans are more risky than even the conventional comparison suggests. Although subject to some ERISA constraints and commonly regarded as "retirement income plans," a major vice of defined-contribution plans—and Individual Retirement Accounts (IRAs) and 401(k) and 403(b) plans—is that they need not operate as *retirement* plans but can be used simply to defer income. When separated from the job; former employees may choose to cash them out or "roll them over" into a new plan; the plan may cash out the benefits, if they are sufficiently small. Most take the money and run. Survey data of federal, state, and local government and private plans indicate that employees offered the return of their own plan contributions usually cash them out. When an employee leaves such a job, he or she may withdraw his or her own contributions (often without interest or only nominal interest). Doing so means losing the value of the employer's contribution. Most employees separating from such plans withdraw despite the resultant loss. In addition, a 1986 study shows most recipients do *not* use the funds for investment let alone retirement. If the tax benefit is conferred on the assumption that plans provide retirement income, that societal goal may well be frustrated. It remains to be seen to what extent the 10 percent tax imposed by the 1986 Tax Reform Act on plan amounts not rolled over into another retirement vehicle will discourage cashing out.

Moreover, nonseparated employees may borrow against the amounts credited to their defined-contribution accounts, although the 1986 Tax Act attempted to tighten the limitations on such borrowing. The interest paid on such loans is credited to the employee's account. That "income" also is tax deferred. The question arises whether we wish to give such favorable tax treatment to "savings" with so dubious a retirement component and so considerable a tax cost.

The Prospects for Pension Plan Coverage

Current Coverage—Less Than Generally Believed

The number of employed people who participate in retirement income plans is one crucial determinant of how many people achieve pension benefits. Unless a person gets on the roster (a job with plan coverage) and gets to play (participation), that person has no chance to score (achieve benefits).

Private Pensions: Chronic Problems

There is little debate over the characteristics of those who do have coverage and those left out and what portion of the working population does have coverage. That is remarkable, because the commonly accepted figures probably overstate current (mid-1980s) coverage. According to conventional wisdom, plans cover about half the private work force. In some data, however, a person gets counted as many times as he or she appears in multiple plans. Thus, the resultant total produces not the total number of different people but the total number of units of coverage. Pension experts have long known that many employers operate more than one plan, especially for managers and executives, usually a defined-benefit plan and a defined-contribution plan and, sometimes, still others.

Baseline Information: The Covered and the Uncovered

For 1983, the U.S. Department of Labor found 66.8 million private plan participants. But, the Congressional Research Service (CRS) deflated the Department of Labor figures for double counting and the inclusion of retirees. CRS concluded that in 1983 the net number of active pension plan participants was "actually 36.2 million," only about one-third of all private employees, not the one-half usually claimed. Even that may overstate coverage. The Census Bureau household survey found only 28.1 million private plan participants. The lower census figure may be partially explained by the fact that it measures coverage in any month while plan administrator reports to the Department of Labor include all who worked within the year. In addition, a large number of people in the census survey reported that they did not know whether they were plan participants.

Table 6.1 (which is consistent with other analyses) provides baseline information for 1975 pension participation for comparison with later developments and prospects. It shows that a small group of plans accounted for the greater part of participants: manufacturing plans constituted only 14.4 percent of private plans but supplied almost half (48.2 percent) of employee participants; though trade and services had 69 percent of the plans, together they accounted for only 16.8 percent of the participating population. (Bear this in mind when looking at more recent data showing numbers of new *plans* in any year.) The formation of new plans does not necessarily mean a net addition of covered employees; during the decade 1974–84, new plans averaged fifty-four participants and often covered employees already participating in another plan. Defined-benefit plans accounted for just over two-thirds (68.8 percent) of participating employees compared with 31.3 percent for defined-contribution and other plan participation. Since 1975, the number of defined-contribution plan participants has grown while that of defined-benefit plans has not.

The industry distribution of plan participants may be critical to future

TABLE 6.1

Estimated Distribution of Pension Plans (Participants)* By Industry and Plan Type, 1975 (as a Percentage of All Plans and Their Participants)

	Defined-Benefit Plans		Defined-Contribution and Other Plans†		Total	
	Plans	Participants	Plans	Participants	Plans	Participants
Manufacturing	6.6	(36.2)	7.8	(12.0)	14.4	(48.2)
Mining	.3	(1.7)	.3	(.5)	.6	(2.2)
Finance	2.7	(4.0)	4.9	(2.8)	7.6	(6.6)
Construction	1.5	(8.4)	4.3	(1.2)	5.8	(11.6)
Transportation	1.2	(10.1)	1.4	(4.5)	2.6	(14.6)
Trade	5.0	(4.9)	17.0	(4.8)	22.0	(9.7)
Services	5.3	(3.5)	41.7	(3.6)	47.0	(7.1)
TOTAL	22.6%	(68.7%)	77.4%	(31.3%)	100.0%	(100.0%)

* The first column in each classification shows the percentage of plans; the figures in parentheses show what percentage of covered employees were in those plans.
† Includes IRA, Keogh, and tax-sheltered annuity plans based on reports that were filed by plan sponsors. The number of participants in each of these three types of plans reflects total participants reported by plan sponsors. For these three types, the number of plans represents one plan for each sponsor.
SOURCE: adapted from ICF analysis of 1975 Employee Benefit Survey data. (ICF, Inc. is a private consulting group.)

private plan prospects. In 1975, plans in manufacturing covered almost half of plan participants, transportation 14.6 percent, construction 11.6 percent, trade 9.7 percent, and service 7.1 percent. Other studies show greater concentration of plans in unionized firms than in nonunion companies.

With the decline in manufacturing employment,[1] the pronounced contraction of unionization, notably in construction and transportation, and growth in the service sector of the economy where plan coverage is less common, the prospects for pension coverage growth seem problematical.

Recession, Retrenchment, and Retirement— The Adverse Impact on Coverage

Manufacturing employment dropped in each of the six recessions that occurred between 1957 and 1982 (see table 6.2). Those contractions ranged from 1,081,000 jobs lost in 1960–61 to 2,372,000 jobs lost in the 1974–75 recession. Most of the unemployment occurred in durable goods industries (like automobiles and major appliances). The 1981–82 job contraction (another 2,136,000 jobs lost) has especially serious implications for pension coverage because the massive job loss in auto, rubber, and steel manufacturing is expected to be permanent. In 1984 robotics put the damper on employment from refreshed auto sales.[2]

TABLE 6.2

Changes in Manufacturing Employment,
Recessions 1957–82

Recession	Percent Change*	Recession	Percent Change*
1957–58	−10.1	1974–75	−11.6
1960–61	−6.3	1980	−6.5
1969–70	−8.8	1981–82	−10.5

*Peak to trough.
SOURCE: Diane M. Nilsen, "Employment in Durable Goods: Anything but Durable," *Monthly Labor Review* 107 (February 1984): 16, table 1.

Industry responded to recession by retrenching—trimming staffs, reducing departments, shutting down whole plants, warehouses and regional headquarters, and spinning off both profitable and unprofitable subsidiaries in attempts to recapture efficiency and profitability and to rejuvenate cash flow.

Many companies attempted to minimize the adverse impact of these actions by offering early retirement incentives, thereby minimizing layoffs. At the close of 1982, for example, Eastman Kodak offered some 8,000 of its 136,500 employees early retirement. Wall Street analysts expressed the belief that about 5,000 Kodak employees took that route. Another 2,700 were laid off and Kodak left some 2,500 jobs unfilled. In all, within a few months about 10,000 jobs disappeared from an employer that had pioneered pension plans.

Other bastions of pension coverage lost large numbers of jobs. Between 1979 and 1982, construction employment suffered 400,000 casualties. For more than a decade, the unionized portion of the industry with heavy pension coverage has accounted for a smaller and smaller portion of construction jobs. Deregulation of the airlines led older, often unionized, companies such as TWA and Eastern to put tens of thousands of employees on indefinite layoff. Truck and bus transportation, following the tortuous route already traveled by the railroads, experienced employment casualties.

Meanwhile, services, which account for comparatively few pension-covered jobs, and operate under conditions inhospitable for pension coverage and pension eligibility, expanded more than any other major category of employment. Small employers and units are common, they have low rates of pension coverage because of comparatively high installation and maintenance costs for plans. They also have a high rate of attrition. Moreover, they employ a disproportionately high number of part-timers and often, as with retail stores, expand and contract employment seasonally.

By EBRI's count, pension coverage for private-sector employees dropped from 55.1 percent in 1979 to 50.3 percent in 1983 (36.5 million).[3] Prediction

"Sir, I'm leaving my high-paying job in the manufacturing industry for a low-paying job in a service industry, because that's what's happening."

Drawing by Fradon; © 1986 The New Yorker Magazine, Inc.

of future employment patterns cannot be precise. But it appears that the number of jobs in areas of heavy pension plan concentration is in relative decline. Manufacturing will most likely account for a progressively smaller portion of total employment than in the past. Similarly, unionization, a major factor in pension coverage, has been shrinking; for the moment, no one foresees a reversal of that trend, particularly in the private sector.

Coverage—by Sex

A larger number and a greater proportion of men than women have jobs with pension coverage. This pattern results in part from the fact that a far larger proportion of women than men work in low-paid and part-time jobs; comparatively few work in construction and transportation (other than the airlines); and a considerable portion withdraw from the labor market for childbearing and rearing, factors that contribute to interruption of employment and part-time work.

The 1984 Retirement Equity Act lowered the mandatory age of plan participation from twenty-five to twenty-one and also prohibited denying retiring workers with service breaks shorter than five years their prebreak plan credits. That should increase the numbers of women covered but may not do much toward their qualifying for benefits large enough to avoid being cashed out by

130

the plan. Nothing ensures employees the right to return after long absences. Even union contracts seldom give recall rights for as long as five years. Hence the protection against breaks shorter than five years may be of marginal utility to women who leave jobs for childbirth and rearing young children. In addition, younger workers are most prone to move or be removed from jobs. Their pension prospects some forty or forty-five years later are little affected by whether they participate before age twenty-five.

Many, EBRI among them, assert that as people get older their chances for coverage, vesting, and benefit eligibility increase. That claim bears exploration.

The Pension Potential of Displaced Employees

Our files bulge with newspaper articles reporting plant and unit shutdowns and large layoffs that include white-collar as well as blue-collar workers. Every day brings fresh news that adversely affects pension expectations:

PHILIP MORRIS DISMISSES 7% OF CORPORATE STAFF

(with an accompanying story that a few weeks before a major PM unit, Miller Brewing Company, had "reduced its work force 8.4%.")[4]

FINANCIAL CORP. TO PARE STAFF BY 20%

headlines a 1984 story reporting the elimination of 1,500 jobs, with the slightly ominous observation by a company spokesperson that "there have been no discussions of 1985."[5]

U.S. Steel laid off *half* of its 72,000 blue-collar work force, and 5,000 white-collar workers beginning in the fall of 1983. MONY's board chairman announced that in its move from Manhattan to Westchester "we will probably lose 20 percent of our middle- and upper-management employees and more than 50 percent of clerical and other workers." Separations included "layoffs, retirements, quits, and dismissals."

In response to our inquiry, Ford Motor Company advised that its salaried employment went from 76,400 to 54,700, a drop of 21,700 or 28 percent between June 30, 1979, and December 31, 1983. (Ford picked the dates.) Chrysler reportedly cut its white-collar staff in half, from 40,000 to 20,000 when facing bankruptcy.[6]

Studies of mass layoffs and shutdowns repeatedly show that separated employees often fare badly in the job market. Once cut adrift, they frequently suffer economic demotions. They have the least seniority at their new jobs, which makes them vulnerable to repeated job loss, even in nonunion firms.

Some notion of the pension potential of displaced employees can be derived from a study of the employment fate of 13.9 million employees separated involuntarily from their jobs because of plant closings or job cuts between 1979 and 1983.[7] Of the job losers, 2.4 million had seasonal work or left for unclassifiable causes. Few seasonal workers (other than those in unionized construction and shipping) can expect to accumulate hours in any one year and years of such credits sufficient for vesting. Of the remaining 11.5 million, more than half (some 6 million) had held their jobs for less than a year. No pension credits or vesting for *them*! The study concentrated on the remaining 5.1 million with at least three years' service at the time of separation. Of those sixty-five and over, somewhat more than half had had more than 10 years on the lost job, with median tenure of 11.9 years. In the fifty-five to sixty-four age group three-fifths had more than 10 years on the job; more than half had 20 years or more. Median tenure was 12.4 years. Among those twenty-five to fifty-four years old, median tenure was 5.8 years; in all likelihood, longer tenure was more common among older members of the group.

TABLE 6.3

Employees Separated Involuntarily after Three or More Years Service, 1979–1983

Age group	Number in Group	Percentage with 10 Years or More of Service	Number with 10 Years or More of Service	Median Years Tenure
25–54	3,800,000	25.1	953,800	5.8
55–64	748,000	61.3	458,524	12.4
65 and over	191,000	54.2	103,522	11.9

SOURCE: Paul O. Flaim and Ellen Sehgal, "Displaced Workers of 1979–83: How Well Have They Fared?" *Monthly Labor Review* 108 (June 1985):4.

Since length of credited service is an important factor in the benefit equation, many plan participants would qualify for only modest benefits. For example, a fairly good blue-collar plan might generate a benefit of $15 a month for each year of credited service; twelve years would produce a monthly benefit of $180. The earlier in working life the credit is vested, the less value it will have at the time of retirement due to intervening inflation.

The same study reports the employment fate of displaced workers within five years after separation.

TABLE 6.4

Employment Status of Involuntarily Displaced Workers
by January 1984 (in Percentages)

Age	Number*	Employed	Unemployed	Not in the Labor Force
20 to 24	342	70.4	20.2	9.4
25 to 54	3,809	64.9	25.4	9.6
55 to 64	748	40.8	31.8	27.4
65 and over	191	20.8	12.1	67.1
Total, 20 and over	5,091	60.1%	25.5%	14.4%

* In thousands.
SOURCE: Paul O. Flaim and Ellen Sehgal, "Displaced Workers of 1979–83: How Well Have They Fared?" *Monthly Labor Review* 108 (June 1985):8, table 4.

Significant groups of job losers, especially those fifty-five and over, withdrew from the labor market, thereby eliminating chances for a new pension-covered job thereafter. Of the 5.1 million studied, 60.1 percent had found work by January 1984. As age rose, the percentage of reemployment fell and the percentage of unemployment rose. Hispanics fared less well than whites, and blacks fared worst of all. In all age categories, women had both lower reemployment and lower unemployment, but higher labor force withdrawal than men of the same age and race.

The report further notes that:

- Former steelworkers fared badly with only 46 percent reemployed.
- The 680,000 employees who relocated succeeded better in reemployment (three out of four) than the non-movers (three out of five). Only 6 percent among those fifty-five and over relocated. Interestingly, a sizeable portion of those who relocate return "home." Relocation is not an option that most displaced workers can or do pursue.
- Of the 5.1 million displaced employees with at least 3 years of service, 2.8 million found new jobs by January 1984: of these, 2.3 million found full-time wage or salary positions; the other half million were self-employed or worked part time.
- Of those who had held managerial or specialty occupations, only half landed similar work.
- Almost half (900,000 of 2,000,000) of those in full-time jobs before and after displacement moved into lower-pay jobs. The lower the pay, the less likely is pension coverage. Slightly better than half (55 percent) obtained equal or better pay.

This study may not be typical of all job losses or all recessions. No one can be sure of future patterns. But these changes in the 1980s look alarmingly similar to large layoffs in the 1960s. They do not support the claim that those separated from pension-covered jobs eventually luck into new pension-covered jobs and live happily ever after. Rather, they suggest that for half of those who had been on a job for at least three years, job loss had no silver lining, that losing often leads to more losing and private pension potential shrinks or disappears.*

1986 Tax Reform Act Changes

Non-discriminatory Plan Coverage and Benefits

Some sponsors install plans to maximize the deferral of taxes on the earnings of corporate officials. Since the Internal Revenue Code of 1942, Congress and the Treasury have sought to condition the availability of that advantage on nondiscriminatory treatment of employees outside that favored group of corporate insiders.

That effort includes a requirement that eligibility be open to a specified percentage of employees in various pay groups and that a specified percentage of them participate. Alternatively, the IRS may approve groupings it finds non-discriminatory. A plan need not be available to all employees, but may be limited to a group with some common characteristics. In applying the percentage test, the group total may exclude part-time and part-year employees. But the sum of all plan benefits, including those provided by Social Security, must be proportional to compensation. Thus, private plans may confer larger benefits on the highly paid because Social Security pays proportionally higher benefits to the lower paid.

The 1942 act required that a plan afford eligibility to 70 percent of the employees in a group and that 80 percent of the eligibles participate. So participation by as small a contingent as 56 percent could pass muster. That requirement did not ensure that rank-and-file employees would participate in nearly the same proportion as company insiders, identified by specified amounts of stock ownership or receipt of high pay. Furthermore, rank-and-file employees are less likely to achieve benefit eligibility because of their higher rate of turnover.

To counteract the advantages of insiders and the disadvantages of rank-and-file employees, which can include middle managers and supervisors, the IRS repeatedly tried to impose early vesting although, prior to ERISA, the tax statute governing plans had no vesting requirement. ERISA's vesting require-

---

* In contrast, job changing does not interrupt the process of accumulating Social Security credits; due to the translation of past wage credits into their current value under Social Security, even permanent job loss is not quite so devastating to program benefits as it is under private plans.

ments appear not to have met the problem. The 1983 Census Bureau Survey indicated that almost a decade after the enactment of ERISA, only about 5 percent of the working population believed themselves eligible for benefits achieved through former employment. That figure included former public program participants.[8]* After enacting ERISA, Congress imposed earlier vesting for "top heavy" plans, that is, those that unduly favored insiders and the highly paid. Top-heaviness is more common and more readily identified in small plans.

Pension reformers remained unsatisfied with the persistent concentration of plan coverage and participation among highly-paid employees and those holding significant portions of stock. The 1986 Tax Reform Act raises the percentage of employees who must participate. Starting in 1989, a plan must meet one of these participation requirements: (1) at least 70 percent of all non-highly-compensated employees participate; or (2) non-highly-paid participants must be no fewer than 70 percent of the highly-paid participants. Obviously, if the highly compensated are relatively few and the rank and file numerous, as is likely, not a very large group of lower-paid people need participate to satisfy the second requirement.

Further the act requires that, taking into account all plan benefits, the average benefit obtained by rank-and-file employees must be 70 percent, measured as a percentage of pay, of the percentage due the highly paid. For example, if the highly compensated average pay of $50,000, and their future annual benefits are 37.5 percent of that, their annual benefit would be $18,750. If rank-and-file employees average pay of $20,000, their average benefit needs to be only 70 percent of 37.5 percent or $5,250. Contributions for such benefits must be similarly proportional. The 70 percent requirement can yield benefits as much as 300 percent greater for the highly paid than for the lower paid. Such disparities, which can be lower or higher (depending on how much the average pay of the groups differs), are offset to some extent by the weighting of Social Security in favor of the lower paid.

Three other major problems persist. Plans may continue to exclude part-time and seasonal employees to the same extent that ERISA allows. How long people work is often within employer control and so can be manipulated. For those newly covered by virtue of these provisions, prescribed benefit improvements will not bear significant fruit for another fifteen or twenty years.

---

* Data showing high numbers and percentages for eventual benefit receipt from pension plans often result from the inclusion of government employee plans, which are classified as "employer-sponsored plans." That comparatively small group of employees has proportionally higher coverage than the rest of the work force and so has higher pension benefit expectations.

Inequity in Plan Integration

Since Social Security benefits replace a larger portion of earnings for the lower paid, the rules forbidding private plan discrimination have been tested by comparing the combined contributions or yield of Social Security and private plans. The process of taking account of Social Security in setting plan contributions or benefits is known as "integration" and the lengthy and intricate IRS regulations and rulings are known as "integration rules."

Although integration* declined in the 1960s, its use expanded in the 1970s and 1980s.[9] By 1984, over half of large plans (defined as those with one hundred or more participants) used integration. More prevalent among plans for white-collar than blue-collar workers. 77 percent of white-collar participants were in such plans, as compared with 34 percent of blue-collar people covered by plans.† These figures are approximate because the basic data are not at all precise. Still, they give some idea of the extensive use of integration. Integration is believed to be even more common among small plans because, pension experts believe, many are devised to serve the interests of their owner employees. Data seem lacking on the integration formulas actually in use in either small or large plans; the pre-1986 limits were amazingly indulgent to those drawing high pay and commensurately unprotective of rank-and-file employees.

The 1986 Tax Reform Act moderates integration abuses somewhat by prohibiting offset plans from reducing benefits below half of what they otherwise would be. In practice that should reduce the permissible percentage of the Social Security benefit that may be subtracted—just how much will vary by plan and individual benefit. Step plans, under the 1986 provisions, may confer benefits no more than twice the rate for pay above the integration level as for earnings below that point. By eliminating excess plans, the 1986 act probably improves the lot of some 1 percent of plan participants. The 1986 program also uses a

---

* Defined-benefit plans may integrate with Social Security in three different ways: (1) Some portion of the Social Security benefit may "offset" the plan benefit—that is, be subtracted from it. As the law stood before the 1986 Tax Reform Act, an amount up to 83.3 percent of the Social Security benefit could be so subtracted, reducing (offsetting) the private plan benefit to little or nothing. (2) The private plan, within specified limits, may replace a higher percentage of high pay than low pay—the opposite of what Social Security does. Plans using that method are known as "step plans" because they have a different replacement formula for pay below a specified level (step) than above that level. The dividing line often moves in concert with the Social Security average wage. (3) The plan may take into account only earnings above the Social Security creditable amount—hence the name, "excess plans."

† Offset plans covered about one-third (34 percent) of large defined-benefit plan participants—again mostly white-collar plan participants. Excess plans accounted for a minuscule 1 percent of plan participants. Presumably (the reports are unclear), the rest of those covered by integrated plans were in step plans.

200 percent limit for defined-contribution plans—limiting contributions above the integration level to twice that for pay below that demarcation line.

The 1986 provisions will curb the most blatant disparities but continue to permit substantially better treatment for high-pay than for low-pay participants. To know how much of an improvement the 1986 provisions will achieve, more information about actual integration practice is needed.

Opponents of existing integration rules argue they credit the employer with half of each employee's *lifetime* FICA contributions made by *all* of that individual's employers, an unduly favorable basic assumption. In contrast, the employer makes contributions only for its plan participants. Thus, the two are not comparable. The plan should instead be adjudged discriminatory or not on the basis of only its own provisions and a realistic apportionment of the particular employer's FICA contributions.

Improved Vesting

The 1986 Tax Reform Act requires that single employer plans fully vest all pension credits after five years of service or partially vest starting after four years, reaching 100 percent after seven years of credited service. Multi-employer plans may continue to use ten-year vesting. Five-year full vesting salvages eligibility for many who fall shy of the ten years of service generally required for full vesting.

However, full vesting after five years sounds better than it turns out to be. Five-year segments often yield paltry benefits whose value is whittled down further by inflation even before payment begins. For vested benefits to amount to anything of significance, an employee losing a pension-covered job would have to combine the vested benefit of prior and subsequent pension-covered jobs. If he or she becomes vested comparatively early in working life—say twenty or twenty-five years before retirement—the period over which inflation erodes the benefit value will be greater and the loss larger. Moreover, once separated from a job, many have difficulty obtaining another pension-covered job.

Cashing Out

ERISA permits small vested benefits to be "cashed out" because administrative costs are out of proportion to the value of the benefit. That indicates how slight the value of some vested benefits generated under ten-year vesting is. Of course, the value of five to nine years of credits is even less. Every year untold numbers of employees withdraw untold amounts from tax-favored plans. Probably most withdrawals occur when people separate from public employee plans (where contributory plans predominate) and private salary reduction/thrift plans in which participants forego current pay. Withdrawals also can take place from IRAs, albeit with some tax penalty for those younger than fifty-nine and a half. Exiting employees with vested rights may receive the cash present value of their vested credits or may "roll over" such funds tax-free into another qualified plan. A recent study shows that withdrawals are rarely used for retirement or other saving.[10]

In order to discourage cash-outs made before death, disability, or reaching age fifty-nine and a half, the 1986 act imposes a 10 percent additional income tax on withdrawals not rolled over into a plan or an annuity. The 10 percent tax does not apply to those above age fifty-five who satisfy plan early retirement provisions; that suggests congressional reluctance to discourage early retirement arrangements outside of Social Security. How much this new impost will discourage cash-outs is unclear. Some regard the impact as substantial.

In sum, ERISA-required vesting frequently adds up to little for retirement.

The Net Effect of the 1986 Reform Act

Using Social Security's II-B assumptions, ICF (a consulting firm experienced in forecasting) projects that by 2015 the reform package as passed by the Senate will produce private plan benefits for 22 million families with retirees sixty-seven and over who, on average, will obtain annual plan benefits that are $1,800 higher. (II-B projects a sixty-five-plus population of about 50 million families at that time.) ICF forecasts that the number of persons receiving pensions would improve by 17 percent and receipt by women especially would improve by 23 percent as a result of improved participation and vesting. In addition, it projects, total supplementary pension benefits should improve by some 22 percent, resulting from more vesting, limitations on benefit reductions under integrated plans, and penalties to discourage cashing out.[11]

These projections may be overly optimistic. First, they make no allowance for plan terminations or reductions induced by several features of the 1986 act.[12] By sharply dropping individual income tax rates, the statute reduces a major incentive for establishing and continuing plans to shelter current income. Simultaneously, the act imposes many new restrictions on plans that make them both more costly and less favorable to upper-income participants. That combination may persuade some sponsors to cancel their plans, others to reduce their benefits, and many new enterprises, especially small ones, not to install them. Furthermore, by using age sixty-seven as normal retirement age, the ICF projections wash out many low-income/low-benefit Social Security participants, a disproportionately large number of whom die before age sixty-seven.

Given the patterns of plan coverage, the extensive part-time and part-year work of women, and the modest survivor benefits required by ERISA (at best

138

50 percent of the husband's full benefit), most improvement will not flow into the hands of those whose benefits most need improvement—older widows. Many argue, perhaps rightly, that private pensions should not be charged with this task. But the plight of older widows is one of society's most stubborn problems. If private pensions can't fix these problems, Social Security's role becomes even more important.

In sum, the 1986 reforms made improvements. But they left unsolved many of private plans' chronic problems.

The Ineffectiveness of ERISA Enforcement

There are too many plans with too many officials for any reasonably sized bureaucracy to ride herd effectively on ERISA compliance. With so many people dealing with plans and so much money changing hands, some will succumb to temptation and take their chances with discovery. In fiscal year 1984, the Department of Labor's Office of Pension and Welfare Benefit Plans (OPWBP) employed five hundred people charged with overseeing the filing of plan reports and assuring compliance with disclosure and fiduciary duties. Of this group about two hundred were investigators and auditors—for 915,000 plans. That office "closed" 2,454 cases; more than half (1,378) found ERISA violations. In all, OPWBP recovered or procured observance of the law's safeguards for $93 million (repeat, million) of plan assets.

A General Accounting Office summary of a 1984 report by an interdepartmental ERISA Enforcement Working Group stated: "ERISA's enforcement program [is] unable to maintain credibility within the employee benefit plan community because there was no assurance that ERISA violations would likely be detected and corrected."[13]

Fiduciary Duties

ERISA declares that plan fiduciaries must observe the common law "prudent man" rule, which requires the exercise of "care, skill, prudence and diligence." Some claimed that making the measure of responsibility what "a person familiar with such affairs would employ" represented the imposition of a higher duty than at common law because it would not excuse trustee ignorance. The limits imposed by such general and amorphous measures can hardly be gauged. ERISA casts the net of fiduciary responsibility more widely than before, imposing such duties not only on plan sponsors but also on all who engage in plan activities

139

that involve discretion and authority to deal with plan assets, investments, and administrative decisions.

Lawyers do a lively business in providing advice and seeking rulings on who is a fiduciary and what fiduciaries may and may not do. Of course, most fiduciaries wish to stay within proper bounds, but the rascals for whom the limits were devised will show as little regard for the new limits as for the old.

Theoretically, fiduciaries negligent or faithless to their duties may be "surcharged," that is, required to make good for their improper activities and, especially, to disgorge any ill-got gains. In practice, the funds they serve insure them against such liability, and the funds foot the cost of the premiums.

The reporting and disclosure mechanism, which had proved a failure under the Welfare and Pension Plan Disclosure Act of 1958, operates on the supposition that the prospect of a probing press and alert participants armed with the reported information would impel plan officials to act honestly and that the information would enable effective prosecution and lawsuits against the few who acted faithlessly. ERISA's use of such requirements was a triumph of hope over experience.

Conflict of Interest

Ideally, pension plans should serve employee and beneficiary interests alone. Practice falls short of the ideal. The "institutional parties"—employers and unions—who shape and administer the plans often have interests that conflict with employee and beneficiary concerns. Even in most negotiated plans, the employer appoints the plan trustees, frequently company officials. They make crucial decisions about investment portfolios. High yields, which normally involve high risks, can reduce employer contributions. Trustees' dominion over funds enables them to make loans to friends and associates—at market rates, of course—who may return the favors. The power to place funds enables trustees to obtain favors from the financial institutions involved, such as loans for unconnected enterprises or advantageous banking terms. When such considerations intrude, they distract from the official goal of plans: to serve participants and beneficiaries. We have no idea how extensive such practices may be. No one does. The problem is that many opportunities exist.

More subtle, but more important, is the problem of conflict of interest in plan design. Employers generally wish to minimize costs and, frequently, maximize the interest of stock-holder employees and key executives and managers. Unions seek maximum benefits at a cost that will not sacrifice other benefits. Both sets of interests lead plan designers to construct eligibility and service requirements and record-keeping procedures so as to minimize the number of rank-and-file employees who achieve benefits.

Private Pensions: Chronic Problems

Indeed, companies and unions (mostly companies) constitute the clients of the pension industry. Pension consultants, banks, insurance companies, accountants, lawyers, and investment counselors seek company business, not the patronage of employees. Many in such firms undoubtedly care about employee interests. But when competing for customers, they do so on the basis of what they can do to advance the interests of plan sponsors—not participants. In that competition, those who demonstrate their superiority in serving institutional interests win the gold. The widespread termination of plans with "excess" funds provides a current example.

Terminating "Overfunded" Plans—Employer vs. Employee Interests

Controversy rages over the propriety of an employer terminating its plan, meeting its obligations to employees and retirees incurred up to that moment, and pocketing the "surplus." A plan may become "overfunded" through better than expected earnings or fewer valid claims against it due to unplanned shrinkage of the covered group—or some combination of these circumstances.

Major amounts of money are involved. During the first five years of the present decade plan sponsors terminated or announced the termination of more than one thousand plans (covering about 950,000 employees) with "excess" amounts of about $11.5 billion.[14] In 1983, of 14,851 large plans studied, some 10,080 were "overfunded" by $57 billion.[15]

Several cases are in the courts. Whatever their outcome, these developments demonstrate that the lure of quick cash available in a pension plan trust can persuade corporate managers to terminate plans. Thus, in addition to the problems of underfunded plans that imperil employee expectations, we have the relatively new problem of the overfunded plan that also frequently defeats employee expectations.

Fear of corporate takeovers increases the possibility of plan termination. In one case, for example, major stockholders informed management that they planned to dispose of their stock. The managers then decided to terminate the defined-benefit pension plan and use the "excess" funds in the plan trust to purchase those shares, thereby thwarting any outside threat to their control. That they paid almost double the current market price for the shares was an especially curious circumstance. The company's profit-sharing plan purchased some of the newly acquired stock; a newly established ESOP acquired another portion, with voting arrangements that ensured continued management control.

In another case, a major energy company acquired an oil company, at a cost of $4 billion. The next year, the acquiring company terminated four plans, including that of the acquired company. These transactions netted the acquiring company some $400 million from the terminated plans (60 percent came from the newly-acquired company's plan). That $400 million went to reduce a part of the debt incurred to enable the original purchase.

In a third case, the plan sponsor spent some $600 million to acquire another brewer. It merged the two companies' pension plans, put all the active employees in a new plan, and terminated the old, thereby obtaining some $80 million in "reversions" (as the excess sometimes is known). The House Select Committee on Aging staff surmised that those funds would be used to reduce some of the debt resulting from the purchase of the former rival.[16]

Critics point to the suspicious circumstances surrounding some of the terminations, in which corporate interests appear to have taken priority over those of employee participants. Companies that take such action argue that by satisfying all plan claims they satisfy all legal requirements and plan promises. They argue that employers get no more than their due. In a defined-benefit plan, the employer promises specified benefits. It then sets out to fund the promise. If the plan's investments fall short, the employer must make good the difference. If the plan investments not only fully finance the promised benefits but earn a surplus, that surplus belongs to the employer, the risk taker. Not all of the risk, however, is taken by the employer. If it underfunds, some of the risk may be shifted to the Pension Benefit Guaranty Corporation.

More important, employees lose the advantages of an ongoing fund. If one takes the view that employees as a group make an implicit trade-off between current pay and deferred income, that calculus includes an assumption that plan arrangements will continue. Technically speaking, that assumption is incorrect, because if the plan is not governed by an agreement with a union bargaining representative, the employer remains free to terminate at any time. Even with a bargaining representative, future arrangements are subject to future bargaining. Nevertheless, the expectation of plan continuation is reasonable. In practical terms, the termination of a defined benefit plan deprives employees of the benefits that the plan would have produced up to their retirement.

By late 1987, there was no legal obligation to provide a substitute plan, and the prospects for such a requirement are remote. In any case, substitute plans do not necessarily fill the void created by terminated plans. Employers installing substitutes often opt to avoid some of the rigors of ERISA that accompany defined-benefit plans by substituting defined-contribution plans. Interestingly, some pension professionals argue that "reversions" must not be inhibited so as not to discourage the installation of new defined-benefit plans.

Serious questions arise as to whether bona fide plan surpluses in fact exist. Recent terminations have been facilitated by high earnings on plan reserves. However, actuarial estimates of plan earnings assume fluctuations in earnings. The expectation is that one period's higher-than-projected earnings will balance out another period's lower earnings. If higher earnings induce terminations, there will not be the proverbial seven fat years to balance the seven lean years.

In practice, when plan termination occurs in a period of high interest rates, many employees are forced to cash out their claims for a comparative pittance. This occurs because a "present value" which assumes many years of high future earnings is placed upon the claims. A union actuary reports that in one termination an employee with a claim to a $100 a month retirement benefit was cashed out for a total of $300—the claim's purported "present value."[17]

One pension consultant serving employers observed that some companies shut down plans to make a "loan" that ERISA self-dealing limitations prohibit.[18] To effectuate the prohibited result, they terminate their plan but substitute one with equal benefits. In this fashion, plan sponsors obtain use of any surplus, which may be temporary, but do not diminish the ultimate value of plan coverage and plan service to employees. But the cost of these maneuvers is considerable. Furthermore, one must question the reliability of a new plan launched by an enterprise that resorts to such unconventional means of making a "loan," a loan prohibited by law, and in the absence of an obligation to provide a substitute of equal value.

Though the rash of terminations may be a passing phenomenon attributable to the unusual bull market since 1982, even if that abates, others fear that the existence of excess funds might tempt management to protect itself from corporate takeovers by plan termination. Moreover, the existence of a plan surplus itself constitutes a lure for raiders.

Do such terminations violate fiduciary duties? Whichever way this question is answered makes private plans look bad: Either such transactions violate ERISA or, if ERISA permits such actions, it affords inadequate protection to participants. A fiduciary problem arises because plan officials often also serve as officers of the company sponsoring the plan. Assuming that termination serves company but not participant interests, the trustees have breached their duties. Their defenders insist that the officials making the termination decision do so properly in their corporate capacity. If this interpretation is correct, then such vital decisions can be made without the protection of the ERISA fiduciary standards, and employee interests lie naked before the employer's interests. On the other hand, if the trustees cannot so easily slip out of their fiduciary skins, the terminations described probably violate those duties. Some in Congress have been pressing for limitations on "reversions"; there have been some hints of possible administration cooperation. That the problem remains unrectified after several years of dispute and dismay is no advertisement for the security of plans and the efficacy of ERISA and its supplements. While the 1986 Tax Reform Act seeks to discourage plan terminations by imposing an additional 10 percent tax on amounts recaptured, there are those who doubt that this will stem the tide.

Generational Conflict Inherent in Private Plans

Some commentators warn that unless Congress curbs Social Security benefits intergenerational conflict will erupt. This assumes that currently younger workers are being heavily taxed to provide overly generous payments for current beneficiaries. Thus, the argument goes, benefits should be reduced in order to forestall rebellion against the system by the young. This argument is shortsighted, since younger workers have several different interests, including the adequacy of disability and survivor features for themselves, and their stake in providing adequate benefits to their parents. Moreover, they have a stake in the adequacy of their own future benefits. So it is hard to see how the interests of the young are better served by less adequate than by more adequate Social Security benefits.

In contrast, private plans *do* involve generational conflict. Economists agree that a large portion of employer contributions to pension plans derive from expenditures that employers would otherwise devote to compensation purposes. So, nonparticipating employees and participants with poor prospects of benefits, frequently younger employees, or those who will derive small benefits from plans, give up part of their compensation to provide benefits to others.

The presence of older employees causes employers to make larger contributions to major fringe benefits plans for several reasons. In pension plans, the older the participant the more likely he or she will achieve benefit eligibility; the older worker starts closer to the winner's circle and exhibits a lower rate of turnover. (Defined-contribution plans also operate in this unequal way until, at least, the young employee achieves vesting.) Most important, the shorter the time period between contribution and the beginning of benefit payment by a defined-benefit plan, the smaller the portion of the benefit attributable to earnings rather than contributions. That pension-cost differential between older and younger employees can be substantial. Thus, every year, older workers earning the same cash pay receive more compensation than younger workers; in non-management jobs they often do the same work.

In contrast, Social Security and Medicare make no cost differentiation by age and so provide no reason for employers to prefer younger to older workers.

Stacking Benefits for the Best Paid

By the mid-1980s it had become possible for high-earning corporate employees to reduce their current income taxes by four different devices: one or more corporate pension plans (including both a defined-benefit and a defined-contribution plan), contributions to a Keogh plan for any "self-employed" income *and* a 401(k) salary reduction plan, *and* an IRA.* This is no theoretical matter; many of the higher paid participate in some or all of these plans. A 1984 EBRI study based on census data documents that 71 percent of those with IRAs in 1983 also participated in corporate pension plans, and 90.6 percent with salary reduction plans also had pension plan coverage. In contrast, of those without corporate plan coverage, only 12 percent made contributions to IRAs.[19]†

Summation: the Problems of Private Plans

ERISA curbed the excesses of private plans and prescribed minimum standards. Subsequent legislation, culminating in the Tax Reform Act of 1986, further enhanced employee participation and vesting requirements, reduced the possibilities of plan discrimination in favor of corporate insiders, and lowered the amounts high income earners could shield from current taxation through deferred income plans.

But significant problems remain. Private plans cover, at best, half the private work force. Small companies, with high installation and administrative costs, short corporate life, and high employee turnover, afford only sparse coverage, and that frequently disappears along with the demise of the enterprise. Service and other low-pay jobs provide little plan coverage and the many people with such jobs, principally women and minorities in part-time and part-year work, generally do not participate. No attention has yet been paid to the needs of agricultural workers.

Plan participation rules have been improved, but disparate treatment in

* The 1986 act permits tax deductibility for IRA contributions up to $2,000 annually only for those without plan coverage, a group for whom such supplementation is desirable and justifiable. It also continues tax deferral of IRA account earnings for those with or without plan coverage. The act also imposes a new lower combined limit on IRAs and salary reduction plans.

† The report of the study did not include information on Keogh plan overlaps. But the data strongly suggest that a sizable group stack this fourth tier on top of the others.

favor of the higher paid remains permissible. Vesting, now mandatory for single employer plan participants after five years of employment, and after ten for those in multi-employer plans, salvages benefits formerly lost. But the dollar amounts that result frequently are small, small enough to be cashed out either by the plan itself or by the recipient; the 1986 Tax Reform Act penalty of 10 percent on amounts employees choose not to roll over may discourage some— we do not know how many—from taking the money and running. Vested benefits of separated employees do not participate in plan improvements; as a result chronic inflation constantly degrades their value even before payment starts. Similarly, inflation outpaces post-retirement benefit improvements which, in any event, are not required by law and are not the subject of mandatory bargaining. The absence of assured inflation-proofing continues as a major drawback of private plans.

Rapid economic change results in shifting economic fortunes for enterprises and their employees. Normal job attrition, aggravated by recurrent recessions, leads to heavy separation of employees from plan-covered jobs. The frequent demotion of such job losers means that many will not regain pension coverage in subsequent jobs, if, indeed, they are reemployed. The steady contraction of the portion of jobs in areas of heavy pension coverage, such as manufacturing, construction, and mining, and the shrinkage of unionization probably translate into shrinking plan coverage, or its continued stagnation.

ERISA set limits on self-dealing and imposed fiduciary standards and a system of reporting by plan officials designed to curb administrative abuses. But, the General Accounting Office reports, enforcement activities have been so flimsy that they enjoy no credibility. Plan sponsors remain in control of plan design and administration. The overlap of corporate and plan officials results in continuing conflicts of interest between company and employee interests dramatically illustrated by the widespread practice of plan termination by plan sponsors seeking to capture the use of "excess" funds. Terminations often result in the substitution of plans that afford fewer employee protections than the defined-benefit plans they replace. Even if terminations are curtailed, and that remains far from certain, they exemplify the opportunities open to plan sponsors who seek to use plan assets for corporate purposes and the protection of managerial interests, purposes often alien to the underlying goal of providing employees with assured retirement income.

Special and Urgent Problems
of State and Local Government Plans

State and local government plans resemble private plans more closely than Social Security. But they need not observe ERISA's participation, vesting, funding, survivorship, break-in-service, and reporting requirements.

About 70 percent of state and local employees participate in Social Security based on their public jobs. Social Security provides their basic coverage and their own public employer's plan acts as a supplement. Such plans "integrate" with Social Security in a variety of ways. In several other states, including Alaska, Colorado, Massachusetts, Ohio, and Texas, most public employees do not participate in Social Security by virtue of those jobs, though they might as moonlighters or from employment before or after their nonfederal public employment. Such plans sometimes offer larger retiree benefits than Social Security, but they frequently do not offer auxiliary benefits to spouses and children (or only less generous ones). Survivor benefits must be elected and usually result in actuarial reductions when a benefit for a surviving spouse is chosen. While many programs offer a limited degree of inflation-proofing, quite a few are not equally generous with survivor benefits.

State and local plans offer vesting but often with longer length-of-service requirements than ERISA permits. Many plans, particularly for those in the protective services, start paying benefits to long-service employees before age sixty-two. Such early retirements are costly to those systems.

The federal government Civil Service Retirement System and many state and local plans are "contributory," that is, employees pay specified portions of their pay as premiums; the public employer may match them or make larger contributions. However, separating employees can withdraw their own contributions. Most do so although they thereby lose the value of the employer's contribution, a forfeiture not permitted ERISA-covered plans. In consequence of such withdrawals, a high percentage of plan participants do not achieve pension eligibility.

The adequacy of their funding varies enormously and ERISA's funding requirements do not apply. A 1979 GAO study reported that among a sample of seventy-two plans (seventeen state and fifty-five local), eleven state plans and forty-two local government plans fell below ERISA standards. Among the fifty-three troubled plans, seventeen attempted no funding at all.[20] Attention to this set of problems has waned.

On ERISA's tenth anniversary, Thomas C. Woodruff, executive director of the President's Commission on Pension Policy, summarized the group's findings regarding state and local plans:

> The final report of the President's Commission agreed with the House Pension Task Force that problems exist in the following areas: vesting, reporting, disclosure, funding standards, fiduciary responsibility, limits on benefits or contributions, survivor benefits, and plan termination insurance.[21]

In a word—everything.

State and local plans present problems sometimes as urgent as those of private plans prior to ERISA. The problems could be especially serious where the participants do not have a base of Social Security protection on which to build.

Preoccupation with the problems of Social Security has diverted attention from the problems and shortcomings of private plans and similar deficiencies in state and local government retirement programs. A full discussion of retirement income policy requires that private arrangements and state and local government plans receive the same critical scrutiny already focused on Social Security.

PART III

CHOICES

Most Americans enjoy unprecedented good fortune. We have both freedom and a productive and resilient economy, two mutually reinforcing elements. Grim necessity does not drive us as it drives so many in the world today and has throughout history. Having broken the necessity barrier, we have gone on to living standards formerly undreamed of. We have available to us a range of choices previously unknown. But because society is changing so quickly, we must choose often.

Making Choices for the Future

Society must make choices among desirable goals because finite resources necessarily place limits on what society can do. In the United States, to say "the economy can't afford that" means, in reality, that we prefer to spend available resources on other goals to which we accord higher priorities.

When the economy grows rapidly, we need only choose how to apply new resources. When the economy slows or remains static, we have the far tougher choice between applying funds to some new purpose and reducing some existing activity. When we choose to expand a major program, such as defense, and do not simultaneously expand federal government income to match, we must curtail other programs or run a deficit or both.

Sometimes the seeming enormity of a problem short circuits choice. So national health expenditures of almost $400 billion (the 1984 total), amounting to 11 percent of the gross national product (GNP), strike some as simply "too much," especially because the totals and their percentages of GNP have been growing. Those totals may be too much if we pay for unnecessary or overpriced care.

But we do not say that we eat too much because feeding ourselves takes one-third of the family budget or that housing costs too much because it commands one-quarter of a family's income, as those functions usually have in modern America. When, however, interest rates drove housing costs above the "traditional" one-quarter, many came to feel them unjust and improper. Perhaps that is just another way of saying that the cost of any important function comes under suspicion and resistance whenever its *share* expands. Then, after a suitable period of expostulation, we examine the necessity of the expansion, swallowing it when we have no choice, scaling down that function if we can, or seeking substitutes. We did all of those things with energy costs and use after OPEC raised fuel costs dramatically. Thus the dimensions of the costs of dealing with a problem should not in and of themselves disqualify it from commanding the necessary resources. But when an activity requires an enlarged *portion* of resources, that, properly, focuses attention on key questions of necessity, fairness, and efficiency.

Also separable are questions of how best to provide remedies to a problem once it is properly defined and described. So the "we can't afford that" has another aspect. It often means a decision that the already enormous federal budget and deficit cannot sustain another burden, for example, health insurance for the unemployed. Such a response often overlooks the costs of *not* providing such coverage. Thus, proposals requiring employers rather than government to provide such coverage would not "save" money. Rather, it would impose these additional costs on either the employer (to the extent that it in fact absorbs that addition), or consumers (to the extent that any part of the additional cost gets passed along in the price of a product), or employees (to the extent that the additional cost gets shifted directly to them or the employer payment substitutes for some other compensation). For any level of protection, the "pure premium," the actual cost of providing benefits or services, does not vary according to whether the government funds them directly or requires employers to provide them or leaves the burden to those who need those benefits and services.

How a program is designed may affect both pure premium and nonpremium costs (administration, advertising, commissions). Program features may provide incentives or disincentives for efficiency and careful determination of eligibility— different, separable problems and important ones.

In exploring and choosing goals we must pursue several different questions:

- What do we desire for our society?
- How much are we willing to spend to achieve these desires? (Which means, what are we willing to forgo?)
- Can we achieve a given goal more efficiently by rearranging methods of delivery?

Choosing a Goal

Choosing a goal not only presents us with choices among desirable activities but also, obviously, distributes benefits and burdens among different groups (retirees, the disabled, employers, employees, consumers, the young, the old).

In a democratic society, those choices are determined by market power and political power. Even unprincipled choices require accurate description of what benefits will be enjoyed by which categories and who will pay and how much. Sheer self-interest, then, requires adequate information and analysis, without which one may not assess where advantage lies.

Principled choice requires all of that, and, in addition, addressing the question of fairness. In A *Theory of Justice*,* John Rawls provides a useful approach to that issue. He posits that each of us is in "an original position" (before we know our role) and that we choose from behind a "veil of ignorance" that prevents us from seeing just what will happen. When choices are made fairly, we choose how to spread opportunities and burdens, taking account of all interests. This is the modern philosophical equivalent of the rule that one "should do unto others as you would have others do unto you." For example, one must decide which arrangements would be fair in the event of either famine or oversupply of food without knowing whether one will be a farmer or a consumer and whether drought or rain will occur. Under such circumstances, probably most of us would choose arrangements that balance the risks and benefits to all concerned groups without exploiting the vulnerability of any to the need for food in the event of great scarcity or the need to make a decent livelihood in the event that food supply markedly exceeds demand. Under ordinary circumstances, we trust the market to set prices that reasonably serve the needs of producers, distributors, and consumers. But in some circumstances, we seek to ameliorate the hardship that calamity produces when only the community can act on the scale required. The rub comes in making such choices because we think we know whether we will be farmers or consumers, but the exercise has some cautionary merit, especially if we bear in mind that our role may change.

In regard to Social Security cash benefits and Medicare, most of us are

* Belknap Press of Harvard University Press, 1971.

both contributors and beneficiaries, albeit at different times. More than that, many of us have substantial interests simultaneously in both the cost of the program and the adequacy of benefits because, even while contributing, we share concern for particular beneficiaries—grandparents, parents, brothers, sisters, nephews, nieces, and friends. Moreover, we can change from taxpayer to beneficiary swiftly and unexpectedly. Thus, we have concerns based on both interest and affection and, often, the realization that benefit inadequacies might require direct contributions from our own earnings or, failing that, impose substantial hardship and guilt for not providing them.

In the Social Security setting, then, self-interest and principled choice tend to be much closer than in most settings. Therefore, the major tasks are: to define the choices (what we want); to identify our interests over our lifetimes; to identify the costs; and then to consider how much we are willing to pay for particular programs, what we are willing to give up to do so or what we refuse to forgo because we prefer it to particular levels of retirement income, benefits for ourselves and others when disabled, and survivors' benefits in the event of death. We also must consider how best to achieve the goals we set—"best" meaning most efficiently, fairly, and reliably and with maximum benefit and minimum damage to other goals, such as economic growth, on which all else material depends.

We suggest that the nation has a greater range of choice about the economic fate of retirees, the disabled, widows, and surviving children than many discussions have assumed. And, we earnestly suggest, most individuals have less real choice about how to prepare for such eventualities and clearly less about their occurence than is often assumed.

For example, few of us shape the pension plan under which we work even if we are lucky enough to be in the category of participants. Others make the general rules and the particular characteristics of the program offered by our employers. Hence, the most significant choices to be made concern what public and private institutions we, as a community, put in place to meet the inevitable economic hazards of modern economic life, and how much of our current income we are willing to deploy to meet the exigencies that befall us all.

The first choices to consider are: What goals do we set for the *systematic* replacement of family income when retirement or death occurs? A corollary question is, when should retirement begin?

In determining future policy, we must first assess where we are today. Do retirees and their dependent family members, and eventually their dependent survivors, have sufficient income and services, or too little or too much? That is one set of questions. Different but related are the questions whether Social Security itself provides too little or too much. Similarly, we must ask whether other programs—state and local plans, private employment-based retirement

154

plans, and deferred-compensation plans—provide too little or too much. In assessing programs for income substitutes we must also ask: Too little or too much for whom? Obviously, certain programs lavish benefits on some but short-change others.

Our analysis persuades us, and we propose to show, that most Social Security beneficiaries have extremely modest resources, that private programs favor the fortunate, but only some of them, and that Social Security is the lowest-cost, fairest, most adaptable, and most dependable vehicle for providing income substitutes to the retired, survivors, and their families.

7 Income and Resources of Social Security Retirees

_____

Fact versus Fiction

In retirement, the most important single income resource for older Americans is Social Security. It has succeeded in providing sustenance to the great mass of older people, saving millions from poverty. It assures most of us that when earnings diminish or cease because of retirement or loss of a mate, we will receive a steady stream of income that does not diminish in purchasing power with the passage of time and inflation. Contrary to the impression of many, however, most of the elderly do not enjoy affluence or opulence.

To fashion income policy for Social Security recipients requires an accurate portrayal of their income and resources. So much has been said of the affluent elderly and so much has been written of the expansion and liberality of Social Security that the belief is common that older Americans are affluent[1] and, indeed, "wealthier" than the rest of the population.[2] In fact, the income of the great majority of older Americans is modest and, with advancing age, for many it declines because non–Social Security income diminishes.

The latest study concludes that the income of older people has not outstripped that of the rest of the population. Rather, since the 1950s, it has simply caught up—particularly due to OASI and Medicare.[3]

Diversity, a hallmark of American society, also characterizes the Social

FIGURE 7.1

Median Income of Persons Twenty-five Years and Over, by Sex and Age: 1981

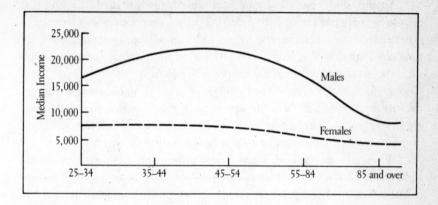

SOURCE: From Cynthia Taeuber, "America in Transition: An Aging Society," U.S. Bureau of Census ser. P-23, no. 128, (December 1983), figure 7, which cites *Current Population Reports*, ser. P-60, no. 134, (1981).

Security beneficiary population. Americans sixty-five and over—the line usually used to classify the "aged"—include the richest and the poorest of our citizenry. Some older Americans continue to work and command substantial incomes; most work less as age advances and reap smaller and smaller incomes. A few elderly have substantial savings, but for most, savings generate little income. A majority possess some modest property, but that too is not a significant source of income, although owned homes save on rent. Many couples enjoy relative comfort, but a significant segment of the elderly, especially single people and widows, live in poverty or close to it.

Realistic assessment of peoples' needs, both in retirement and as survivors, requires attention to the diverse circumstances in which people find themselves as their earnings decline and then end. It helps to group them by age, marital status, sex, race, and, most important for Social Security policy, by whether they draw OASDI benefits.

Age and Income Patterns—A Quick Look

Figure 7.1 provides a recent snapshot of the median income of adult men and women in various age groups. Among the youngest group of men, median income was just over $15,000. Contemporaneously, older groups of men enjoyed progressively higher income; those in their early fifties enjoyed the highest income, and each successive older group of men had lower income. In contrast, women's income was relatively flat from the youngest group to those in their

157

early fifties; thereafter each older group of women received somewhat lower income with the income line flattening out for those in their sixties and over.

Another study[4] looked at groups as they themselves aged. It found that prior to age sixty-five each group of working people, except for nonwhite women, experienced generally increasing wages, with men's earnings peaking a year or two before age sixty-five. Nonwhite women's earnings generally improved, with slight dips for recession years, but did not peak before age sixty-five. Each later-starting group, that is, each wave of younger people, had higher average earnings than its predecessors at the same age in prior years. Hidden within the age-group averages are fluctuations that many individuals would experience. Except for non-white women, earnings drop at age sixty-three or sixty-four.

When considering how Social Security recipients compare with others, age sixty-five is not a good reference point since most people begin the receipt of Social Security benefits before then, and the greater portion of them at age sixty-two, the first age of eligibility for retirement benefits. The fifty-five-through-sixty-four age group, whose finances are often compared with those of the "aged," include millions of retirees from other programs and disabled already receiving Social Security.

We present data (where it exists) in pertinent age groups: those fifty-five to sixty-one (when a majority of people still work and most of the relatively small group of Social Security beneficiaries draw disability benefits); age sixty-two (the age of first eligibility for Social Security retirement benefits) through sixty-four; and sixty-five (the age of "normal" retirement when "full" benefits start) and over. In each category the financial resources of beneficiaries are emphasized and compared with those of nonbeneficiaries. Also, where possible, income and resource data are presented for the sixty-five-and-over group in several different groups: the "young old," aged sixty-five through sixty-seven (when some, especially members of couples, work); sixty-eight through seventy-two (when earnings disappear for most); the "middle old," aged seventy-three through seventy-nine (when widows predominate); and the "old old" aged eighty and over (a growing group).[5]

At the outset, it is important to get some basic ideas straight.

The Misleading Mean

Unfortunately, accounts of the 1985 annual report of the Council of Economic Advisors lent credence to the myth of the affluent elderly. Press accounts of a chapter entitled the "Economic Status of the Elderly" reported passages that emphasized how financially well off the elderly had become. The *New York Times* story stated that "couples who are 65 and over are, on average, more financially secure than the rest of the population. . . . The report says that the average elderly couple is wealthier than the rest of the population, receives as much income and pays lower taxes. . . . Over the past two decades," the news account continued, "income of the elderly has increased faster than the income of the non-elderly population."[6] Another *New York Times* story on the report declared that the income of the elderly had caught up and surpassed that of the rest of us. The report made those points in large part by presenting the *"mean"* money income of the group and stressing the per capita income of "average" older Americans.[7]

Using the mean (the arithmetic average derived by dividing all income by all income recipients) can mislead; in this instance, it does not show the income of the bulk of the elderly. To illustrate, take the income of ten people. If one person has an annual income of $100,000 and each of the other nine has an income of $10,000, the *mean* income of all ten is $19,000. The mean misleadingly attributes a large part of the income of the uniquely wealthy member of the group to all the other group members. In contrast, the *median* income (which means that half the group has an income above and half an income below) is $10,000, a more accurate portrayal. The council reported that in families headed by a person sixty-five or over, 1983 mean income was $21,420, and the mean for individuals was $10,040. However, later in the text one finds: "In 1983 most of the elderly (60.8%) had before-tax income between $4,000 and $15,000." That presents quite a different picture! Indeed, the report observed that those sixty-five and over "are more likely [than those in younger groups] to have income below mean levels for their age groups."[8]

A *Washington Post* "Outlook" section article, using a similar approach, headlined "The Coming Conflict As We Soak the Young to Enrich the Old" declared at the outset: "America's elderly are now better off than the population as a whole."[9] Then the author paraded a set of claims that led him to declare the desirability of "reconstructing Social Security."

Among the elderly, those with income from work enjoy far larger incomes than those who do not have such earnings, except for a small group with significant income from assets. To lump together people in such varied circumstances and use average (per capita) income makes as much sense as saying that a slum neighborhood experienced an average per capita increase in income with the arrival of a stray billionaire.

In deciding policy issues about the need or desirability of income, the *number* of people at various income levels constitutes the more pertinent information for Social Security policy purposes. Where we do not have data showing income distribution, the median comes closer than the mean to telling us what we want to know: how *many* people fall above or below a particular level.

159

The Myth of Elderly Affluence

A study of "discretionary income" by two prestigious agencies similarly added to the myth of the affluent elderly. In reporting a late 1985 release of a Conference Board and Census Bureau study, an Associated Press story observed:

> . . . contrary to reports of impoverished elderly, the over-65 segment also was found to have substantial discretionary spending power. Linden [a Conference Board official] said, "One of the most dramatic findings is the affluence of the new old, the generation of people retiring now."[10]

Linden made the observation in a news conference. The report itself made no such claim.

Such a characterization of the over-sixty-five segment is misleading. The article stated that the study "calculated the normal costs of living, added an additional 30 percent to allow for what they considered a comfortable lifestyle, and labelled any income above that as discretionary." Almost but not quite right. Actually, the study set income 30 percent higher "than the *average for similar families*" (emphasis added) as its measure of disposable income.[11] That is a very different thing, especially when applied to the sixty-five-and-over group. With that definition, a segment of any age group would appear to have "disposable income" even if the age group's average income were below the poverty level.

The study "found" that those sixty-five and over had as a total among them the largest amount of "spendable discretionary income." That is hardly remarkable when one takes into account that the over-sixty-five group contained 17.7 million people while all others were grouped in five-year age spans with only 6.1 to 9.4 million people in each group. Even so, the sixty-five-and-over group accounted for 21.1 percent of all households, but only 18 percent of those with so-called discretionary income.

In fact, the study presented data showing that *the sixty-five-and-over households had average before-tax income below that of all but the under-twenty-five group*. The vaunted affluence, the supposedly large hunk of discretionary income attributable to the elderly, will be met by most older Americans with wry disbelief.

Misleading Comparisons of Improved Income

Some discussions of Social Security policy suggest that during the 1970s and early 1980s the aged have fared so well in comparison with the nonaged that Social Security is too generous. Or, as some put it, the nonaged have fallen behind, implying undue generosity to the older group. However, the aged/

160

TABLE 7.1

Percentage Change in Annual Total Money Income of the
Aged and Nonaged, 1950–80*

Economic Unit and Time Period	Mean		Median	
	Aged (%)	Nonaged (%)	Aged (%)	Nonaged (%)
Families:				
1950–60	25	39	24	41
1960–70	24	35	33	38
1970–80	12	1	20	−1
Families Per Capita:				
1970–80	15	(11)†	(1)†	(1)†
Unrelated Individuals:				
1950–60	33	37	32	36
1960–70	34	46	41	47
1970–80	17	6	24	−2

* Adjusted for inflation using 1967 as the base.
† Not available.
SOURCE: Susan Grad, "Income of the Aged and Non-aged, 1950–82,"
Social Security Bulletin 47 (June 1984): 8.

nonaged comparison looks different when account is taken of the income levels in the 1950s and 1960s.

Table 7.1 shows that during the 1950s and 1960s, the income of nonaged families and individuals improved more substantially than that of the aged— whether measured by mean or median. In the 1970s, the aged played catch up, and a good thing, too, given the high incidence of poverty among the aged in the 1950s and 1960s.

The comparisons contrast older people who have had a lifetime of earnings with a heterogeneous younger population. This younger group includes many people who are just getting started in economic life and have low earnings, a substantial group who live in families headed by women, many of them with marginal earnings, and young adults, a large percentage of whom do not work. In addition, in the recent past, the youngest group of nonaged adults has grown relatively larger, with the major influx at the lower ages. That factor alone would tend to lower average income of the nonaged. Little wonder that, *on average*, the per capita income of the older group, aided by Social Security, slightly exceeds the average income of the nonaged.

The Inappropriateness of Comparing the Aged and the Nonaged

The categories aged and nonaged or elderly/young do not describe the crucial element pertinent to Social Security policy: the end or reduction of earnings. Age sixty-five, the usual line used to differentiate between the young and old, serves that function poorly. People age both physically and mentally at different rates. Retirement sets in at different stages depending on countless circumstances. In addition, for many years now, the majority of working people have begun receipt of Social Security benefits before reaching age sixty-five. A smaller group, usually the healthiest and wealthiest, do not begin Social Security benefit receipt until after sixty-five. So the nonaged group includes significant numbers of Social Security beneficiaries and the aged group includes some unusually fortunate nonbeneficiaries.

The aged/nonaged classifications are too large and too gross to isolate elements pertinent to policy choices and lead to inappropriate decisions based on that distinction. For example, among the nonaged, two major and contra-dictory developments have been taking place in recent decades. On the one hand, female-headed households, in which low earnings and poverty are common, have grown in both numbers and proportion. Simultaneously, two-earner households, typified by higher earnings, constitute an ever larger portion of married couples. These two very different trends almost cancel each other out when the average income of the nonaged is calculated. To observe simply that during the 1970s average real income among the nonaged dropped would obscure these two developments.

Moreover, family composition and income sources differ so markedly that the utility of aged/nonaged comparisons is dubious, especially comparisons that turn on per capita income. The elderly live in couples, rather than with children, and the poorest of the elderly, widows, live alone. In contrast, many of the nonaged live with children. These larger groups have economies of scale for rent, utilities, and food; hence even lower per capita income, as compared with the elderly, often will provide an equal or even better standard of living than enjoyed by oldsters with higher per capita income. On the other hand, the income of nonaged couples must support children, must go farther, must cover more people. And, it usually does, because younger families enjoy—on average—higher income than the retired. In sum, per capita income data do not usefully compare well-being of the aged and nonaged.

FIGURE 7.2

Median Income for Persons in Selected Age Groups, by Marital Status, 1982

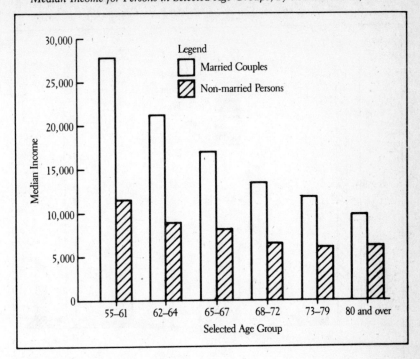

Income Portrait of the Older Population

Susan Grad's "Income of the Population 55 and Over"[12] provides the most complete data about the sources of income and percentage of income from those sources to the population fifty-five and over. The study reports on "units," either a couple or a single person.

Figure 7.2 depicts the comparative median income of older single people and couples. The older the group, the lower the income. As age advances, couples constitute a progressively smaller contingent of older people, and singles a growing segment.

Figure 7.3 charts the percentage of the units according to different age groups who receive *at least* 50 percent of their income from earnings, Social Security, government pensions, private pensions, assets, or public assistance.

As can be seen, at each age past sixty-two, earnings constitute a progressively less important source of income for most people. At each higher age, Social Security provides a larger segment of that population with the major portion of its income.

FIGURE 7.3

Percentage of Units Receiving at Least 50 Percent of Income from Specified Income Sources, by Selected Age Group, 1982

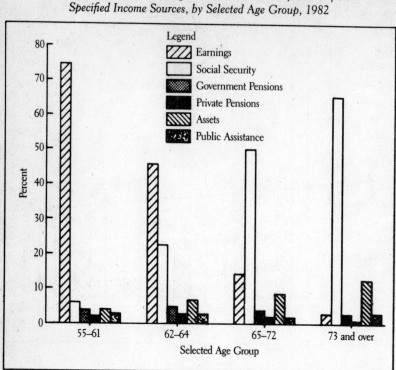

The Group Aged Fifty-five through Sixty-one

In this age group, four out of five had earnings, which provided the greater part of income for 76 percent of all units. About one-fifth drew *some portion* of their income from private and public pensions, including Social Security. Social Security income, the largest pension plan source for over 1.3 million, came mostly from Disability Insurance (DI) and young widow or widower benefits, payable to a widowed parent with young or disabled children.

To summarize the fifty-five to sixty-one age group profile:

- Seventy-five percent earn the majority of their income from work;
- Twelve percent receive over half of their income from pensions;
- Social Security constitutes an income source for a very small group;
- Governmental and private pensions also serve significant groups, but the latter do not often provide the major source of income;
- A small group receives public assistance, and those who do are heavily dependent upon it.

Income and Resources of Social Security Retirees

The Group Aged Sixty-two through Sixty-four

The 4.2 million in this group present a very different picture. A decidedly smaller proportion had earnings than in the younger group, and earnings accounted for a smaller portion (58 percent) of this group's income. Only 46 percent relied on earnings for over half of their income.

Retirement plan income flows to much larger segments of both marrieds (61 percent) and singles (64 percent) than in the fifty-five-through-sixty-one group. The great majority of Social Security eligibles start receipt of benefits *before* age sixty-five (see chapter 8). Furthermore, Social Security benefits account for the lion's share of retirement plan income. As with the fifty-five-through-sixty-one group, the unmarrieds derive a decidedly larger portion of their income from Social Security than do the marrieds, probably because earnings of one partner remain significant for many couples in this age group. Forty-two percent of Social Security recipients, 45 percent of governmental pensioners, and 15 percent of those receiving private pensions count on such benefits for over half of their income. Data from another study show that private plan benefits for those retiring at sixty-two with twenty years of service ranged from 16.5 to 18.5 percent of salary for those with final income of $10,000, to 22 to 25 percent for those with $50,000 final income. State plans replaced a nearly flat percentage of salary at all salary levels, almost 27 percent after twenty years of service.[13]

Public assistance, though a small portion of income, appears far more important for unmarrieds. SSI for the blind and disabled probably constitutes the largest portion.

The Group Aged Sixty-five and Over

In 1982, the total population of those sixty-five and over was 27.9 million, or 19.7 million units. Of these, some 18.5 million units received some retirement pension income: 17.7 million from Social Security and 6.6 million from government or private pensions.

Table 7.2 reports the numbers and percent of units aged sixty-five and older and what percent of income they received from various sources.

Social Security. Of the 17.7 million units who received benefits from Social Security, sixty-five percent derived at least 50 percent of their money income from this source; more than one-quarter obtain 90 percent or more from it.

The lower one's total income, the higher was the proportion provided by Social Security. Even in the $10,000 to $19,999 income group, almost half

165

TABLE 7.2

Relative Importance of Income Sources in Percent by Levels of Total Money Income:
Aged Units Sixty-five and Older, 1982

Proportion of income (recipients only)[a]	Total	Under $5,000	$5,000– 9,999	$10,000– 19,999	$20,000 more
Retirement pensions[b]					
Number (in thousands)	18,539	4,117	6,042	5,071	3,308
Total percent	100	100	100	100	100
50 or more	78	97	90	71	42
90 or more	40	68	51	27	6
100	19	43	24	7	1
Social Security[c]					
Number (in thousands)	17,746	4,030	5,780	4,861	3,076
Total percent	100	100	100	100	100
50 or more	65	96	86	48	8
90 or more	27	64	34	4	0
100	15	41	16	1	0
Government employee pension[d]					
Number (in thousands)	2,330	99	470	862	900
Total percent	100	100	100	100	100
50 or more	33	29	31	32	34
90 or more	4	12	6	4	2
100	1	7	3	1	0
Private pension or annuity					
Number (in thousands)	4,333	152	1,052	1,869	1,260
Total percent	100	100	100	100	100
50 or more	6	24	5	4	7
90 or more	1	18	2	0	0
100	1	16	1	0	0
Earnings					
Number (in thousands)	4,239	206	753	1,550	1,730
Total percent	100	100	100	100	100
50 or more	40	25	24	35	52
90 or more	12	18	9	9	15
100	3	14	5	3	2
Income from assets					
Number (in thousands)	13,386	1,558	3,865	4,495	3,469
Total percent	100	100	100	100	100
50 or more	16	9	7	16	28
90 or more	1	7	0	0	1
100	1	7	0	0	0

[a] Units with zero or negative total income are excluded from this table. In addition, units with negative earnings are excluded from the earnings section; units with negative income from assets are excluded from the income from assets section; units with a person receiving both Social Security and railroad retirement are excluded from the Social Security section; and units with a person receiving both a government employee pension and a private pension are excluded from both the government employee pension and private pension sections.
[b] Retirement pensions include Social Security benefits, railroad retirement, government employee pensions, and private pensions or annuities.
[c] Social Security beneficiaries may be receiving retired-worker benefits, dependents' or survivors' benefits, transitionally insured, or special age-seventy-two benefits.
[d] Government employee pensions include Federal, State, local, and military pensions.
SOURCE: Susan Grad, "Income of the Population 55 and Over, 1982," Social Security Administration, Office of Retirement and Survivors' Insurance and Office of Policy, SSA Publication No. 13-11871 (Washington, D.C.: U.S. Government Printing Office, March 1984), table 43, p. 74.

received at least half of their monetary income from OASI. In contrast, only 8 percent with income of $20,000 or more relied on Social Security for at least half their income. For this highest income group, other government pensions, asset income, and earnings all provided a greater share of income than Social Security. Of course, as earnings diminish, many will derive a greater share of income from Social Security.

Other Pensions. While private pensions and annuities provided income to 4.3 million, only 6 percent depended upon that source for half or more of their income. In contrast, of the 2.3 million units receiving government pensions, 33 percent derived half or more of their total income from that source. Government pension recipients and high-income earners account for two of the largest groups who did *not* rely on Social Security for at least half their cash income.

Earnings. Only about 20 percent of those sixty-five and older had any earnings. Of those who did, about three-quarters had income exceeding $10,000. Significant earnings will sometimes reduce whatever Social Security benefits would be otherwise payable. For both the high earners and those with large asset-derived income, the tax on half their Social Security benefits reduces the net OASI component. Figure 7.3 shows that. As age increases, earnings play a progressively smaller role. The 1985 report of the Council of Economic Advisors indicates that in 1980 about one-third of the men and almost two-thirds of the women sixty-five and over worked part-time, larger percentages than in former years. However, on average, such part-time work lasts only three years. As age increases, the portion of each age group with earnings shrinks, although in the age group seventy-three through seventy-nine, 15 percent of the units still had some earned income.

Assets. Although 13.4 million of the 18.5 million reported some asset income, only 2.1 million relied on that source for half or more of their income; the greatest number were in the highest income bracket.

Welfare. Of the 17.7 million units over sixty-five receiving Social Security benefits, 1.2 million also received public assistance. Only 8 percent of these received at least 50 percent of their income from public assistance (welfare).

Of the 1.9 million units sixty-five and over who did not receive Social Security benefits, the largest group—some 700,000—had earnings. Most with earnings derived almost all or the better part of their money income from that source.

TABLE 7.3

Median Income in 1982 of Social Security Beneficiaries (in Dollars)

	Total Cash Income	Social Security Income	Non–Social Security Income	Private Plan Benefits
Beneficiaries				
55–61	9,860	4,010	4,930	3,570
62–64	11,230	4,630	6,050	3,750
65 and over	8,890	5,170	2,890	2,530
65–67	n.a.	5,350	n.a.	n.a.
68–72	n.a.	5,550	n.a.	n.a.
73–79	n.a.	5,230	n.a.	n.a.
80 and over	n.a.	4,780	n.a.	n.a.
Nonbeneficiaries*				
55–61	21,530	0	21,530	4,640
62–64	19,630	0	19,630	4,160
65 and over	6,760	0	6,760	3,250
Median Asset Income (of entire age group)				
55–61	830			
62–64	1,160			
65 and over	1,540			

* By definition, these groups receive no Social Security benefits.
SOURCE: Susan Grad, "Income of the Population 55 and Over, 1982," Social Security Administration, Office of Retirement and Survivor's Insurance and Office of Policy, SSA Publication No. 13-11871 (Washington, D.C.: U.S. Government Printing Office, March 1984), tables 13 (pp. 31–32), 18 (p. 41), 21 (p. 46), 32 (p. 58), 36 (p. 62).

Beneficiaries and Nonbeneficiaries Compared

Table 7.3 shows the extremely modest amounts of total cash income received by Social Security beneficiaries in all age groups especially when compared to nonbeneficiaries below age sixty-five. Social Security beneficiaries *prior* to age sixty-five enjoy far more modest income, primarily because a larger group of nonbeneficiaries still work. As they move from work to retirement, beneficiaries of any age group also move to decidedly lower levels of income. Each older group of beneficiaries receives lower income because work income and the value of second pensions decline.

While most elderly own assets, those assets produce little income of significance for most older people. Beyond that, only about one-quarter of Social Security beneficiaries receive private pension benefits and those benefits are extremely modest.

To summarize the findings of the Social Security report of 1982 for the 19.7 million population units over sixty-five:

· 17.7 million received Social Security benefits;
· 4.3 million received private pensions and annuity benefits;

TABLE 7.4

Percentage of Beneficiaries Age Sixty-five and Over with Earnings

Marital Status and Sex	NBS[a] (%)	1982 55-and-Over[b] Survey (%)
Married Couples	44	33
Unmarried:		
Men	22	15
Women	30	9

[a] Includes only married men, retired workers, and their wives, and unmarried retired workers interviewed in October–December 1982 who received a first retired-worker benefit payment during mid-1980 to mid-1981.
[b] Includes all couples and unmarried persons aged sixty-five or older in 1983 who reported receipt of Social Security benefits in 1982 in the Current Population Survey (CPS) March 1983 Income Supplement.
SOURCES: (a) "The 1982 New Beneficiary Study," *Social Security Bulletin* 48 (January 1985) table 1; and (b) Susan Grad, "Income of the Population 55 and Over, 1982," Social Security Administration, Office of Retirement and Survivor's Insurance and Office of Policy, SSA Publication No. 13-11871 (Washington, D.C.: U.S. Government Printing Office, March 1984), table 3.

- 2.3 million received government pension benefits;
- The lower one's total income, the higher was the portion provided by OASI;
- The higher one's income, the greater was the portion provided by earnings or assets;
- While many possessed assets, few derived significant income from them;
- 1.2 million received public assistance, of greatest significance for those who did not receive Social Security benefits.

The "New Beneficiary" Survey

The 1982 study just discussed presents a snapshot of the entire population fifty-five and over and shows the differing financial resources of the elderly, many of whom have been retired for significant periods. The 1982 New Beneficiary Survey (NBS)[14] provides information about *new beneficiaries* who began benefit receipt in June 1980 to May 1981. This is a younger group because most started to receive benefits before age sixty-five. Although the NBS includes some sixty-five and older, they are the *new* retirees only and constitute only a small fraction of the much larger group that age who already retired. The picture of *all* over fifty-five indicates the continuing effect of earlier patterns. The NBS provides a sense of the impact of recent developments. As table 7.4 shows, the two surveys produce these quite different pictures of retirement earnings.

Table 7.5 shows the relative importance of various sources of income among those newly retired during the period June 1980 to May 1981.

TABLE 7.5

Percent of Mean Total 1982 Monthly Income from Major Sources, by Percentile of Total Monthly Income Distribution: Married Men and Their Wives and Unmarried Persons Who First Received Retired-Worker Benefits in June 1980–May 1981

Percentile of Total Income Distribution	Mean Total Monthly Income	Percent of Mean Total Monthly Income From:					
		All Sources	Social Security	Pensions	Assets	Earnings	Other Income
Married Men and their Wives							
1st–10th	$ 521	100	77	4	4	9	6
11th–20th	843	100	67	10	7	12	4
21st–30th	1,068	100	59	14	9	15	3
31st–40th	1,257	100	54	20	11	14	2
41st–50th	1,427	100	48	20	12	17	3
51st–60th	1,630	100	44	22	16	15	3
61st–70th	1,880	100	38	24	15	20	3
71st–80th	2,225	100	32	23	20	22	3
81st–90th	2,829	100	25	26	23	23	3
91st–100th	5,895	100	13	14	39	27	8
Unmarried Men and Women							
1st–10th	$ 248	100	87	1	2	3	7
11th–20th	375	100	80	2	4	6	8
21st–30th	478	100	71	5	6	6	12
31st–40th	588	100	70	7	6	13	5
41st–50th	708	100	61	12	9	13	4
51st–60th	839	100	52	18	10	15	5
61st–70th	983	100	43	21	17	16	4
71st–80th	1,189	100	42	22	17	15	4
81st–90th	1,520	100	34	25	21	15	5
91st–100th	3,287	100	17	19	34	18	12

SOURCE: Linda Maxfield and Virginia Reno, "Distribution of Income Sources of Recent Retirees: Findings From the New Beneficiary Survey," *Social Security Bulletin* 48 (January, 1985): 13.

The NBS study found that Social Security accounted for at least half of the income of 45 percent of the couples and 55 percent of single persons in that group. Data in this study show that the lower the beneficiary's total income, the greater is the proportion supplied by Social Security. Pension income (including that from public employee as well as private plans) provides no more than one-quarter of all cash for any income group. The higher the total income, the greater is the share provided by earnings or asset income.

As those beneficiaries get older, real earnings will decrease in amount and importance and, as a result, so will total real income. On the other hand, Social Security benefits will not shrink in value and will increase as a proportion of income.

Taking Account of Housing, Medicare/Medicaid, Food Stamps, and Tax Breaks in Assessing Income Adequacy

Although relatively few receive food stamps, many beneficiaries, in addition to cash income, own their own homes, qualify for Medicare at age sixty-five, and obtain Medicaid. These programs supplement cash income. The difficult question becomes: how should noncash benefits or potential benefits be valued when considering Social Security policy and in comparing Social Security beneficiaries with others? No one has precise answers to this question, but it should not be ignored.

Needs-Tested Benefits

Needs-tested benefits, such as Medicaid, food stamps, and housing subsidies, can be regarded in three ways. First, they help make ends meet. Second, the need for them indicates the modesty, indeed inadequacy, of other non-needs-tested income. Their receipt by beneficiaries who did not formerly resort to them indicates that Social Security benefits are too low and that supplementary benefits are not sufficiently widespread and substantial. Third, needs-tested benefits must be included in totaling what the community spends for the elderly and the disabled.

Owned Homes

Without debate, owned homes constitute the largest asset most older people possess. Several different 1983 surveys found that about 75 percent of those sixty-five and over live in their own homes.[15] Home ownership relieves the owner from rent payments. But to the extent that mortgage payments remain, as in about 20 percent of the cases, and property taxes, repairs, maintenance, and utilities must be paid, the advantage disappears. (Some states and localities give special property tax breaks to the elderly, some conditioned on specified low income.) The mere fact of home ownership should not be equated with rent-free housing. As age advances, the elderly become less able to do their own repair and maintenance work, thus increasing such outlays. This undoubtedly is one major reason that home ownership diminishes with advancing age.

171

Medicare and Medicaid

Medicare and a sizable portion of Medicaid (the needs-tested program for the medically indigent) expend vast sums to provide hospital, surgical, physician, nursing home, and home health care to the elderly and the disabled. While few of us feel enriched when we receive medical care, were Medicare and Medicaid not provided, beneficiaries would have to pay amounts roughly equal to the Medicare and Medicaid expenditures made on their account or forgo care.

However, it does not follow that the value of these in-kind benefits should be added to the cash benefits when measuring the adequacy of total benefits in comparison with former income, given that the greater part of the employed participate in health insurance provided in some measure by employer contributions. Overall, such private employment-based group health insurance meets the cost of about one-third of private health care expenditures.[16] Medicare meets almost half of such costs for beneficiaries,[17] although the beneficiary population undoubtedly has larger per capita medical expenditures than the younger population.

That overstates the position of Social Security beneficiaries before the age of sixty-five, however, because, prior to that age, they are not covered by Medicare unless receiving DI benefits for twenty-four months or more. In addition, most employment-based health insurance affords coverage for one's spouse and children, for a charge to be sure, while Medicare provides similar coverage for a spouse only when the spouse reaches sixty-five. This is no insignificant matter inasmuch as a large proportion of wives, who are on average three years younger than their husbands, work in low-pay, part-time, or part-year jobs that infrequently provide health insurance coverage.

In any case, precise measures of value of the noncash possessions and in-kind benefits and the comparative well-being of beneficiaries and nonbeneficiaries do not exist. Some studies that purport to make the comparison simply tote up the value of Medicare and other in-kind resources for the aged but omit health insurance and other fringe benefits enjoyed by the employed in assessing comparative well-being. This approach overstates the comparative position of older Americans.

In sum, Social Security beneficiaries enjoy modest total cash income. Their Social Security benefits are far from munificent, and their private plan benefits are less substantial. The data dispel the myth of opulence. In the real world, Social Security serves a vast population with modest income and even more modest resources.

8   Retirement Age

Some of us can choose when to retire, but sooner or later, we all reach a point at which something gives out: our body, mind, memory, skills, employer, industry, locality, or the economy. Much of the public discussion about retirement age in the 1980s proceeds on the assumption that most older people retain a choice whether or not to work.

Several considerations have shaped the discussion of what is the proper "normal retirement age." Foremost was the argued need to trim the Social Security cash program. All other things being equal, the higher the normal retirement age, the lower the outlay for benefits.

Second, longevity has increased. Experts expect that trend to continue, although at what rate and with what upper limit is unclear. Thus, while the good news is that the lifespan has been lengthening, the bad news is that longer-lived people draw retirement benefits for longer periods unless they work commensurately longer. If the elderly population grows more rapidly than the younger "working age" population, the problem gets worse, according to popular analysis. The energetic and the logical find a solution in redefining "elderly" and "working age." If we shift the dividing line upward, the aged-dependency ratio problem (too few young people to support a growing number of dependent elderly) disappears, by definition.

But the problem is not so obliging. Many do not fit the new definitions because of inadequate health or skill or the infirmities of their employer, industry, or region. We ought to regard as significant the fact that the majority of working Americans start to collect Social Security benefits before age sixty-five.

What do we mean by choosing when to retire? We must mean to stop work voluntarily and at the same time obtain sufficient income. And at what level of comfort should retirement income enable us to live: subsistence? enjoyment? the crowning experience of a life of labor?

173

Those who debate these issues in government, industry, and the universities have the best jobs, the lightest, cleanest, best-paying, and most prestigious work. These fortunate decision-makers also have, or think that they have, the expectation of comparatively generous retirement income arrangements. They feel relatively little apprehension over the future because they like their work—*until* they get fed up with the pace, the demands, the wear and tear on family and psyche, or they become ill, injured, or are considered surplus or obsolete. When removed from the charmed circle of deciders, many discover that they are losers rather than winners in the retirement income gamble or smaller winners than they at one time expected.

People age at different rates depending on their genes, health, work, and economic circumstances. Those with poor constitutions, reared on meager rations, poorly clothed, and miserably housed will probably get "used up" or "worked out" earlier in life than the more fortunate.

Economic "fitness" also varies across a wide spectrum of personal and outside circumstances. Fortunes may change if an accident, physical or financial, intervenes. Many suffer severe reverses when their marriage fails, their spouse dies or becomes disabled, their industry shrinks, their plant shuts down, or their department is phased out.

Few Social Security issues surpass in importance the change in retirement age enacted in 1983; in 2003 normal retirement age (NRA) begins to move from sixty-five to sixty-six and in 2027 reaches sixty-seven. Congress took that action so as to reduce the cost of OASI in the next century. However, the change also will mean lower benefits at any given age for many now at work compared with pre-1983 arrangements.

Delaying the age of retirement was hastily enacted and the implications were not widely understood, although specialists had discussed such a change for several years. If some or all of the "savings" to the Social Security trust fund that the higher ages produce are deemed necessary, there are preferable methods of achieving them.

Needed: A Philosophy of Aging

Modern society holds reasonably clear ideas about the role of the young. We deploy enormous public and private resources for their nurture and training. The family supports the child—housing, feeding, clothing, and socializing youngsters. Society mobilizes its largest and most sustained and organized effort to school the young to prepare them to function and work in society.

Retirement Age

We hold less clear ideas about what society and older people should expect of one another. We should attempt to clarify our ideas about work and retirement, and we must make realistic choices that match our resources and our aspirations.

What Retirement Means

Our society holds several different views about retirement, not all mutually consistent. We see retirement as:

- A reward for a lifetime of productive work;
- A way to enjoy the closing years of one's life while still able to do so;
- A means to enable former workers to live out their lives when they become incapable of work;
- A method of increasing job opportunities for younger workers;
- An unfortunate fate fastened upon individuals who desire to work, can work, and, often, need work income;
- A device whereby employers oust higher-paid employees and replace them with lower-paid younger people;
- A means of removing workers with declining capabilities and replacing them with people possessing more current skills and greater stamina;
- A drag on the economy, burdening it with unproductive persons requiring support;
- The end of pain, boredom, exhaustion, and lack of status where those are the main job "rewards."

Retirement may signify the end of working, the departure from a regular full-time job but continuation at other work, the beginning of pension payments (which usually requires departure from the job on which they were earned), and/or the commencement of Social Security retirement benefits (which does not require but often accompanies the cessation of work). Studies differ in the concept of retirement employed. When the data permit, we use the Social Security definition, which is the beginning of benefit payments, although considerable work may continue. (The Social Security earnings test reduces and eliminates benefits only when earnings exceed specified amounts.)

Retirement serves so many different purposes, depending on personal endowment and circumstances, that there is a lot to be said for maximizing individual choice and minimizing compulsion.

What "Retirement Age" Means

"Retirement age" also can mean different things: the age at which particular people retire; the average of ages at which people retire; the age at which retirement becomes mandatory. Each meaning is common. But in pension plans

175

and the Social Security system, it usually stands for "normal retirement age" (NRA), the age at which a full benefit first becomes payable. It serves as both a benchmark and part of a formula.

If a plan pays retirement benefits prior to normal retirement age, usually that benefit will be lower in accordance with a prescribed formula. Social Security currently sets NRA at age sixty-five, but actuarially reduced retirement benefits can be drawn as early as age sixty-two. On average, the lower outlays paid over longer periods equal the higher payments made for shorter periods. Therefore, the earlier availability of lower benefits does not cost the system more on the benefit side.

Private pensions have somewhat similar arrangements, with age sixty-five remaining the typical NRA. However, they usually offer benefit payments starting at earlier ages. In 1983, the *median* age was sixty-two (compared to sixty three under Social Security). Frequently private plans pay *more* at pre-NRA ages than the actuarial equivalent, and occasionally offer extra inducements to ease or encourage early retirement.

In 1967, Congress enacted the Age Discrimination in Employment Act (ADEA) which prohibits employers from refusing to hire people in the forty to sixty-five age bracket or firing them on the basis of that age. In 1978, Congress raised that protective band to age seventy, and then, in 1986, prohibited mandatory retirement ages with limited exceptions, most of which will expire in a few years. Such protection against age discrimination has no direct connection with Social Security's normal retirement age. Some confuse the two and erroneously assume that Congress expected people to work until age seventy or beyond.

The ADEA hearings treated us to a parade of superstars in their seventies, eighties, and nineties carrying the message that being old has become passé. The *Washington Post*[1] headlined a 1985 piece, "The New Definition of Old"; its subhead trumpeted: "Today 65 Is Just Another Number" and featured Representative Claude Pepper, a prodigious force at eighty-five (as he was then), and Edward Bernays, the putative papa of public relations, who at ninety-three reportedly works every day. Clearly, forcing such spectacular people to retire would be wasteful, but their experiences do not point to proper public policy for most of us.

Retirement Age Policy Goals

Retirement age policy must accommodate a wide variety of personal circumstances and must serve goals that tug in different directions. For those with ill health or outmoded skills, relatively early retirement in reasonable comfort must be possible. But we also want to give the able-bodied and adequately skilled the incentive to keep earning and producing. We want a policy that will realistically balance incentives to stay at work with the supply of jobs, in the interest of all age groups. The young want retirement policies that enable them to stay employed, to move ahead, to prosper—*and* to retire in comfort when the need or desire arises.

Not least, we ought to recognize that it is honorable and desirable for paid work to come to an end for those who desire it. Some of us believe that we never will want to stop working. Fine. As long as we feel that way, can get a job, and cut the mustard, impediments should not be put in our way. But others may properly feel that enough is enough, that work has had its due, that there are other things to be done while we can still do them. In a productive society, a variety of options should be possible.

Retirement age policy should be set by recognizing that not only Social Security but other pension programs affect retirement decisions by employers and employees. Moreover, programs other than Social Security entail costs, both directly by contributions and indirectly by favorable tax treatment and consequent loss of tax revenues otherwise payable.

Present Law Meets Differing Needs

Discussions of retirement age frequently assert that the choice of age sixty-five as the normal retirement age for Social Security: (1) lacked any scientific basis, (2) was made arbitrarily, and (3) has remained fixed without further thought of its purpose. A review of the literature of the first third of the century, however, provides a different view. Civic, charitable, and governmental agencies studying problems of old-age dependency regularly used age sixty-five as the line of demarcation. Several studies reported in Abraham Epstein's classic book, *Insecurity*, noted the sharp increase in unemployment after age sixty-five.[2] To say that Social Security simply perpetuates the arbitrary Social Security retirement age decision made in 1935 overlooks more than a quarter of a century during which Congress made successive adjustments to meet evolving circumstances, each time continuing sixty-five as the normal retirement age but adding alternatives with gradations. As now constituted, Social Security recognizes that the interaction of personal and economic circumstances makes retirement appropriate for different people at different ages. Social Security recognizes these differences and allows for them with disability insurance, early retirement, and delayed retirement, each with appropriate variations in benefits. This adaptability to differing patterns is one of Social Security's great strengths.

Retirement Age and Private Pensions

Private plans usually provide for benefits earlier than age sixty-five, most often without reducing benefits by the full actuarial equivalent of the earlier retirement. Frequently full benefits are payable at age sixty-two, and many plans pay benefits as early as age fifty-five.[3] Such widespread arrangements argue that many (perhaps most) employers as well as employees see that the ready availability of early retirement offers advantages to enterprises as well as to individuals.

Many employers use Early Retirement Incentive Programs (ERIPs) in response to company needs to trim staff. The extra incentives for retirement can be additional cash payments, larger than usual benefit payments until Social Security eligibility age is reached, and the continuation of health insurance. In the late 1970s and early 1980s, AT&T, Bethlehem Steel, Dupont, Gulf Oil, IBM, Kodak, Polaroid, R. J. Reynolds, and Xerox all used them.[4] Again, in 1986, Xerox offered enhanced early retirement benefits to four thousand "senior employees," more than 6 percent of its American employee contingent.[5]

Some advocates argue that ERIPs do not run counter to the policy implicit in the 1983 Social Security amendments encouraging later retirement, because they are "one shot" affairs. To the extent that they avoid laying off others, ERIPs do not adversely affect FICA collections.

No one advocates curbing ERIPs (however, there is concern that employees be free to choose without pressure, such as the need to make an election on a few days' notice). ERIPs appear to be a reasonable response to fluctuating economic conditions. Their use demonstrates that people often lose jobs in their fifties and sixties for reasons beyond their control.

FIGURE 8.1

Workers Retiring by Selected Age Groups and Sex (1982 Survey)

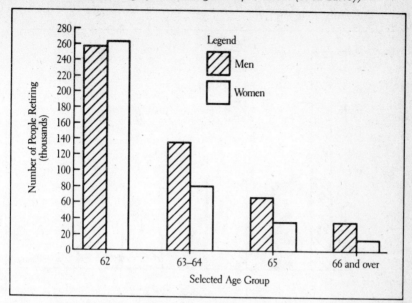

SOURCE: Sally R. Sherman, "Reported Reasons Retired Workers Left Their Last Job: Findings from the New Beneficiary Survey," *Social Security Bulletin* 48 (March 1985): 27, table B.

When and Why People Retire

One major issue in the debate over retirement age must be how many retirees choose the age at which they retire and how many have retirement thrust upon them. The majority of Social Security retirees begin receipt of benefits before age sixty-five. The trend to steadily lower labor force participation by older men reaches back to at least the late 1940s. Some commentators attribute this phenomenon to the availability of Social Security benefits. Others puzzle over the same data and are not so sure.

The New Beneficiary Survey probed the reasons given by those retiring under Social Security in the early 1980s.[6] Most useful for our purposes are the responses separated by age—those retiring at sixty-two, at sixty-three and sixty-four, and at sixty-six or over, the oldest and smallest group. "Retirement" here means the commencement of benefits; at sixty-five it may mean registering to qualify for Medicare.

As Figure 8.1 shows, the majority of both men and women surveyed in 1982 retired at age sixty-two; indeed, many had already stopped working (45

179

FIGURE 8.2

Involuntary, Voluntary, Family and Other Reasons for Leaving Last Job:
Number of Retired-Worker Beneficiaries for Selected Age Groups, 1982 Survey

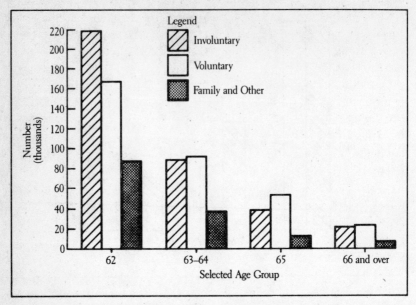

SOURCE: Sally R. Sherman, "Reported Reasons Workers Left Their Last Job: Findings from the 1982 New Beneficiary Survey," *Social Security Bulletin* 48 (March 1985): 29, table B.

percent of the men and 54 percent of the women) and begun receipt of benefits at the first moment possible.[7] Of the 496,000 men, 80 percent began benefits *before* age sixty-five, and 256,000 of them first received benefits at age sixty-two. An even larger proportion of women first received benefits at age sixty-two, 86.7 percent retiring before age sixty-five and two-thirds beginning benefit receipt at age sixty-two. Relatively small groups retired at age sixty-five—13.5 percent of the men and 9.4 percent of the women. Only 7.3 percent of the men and 3.7 percent of the women delayed retirement to age sixty-six or later.

These numbers suggest that powerful forces must be at work because retirement before age sixty-five carries financial disincentives under Social Security: it results in a lifelong reduction in benefits. In addition, eligibility for Medicare does not begin until age sixty-five, and qualifying for Medicaid is difficult.

Figure 8.2 summarizes the reasons for retiring given by retirees in different age groups.* The reasons given for "involuntary retirement" are: health, business bad or lost job, and compulsory retirement. Until age sixty-five, health was far and away the most important reason, followed by business bad or lost job. Reasons given for "voluntary retirement" are: desire to retire, the most often cited reason; eligible for Social Security; and eligible for second pension. "Family reasons and other" are not further identified in the study; women cited "family reasons" more frequently than men.

It is not easy to know whether to consider "family reasons" as voluntary or involuntary. Caring for elderly parents or an ailing spouse might be regarded by some as a necessity, by others as a choice. A husband's retirement may be the signal for the couple to move closer to children and grandchildren or to a more benevolent climate. Under those circumstances, is a wife's retirement voluntary or involuntary?

The study found that large percentages, especially those who started benefit receipt at age sixty-two, stopped work *before* they began collecting Social Security benefits: 59.7 percent of the men and 67.8 percent of the women. The bulk of them had been unemployed for more than half a year before benefits began. Clearly they were not lured from work by benefits.

Table 8.1 presents the data underlying figure 8.2, providing the reasons given for retirement in the 1982 survey.*

Involuntary retirement predominated among those retiring before the NRA of sixty-five and comprised a significant portion of retirement at sixty-five and beyond. Single men and women more often ascribed their retirement to involuntary causes than did their married counterparts.† Starting at age sixty-five, the majority retired voluntarily.

Pension eligibility, either for Social Security or other plans, was cited as the major cause for less than 5 percent of retirements. Of course, such eligibility does facilitate retirement for other causes, such as "desire to retire." The availability of a second pension in addition to Social Security may be far more important in prompting retirement than Social Security alone. The fact that the

---

* Some distrust survey data derived from querying beneficiaries. They say that these respondents do not have good memories for financial details (not pertinent here because quantities of money received are not involved) and many give answers they regard as laudable or acceptable. For example, it may be thought acceptable to retire for poor health but questionable or even blameworthy to retire just because you feel like it. The data in this survey do not seem susceptible to this criticism as substantial numbers had no hesitancy in saying that they retired because they wanted to do so. And the consistency of the data among different age groups argues that real rather than fabricated reasons were expressed.

† Curiously, mandatory retirement accounted for small but significant percentages of retirement in all groups (except women retiring at sixty-two), and that cause rises in relative importance with age between sixty-two and sixty-five. This is odd because the 1967 Age Discrimination in Employment Act (ADEA) and its later amendments prohibited mandatory retirement at any age in most federal civilian employment. However, the ADEA exempts small employers (defined as those with fewer than twenty employees). With the nearly universal federal law prohibition of mandatory retirement ages, undisguised compulsory retirement should become less significant.

TABLE 8.1

Reasons Workers Gave for Leaving Their Last Job (in Percentages by Age and Sex)

	Men (in years)			Women (in years)		
	62	63–64	65 and over	62	63–64	65 and over
Involuntary Retirement, 1982						
Business bad or lost job	11.8	11.0	6.7	14.8	9.8	7.7
Compulsory retirement	4.0	7.3	13.9	.8	5.9	8.0
Health	31.5	24.3	14.6	22.8	21.8	25.0
Total	47.3	42.6	34.9	38.4	37.5	40.7
Voluntary Retirement, 1982						
Desire to retire	36.1	41.5	47.8	21.9	32.5	35.7
Eligible for Social Security	2.5	4.1	4.0	1.3	2.2	3.3
Eligible for Second Pension	1.6	.7	1.8	1.0	.6	.6
Total	40.2	46.3	53.6	24.1	35.3	39.6
Unclassified						
Family reasons	2.9	2.5	2.5	19.0	13.7	8.5
Other	9.5	8.6	7.0	18.5	13.4	9.9
Total	12.4	11.1	9.5	37.5	27.1	18.4

SOURCE: Derived from Sally R. Sherman, "Reported Reasons Workers Left Their Last Job: Findings in the 1982 New Beneficiary Survey," *Social Security Bulletin* 48 (March 1985):29, table B.

median age of retirement for those with pensions other than Social Security has become sixty-two—that is, with half retiring prior to age sixty-two—strongly suggests that other plans provide a significant magnet.

Experts do not agree about the *extent* to which particular factors affect decisions to retire.[8] Economist Henry Aaron concludes that the retirement decision is necessarily a complicated one in which many variables operate in ways not well understood.[9] Philip Rones also cautions how difficult it is to isolate the reasons impelling people to cease work.[10]

In one study, which explored the circumstances under which retirees would become available for work, more former blue-collar than white-collar employees said they would return to work. The same study found that when the retiree had a second pension in addition to Social Security, "unavailables" outnumbered availables by more than 2 to 1 among married men, and the ratio was nearly as large among women and nonmarried men. "When [second] pensions were absent, married men were as likely to be available as to be unavailable but, among women and nonmarried men, the availables far outnumbered the unavailables."[11] The NBS provides data of conduct consistent with that pattern. Among women whose Social Security benefits had recently begun, those "who had no [second] pension were almost three times as likely to be working as those receiving pension benefits—about 26 percent, compared with 9 percent. The

TABLE 8.2

Pension Status, Sex, and Marital Status: Percentage Distribution and Employment
Rates of Retired-Worker Beneficiaries Receiving First Payable Benefit
in June 1980–May 1981*

	Women			Men		
Pension Status	Total	Married	Unmarried	Total	Married	Unmarried
Percentage Distribution						
Total Number (in thousands)	551.7	368.3	183.4	692.5	579.9	112.5
Total Percent	100.0	100.0	100.0	100.0	100.0	100.0
Pension	29.8	23.6	42.2	50.8	52.8	40.8
No Pension	70.2	76.8	57.8	49.2	47.2	59.2
Employment Rates						
Total	21.1	17.5	28.6	24.6	25.6	19.9
Pension†	8.6	7.5	9.9	13.7	14.0	11.1
No Pension	26.4	20.6	41.8	36.0	38.5	25.9

* Data from New Beneficiary Survey, October–December 1982.
† Means pension in addition to Social Security benefits.
SOURCE: Howard M. Iams, "Employment of Retired-Worker Women," *Social Security Bulletin* 49 (March 1986):7.

difference is particularly large among unmarried women (43 percent, compared with 10 percent)."[12] As Table 8.2 shows, men follow much the same pattern.

These survey data suggest that second pensions constitute a critical factor in the retirement decision. It may be that people retire because they want to and the availability of both Social Security and retirement plan income makes them believe that it is feasible to do so.

John Wilkin of the Social Security Actuary's office reports a correlation between choosing to work or retire based upon the degree of difference in income rather than any absolute amounts involved. Those who can choose will have some "price" at which continued work is preferable to retirement with reduced income. People's prices differ depending upon many factors including the ease and congeniality of the work available and the income it provides.

Raising Retirement Age: Justifications and Consequences

Under Social Security, raising retirement age means raising normal retirement age (NRA) above sixty-five and paying essentially the same benefit at the new higher age that would be payable at sixty-five under the current benefit formula.

The arguments for raising retirement age boil down to three: (1) the Social Security system allegedly cannot afford benefits based on an NRA of sixty-five;

TABLE 8.3

*Comparison of Percentage of PIA Payable as Monthly Benefit Amount under Current Law and with 1983 Changes in NRA and DRC**

Year of Attainment of 62	Age at Entitlement								
	62	63	64	65	66	67	68	69	70
(1) 1986	80.0	86.7	93.3	100.0	103.0	106.0	109.0	112.0	115.0
(2) 1999	80.0	86.7	93.3	100.0	106.5	113.0	119.5	126.0	132.5
(3) 2005	75.0	80.0	86.7	93.3	100.0	108.0	116.0	124.0	132.0
(4) 2022	70.0	75.0	80.0	86.7	93.3	100.0	108.0	116.0	124.0

* Delayed Retirement Credit.
NOTE: NRA is sixty-five in 1987, sixty-six in 2009, and sixty-seven in 2027. Until 1990, a 3 percent DRC is payable for each year retirement is delayed after NRA. The DRC starts to increase in 1990, reaching 8 percent a year in 2009.
SOURCE: Social Security Administration, Office of the Actuary, February 25, 1986. Prepared in response to authors' inquiry.

(2) people live longer and so can work to older ages; (3) in the next century the NRA of sixty-seven will provide working people with the same proportions of work and retirement as age sixty-five does today. However, we believe that the consequences of the higher NRA are not widely understood.

Lower Benefits

The asserted purpose of raising retirement age was to induce later retirement by making it financially less attractive to begin benefit receipt earlier rather than later. The actual consequence is to reduce benefit payments at any given age below what the current formula would provide.

To understand the net effect of what Congress did about retirement age, one must also understand that Congress raised the delayed retirement credit (DRC). Critics asserted that the less-than-actuarial DRC discouraged people from working longer. (The DRC is payable only to those who draw no benefits, that is, their earnings not only exceed those permissible under the retirement test but are so high that those earnings cancel all benefits.) While Social Security total lifetime benefits may be lower for those later retirees, their overall economic well-being is substantially better. Nevertheless, the 1983 amendments gradually raise DRC beginning in 1990. By 2009, it reaches 8 percent for each year of delay (up to age seventy), considered by the Social Security actuary to be the full actuarial equivalent of benefits begun at NRA. Some disagree. After the DRC change becomes fully operative, *total* lifetime benefits, on average, will *not* improve by delaying retirement. That aspect of the reduction provides no inducement to delay; rather, the DRC becomes a neutral factor.

Table 8.3 shows the result of the interaction between NRA and the rise in DRC in terms of the percentage of PIA payable to beneficiaries at critical future dates. Line (1) shows the current situation. Line (2) shows the effect of the creep of DRC to the point just before NRA starts to move to sixty-six. Line (3) shows the percentage of PIA received for beginning benefits in 2009 at different ages when the NRA of sixty-six is fully in effect (hence age sixty-six shows 100 percent) and the new higher DRC of 8 percent reaches full effect. Line (4) shows the effect of having raised NRA to sixty-seven starting in 2027.

Starting in 2009, at any given retirement age the benefit paid a retiree is roughly the actuarial equivalent of benefits paid at any other age. Lower total benefit payments come from paying at age sixty-six (sixty-seven by 2027) what formerly would have been payable at age sixty-five and by making proportional benefit reductions at both lower and higher ages. After the changes, those who retire before age sixty-eight will obtain less in total benefits than they would without the changes in NRA, and those who retire after a few months beyond sixty-eight will do better than they would without the changes. Early retirement benefits still may be drawn at age sixty-two but are reduced 25 percent in 2005 and 30 percent in 2022 from that payable at NRA, rather than the current 20 percent. Similarly, at all other ages before the new NRA, the benefit is less than with NRA set at sixty-five.

On the payout side there will be no total savings to the trust funds by anyone's delay in retiring. The Social Security Office of the Actuary projects that most beneficiaries will start benefit receipt before the new NRAs. The Actuary contemplates that the *two* raises in NRA will produce an average delay in retirement of only eight months beyond the current average—age sixty-three.

The OASI trust fund gains by delayed retirements only *if* the reduction in benefits induces some people to work longer than they otherwise would, producing more payroll taxes as a result, but then only if the person's continued work represents a net addition to all taxable income due to work that would not otherwise be done. The bottom line is that the "savings" of raising retirement age will come mostly from paying lower benefits after 2000 than under the current formula.

Even so, those retiring in the next century probably will not be worse off than current retirees. If, as expected, real earnings improve rather steadily, the real value of retirement benefits will improve. Those higher real earnings would more than offset the fact that at any given age the benefit formula will be less advantageous than now. Table 8.4 shows the net effect of the combined changes in benefit formula and real earnings.

TABLE 8.4

Projected Benefits for Persons First Receiving
Retirement Benefits at Age Sixty-five

Year Reaching Age 65	Monthly Benefit For Workers Earning Average Wages[a] (in 1985 dollars)	Maximum Monthly Benefits For High-Income Workers[b] (in 1985 dollars)
1985	548	717
2000	659	950
2015	761	1190
2030	873	1371

[a] For hypothetical worker with average earnings throughout his or her working life.
[b] For hypothetical worker with maximum taxable earnings throughout his or her working life.
Projected benefits based on Alternative II-B Intermediate Assumptions used in the *1985 Trustees Report* adjusted to reflect the actual figure for the 1984 average wage.
SOURCE: Reprinted with permission, from Eric R. Kingson, Barbara A. Hirshorn, Linda K. Harootyan, *The Common Stake: The Interdependence of Generations* (Washington, D.C.: The Gerontological Society of America, 1986), p. 24. Copyright © 1986, The Gerontological Society of America.

Higher Retirement Ages and the Problem of Ill Health

Two major questions arise concerning the relationship of higher NRAs to health: Can we anticipate improvements in health to such a degree that ill health will disappear as a major compelling reason for retirement? If so, can special, more lenient DI eligibility rules meet the needs of the assumed small number who retire for health reasons? Proponents of the higher NRA aver that the first is happening and that the second can.

Robert N. Butler, then head of the National Institutes of Aging, and Jacob J. Feldman, associate director of the National Center for Health Statistics, testified before the National Commission on Social Security Reform that no one knew whether improved longevity would also mean improved health and ability to work to higher ages. They both stated that in all likelihood greater longevity will be accompanied by a higher incidence of chronic ill health. The upward creep in the DI rolls already under way may suggest that, even prior to age sixty-five, recent improvements in longevity may not produce commensurately improved ability to work. (These increases, or some part of them, may be due to differences in administration of the DI program resulting from 1984 legislation to counter the harshness that removed hundreds of thousands from the DI rolls in the early days of the Reagan administration.) Whether higher DI rates will persist, and for how long, are matters for conjecture. We cannot be sure that lower death rates also imply improved work capacity at higher ages.

Some recent research indicates improved health among those in their early sixties.[13] In 1968, 54 percent said they left their last job for health reasons; in 1982, 29 percent identified health reasons. Although the two groups were not strictly comparable, a *Social Security Bulletin* article concluded that ill health declined dramatically as a factor. That analysis overstates the change because the higher percentage in 1968 applied to a smaller portion of retirees *who had stopped work* (60 percent) than the comparable group in 1982 (78 percent). *Thus, in 1982 a substantial group, roughly 30 percent, retired at age sixty-two because of poor health.*

We cannot be certain of how healthy people will be in the future. Whether exercise and sound diet will outdistance beer busts and fast food cannot be foretold, although beer and hamburgers seem to command the larger advertising budgets. Even a small percentage of ill and impaired people below the age of sixty-six, and then sixty-seven, will produce formidable numbers who cannot delay retirement. Those whose health prevents continued employment should not suffer a reduction of income beyond the 20 percent now applicable to benefits for retirement at age sixty-two. This benefit reduction and the absence of Medicare protection before age sixty-five already provide substantial disincentives to retire for those who still have the ability and opportunity to work.

Proponents of a higher retirement age suggest meeting the special needs of people who are in poor health by making the Disability Insurance (DI) standards less exacting for ages between current and future NRAs. But no concrete proposals are on the current agenda.

Achieving eligibility for DI is extremely difficult (see chapter 1). To meet it on medical criteria alone one must be terminally ill or dramatically impaired. The disabled with some residual physical capacity can qualify only if they cannot perform sedentary jobs. If they theoretically have the capacity to do any jobs that exist in the national economy, even if no such positions are available in their vicinity, and regardless of whether or not they would be hired for such jobs, they do not qualify as disabled. The more extensive their education, the greater range of jobs they could theoretically perform.

Although current law and regulations moderate these requirements for those aged sixty through sixty-four, denial rates in this age group have been high. Administration of the DI program has provoked widespread criticism that many have been improperly denied benefits or removed from the rolls. The program as it now operates provides no ready haven for people with health problems that impair their ability or their employability. For all but the most obviously disabled, the definition is already too Delphic. A recasting of the verbal formula, however clear the intent to expand eligibility for those sixty-two and over, could present many of the same problems of application that present criteria do. Modifying the DI program to assist those who take early retirement because of poor health does not seem a dependable way to avoid hardship for those who cannot delay retirement to the new higher NRAs.

Ill health or impairment, especially if visible, combined with older age make a deadly combination for a job applicant. Employers are ever more conscious about the costs of health care and try to keep them down by rejecting or separating those with known or suspected health problems.

Additional Private Pension Costs

Many employers offer retirement at ages as early as fifty-five because it facilitates easing out older employees under a variety of circumstances. Hence, we can expect that some employers will make larger contributions to pay for greater private plan benefits to offset the Social Security benefit reductions. In effect, they will pay more compensation for less work.

To the extent that private plans boost their benefits to counteract reduced benefits resulting from higher Social Security retirement ages, the economy has neither saved on retirement nor maintained the avowed purpose of the Social Security change, inducing people to work longer. It would be difficult to prohibit changes in private plans designed to cancel or mitigate the lowered Social Security benefits. Furthermore, prohibition could be readily side-stepped by generous determinations and benefits for disability by private plans. Policing the administration of private plan disability benefits on any large scale would be difficult, probably impossible.

The Better Way

Encouraging and facilitating work for the able seems far preferable to attempting to compel everyone to work longer. Before resorting to the attempted compulsion of higher NRAs, we ought to consider the employment scenarios likely to occur when the new provisions are due to take effect. And we ought to clean up existing law and practices that interfere with employment opportunities for older people.

Reliance on Market Forces

A *Tight Labor Market*. Concern over the projected adverse aged-dependency ratio implies that we will need more people at work than will be available. If projected demographic shifts occur and a tight labor market results, market forces should induce some delayed retirement, producing net additions to the work force. If employable people aged eighteen through sixty-four become scarce, employers will offer higher wages and lower employment barriers to others. Such developments could lure older people into continuing at work or returning to it. A tight labor market could result from several other developments in addition to a smaller number of workers in the so-called "prime" work ages. New markets in the third world, new technology, new sources of raw materials, new industries, new products, and expanded demands for services could combine to make a relatively tight labor market at all ages. For example, developments in deep sea mining could create entirely new labor markets where none now exists. In the 1880s, almost no one foresaw the advent of the internal combustion engine and the revolution tractors, cars, and trucks would produce in agriculture, industry, and the entire economy. In short, no one a century ago anticipated the economy that existed by 1920 and 1960, let alone that of today. We can hardly anticipate the impact of our current computer revolution. We cannot now foresee what the computer revolution, biotechnology, space manufacturing, and developments now unknown will produce in fifty to seventy-five years. But we already have a glimmer of a superconductor revolution, bringing more efficient, less costly power just for starters.

A Slack Labor Market. On the other hand, a slack labor market does not automatically translate into a limping Social Security system. With increased productivity, the economy could produce more with less work, a continuation of the trend in the United States and Western Europe in the twentieth century. Greater productivity means that the economy can afford to sustain a larger dependent population than it currently does.

Removing Barriers to Employment for Older Employees

Present policies often create impediments between competent older workers and employment. We should remove those obstacles where possible. Furthermore, flexible arrangements, such as partial retirement, could encourage the employment of older workers.

Health Insurance for Those Sixty-five and Over. Before 1982, employment-based health insurance operated as a supplement to Medicare for employees over sixty-five, picking up costs not covered by Medicare, including deductibles and copayments. Congress changed this rule to require that, at the employee's option, employment-based insurance could become primary and Medicare supplementary. In 1984, Congress required most employers with health plans to offer health insurance to a spouse of an employee sixty-five or over. In 1986, Congress adopted the administration proposal to extend like requirements to employees' spouses sixty-five or over to "save" money for Medicare.

Cost-conscious employers know that they must pay more for medical care insurance for older employees than for younger employees. By increasing the cost of employing people over sixty-five or with spouses over sixty-five, the 1982, 1984, and 1986 changes can discourage employment of older people.

If we seek to promote the employment of older people, it behooves us to minimize arrangements that discourage such employment in a manner inconsistent with Social Security policy to encourage working longer in life.

Promoting Continued Employment: Partial Retirement under Private Pensions.   Private pensions usually require total retirement from a job to establish benefit eligibility. Partial retirement accompanied by a partial private plan benefit might encourage some to continue at work, part time or part year, in ways employers and employees find mutually advantageous. Some enterprises already use such devices to wean employees from full-time work, to enable others to test the retirement waters, and to adjust habits and routines. The growing use of part-time work suggests that it is feasible.

A Proposal: Raise Retirement Age—Without Cutting Benefits

In aid of maximizing incentives to continue at work, the NRAs could be changed in the next century as now provided in law. But, to avert financial hardship to those who do not or cannot persevere at work to the new higher NRAs, benefits should be the same as those achieved with an NRA of age sixty-five and an 8 percent DRC. That can be accomplished by simply adapting the benefit formula to produce a benefit at age sixty-seven equal to what current law provides. That done, it would be harmless to set the NRA at age sixty-six and then age sixty-seven. Those who must retire before age sixty-seven, sixty-six, or sixty-five would be no worse off than under current law. Those who can delay past those ages would have the same incentive to delay retirement claimed for the scheduled higher NRA arrangements.

That would be fair to those who have no choice but to stop work, but holds out a carrot to encourage working longer. Such an arrangement would cancel most if not all of the "savings" from the increase in retirement age. But if the incentive effect of higher NRAs has the efficacy claimed, and if jobs exist and unemployment is low, overall production of goods and services would be greater, so that the economy would have more to share.

If the trust funds require additions in the next century, a 0.5 percent (one-half of one percent) FICA/SECA rate increase would produce trust fund income equal to the projected savings attributed to the higher NRAs. That is less onerous than it sounds. All of the four actuarial projections, including the pessimistic one (III), forecast a steady improvement in real earnings. The II-B improvement factor projection of roughly 1.5 percent each year would result in average wages and salaries 35 percent higher in real terms (not just numbers of dollars) in 2008 as compared with 1988. An annual improvement of 1 percent real growth would produce an improvement in the standard of living of 22 percent from 1988 to 2008. Those increased real earnings would substantially exceed the amount of payroll tax increase suggested. In consequence, FICA/SECA with a 0.5 percent payroll tax increase would impose smaller burdens than current FICA/SECA rates do today.

For those reaching age sixty-two after the year 2000, the availability of Social Security benefits unreduced by the rise in NRA would probably be regarded as a good trade for the somewhat higher FICA rate, especially if the questionable chances of staying at work until age sixty-six or sixty-seven are understood.

Facilitating Choice of Retirement Age

At what juncture in life—short of necessity—does retirement become appropriate as a matter of principle? On this question, we as a society have more real choice than usually thought, while the individual has less choice than is often assumed.

The choices focus on how to allocate earnings over the life cycle. As individuals, most of us indulge in current consumption and stint the future. Moderating current consumption to accumulate resources for use later in life is like going on a diet; good intentions frequently outdistance performance. We can make allocation choices more readily and effectively by formulating public policy made mandatory by law. A Social Security system providing more protection—and costing more—would make such a shift. Our economy does not provide special incentives to start work early. Rather, we recognize the utility of long preparation for work, do not try to control what people prepare for, and do not attempt to penalize people who begin work later even though those preparatory years consume public and private economic resources. During those periods of preparation, covered work often will be insubstantial in terms of FICA/SECA contributions. We do not penalize such a result. Consider the variety of starting ages for employment—eighteen or nineteen for high school graduates, twenty-two for college graduates, and twenty-five, twenty-six or later for professionals and mothers entering the work force. Imposing a uniform time for ceasing work seems equally inappropriate. Given the variety of our circumstances, we must recognize the need for a variety of possibilities.

191

Assume that most people work from necessity rather than from the joy of the job. Assume a job like removing panes of glass from a moving belt and stacking them in boxes, at the rate of 12 a minute, 720 an hour, 5,760 a day, 27,800 a week, year after year. When does a worker so employed earn a respite, to fish, sleep in, travel, dandle grandchildren, and clean up the garage?

Actuarially, if not actually, after the two increases in retirement age take place, the lifetime primary benefits of people retiring at age sixty-seven will equal the lifetime benefits of persons retiring at age sixty-two, sixty-three, or sixty-four. Of course, the *monthly* benefits of those retiring earlier will be lower than those paid to those with equal creditable average earnings retiring at or after age sixty-seven. For the earlier retirees without a real choice, this often will mean low benefits. Moreover, the Congressional Budget Office has identified a group of low earners among the early retirees who die earlier than the average. For them, the reduction means that their lifetime benefits will be lower than those with better health who retire later. Many later retirees do not need any Social Security incentive to continue at work because their ample earnings render Social Security benefits an insignificant factor in their decision to continue at work.

After NRA goes up, everyone at every age, except the longest working and highest paid, will get lower monthly benefits than they would under current arrangements. Unless the longevity, health, and employability of all increase commensurately, the losers will be those with least promising longevity who must retire early for reasons of ill health—their own or the economy's. Even if improved personal health improves ability to continue work, there is no assurance that skills and opportunity also will move in tandem. Those who will lose least are the best off in terms of longevity, health, and employability. Indeed, many of them will lose nothing because they often can command tax-subsidized private plan improvements to offset any Social Security benefit losses. The projections of the Social Security actuary that average time at work will increase only eight months while NRA increases by twenty-four months tell us that the bulk of the "savings" on higher retirement ages derives from paying lower benefits—lower monthly and lower total benefits over the retirees' and survivors' lifetimes than under the present benefit formula.

All of these considerations argue for a sober, probing, considered debate on retirement age.

9   Choices in Seeking
Income Adequacy
for the Elderly

Deciding the relative roles of Social Security and other retirement income security devices depends on what one can reasonably and realistically expect of each category. If we all could and did save dependably and adequately throughout our working lives, group pension plans and Social Security would be needed primarily for disability and medical care. If pension plans covered everyone, always paid off, and provided benefits that enabled us to maintain former living standards and keep pace with inflation, we could dispense with Social Security. Or if Social Security not only covered everyone (it just about does), not only always paid off (it has not missed yet), not only kept pace with inflation (it does), but also replaced a large enough portion of former income (ay, there's the rub), we would need no other program.

As it is, no income replacement program does the whole job for everybody, so we must attempt to determine how to combine all devices to do what we desire in the most dependable, most efficient, most economically productive, and fairest way. The role assigned to private arrangements and Social Security should depend on the actual track record of each and whether and to what extent its shortcomings can be remedied.

What Role for Private Pensions?

Private pension plans might conceivably play various roles: continuing to supplement Social Security, primarily for the better paid; providing supplementation for more people through better coverage and more generous benefits; supplanting Social Security; supplying smaller supplements, with Social Security assuming a larger responsibility. Alternatively, principal emphasis could be placed on individual plans, like IRAs, putting people on their own (see chapter 10).

Supplementary private pensions are, as now structured, undependable. They cover only about one-half of the private work force, at best. Claims of improving coverage are scarce. Claims of improved yield in the future should be viewed skeptically given the accelerating rate of change in the economy and the demonstrated instability of employment. Even with the five-year vesting required by the 1986 Tax Reform Act, the odds do not favor splicing together sufficient pension credits to add up to a substantial benefit for most working people. And even the fortunate who receive benefits will usually see their value eroded by inflation.

Private Pension Reform—What Might Be Done[1]

The question arises whether these shortcomings can be overcome by some redesign. Improving plan coverage, vesting, protection against the ravages of inflation, and effective representation of retiree interests are features that merit exploration even if these improvements cannot guarantee perfection.

Improving Plan Coverage: MUPS—Making Plans Mandatory. The President's Commission on Pension Policy, launched in the Carter administration, chose pension coverage as the most salient problem pension policy faced. The commission assumed that Social Security benefits were too low to sustain preretirement living standards. It further assumed that expanding Social Security's role was undesirable, although it did not explain why. It concluded that adequate retirement income depended on supplementing Social Security with an additional layer of retirement income for all employees. Its 1981 report[2] recommended a Mandatory Universal Pension System, frequently known by the acronym MUPS.

The proposed system would require all but the smallest employers to make a minimum pension contribution for every year of service beyond the first. With full vesting after one year of service, a large part of lifetime employment would

194

produce retirement savings. Spread over almost all employees and their full working lives, each unit would be low-cost—a key element to make the proposal attractive. Only small amounts would be contributed, estimated to start at 3 percent of pay. Before the resulting supplement could create a significant benefit, fifteen or twenty years of plan life, in many cases longer, would be required. Social Security met that start-up problem by granting benefits exceeding the actuarial value of the contributions made for individuals who retire in the early years of the program or of program improvements. Private defined-benefit plans typically give past-service credit for periods worked prior to plan inception, thereby providing more adequate benefits for those who retire early in the life of such a plan. But the past-service liability thereby incurred can be substantial. Plans that would come into being only in response to MUPS would be in the employment sectors now hardest to cover and least able to fund pensions. MUPS proponents did not propose providing past-service credit.

Most economists regard pension contributions as part of the total compensation package, a total which, over time, is fairly inelastic. An expenditure for one benefit comes from funds that would otherwise go into cash pay or another fringe. MUPS's greatest impact would be upon companies without a plan— typically small, low-pay enterprises; many such companies would respond by reducing employee pay or not improving it as they otherwise would. That result would not be cushioned by the earned-income credit and benefits weighted in favor of the low paid, devices used in tandem with Social Security to offset the burdens of the payroll tax. Some employers, on the other hand, do not accept the proposition that added fringes come out of other pay. Rather, they regard any new benefit as an addition to employment costs, which they resist. In any event, the cost of MUPS would get passed back to the employee, forward to the consumer, or both.

Despite the fact that pension credits would vest after only one year and ERISA's requirement that an employer not discriminate against an employee because of his or her eligibility for an entitlement, such antidiscrimination provisions are difficult to enforce. Frequent employee separation of low-skilled workers during the first year of employment would subvert both MUPS and ERISA. The enforced savings of both MUPS and Social Security would impose a higher rate of savings on the low paid. This double burden might subvert the integrity of Social Security if it led to reduced contributions to that program.

Whatever its merits, MUPS has produced little enthusiasm. The fact that a Carter-appointed commission reported the plan in the first days of the Reagan administration undoubtedly did not help. In any event, MUPS has no powerful patron pushing for its passage, despite the initial ardor of a few respected private pension specialists. So improved coverage will have to come from someplace else. For the moment, no one knows where that will be.

195

Defrosting Vested Benefits. In practice, five-year vesting will produce little benefit improvement. For those who qualify, even ten-year vesting promises only modest benefits, all the more so because vested benefit amounts remain frozen from the time of vesting. No one has yet suggested crediting exiting employees with plan improvements made between the time of separation and retirement. However, that would often improve benefits and achieve treatment equal to that for employees not separated. Equal pay for equal work has come to be regarded as fair. By freezing vested benefits, exiting employees receive less compensation for the credited years than employees who stay in the plan and participate in plan improvements based directly or indirectly on those same years of work.

Vesting that incorporates plan improvements would increase plan costs, which is the major reason that no one has proposed it.

Since five-year vesting promises often paltry benefits, widespread cashing out, which remains permissible,* may continue to be the rule. In addition, vested benefits which the employer or employee does not cash out stay "frozen" within the plan in which they are earned.

Pension Clearinghouse. What would be achieved if the present value of the vested benefit were transferred to the exiting employee's credit in a central fund or to a new plan that he or she joined; that is, if vested benefits were to achieve "portability?" Originally proposed in 1964,[3] a pension credit clearinghouse could:

- Combine bits and pieces of vested credits earned with different employers;
- Finesse the problems encountered in transferring vested credits into employees' next plans;
- Provide separated vested employees with a chance to have their credits participate in economic growth;
- Enable separated employees to invest their vested credits in an expertly-managed and diversified fund;
- Relieve plans of the bother and expense of keeping track of vested credits for former employees.

Many vested credits simply are so small that they do not warrant the cost and bother of investing, which is why ERISA permits employers to cash out benefits with a present value below $3,500. Further, many employees lack adequate information about investment choices and their value. A clearinghouse that meets standards prescribed by statute and regulation could provide a means of reinvesting the credits in a retirement fund. With standardized procedures

---

* The 1986 Tax Reform Act requires separating employees who do not "roll over" amounts distributed into another qualified plan to pay a 10 percent additional tax.

196

such a transfer could be as easy and inexpensive as shifting a modest bank account when moving to a new city. To facilitate reinvestment of vested credits and to discourage cashing out, most employees need the financial equivalent of McDonald's, Burger Chef, and Wendy's—not sophisticated fare, but a known and readily accessible option.

The availability of such a device might warrant mandatory preservation, "locking in" of vested credits, even small ones. That becomes justifiable if separating employees have a reasonable expectation of obtaining credits from more than one job. If vesting were required after one year of service, more employees would obtain vested credits from more jobs than under five-year vesting. As a clearinghouse program matures, the plan for the last employer prior to retirement would bear less of the burden. (Currently it supplies most or all of the benefits to be obtained from private plans.) That, in turn, would enable plans to reduce the benefit attributable to each year of service, thereby lowering per capita per annum costs and facilitating the installation of plans and the introduction of early full vesting.

A clearinghouse avoids a major problem presented by vested credits: translating such credits into credits in another employer's defined-benefit plan. Instead, a clearinghouse lodges vested credits in a money-purchase plan operated for thousands of others similarly situated.

At the same time, a clearinghouse relieves a plan from which an employee exits from the cost and bother of carrying the value of vested credits or administering future benefits, which differ from those of employees whose employment continues. Not unimportant, even if former employees keep track of their entitlements from former jobs (which ERISA instructed the Social Security Administration to do for them), the plans and the former employees may not keep track of each other. If a plan terminates, combines, or is transformed into another financial arrangement, the former employee may not be able to locate the responsible party, if there is one, when the time comes to make a retirement benefit claim.

A most important reason for establishing clearinghouse arrangements would be to give former employees with vested credits a fighting chance to have those credits participate in economic growth. Investing the value of the credit in the clearinghouse might enable their credits to grow with the economy. However, when a plan pays out the present value of a vested credit, it discounts the assumed earnings of that credit during the years until a benefit will be drawn. In order for the value of the vested credit invested by the employee—in a clearinghouse or otherwise—to increase, the interim actual earnings must exceed the earnings rates assumed in setting the present value. Nothing about a clearinghouse overcomes those discounts unless the permitted discount is held low enough by regulation to make improvements likely to exceed the rates assumed.

PBGC now sets the interest rate assumption for cashing out benefits into their present value. The resulting rates have not provided much protection to employee interests.

So, the principal utility of a clearinghouse would be that it salvages credits that otherwise would be cashed out. While that problem could be met by prohibiting cash outs, the bits and pieces of vested benefits thereby preserved require a device for their accumulation; otherwise administrative costs can be disproportionally high.

A clearinghouse, or a series of clearinghouses with transfers among them, could be either public or private entities. The latter would minimize the problem presented by private investment decisions being made by public officials. A private enterprise might well be more acceptable than "another federal bureaucracy."

In addition, a private clearinghouse arrangement also might offer basic plan coverage for small employers. The availability of such a carrier, with prescribed minimum benefits keyed to the needs of small companies, could facilitate the installation of plans in an area where the costs and bother of plan installation and administration now discourage plans.

However, such a scenario requires starting somewhere. As the preceding discussion of MUPS indicates, instituting a new program while maintaining existing programs (Social Security and supplementary programs) commandeers additional resources for retirement income purposes when other demands often are more urgent, especially for low- and middle-income earners. As with MUPS, many years must pass before substantial improvement in retirement income would result.

The Chances for Inflation Proofing.   The rarity of inflation-proofing provisions in private plans demonstrates what a formidable undertaking such a guarantee constitutes. Indeed, state and local plans, even those with a large base of participants, do not tackle full indexing. It seems that no entity other than the national government or a national plan of near-universal coverage can manage that job. A few large employers offer a partial inflation offset to plan participants under which retirees elect a smaller benefit in exchange for a promise that the plan will pay the reduced benefit with some limited COLA. The ability of plans to make good on such promises must be questioned. If many participants elect such an option, plan costs could become unmanageable. In the event of serious inflation accompanied by reduced revenues for the employer (a perfectly possible combination for individual enterprises although less likely for the economy as a whole and employers in general), the ability to sustain the underlying plan let alone the guarantee would come under stress.

Full inflation proofing by plan sponsors seems not in the cards. Partial or capped inflation proofing, but with the cost borne by the beneficiary in lower basic benefits, seems more likely. Whether participants find that a good trade and whether, if made, it proves a good one, remain to be seen. Furthermore, in the event of plan termination, it is not clear whether and to what extent the Pension Benefit Guaranty Corporation's (PBGC) guarantee would include indexing. PBGC's full guarantee runs only to benefits that have been in force for five years. The limit is designed to discourage promises a plan might be unable to sustain. An increase in any one year due to inflation arguably would be a new benefit. PBGC, its own funding already wobbly, might well resist paying in full a benefit addition which had not itself been in force for five years.

RETIREMENT BONDS.[4]   Some economists advocate that the U.S. Treasury issue inflation-proofed long-term bonds to enable plans and individuals to assure steady benefits that would not lose value through inflation. Such bonds would repay both principal and a stated interest rate adjusted for inflation. Proponents argue that Treasury could sell such bonds at interest rates lower than those otherwise necessary because bond purchasers seek rates of return that promise a high enough real rate of return to constitute a hedge against inflation. With inflation-proofed bonds, they anticipate that Treasury would obtain money at lower and steadier rates unaffected by the gyrations of inflation and changing investor estimates of it.

The question arises whether employers sponsoring defined-benefit plans would purchase such bonds. Under current arrangements, when earnings on plan reserves exceed the rate assumed for the plan, the sponsor may properly reduce contributions. Inflation-proofed bonds with lower yields than riskier investments would offer less opportunity for reserves to produce returns enabling the sponsors to make such reductions. In the 1950s and 1960s, the rapid growth in value and earnings on plan reserves stimulated plan expansion and improvement. In contrast, plan response to a private inflation-proofed certificate of deposit offering reportedly was tepid, suggesting that plan sponsors may not embrace such a device.

Alicia Munnell suggests that such bonds could be offered by Treasury as tax-free IRA investment instruments, avoiding the tax complications otherwise attendant upon such a bond. Here, too, we cannot be sure whether IRA holders will find such instruments attractive, whether IRA holders would prefer inflation-proofed bonds to bonds without a COLA element but with higher rates.

Some argue that widespread use of inflation-proofed bonds would reduce public pressure against governmental actions that stimulate inflation because investors need not be concerned about inflation.

Whether maintaining large OASDI reserves would leave the Federal Reserve Board without enough private holdings to enable it to exercise monetary

199

control is a concern. It would seem to follow that large Social Security reserves would make Treasury unable to issue indexed bonds in any great quantity. Despite the backing of eminent proponents, interest in retirement bonds remains limited but may well warrant more attention.

VARIABLE ANNUITIES AND OTHER ATTEMPTED HEDGES.   Through the 1940s, annuities were funded by fixed income investments, primarily bonds, which were regarded as prudent investments with regular, equal interest payments and a debt claim against the issuing enterprise. A decjdedly conservative philosophy dominated investments for annuities. Only a minor portion of a portfolio might be invested even in "blue chip" stocks.

In the late 1940s, William C. Greenough, later chairman of the Teachers Insurance and Annuity Association (TIAA), devised the "variable annuity," a new financial instrument designed to harness the growth potential of stocks (known more technically as "equities"). His study[5] found that a wide selection of shares over a period of several decades did keep pace with inflation. He proposed the variable annuity based on stock investment which would pay periodic benefits from a fund whose equity holdings grew in value. TIAA launched the College Retirement Equity Fund (CREF) embodying that design. Greenough recommended that individuals balance CREF with the more traditional fixed annuity arrangement.

During the 1950s and 1960s the stock market boomed along with the U.S. economy. CREF unit values grew handsomely and dividends were grand. But the movement of CREF values and income often diverged from the movement of the Consumer Price Index (CPI). As one analyst observed: "Imagine the plight of a CREF beneficiary who started receiving his benefits in 1967 . . . with a current dollar value of $609.76 per month. In 1978 his monthly benefit would have been $444.72 in current dollars and only $222.56 in terms of 1967 purchasing power."[6]

The variable annuity has not proven equal to supplying a method of systematic personal or group savings that reliably protects against inflation. Mutual funds, which offer participation in a variegated pool of investments for many individuals, suffer from a similar shortcoming. Commodity futures, which some thought might mirror the movements of consumer prices, did not answer the problem either, because as some commodities prosper, others decline. All in all, the search for a method to inflation-proof private retirement savings has not found much success.

Bargaining Rights for Separated and Retired Employees.   Collective bargaining sometimes produces plan improvements to help catch up with the effects of inflation and also to reflect economic improvements. Without such changes, inflation degrades the value of the pension benefits of employees who persevere to retirement. Once separated or retired, however, even those formerly represented by a union no longer get the protection of collective bargaining. Since a 1971 Supreme Court decision (*Allied Chemical & Alkali Workers* v. *Pittsburgh Plate Glass Co.*, 404 U.S. 157), employers have not been obligated to bargain with the unions representing their current employees over the pension rights of *former* employees.

Although many employers refuse to discuss or make postretirement cost-of-living adjustments, some employers do improve benefits for retirees, sometimes as a result of bargaining and sometimes without bargaining. Studies show, though, that those postretirement improvements do *not* keep pace with inflation.[7] What results might be achieved if the law required employers to bargain about former employees cannot be known. But the fact that many employers assert the right not to bargain on the subject suggests that *they* think it makes a difference.

Ironically, the 1971 Supreme Court decision reasoned that employees and retirees may have differing interests and that unions might not faithfully serve retiree interests since only current employees can vote out the union representative. That reasoning overlooked the fact that former employees often are related to current employees; children often follow their parents into a plant, mine, warehouse, or store; and people get job leads from family and friends already at work for a company. So retirees often are relatives, friends, and neighbors, as well as former coworkers, of employees. Furthermore, current employees may be anxious to set favorable precedents for retirees against the day when they join the retirement ranks. More than that, some unions continue retirees as members, frequently with low or no dues. Thus, retirees figure in the affection and concern of employees and even participate directly in the electoral politics of some unions. For all of these reasons, some unions may respond to retiree interests, and those interests might not diverge from those of employees to the extent that the Court apparently believed.

Congress could amend the National Labor Relations Act to require employers to bargain about benefits after retirement with representatives chosen in National Labor Relations Board elections by former employees with vested pension rights and by retirees. Indeed, former employees should have such a right to choose a spokesperson whether or not the plan originated from bargaining. Such former employees might choose the union representing current employees or some other organization, not necessarily one that represents employees. The American Association of Retired Persons and the National Council of Senior Citizens, for example, might perform such tasks.

When such bargaining was first proposed, some objected that nonemployees would lack bargaining power because they could not strike. But their first amendment rights to free speech give them the right to picket. Indeed, they

201

can legally picket where "employees" cannot because the secondary boycott provisions of the National Labor Relations Act, which limit most picketing to primary strike locations, apply only to labor organizations, entities that represent "employees." Further, former employees could publicize their needs and claims in the media, bringing public opinion to bear if they present a persuasive story to back demands. Such efforts by former employees might not require the sanction of law, but a need for orderliness and for a binding bargaining process conducted by a democratically-chosen representative makes a statutorily-prescribed procedure desirable.

Once the idea of bargaining catches on with retirees, they have the numbers and the leisure time to organize effectively. Indeed, such efforts might speed the demand for implementing legislation. So far, little interest has been shown by unions and retirees in such efforts. But today groups organize to vindicate their interests far more readily and effectively than in the past. Organizations of older Americans exist and have power they formerly did not enjoy. Retiree bargaining deserves fresh attention.

Private Plan Costs to Employers and Taxpayers

Private plan costs to the taxpayer seldom have figured in debates over the costs of Social Security, even at the height of anxiety over budget deficits. We should be asking whether taxpayers get their money's worth from private plans.

Pension plans cost vast sums in tax money not collected as a result of their tax advantages. In 1986 the congressional Joint Committee on Taxation estimated that tax credits for employer pension plans would deprive the Treasury of $58.9 billion in fiscal year 1987, and $64.3 billion in 1988. By 1990 employer plans were estimated to reduce Treasury collections by $83.9 billion in one year, with Keoghs taking another $3.1 billion.[8]

The lower personal income tax rates of the 1986 Tax Reform Act translate into permanent loss of tax revenues, just as the lowered rates of the 1981 act did. Pension contributions are not subject to income taxation when made, nor are fund earnings attributable to them. Eventually, however, contributions and earnings do get taxed when drawn as benefits. The permanent loss to the Treasury consists of the difference between the tax that would have been paid but for the special tax treatment and the tax paid when the eventual benefits are drawn, plus the interest the Treasury had to pay for amounts borrowed to make up for each year's uncollected amounts. By cutting tax rates drastically in 1981 and again in 1986, Congress presented an enormous windfall to pensioners on amounts deferred prior to those tax cuts. So, although the Treasury tax loss for each year in the near term is lower for each year after the tax rate cut, the value of the deferral—and hence the tax loss—is commensurately increased for all contributions and the earnings on those amounts made prior to the rate reductions. This was a massive hidden windfall in the tax acts of 1981 and 1986. A surtax on deferred plan income correlated to the years of plan participation prior to the effective date of the tax cuts would recapture some of the windfall bestowed by the acts. Such a 5 percent tax imposed on plan and IRA benefits would yield some $117.6 billion for the years 1988–1992.[9]

Deficit Reduction by Lowering Private Plan Upper Limits

Employers now may obtain tax deductions for contributions to defined-contribution plans up to 25 percent of an employee's pay or $30,000 a head, whichever is less. Further, defined-benefit plan contributions are deductible if they produce a yearly benefit no higher than $90,000 or 100 percent of a person's pay. Those limits will strike most wage earners as extremely generous. Starting in 1988, the so-called limits will be indexed to increase with inflation. We have not heard senators who voted in 1985 to freeze the Social Security COLA limits suggest that these "top-hat pension" limits be frozen.

In 1987, the Congressional Budget Office (CBO) estimated what lower limits on such plans would yield in tax revenue. Reducing the defined-contribution limit to $15,000 and the defined-benefit upper limit to $45,000 would improve collections some $12.9 billion, even permitting upward movement with inflation.[10]

Another candidate for pruning is the 401(k) deferred-income amount, and comparable nonprofit organization provisions, by which an individual can fictitiously take a "pay cut" yet be assured that the funds will come his or her way, with earnings, when the participant chooses. The CBO estimated in 1987 that repeal of this arrangement would raise about $29.8 billion from 1988 through 1992.[11] Treasury #1, the first Treasury version of tax reform in 1985, called for the elimination of 401(k) plans. The 1986 Tax Reform Act set an annual limit of $7,000 or 25 percent of pay for a combination of 401(k) and IRAs.

In addition, in 1986 Congress drastically pruned IRAs to prevent tax losses on the order of $20 billion a year in the near future. Congress made deductibility of IRA contributions unavailable to high-income individuals with employer pension plan coverage and, indeed, couples with one earner covered by an employer plan if their earnings exceed $50,000. The new limits do not adversely affect amounts already dedicated to IRAs, and earnings on both past and future IRA accumulations remain eligible for tax deferral. Those with money to spare may continue to make IRA contributions, especially if they are unaccustomed to shopping the securities markets.

A surtax on plan benefits when received and reductions of the amazingly generous upper limits on employer plans and income deferral arrangements would produce substantial amounts to apply toward deficit reduction. In terms of retirement income policy, these savings might reduce pressure to trim benefits for *all* of the elderly, such as increasing premiums for Part B of Medicare, and would provide revenues to serve the needs of all generations.

The High Cost of Improving Private Plans

Private plans remain unreliable for a multitude of reasons already explored. The most basic is that for the most part employers as plan sponsors dominate plan design and administration. Often their agenda only incidentally address general employee welfare. Instead, tax savings and good deals for corporate owners, insiders, and managers frequently shape their pension plan strategy, as the rush for "reversions" demonstrates. Employee interests often come second. Even some managers and executives discover they are vulnerable only when they, too, fare less well than they originally expected.

Despite their various elements of undependability, supplementary plans cost the Treasury billions. Plan improvements would increase costs both to sponsors and the Treasury. The private economy seems unwilling to spend more to achieve full coverage, immediate vesting, and inflation proofing. However, proposals for improving coverage and eventual receipt of private pension benefits merit thoughtful consideration. Furthermore, they may be worth doing *if* those covered are dealt fair payouts, the benefits serve the great bulk of the workers covered, and the public treasury is not tapped to subsidize pension payouts primarily to a high-income segment of the retired population.

The structure of private plans makes implementation of improvements both slow and costly. For the most part, congressional reform of private plans has been made prospectively so as to give the hundreds of thousands of existing plans time to conform and to adjust. Even the ERISA requirement for counting pre-ERISA service for vesting purposes could be avoided by following little-heralded, little-understood provisions of the act. For inflation-proof plans upon which all employees can depend, we must look beyond private pensions.

In sum, only about one-quarter of retirees receive any private pension benefits. In the short run, a larger portion of the population may receive private plan benefits as existing plans "mature." However, the decline in overall supplementary pension coverage registered since 1979 tends to reduce the percentage of the working population who will receive pension benefits. Writing in 1985, EBRI's Emily Andrews observed that "currently few continue to believe that the pension coverage gap will dissipate naturally."[12]

The Preeminent Role of Social Security
Retirement Income

Social Security provides an ever larger portion of the income of the elderly because of: (1) the extension of Social Security coverage; (2) the constantly smaller role of currently earned income as people get older; and (3) the fact that Social Security benefits are indexed to keep pace fully with inflation. If, as seems possible, Congress requires all state and local government employees to participate, no significant group of employed will remain outside the system.

How Big a Role for Social Security?

A bipartisan consensus of experts concludes that Social Security can be relied on to make good on its promises at least until the middle of the next century (see chapters 2 and 3). That answers the biggest concern that most people have about Social Security.

Some, however, question what those promises ought to be, claiming that Social Security plays too large a role, that its benefits have become overgenerous either to the low paid or the high paid or, indeed, to everyone. Some claim that Social Security ought to be needs-tested to make it more purposeful and efficient. In addition, some assert that it has strayed from its original charter, attempting to do too much for too many. On the other hand, Social Security's supporters seek universal coverage for both effectiveness and fairness. Critics claim that Social Security depresses the rate of private savings and thereby slows economic growth, assertions vigorously disputed by others. Yet, as we shall see later in this chapter, the claim that private pensions constitute a pool of net savings, a major justification for tax subsidization of such plans, is itself questionable. These major questions merit discussion.

Are Benefits Too High?

Probably by most people's standards, the median Social Security benefit is not "too high," certainly not for themselves. Table 9.1 shows just how modest the median benefits were in 1982.

Nevertheless, critics allege that benefits are too high—at least for the low paid and the well-to-do. On the one hand, they insist that replacement rates are too high for the low paid; that their benefits can approach or exceed former

TABLE 9.1

1982 Median Social Security Benefits for
Persons Sixty-five and Over

Married Couples' Benefits	
White	$6,080
Black	4,350
Unmarried Individuals' Benefits	
White men	$3,970
Black men	3,310
White women	3,620
Black women	2,490

SOURCE: Susan Grad, "Income of the Population 55 and Over, 1982," Social Security Administration, Office of Retirement and Survivor's Insurance and Office of Policy, SSA Publication No. 13-11871 (Washington, D.C.: U.S. Government Printing Office, March 1984), table 12, p. 98.

pay, at least for a one-earner couple, especially when the value of Medicare benefits are added on top. On the other hand, the charge is made that the well-to-do get benefits that they do not need. Some even conclude that average income earners get too generous benefits. The implication is that the "rest of us" are paying too much because benefits are overly generous.

Are Benefits Too High for the Low Paid?   First consider the charge that benefits replace too large a percentage of earnings for the low paid. Typically the argument proceeds in this fashion. A lifetime minimum-wage worker receives a primary insurance amount (PIA) at age sixty-five that replaces 70 percent of his or her pre-retirement pay. Adding a spouse benefit of 50 percent of PIA, OASDI replaces 105 percent of former earnings. In some versions, the value of Medicare is added, which, when treated as a net addition to income, appears to raise the replacement rate even further above 100 percent.

But this analysis errs on several counts. In the first place most workers retire between sixty-two and sixty-four. At age sixty-two, the retiree's own benefit replaces about 55 percent of former earnings; the spouse's auxiliary benefit raises the total replacement rate to 83 percent. However, even 105 percent of $6,968 (yearly minimum-wage income in 1987) can under no circumstances be considered excessive for an elderly couple. Moreover, at such low income levels a second family member, usually the spouse, works. In that common situation, the retiree's own benefit plus the spouse's benefit often replace less than either the 105 percent or even 83 percent of the *couple's* former earnings.

If the retiree had health insurance coverage on his or her former job or qualified for Medicaid, Medicare coverage (which does not start until age sixty-five) essentially *replaces* that coverage; so it usually is not appropriate to add

206

FIGURE 9.1

Percentage of Social Security Beneficiaries Below Poverty Line
and 125 Percent of the Poverty Line by Marital Status, 1982

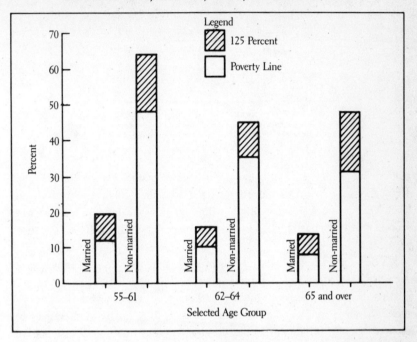

SOURCE: Susan Grad, "Income of the Population 55 and Over, 1982," Social Security Administration, Office of Retirement and Survivor's Insurance and Office of Policy, SSA Publication No. 13-11871 (Washington, D.C.: U.S. Government Printing Office, March 1984), table 49, p. 84.

the value of Medicare when measuring how much of former pay is replaced. Moreover, the retiree's job-based health insurance often also covers a spouse; Medicare does not replace that coverage for a spouse under sixty-five. For retirees who did not have health insurance, Medicare constitutes a net addition; in such circumstances, few if any would assert that it adds too much.

Even using the abysmally low measure provided by the poverty line, figure 9.1 shows that, in 1982, 27 percent of all the beneficiaries in the fifty-five-through-sixty-one age group fell below it, while 39 percent fell below the near-poverty line.* Forty-eight percent of the unmarried beneficiaries fell below the

---

* The poverty line was set by taking the Department of Agriculture's minimum emergency food budget, itself an austere measure not designed for long use, and multiplying by three based on the notion that at low levels of income about one-third of one's budget goes for food. In fact, a smaller portion, more on the order of 28 percent, gets so used; hence, using three as a multiplier understates the total money needed to remain above the poverty line. The near-poverty line is 125 percent (1.25 times) the poverty amount. None of us would choose to live at those levels or, if we worked long enough to qualify for Social Security, feel that we deserved to.

TABLE 9.2

Trends in Cash Transfers and Poverty Among the Elderly

Year	Number of Elderly Poor (thousands)	Poverty Rate	Cash Social Insurance (1982 dollars)
1959	5,481	35.2%	$ 39.1 billion
1966	5,114	28.5	73.5 billion
1973	3,354	16.3	129.7 billion
1982	3,751	14.6	194.6 billion

SOURCE: "Poverty Rate Increase," Hearings before the Subcommittee on Oversight and Subcommittee on Public Assistance and Unemployment Compensation of the Committee on Ways and Means of the House of Representatives, 98th Cong., 1st sess., 1983, table 5, p. 239.

poverty line and 64 percent below the near-poverty line. Even among couples, 12 percent were below the poverty line and 20 percent below the near-poverty level. Most beneficiaries aged fifty-five through sixty-one draw DI benefits; most such beneficiaries have had lives of manual labor, low earnings, and low levels of education.

For beneficiaries aged sixty-two through sixty-four, mostly early retirees (plus the disabled), poverty and near-poverty rates were deplorable: 16 percent of couples and 45 percent of the singles were below the near-poverty line. For those sixty-five and over the rates decline somewhat for married couples but increase slightly for single people. Regrettably, even among Social Security beneficiaries, large contingents hover below and near the poverty line.

Social Security as an Antipoverty Weapon. Given the fact that for about half the beneficiary population Social Security benefits constitute half or more of cash income, the absence of Social Security benefits would produce disastrous rates of poverty and near poverty. Remember that for those surveyed in 1982 the general level of income for beneficiaries was extremely modest, $8,890 (median) for the sixty-five and over beneficiaries, declining to $4,780 for those eighty and older.

An analysis by the Office of Management and Budget presented by David Stockman in 1984 shows that Social Security cash benefits play an enormous role in ameliorating poverty for the elderly (see table 9.2).

The Stockman analysis indicates that the poverty rate among the elderly plummeted from 35.2 percent in 1959 to 14.6 percent in 1982. Stockman further estimated that, without social insurance transfer payments, the poverty rate among the elderly in 1982 would have been 55.1 percent.[13]

By 1984, the elderly poverty rate had been reduced to 12.4 percent, "largely because of Social Security," the Congressional Budget Office noted.[14] Social Security is our largest and most effective antipoverty program.

Choices in Seeking Income Adequacy for the Elderly

Are Benefits Too High for the Well-to-Do?   In 1982 about 11 percent of all beneficiary units had total money income at or above $30,000.[15] Most of them were couples. The 1983 amendments subject up to half of the Social Security benefit to federal income tax for couples with total income, including asset income and half the benefits, of $32,000 or more. Only a small group of single beneficiaries (about 2 percent) enjoy total income at or above $25,000, the point beyond which up to half of their benefits become taxable. Whatever one's definition of "too high," those whose benefits are subject to tax have income well above average for beneficiaries of their age and for the average employed person.

In the future, increases in real income and inflation will subject a progressively larger group of beneficiaries at the upper end of the income scale to federal income tax, because the $32,000 and $25,000 levels for such taxation do not rise with inflation although incomes and benefits will. Ultimately all beneficiaries with income *above* the deductions—the point up to which a person pays no tax—will have up to half their benefits subject to tax.*

The taxes so obtained are credited to the Social Security trust funds. The effect on beneficiaries with high income is to make their Social Security benefits less generous and the trust funds larger. In addition, those with high income will pay higher income tax rates on their benefits. Thus, if their benefits are "too high," income taxation returns some of the benefit to the trust funds.

In fact, we suggest that the replacement rates for upper-income earners be improved. Many in that group feel that Social Security gives them a return on their contributions inferior to that enjoyed by lower-income participants and less than they could earn on their own. Although many underestimate how substantially Social Security provides earnings replacement for middle- and upper-income participants, that commonly held view leads to increased pressure for greater availability of tax-favored supplements, such as salary reduction plans and IRAs, which the well-to-do use more extensively than lower-income earners. Improving Social Security replacement rates for those with high average earnings would reduce pressure for extensive private supplements, increase congressional resistance to those supplements, and improve the support for Social Security by upper-income groups. The net cost would be less than first appears when the resultant savings to the Treasury on supplementary plans are taken into account. As noted, we advocate a tax surcharge on receipt of deferred income attributable to deferred income from plan years prior to the 1986-mandated tax rate cuts. That reaches windfall benefits, not the basic benefits supplied by Social Security. The question whether upper- and middle-income earners get unwarranted benefits relates to the question whether need should be the touchstone of eligibility.

* The 1986 Tax Reform Act raised the income threshold at which income taxes first become payable, eliminating some six million people from the income tax.

209

Should Social Security Serve Only the Needy?

Some propose that Social Security be transformed into a needs-tested program that excludes those with adequate resources of their own. With public resources scarce, they argue that Social Security benefits should be limited to those who need them as objectively demonstrated by low income and meager assets.

The major claims made for a needs-tested program are that it would provide focus, efficiency, and lower cost. Given the fact that we already have such a program—Supplemental Security Income (SSI) for the aged and disabled, and Medicaid for the medically needy—we presumably would not need OASDI at all. However, we would need to expand SSI enormously to pay larger benefits to replace the Social Security benefits that now keep millions out of poverty.

Proponents of needs-testing also argue that consumers overuse medical care because Medicare foots their bills. If people who could afford medical services had to pay their own bills, the argument goes, they would discipline the providers (see chapter 11).

Since its inception a key tenet of Social Security has been that "need," as measured by some specified low income and low level of assets, plays no part in eligibility. Lack of a needs test, perhaps above all else, accounts for the wide popularity of the program. Participants work to build and sustain the economy, contribute to the trust funds, and in return qualify for benefits.

Several major considerations justify benefit eligibility without a needs test. First—and above all—is respect for human dignity. After a lifetime of work and self-support, most of us feel demeaned to seek benefits, even those essential to survival, if we must plead and prove poverty. Many would rather go without than to pay this price, despite their need, despite their entitlement. This is no theoretical matter. The "take up" rate for needs-tested programs consistently runs far below the numbers who actually qualify. This is particularly true of the elderly.[16]

Second, and little understood, is that the absence of a needs test encourages private savings. If applicants must prove poverty in order to qualify, those of modest economic means and expectations would save little, even, some cynics say, give everything of value to their children.

Third, needs testing requires enormous administrative expenditures in proportion to benefits paid. The Social Security cash programs are an administrative bargain, incurring operating costs slightly above 1 percent of collections and benefits, paid from their own revenues. In contrast, SSI spends roughly 7.6 percent on ascertaining need and on administrative expenses.[17] A program paying needs-tested benefits to over 15 million people who would be thrown below poverty levels without Social Security would impose enormous administrative costs.

Fourth, most recipients do in fact need their benefits either to keep from skidding into poverty or to avert a sharp decline in their standard of living. The rapid improvement in the financial condition of the older population has been confused with affluence.

The bottom line, however, is that a needs-tested program paying decent benefits simply may not be feasible. A needs-tested program could not be financed as Social Security now is. Wage earners accept the present FICA tax burden in anticipation of future benefits. If only the needy qualified for benefits, the present connection with near-universal contribution would be severed. The most likely substitute source of financing would be general revenues, the source for SSI and Aid to Families with Dependent Children (AFDC). Experience demonstrates that Congress and the taxpayers tend to be close-fisted with these needs-tested welfare recipients, especially when compared with the far more benevolent attitude exhibited toward programs in which they and theirs will participate. For decades the major congressional committees concerned with the program have been philosophically committed to universal coverage as a Social Security goal. So have the major concerned organizations in the business community, such as insurance companies, the United States Chamber of Commerce, the National Association of Manufacturers, and organized labor. Limiting income-maintenance programs to the needy would undermine a major reason for that support.

Does Adequate Social Security
Lead to Shortchanging the Poor and Children?

In 1970, 14 percent of children under age fourteen lived with families below the official poverty level; by 1982 that figure had grown to 23 percent. Meanwhile, the reverse took place with those sixty-five and over as demographer Samuel H. Preston noted.[18] Although most of the improvement for the elderly is attributable to Social Security improvements enacted prior to 1977, some deduce that there is a causal relationship between the inadequacy of programs for the young and what is perceived as largesse for the elderly. Preston did not attribute the reverses suffered by children's programs directly to the expenditures made for the elderly. Rather, he wrote, "I am primarily concerned about the fate of children and, in that context, the elderly serve largely for comparison." He went on, "Nevertheless, it is unrealistic simply to wish away the possibility that there is direct competition between the young and the old for society's resources." He cited growth in Medicare as a major example of generosity to the elderly. The amounts devoted to Aid to Families with Dependent Children

(AFDC), the major federal welfare program to help children, illustrated reduced support for children.

In making this comparison, Preston did not describe what program changes led to the declining adequacy of AFDC, nor did he mention that the states, not the federal government, determine eligibility. In that period the states were gripped by "Proposition 13" fever (named for the California initiative mandating reduced taxes) at the same time the federal government reduced its general financial aid to the states.

Meanwhile, four major adverse developments increased the *number* of youngsters in poverty: greater unemployment; larger numbers of families headed by women; more illegitimate births; and the growth in the rate of divorce, which often results in inadequate or no support from fathers. Hence, the numbers and proportion of children in poverty grew substantially, but the states did not expand their programs to keep pace.*

In all likelihood, not many people followed these interacting developments. Even in the booming 1960s, before public budgets came under critical public scrutiny, AFDC lacked powerful defenders. Indeed, it caught hell from both the right (for allegedly removing incentives to work) and the left (for allegedly "buying off" the poor). Many programs to aid the poor faced skepticism, distrust, and considerable opposition while Social Security enjoyed strong public support, as demonstrated by the 1965 enactment of Medicare.

It might be argued that the tight-fistedness shown programs for children and the poor starting in 1981 was intensified by the fact that Social Security payroll taxes reduce take-home pay and so reduce willingness to pay other taxes to fund programs more adequate for the poor. That line of argument would have more cogency if Congress had not already enacted the earned income credit to reduce the impact of Social Security taxes. That vast expenditures for a 600-ship Navy accompanied and followed the huge 1981 cut in federal taxes suggests that the Administration and Congress followed their druthers rather than a plan by which Social Security payment increases were balanced in part by cuts in food stamps, public housing, and well-baby clinics. Indeed, soon after the tax and social program benefit cuts began, the Administration, in the spring of 1981, also proposed enormous cuts in Social Security. Public outcry defeated those Social Security proposals quickly and decisively. The process of cutting or neglecting programs for the poor was already under way and encountered no such resistance.

---

* The long, sad, and complex story is recounted in greater detail in "Children in Poverty," House Ways and Means Committee Print (WMCP 99-8, May 1985), prepared by the Congressional Research Service and the Congressional Budget Office. Pp. 177–178 document that federal outlays for children grew in nominal terms but shrank in value because of inflation, while the population of poor children grew about 30 percent. Meanwhile, median state AFDC benefits declined in real terms even after taking account of greater use in the AFDC program of federally-paid food stamps.

Choices in Seeking Income Adequacy for the Elderly

Skimping on AFDC, health care, and education for young people is not only inhumane, it constitutes poor investment policy. All generations have a stake in healthy, well-trained and educated children and young people. In addition to the affection we bear them, we need them to produce the goods and services of tomorrow. The Social Security program recognized this by adding auxiliary benefits for surviving children and youngsters of those drawing DI benefits.

The choice to spend for one purpose makes that amount of money unavailable for any other purpose. But concluding that funds allocated to Social Security deprive the poor and children of like amounts or some portion of them does not necessarily follow. Were Social Security diminished, there is no assurance whatever that an equal amount of funds or even a substantial share would flow to the poor or to children. But any such reduction in Social Security would, for a certainty, reduce the substantial help which Social Security provides to the 3.3 million children, and other beneficiaries who support youngsters, who would be beggared by lower benefits.

Does Social Security Tackle Too Much?

Some complain that over the years Social Security strayed from its original concept and thereby (to change the figure) bit off more than it could chew. The original law, enacted in 1935, established only a retirement program—for two major reasons. Economically, the most urgent needs were to enable superannuated workers to live and to make retirement feasible in the interests of opening jobs for the younger unemployed. Politically, the New Deal had to field an alternative to the Townsend Plan, and variants like "Ham and Eggs Every Thursday," which simply proposed to give money to the elderly with the sole proviso that they spend it.

Assuredly, Social Security covers more people and more conditions than the 1935 act did. It is also paid for by a greater number of people. At bottom, however, the additional protections address the problems caused by lost earnings.

Auxiliary Benefits.   Even before the first benefit payments were made in 1940, an Advisory Council recommended "auxiliary" benefits for spouses and surviving widows and children so as to meet family needs. Clearly, a retiree with a non-employed spouse needs more income than a single retiree. Similarly, spouse and children depend on the income of an earning adult. When a working and earning adult dies and his or her earnings are lost, protecting the family requires providing at least a partial income substitute. The council recommended and Congress enacted survivor benefits for spouses—originally only widows— and children. A "young widow," one under age sixty, qualifies if she has minor children in her charge. Widowers now enjoy the same protections.

Obviously, these auxiliary benefits went beyond the original program. Equally obviously, the auxiliary benefits addressed the same problem the original act was meant to ameliorate—family loss of earned income by hazards common to us all.

Auxiliary benefits did introduce a new concept. Adding benefits for wives, widows, and orphaned children meant that insured workers with such family members might receive larger benefits than those with equal earnings but without such family members; and the more family members eligible, the greater the benefits. A principal advocate of this change, Reinhard Hohaus, a vice president and actuary of the Metropolitan Life Insurance Company, pressed for a balance between "equity" (returns based on the amount one had contributed) and the socially desirable goal of benefit "adequacy." That balance led to the benefit formula that pays larger benefits for higher covered earnings, replaces a larger portion of low earnings, and pays (up to a family maximum) for family members who could be reasonably regarded as dependent upon the insured worker's lost earnings. That approach puts the "social" in "social insurance." Assuming it makes good social policy, is such an arrangement fair?

Most families do fit a pattern of marriage, children, survivng spouse, and dependency, at some time, by all family members on the earnings of employed parents. Even if adults never marry or never have children, all of us can. Marriage and the addition of children (adopted children qualify) can occur at any time of life. In other words, all of us have a potential stake in auxiliary benefits.

Proposals for higher or lower contributions according to marital status and numbers of children present problems. They would be difficult to administer. If only "equity" (the amount of contributions) were to determine survivor benefits, a large family of survivors might receive no more than a small family despite obviously differing needs. For those who marry late in life, benefits would be lower no matter what the number of survivors or their specific needs. Young children, necessitous for a longer period than older children, might receive smaller benefits despite equal or possibly greater needs where the dead wage earners had had equal earnings.

Auxiliary benefits seem socially warranted. As none of us can know what our family fortunes will be, all of us should contribute on the same basis to the program that meets the hazards we all may encounter. Beyond that, we all have multiple interests in protecting all families, not least our own, including parents, children, brothers, sisters, cousins, nephews, and nieces, as well as other families. Often, society pays in one way or another for people unable to pay for themselves.

Disability Benefits.   Although the disability program appears to be something different from age retirement and survivorship, disablement has the same financial impact on working people and their families. In sober truth, the financial consequences of severe disablement are worse than death, because the disabled person often needs care that costs time and money.

Other, non–Social Security programs directed to the disabled do not meet these needs. While all states now maintain workers' compensation programs, extreme disablement seldom results from traumatic job-related injury, an essential element of workers' compensation benefit eligibility. Most disabled workers suffer from degenerative conditions and chronic illness. Furthermore, the time limits on benefits common to the state programs do not extend for the duration of need for those who lose earning capacity permanently, as most DI beneficiaries do, or pay auxiliary benefits for eligible family members. Surprisingly, only about two percent of DI primary beneficiaries also receive workers' compensation. It is clear that the Social Security disability program meets income replacement needs any of us might have that are not being satisfied by other programs.

Expanded Coverage.   Between 1937 and 1950 only about 60 percent of the private work force participated in Social Security. By the 1990s, more than 95 percent of the work force will be covered.

Some believe that such expanded coverage costs Social Security more than it gains in contributions and taxes.

In fact, the reverse is true: the exclusion of earnings derived from non-covered employment deprives the trust funds of employee and employer contributions; because contributions precede benefits by many years, they provide a cushion and additional earnings to the trust funds. Most who do not contribute for substantial periods of their working lives nevertheless qualify for benefits. Years of nonparticipation reduce the individual's average Social Security creditable earnings, thereby possibly qualifying him or her for benefits which provide a higher rate of replacement than if lifetime earnings were counted; but the 1983 amendments reduce this possibility.

Medicare.   Undoubtedly, Medicare, added by Congress in 1965, was a vast improvement in protection for the elderly and disabled. Where OASDI provides cash benefits, Medicare enables participants to obtain a service, health care, an urgent need of both the elderly and the disabled.

The main rationale of Medicare follows that of OASDI—to protect working people when disabled or retired against economic disaster with the loss of earned income. Health care costs often occur unpredictably and so defy budgeting; and they so often outstrip individual and family resources (and health insurance is so expensive for the elderly and disabled) that OASDI benefits, even when supplemented, simply do not suffice. Few families of any age can meet the costs of serious illness unaided by such insurance.

OASDHI is not overextended. Rather, it has become more adequate for more people by providing social insurance for income and insurance lost by virtue of retirement or disability. In reality, the "improvements" fill out the program originally contemplated; even replacement rates are quite similar.

New Patterns for Women—Problems and Proposed Solutions

Over the past twenty to twenty-five years, women's work and work expectations have undergone a revolution. Today, more women than ever before both desire and need paid work. They have the same ambitions for opportunity, advancement, and recognition as men. Nevertheless, residual prejudice and the demands of childbirth and nurture make it unlikely or even undesirable that women's work patterns mirror male patterns.

Whatever the eventual patterns and despite the need for equality in the workplace, women face special difficulties in employment that will doubtless continue for some time. On average, they earn less money than men. When employed, they must interrupt work more frequently, usually for family reasons such as childbearing and rearing or to manage a wide range of family emergencies. The persistence of "women's jobs," characterized by lower pay and part-time or part-year employment, plus absence from the workforce for family purposes reduce chances for qualifying for a public or private supplementary pension. Should they qualify, retired women on average achieve lower benefits than men. Married women generally outlive their husbands by many years, thus having a widowhood without the economies of a two-person household. Since many private and state and local pension plans do not effectively provide survivor benefits, they also often lose whatever income the two of them had from the husband's supplementary pension. If divorced after a marriage of less than ten years, they do not participate in any of the former husband's Social Security benefits. (If the marriage lasted ten years or more they and any of the former husband's other wives of ten years or more are entitled to half of his PIA.) The spouse's benefit of 50 percent is fine, even generous, for a woman living with her husband, but totally inadequate for a divorced person heading her own household. These are the realities for countless women, particularly of older generations.

In addition, many working women complain that due to Social Security's provisions for spouse and survivor benefits, their earnings and contributions do not produce commensurately higher benefits than those received by nonworking

216

TABLE 9.3

*1982 New Beneficiary Survey of Married Women
Receiving Benefits (in Percentages)*

Worker's Benefit	
Dually entitled	25
Worker's benefit higher than spouse's benefit	27
Worker's benefit, husband not retired	13
TOTAL	65
Wife's Benefit Only	35

SOURCE: Virginia Reno et al., "Women and Social Security," *Social Security Bulletin* 48 (February 1985): 20.

women by virtue of their marriage. Put another way, one-earner couples can obtain higher benefits than two-earner couples with equal earnings.*

On average, two-retiree couples draw higher benefits than one-earner couples.[19] Nevertheless, it galls some working women that their work results in Social Security benefits that do not fully reflect their Social Security contributions, and that women who did not work nonetheless obtain benefits. They protest that the family patterns on which spouse and surviving spouse benefits were based, a mother in starched apron at home with Dick and Jane while Dad slogs away in the world of "work," have become relics of the past. In fact, the work patterns of women today vary considerably. While more and more women "do it all," there are still a significant number of women who step out of the work force for extended periods of their adult lives, some by choice, many by necessity. A smaller percentage of women work than men; many women now in their forties, fifties, and sixties did not have either the pattern of full-time work or the opportunity for it enjoyed by their younger sisters.

The 1982 New Beneficiary Survey (see table 9.3) reflects the variety of work and benefit patterns among married women. Roughly one-third (35 percent) drew benefits as spouses while two-thirds (65 percent) drew benefits as insured workers. Among the latter group, 27 percent earned higher benefits on their own accounts than as wives; but 25 percent had dual entitlement, consisting of the benefit obtained by their own paid work and a supplement provided as a spouse's benefit. Yet another 13 percent, whose husbands had not retired, received retired worker benefits.

Twenty-four percent of new beneficiaries in the 1982 Survey started benefits as widows. In that group, 56 percent claimed benefits solely as widows rather

* Discussions of the comparative disadvantage of two-earner couples often omit consideration of the fact that working women frequently earn Social Security Survivor and Disability Insurance eligibility as well as entitlement to retire before their husbands do, thereby gaining more from their work and earnings than shown by a comparison limited only to retirement benefits after a husband's retirement.

than on their own account; only 14 percent had dual entitlement. (The different patterns among retired women with husbands still alive and widows comes as no surprise because the spouse's benefit, at age sixty-five, is 50 percent of the husband's PIA benefit while the widow's is 100 percent, also at age sixty-five.)

These figures warn us that, despite changing work patterns, many married women retirees and widows draw heavily on their husband's accounts. Although we can expect that an increasing number of women will draw benefits solely or primarily on their own accounts, with smaller portions of their benefits supplied by their husbands' work records, it will be many years before women's paid work will provide benefits comparable to those now made possible by the spouse's benefit, widow's benefit, and dual entitlement.

In order to equalize benefits for couples with two earners and to mitigate the adverse effects of divorce upon Social Security benefits, several changes in Social Security have been proposed.

Earnings Sharing—A Possible Answer to Women's Problems.   "Earnings sharing,"[20] which has received the most attention, regards marriage as a partnership which extends to the financial affairs of the couple. Whatever the roles of the spouses in working for pay and working in the home, the partnership theory regards both types of work as enabling the unit to carry on and produce earnings. As the couple lives on the earnings of both, in retirement a two-earner couple requires a benefit geared to their total former earnings, not just that of the higher earner.

Under earnings sharing, the earnings of both spouses during each year of marriage would be added together and half of the total then credited to the account of each. Such an arrangement would produce equal treatment for all couples with equal total earnings regardless of whether or how much either spouse worked for pay. The arrangement would for the first time give credits (half the couple's total) to nonworking spouses. In the event of divorce, a nonworking spouse would have earned credits for the years of marriage in which the other partner worked. Similarly, a spouse working part time would obtain credit for some of the pay received by the higher-earning spouse.

Earnings sharing accomplishes four things: it equalizes the benefits of all couples with equal earnings; it credits current earnings to both partners so that in the event of divorce the spouse with the lower cash earnings or none will get equal treatment with the spouse for the period of the marriage; it takes account of all the couple's earnings in providing a retirement benefit; and, very importantly, earnings sharing facilitates qualifying as "disability insured" for women who work in the home or sporadically outside of it. The disability feature accounts for the greatest portion of earnings-sharing costs.

218

In one respect, earnings sharing saves money for the trust funds by no longer paying a spouse's benefit based on a life-time record for a marriage that lasts less time. It also avoids paying a full spouse's benefits to each former mate of a multiply-divorced insured. Under current law, the higher-earning spouse, generally the husband, suffers no financial ill effects from divorce, no matter how often divorced and no matter how many former spouses qualify for spouse's benefits on that record. Indeed, the family maximum does not apply to multiple spouses' benefits for divorced people. Spouses with fewer than ten years of marriage, however, get nothing from their spouse's records for those years under Social Security.

Earnings sharing results in higher benefits for the lower-earning spouse and lower benefits for the higher-earning spouse when each comes to draw on his or her own record. In the event of divorce, such an outcome seems appropriate—divorcing couples divvy up their common property, either by agreement or court-imposed apportionment. Community property states treat property acquired during marriage as owned equally by husband and wife. In the typical divorce situation, earnings sharing usually will result in lower Social Security benefits for the former husband. All that sounds eminently fair, but, some fear, men might resist such a change.

To make earnings sharing more acceptable some propose that the higher-earning spouse continue to draw benefits equal to those under current law (a hold-harmless guarantee) at least for a time. Such a guarantee, however, would be costly and defeat the goal of achieving equal benefits for couples with equal earnings. Moreover, a guarantee would reduce the adverse financial results of divorce for the higher-earning spouse. There seems no principled justification to provide such a cushion. However, something more than half of the earnings sharing credit, but less than the full undiminished benefit, may be the price of gaining acceptance of earnings sharing.

In the event of disablement of the higher-earning spouse, auxiliary disability benefits would be lower, an unintended and undesirable result. Disability insurance benefits are designed to provide a replacement for the lost earnings of the disabled person. Applying the sharing concept when a spouse or parent becomes disabled defeats the purpose of replacing those lost earnings and could produce a benefit that is arguably too low. In the reverse situation, the disablement of the lower-paid person, not applying earnings sharing would produce "too high" a replacement. However, that lower-earning person probably has provided the larger share of homemaking and child-tending services and so a cash substitute often is needed to purchase some of the services formerly provided, without pay, by that spouse.

Earnings sharing presents some major problems and innumerable minor ones. Therefore, in addition to straight earnings sharing, sometimes called "generic (or pure) earnings sharing," there have been proposals for "earnings sharing plus," the name given to modifications of "pure" or "generic" earnings sharing.

Pure earnings sharing would eliminate widow(er) benefits. That would be devastating for many survivors. Now widow(er)s receive a benefit equal to 100 percent of the dead spouse's benefit if it is higher than the benefit payable solely on the survivor's own account. Under pure earnings sharing, the surviving spouse would receive only half a benefit based on the couple's combined credited earnings. Since a couple achieves an economy of scale by living together, the survivor requires more than half a benefit to maintain current living standards. Earnings sharing plus could meet *that* problem by crediting the surviving spouse with the earnings record of the dead partner in addition to his or her own (up to the maximum creditable for one person). Divorced surviving spouses who get no spouse or survivor benefits under current law would be helped if they had no or low earnings during many years of marriage due to childbearing, child care, and other family obligations now borne mostly by women.

Earnings sharing presents additional questions of less magnitude. For example, when only the lower-earning partner retires, should he or she draw on the shared account? The solution to this and other dilemmas probably should be that if any of the purposes of sharing would be served, then earnings should be shared; if not, no. No such purpose is served by sharing *while* the lower-pay partner alone is retired but the other works for pay; but when both have retired, sharing does serve the principle's purpose.

Perhaps the simplest solution is to use earnings sharing for couples' retirement benefits and spouse's and divorced spouse and survivor benefits (including "inheriting" the dead spouse's earnings credits, for years of marriage up to some maximum) and to leave all other arrangements as they are now. Historically, that makes sense because benefits other than the spouse's benefit, especially children's benefits, were all adopted and improved to meet recognized familial economic problems that have not substantially changed.

The Net Effect of Earnings Sharing.   A major purpose of earnings sharing is to withdraw the "unearned" spouse and widow survivor's benefit and substitute benefits based upon the combined paid work and household contributions of both the marriage partners. It gives credits to women who, while married, do not work for pay or work only part time or part year. The change enhances their chances to earn disability insurance protection and survivor benefits for their immediate family members, as well as for themselves in the event of divorce.

According to the Congressional Budget Office's (CBO) simulation study of earnings sharing,[21] *average* benefits would stay about the same as under present law for both couples and widows. Nonetheless, there are gainers and losers. The key element differentiating them is the length of time the women work. The longer the period of earnings, the greater the gain; the shorter the period of paid work, the greater the loss as compared with current arrangements.

Wives, widows, and divorcées who survive a present or former spouse and who have fewer than thirty years of paid work are among the significant "losers" under pure earnings sharing. Nonworking wives of rich husbands are meant to be losers. But many spouses who do little paid work, who bear and rear several children, who care for other family members, or who have the fewest and poorest work opportunities, deserve income protection. As no one has come up with a litmus test to figure out who falls into which category, a phased change that seems sufficient to accord with the changing realities of most women's family and financial roles seems justifiable. But achieving full equality will take time; that argues for a substantial paid guarantee.

Divorced women would benefit from earnings sharing because current law affords them little (at most 50 percent of the former husband's PIA) or nothing (for those with fewer than ten years in a marriage). The few losers among them would be those who would get 50 percent of a former spouse's benefit under current law and had little or low-paid work themselves.

Divorced men would sustain the largest (average) percentage losses from pure earnings sharing. According to the CBO study, between now and 2030 their average benefits would drop 7.9 percent, resulting in an average annual benefit reduction of $1,590 (using II-B assumptions). On the other hand, many widowers (a comparatively small group) would receive larger benefits under earnings sharing.

The Cost of Earnings Sharing. These effects argue for a transition period in which those who fare better under current law than under earnings sharing would have a guarantee against worsened benefits, at least in part and at least for some years. The transition, however, could offer a diminishing guarantee in recognition of the expectation that the factors warranting a guarantee will exercise less and less influence upon benefits as time passes. The larger and longer the guarantee, the more expensive the changes will be.

A major objection to earnings sharing has been that it increases program costs. Since 1977, any such increase has been unthinkable. However, as apprehension over the cash programs abates, more serious attention may be paid to achieve greater equity for women earners, to alleviate the harsh financial consequences of divorce encountered by women, and—quite apart from earnings sharing—to improve the financial lot of widows, especially older widows.

The costs of earnings sharing vary according to the speed of its introduction, whether it is modified to guard against benefit reductions in the case of disability and survivorship, whether and what guarantees are given during transition periods to divorced men and women who did not work or who worked for short periods and/or for low wages.

Generic earnings sharing would reduce program outlays. But that option produces unintended hardships. At the other extreme, a "no-loser" guarantee would boost costs by 1 percent of payroll under CBO estimates. Depending upon the mix of modifications and transitional provisions, some form of earnings sharing could be achieved, based on estimates in those studies, for between 0.39 percent and 0.73 percent of payroll.

So far, the requisite willingness to pay for modified earnings sharing has been absent. But, then too, our attention has been elsewhere and until recently proposals were not as well defined as they have become. Before long, earnings sharing will be an active issue.

Problems of Transition. When to make the earnings sharing effective constitutes a major problem, at least for some aspects of the change. Experts agree that there is no possibility of reconstructing records so as to implement earnings sharing for periods already passed. Apportioning credits for those who marry and divorce after earnings sharing goes into effect would be simple because all relevant events occur after the new system kicks in. But for those who are already married prior to implementing the change, the lower-earning spouse could get earnings credits for only those years of marriage after the change. If he or she would qualify for a spousal or widow(er) benefit under current law and retires or survives soon after implementation of earnings sharing, it would seem appropriate to use current rather than the new arrangements. The question arises, for how long should such a transaction extend? Similarly, if it is deemed desirable or necessary to cushion the benefit results for the higher-earning spouse, how long should such a guarantee last and for what portion of current-law benefits?

Assuming earnings sharing went into effect in 1990, it would be 2030 before participants had worked under the new arrangements for all creditable years up to the first year of retirement eligibility (from age twenty-one to sixty-two). Some might argue that only in 2030 would it be fair to shift entirely to earnings sharing. How then should those who retire and survive during the next forty years be treated? The tendency of earnings sharing to reduce benefits for couples and widows when one spouse works fewer years and to increase the retirement and survivor benefits of couples and widows when one spouse works longer and with higher earnings must be recognized. Furthermore, we must take account of the fact that women retiring and surviving during the next two or three decades will be those who probably will have had less opportunity for paid work or equal pay than their younger sisters. But by 2030, a very high proportion of women will claim under their own earnings record in any event.

A First Step—The Ball Proposal.   Former Commissioner of Social Security Robert Ball suggests two related steps to meet two pressing problems: the disparity in benefits between one- and two-earner couples and the frequently meager benefits of those without partners, especially older widows. Increasing PIA by 7 percent and reducing the spouse's benefit from 50 percent to 40 percent of PIA would narrow the one-earner-couple/two-earner-couple differential. Simultaneously increasing PIA improves the benefits payable to singles, including widows, or to members of couples claiming on their own accounts. He notes that the proposal is not inexpensive; it would require a 0.3 percent point increase in the contribution rates for both employee and employer.

In tandem with this, he proposes earnings sharing in the event of divorce, the most urgent purpose of that device. Alternatively he puts forward the notion of a benefit for divorced persons that varies with the length of their marriage, which might do enough justice for periods of no or reduced earnings while avoiding the stacking up of benefits for the divorced spouses of those with multiple marriages.

Alternatives to Earnings Sharing.   Other proposals consist of simpler devices to accomplish some but not all of the purposes of earnings sharing.

Conferring earnings credits for periods when children are young—say up to seven years, possibly older—would boost benefits for women who later divorce and would help in establishing eligibility for their own disability benefits and survivor benefits for the family. If such credits were confined to those who do not work at all or have earnings under a low ceiling, the arrangement would discriminate against those who juggle job and family, those who may not have it all but do it all. That objection might be met by giving credit for *both* child (or invalid) care and earnings—at additional program cost. If specifically limited to women, the provision would surely not pass constitutional muster. That objection could be overcome by providing such credits only to the lower-earning marriage partner or to a single or widowed parent.

Another proposal to expand the number of drop-out years from five to ten when computing the PIA would help women eliminate periods of no or low-earning from their earnings records. This would enhance benefits for divorced women whose earnings were reduced by fulfilling family obligations, but it would not improve their chances for survivor or disability benefit eligibility. It also might boost benefits for spouses of wealthy earners, especially for periods before that earner retires and the wife claims benefits on her own record.

Meeting Needs of the Older Elderly—Mostly Widows

A widow(er) loses both a portion of the couple's benefit and the partner's services. Meanwhile, the benefit, although sustained by cost-of-living adjustments, tends to fall behind the earnings of those employed—given the generally steady advance of earnings. This accounts for the observed higher incidence of poverty among older people. The low income of the older elderly, especially widows, is the most pressing problem warranting program improvement. Few would disagree. The older elderly, in addition to their need for cash income and medical care, often have an increased need for services.

But not all older elderly have the same needs, nor do the needs increase strictly according to age. The questions arise whether additional help—either cash or services—should be available, should be needs tested, and whether services targeted to identifiable problems should be provided rather than cash supplements. Surely it would be especially poignant if people who make it without needs-testing to age seventy-five or eighty, or whatever watershed age might be chosen, were subjected to it at advanced ages.

Providing services has the advantage of being geared to common needs such as assistance with homemaking, home repair, shopping, transportation, and the like. Organizing services requires a bureaucracy. To help offset objections on that ground, services directed to the elderly might be arranged so as to encourage employment of the elderly, thereby providing manageable part-time work and additional income. Utilizing people with life experiences similar to those of the older elderly could provide sympathetic help and comfortable companions. In sum, using services as a supplement answers several different needs.

Cash supplementation, however, enables the recipients to allocate the additional resource in accordance with their own needs and priorities. Moreover, benefit recipients could still, if they desired, utilize the services of older people if public or private agencies organize and fund such sources of service. Therefore, higher cash benefits could serve multiple purposes—with the added tang of possible competition among providers and control over the allocation of resources by the recipient.

Cost is the problem. As the population gets older, as more people see the problems of the elderly close up, the desirability of meeting the more urgent needs of the older elderly should take on greater urgency for all age groups. If and when that happens, the additional funding may be found.

Extending Coverage to State and Local Government Employees

The only significant group remaining outside of the OASDHI program consists of roughly one-third of state and local government employees. Today, Alaska, California, Maine, Massachusetts, Nevada, Ohio, and Texas keep large numbers of their employees out of the Social Security program. Some other states and some localities keep out particular groups, often teachers.

Mandatory coverage would better serve both the excluded employees and the financial health of the OASDHI trust funds. Beyond that, universal coverage treats people in equal situations equally—the very essence of fairness.

A large percentage of state and local government employees work in other Social Security–covered employment during some of their working lives. But working outside OASDHI can impair eligibility for Social Security benefits. State and local plans are notably weak in providing disability and survivor benefits. Working under OASDHI at some times and under nonparticipating public systems at others leave some individuals without disability or survivor protection under either.

Coverage under a state and local plan, even for considerable periods, does not always ensure qualifying for its benefits. Just as with private employment, enormous numbers of state and local government employees leave those jobs or those jobs leave them. For example, during the 1960s some 10,000 people left the Ohio State Teachers Retirement System annually without benefit eligibility. Some state and local programs do not offer any vesting or exact longer service for vesting than ERISA requires. But even if a person exits such a program with vested rights, most people cash out their own contributions, often receiving little or no interest on them, and losing the benefits attributable to their public employer's contributions.

By remaining outside of Social Security for significant periods, people lower the amount of benefits they eventually will draw from Social Security, because these benefits depend on averaging lifetime Social Security–creditable wages. Many who work outside Social Security end up losing on all fronts—both with the state or local government plan and with Social Security. The 1983 amendments eliminated some of the "windfall" cash benefits available to retirees with much non-covered work and sporadic Social Security–covered work.

Medicare gets an especially rough deal. When one member of a couple works outside of Social Security, he or she qualifies for Medicare upon reaching age sixty-five based on the other spouse's Social Security eligibility despite few or no contributions of his or her own. In contrast, a two-earner couple both working under Social Security make contributions to the Hospital Insurance trust fund based on their full pay. The unfairness of this can be deduced from the fact that the majority of retirees under the Ohio State Teachers Retirement System qualify for Medicare although no part of their Ohio employment obliged them to pay into the Medicare trust fund. They obtain all of Medicare's benefits but contributed less than most other Medicare beneficiaries with equivalent earnings. Federal legislation in 1986 makes Medicare coverage mandatory for new state and local hires.

Before the 1983 amendment, some couples found Social Security non-participation to their apparent advantage. One spouse could qualify for Social Security, complete with the spouse's and/or widow's benefit and Medicare eligibility for both. The other spouse could qualify for the state or local plan's benefits. Of course, the Social Security spouse's benefit was not designed for such a couple but was designed for a couple in which one partner had no significant earnings. The 1983 Social Security amendments reduced the apparent advantages of such an arrangement. Those retiring after the amendments and drawing a benefit from a public program who do not have thirty years of Social Security coverage receive a reduced Social Security benefit. Furthermore, a full spouse's benefit is not payable to a spouse who draws a pension from a public program. Though the advantages of playing this double game have been reduced, the chances of an unfavorable outcome to Social Security nonparticipants have not. Indeed, given the shrinkage in state and local government employment because of budget cuts and the diminished job opportunities for public school teachers, who compose the largest group of such employees, the odds against obtaining that state or local pension have increased. Add to this the questionable solvency of some state and local plans and the hazards to employees of non-participation appear daunting.

In sum, the Social Security trust funds get shortchanged by those who work outside its coverage for significant periods yet qualify for its benefits. Those who remain outside run the risk of losing valuable Social Security coverage for themselves in the event of disablement and for their survivors in the event of premature death. They almost surely reduce their eventual Social Security benefits as well.

Requiring participation by all state and local government employees would improve the long-run financing of the OASDHI trust funds, especially for Hospital Insurance. In 1982, the Social Security actuary estimated that the long-term savings to the OASDI trust funds achieved by covering all *new* state and local government plan participants would amount to one-quarter of 1 percent of payroll over the ensuing seventy-five-year period. For Medicare it would save almost the same for the following twenty-five years (the period for which HI estimates then were made). Considering that the Social Security deficit hue and cry in the early 1980s was about a projected deficit of 1.58 percent of payroll, these are significant amounts.

Eliminating some of the windfall reduces the loss of OASDI revenue, but revenues lost during non-covered periods remain significant. Requiring that only new hires be covered by OASDI would provide a substantial period of transition for state and local governments to adapt their plans. The shift to Medicare coverage does not require such a transition because state and local program medical care components, where they exist at all, do not help the financing of those programs—probably the opposite is true. Whether all are required to participate in OASDHI or only new hires, such plans would have to make major modifications to meet their changed circumstances. Mandatory Social Security coverage reduces the extent of benefit payouts of future hires on the state or local plan, but it also reduces the state or local plan income stream. Funding for some plans has been questionable or inadequate. Adapting these plans to a new regime, however, may force state and local authorities to confront future expectations and funding realistically. Attention focused on the financing of state and local plans also may help participants wake up to their weaknesses in the areas of survivor benefits and indexing against inflation.

In 1985, the Supreme Court implicitly answered the question of whether federal law could constitutionally require state and local governments to participate in Social Security.[22]

Given the margin of decision and changes in the Court membership, the staying power of that decision is open to question. But even if it does not survive, Congress can constitutionally require all *employees* to participate without coercing the states; such a device can readily finesse constitutional objections and put state and local employees on a par with all other employed and self-employed persons who must participate in Social Security. In effect, those not covered would be treated as the law treats the self-employed.* As a practical matter, employee pressure would surely make public employers remit the employer's share and elect coverage. It would be desirable to couple such an enactment as a backstop to direct mandatory coverage, thereby avoiding the expense and uncertainty that litigation challenging the constitutionality of mandatory coverage would otherwise produce.

Universal coverage makes a stronger system, a better funded system, and a fairer system. Everyone, especially employees now under programs of questionable dependability, would be better off if all state and local government employees came under the umbrella of Social Security.

---

* The law already does something like this in regard to ministers; they are covered as if self-employed. Some few may opt out on the ground of religious principles.

The Impact of Social Security on Savings

Some charge that Social Security decreases the incentive for private savings because people count on Social Security for their old age. This, in turn, reduces capital investment, reduces the productive capacity of the economy, and thereby makes us all the poorer. The allegation remains unproved and is challengeable at all of its critical points. Similarly, the claim is made that private pension plans constitute our largest pool of savings for investment and so should remain undiminished for that reason. Recent data and our analysis cast doubt on the accuracy of that claim.

Nobel Laureate Franco Modigliani, the great theoretician of savings, posits two conflicting effects of Social Security. On the one hand, awareness of future benefits lessens concern over retirement income and so reduces the inducement to save. However, since Social Security makes retirement possible and probable at an earlier age, workers save for the longer retirement haul, a point that he has credited to Alicia Munnell. Others contend that Social Security has made the working population more aware of retirement and the need for resources in retirement and so stimulates savings. The fact that the spread and improvement of Social Security occurred during a period of unprecedented economic growth and a degree of affluence hitherto unknown complicates analysis of these propositions.

Since World War II, consumer credit has exploded. Undoubtedly the new ease of purchasing on credit decreases personal savings. Today, lending institutions huckster credit cards to a population ravenous to consume; banks and businesses eagerly provide easy credit, car loans, and mortgage loans in sharp contrast to the chilly inspection lenders accorded would-be borrowers as recently as the 1950s. Beyond that, steady and often dramatic price inflation has encouraged debt and discouraged savings because borrowers expect to repay with dollars of lower value. Before the 1986 Tax Reform Act, the deductibility of debt interest for income tax purposes also stimulated borrowing. Among the many powerful forces at work, the claimed adverse impact of Social Security upon savings seems difficult if not impossible to isolate.

Professor Martin Feldstein, writing in 1974, claimed to demonstrate that by 1971 Social Security had lowered personal savings by 50 percent.[23] Two other economists, Dean R. Leimer and Selig J. Lesnoy, challenged Feldstein's conclusion, demonstrating that he had used a faulty computer program and so obtained incorrect answers.[24] Feldstein countered that new and better numbers supported his original conclusion.

Others, however, have found the revised arguments unconvincing.[25] Five later studies by economists have analyzed the Feldstein claim and concluded

228

that he was wrong both times. Summarizing four of those studies, Professor Louis Esposito, writing in 1978, declared that "the empirical analysis of [the kind of data] Feldstein used has not been able to isolate or capture this effect" (that is, that Social Security reduces savings).[26] A trio of economists writing in 1985 concluded that "evidence on the impact of Social Security [on savings] is inconclusive."[27] The 1985 study, using Census Bureau data specially gathered to explore Social Security, pension, and savings activities, added that Social Security showed an impact on savings "so small in size [that] they are not significantly different from zero." In 1982, Brookings economist Henry J. Aaron, a leading student of Social Security, also found the claim unsubstantiated.[28] So the claim that Social Security reduces savings is, at the least, unproven.

Moreover, studies of other countries discovered no such adverse impact. One by Modigliano found "that the Social Security benefit effect and the retirement effect roughly offset each other, indicating that the net impact of Social Security on savings is close to zero." Yet another study of fourteen industrialized countries attributed a positive effect upon savings to Social Security.[29]

In 1985, economist Robert Lampman summarized the conclusions: "The weight of professional opinion among economists is that empirical study of this question leaves the issue unresolved."[30]

Even assuming that Social Security reduces personal savings, it does not follow that investment in a new productive capacity suffers as a result. Historically, most capital for investment has been derived from *within* enterprises that, when successful, make much new investment from retained earnings rather than from new stock or bond issues or other borrowing. The high priest of productivity, Edward Denison, concluded in 1983 that the rate of personal savings has been irrelevant to past changes in productivity. He wrote:

> In the four most recent years (1978 to 1981) the annual percentages [of capital investment] ranged only between 16.40 and 16.66%; all these years were very close to the 1948–80 average. *Stability prevailed despite* major changes in rates of inflation, interest rates, the level and structure of taxes, real per capita income, *government and private retirement programmes*, other forms of public and private insurance against contingencies, and many other aspects of the economic environment. It suggests that policymakers should be cautious in appraising their ability to influence private saving behaviour. . . . It seems clear to me that during the period of slow productivity growth *investment was limited only by investment demand and not by a saving propensity too weak to support larger investment.* I also believe that any programme to stimulate growth of capital stock over an extended period would do better to try to strengthen incentives to invest than incentives to save [emphasis added].[31]

If the solutions to our productivity problems do not lie in the savings rate, then the issue of Social Security's effect on savings becomes irrelevant. When that element of the Social Security debate disappears, so does the argument for expanding private programs based upon their claimed role in fueling the economy with more personal savings for investment.

The Questionable Claims
that Private Plans Add Significantly to Savings

The claim is made repeatedly that private pension funds constitute our most important source of savings and for that reason should not be limited. However, data show that may not be so. On the contrary, their net effect may be to reduce savings!

Alicia Munnell postulated that private pension plans *reduce* individual savings, and she estimated that for each dollar of private plan contributions individuals reduce their own savings by about 65 cents.[32] A 1985 study by Avery, Elliehausen, and Gustafson, economists for the Federal Reserve Board, comes up with a figure of 66 cents, confirming Munnell's guess.[33] More than that, the trio's study found that for each $1 contributed to thrift plans (profit-sharing plans and the like), individuals reduce their nonpension wealth by $1.20.

Furthermore, we would add, the 34 cents apparently "saved" are more than canceled by the increase in the public debt that they cause through tax deductibility. So in 1984, the last year for which comparable data exist, the estimated net savings of private plans was $22.9 billion.* For the same year, the Congressional Budget Office estimated that the combined tax forfeitures of private plans, federal civil service, and state and local government plans were about $50 billion. The tax expenditure is a subtraction from savings in any period of budget deficit and outstanding public debt. By subtracting 19 percent, roughly the portion attributable to civil service and state and local plans, the estimated tax *loss* for private plans came to roughly $40 billion. In other words, private plans may have reduced net savings by $17.1 billion, possibly more. With lower tax rates, the 34 percent "savings" roughly equals the marginal tax rate of participants with substantial earnings—so they just about cancel each other out.

The conventional wisdom that Social Security reduces savings and that private plans increase savings is probably half wrong and may be totally wrong.

---

* Based on the $67.5 billion of private plan contributions reported by the Commerce Department's Survey of Current Business as multiplied by the Federal Reserve study estimates of 34 percent as savings.

Choices in Seeking Income Adequacy for the Elderly

Social Security Receives Greater Scrutiny

The procedures for shaping Social Security policy provide far greater assurance of fairness and reliability than the processes for the design and administration of private plans. Social Security receives much more extensive and varied scrutiny than do the hundreds of thousands of private programs.

Private plan sponsors and designers seek a variety of goals, some of them self-serving. Legislation and regulation fitfully attempt to keep them within acceptable bounds. Private plan regulation has not been subject to the kind of scrutiny and debate that Social Security receives. Financial institutions, big business, and corporate insiders have greatly influenced such legislation and regulation. No natural adversary group has shown sufficient numbers or power to ride herd on private plan legislation. The vast tax expenditures cost of private plans to U.S. citizens has engendered little significant public attention or opposition, though the urgency of huge benefit deficits has recently directed some attention to that preferential treatment.

In contrast, the fact that almost everyone has a stake in Social Security assures close scrutiny and extended public debate. Of course, some decry the influence of demagoguery in shaping Social Security policy. But the fact of great public visibility, the existence of major contending groups, and the dual roles of most Americans as both contributors and beneficiaries, provide protection against demagoguery. If, as some insist, political power overwhelms principled design, at least it operates on behalf of the many.

A major strength of Social Security as a system is that, soon, almost 100 percent of the working population will contribute and benefit; for the majority it will continue to be the major and most dependable source of retirement income. Not only is it adequately financed, Congress and the American people will make sure it remains that way.

10 Going It Alone: Substitutes for Social Security

Abolish Social Security?

Some economists and young people seriously advocate scrapping, curtailing, or privatizing Social Security because they never did like it, regard it as fatally flawed, or believe that they can invest their contributions elsewhere more advantageously. However, not only are such assumptions shaky, but any such changes would pose enormous questions of fairness, prodigious practical problems, and produce alternatives that fail to satisfy society's needs for retirement income security for all.

Fairness Problems

In fiscal year 1986 over 120 million individuals and employers made Social Security contributions amounting to over $180 billion. Most have done so for years and years.

If the system comes to an end and revenues cease, the cupboard would soon be bare for those already on the rolls, and for future claimants as well. Would—could—those tens of millions of contributors be told that they contributed in vain? That they had supported millions of beneficiaries but would see nothing themselves?

232

Going It Alone: Substitutes for Social Security

In all fairness, neither beneficiaries nor those still contributing could be told that the system had ended no matter what their contributions, their expectations, or their dependence on that source.

Practical Problems

Fairness aside, such an outcome is politically unthinkable. All of the beneficiaries, all of those family members who would be confronted by some burdens to provide substitutes for benefits, and all those who had made contributions—in other words, just about the entire population—would not stand for it.

Well, then, phase it out, say the advocates of alternatives. Nevertheless, some cutoff, possibly of age or length of contribution, would eliminate at least some claims. What principled bases would serve to select those who would retain all or some of the claims to which their contributions entitle them? Even if one can construct such a principle, could it pass muster politically? Possibly, if the principle excluded very few. But if it did only that, the problem of meeting claims would be reduced very little.

If Social Security were continued for all current participants, but excluded new entrants, the system would lose contributors, would require increases in contribution rates and/or huge transfusions of general revenue to sustain benefits under existing formulas. Only after eighty or more years would Social Security reach the point at which the last of those now earning eligibility die. We would be faced with a "closed system" with trillions of dollars of obligations but diminishing resources with which to meet them.

Financing would be required on some new basis for the tens of millions who remain in Social Security, presumably with undiminished claims; *simultaneously*, a new scheme of retirement income would need to be financed. Thus, to phase out Social Security while phasing in a new system requires that the total share of the economy dedicated to funding retirement income increase enormously, unless the alchemists find a way of increasing retirement income without enlarging the amounts devoted to that purpose.

Presumably abolition of Social Security would occur only because enough of the populace deemed some other, new scheme as preferable. Any new scheme immediately poses a dilemma: if constructed along the lines of current pension plans in which length of service is a critical factor, it would take decades of credited service to achieve a benefit considered adequate. If a new scheme did not make special provision for older workers, those closer to the retirement age would earn inadequate benefits if limited to years of service after the inception of the new scheme. In consequence, pressure would build to do what Social Security and some private plans did, give a disproportionately good benefit to those retiring in the early periods of the new plan. That requires starting the plan with an unfunded liability for "past service." Alternatively, those above the age at which future credits would yield inadequate benefits have a strong claim not to have their Social Security benefits docked.

Contracting Out Problems

A major battle, *the* major battle, preceding the adoption of Social Security in 1935 was over "contracting out," which means making an exception from compulsory coverage for those who choose to obtain some statutorily-prescribed alternative coverage.

Proponents of contracting out claim that it serves two major and salutary purposes: individual freedom of choice and enlargement of the private sector. Since Congress did not choose contracting out, the arguments against it must be powerful. They are.

First of all, contracting out erodes the base of any insurance program, with often unhappy results for those who do opt out.

Second, insurers, banks, and others offering plans lure the most lucrative accounts away from the public program. Opting out would be most attractive to high earners, because Social Security replaces a lower portion of high average earnings than low average earnings. The system would lose those who make the largest contributions and take proportionally less in benefits. In addition, such people often believe that they have superior investment acumen. Many will guess wrong about where the advantage lies in making the choice of whether to opt out. High pay is not a lifetime condition. Changes in the economy, one's industry, or health may drop one slowly or precipitously down the earnings scale. But that only happens to the "other guy." Even so, other guys abound and could be us.

Moreover, considerable doubt exists whether money diverted from Social Security could obtain coverage comparable to that afforded by the public program. No existing private program comes close. Whatever *minimum* protection the statute required for those who contract out undoubtedly would offer less than Social Security provides.

Individuals could take an amount (possibly equal to his or her Social Security contributions and the employer's or some portion) and either purchase a package offered to members of the public, design one for him- or herself, or simply spend it. Any of these courses seems risky and presents opportunities for marginally scrupulous hucksters to sell shoddy coverage. By way of example, judging from television ads, a considerable market for "cancer insurance" exists. Without known exception, insurance experts regard such coverage as a bad buy. But former Hollywood stars deliver their insurance pitches with the same sincerity that brought tears to viewers' eyes at yesterday's grade-B movies. Grade-B actors

234

apparently can sell class-A junk. If employers were required to pay as much for an employee opting out as for one covered by Social Security, they would have little incentive to put together an attractive group package. Employees would likely be on their own in a sea of sellers not all telling the truth, the whole truth, and nothing but the truth.

For how long would/could one opt out? Once out, would one have to stay out, no matter how circumstances changed? That sounds harsh and inflexible for the individual. However, if one were permitted to come and go, Social Security would have to pay lower benefits to the less steady participants, many of whom would only belatedly realize their need for coverage.

Would those opting out receive the kind of favorable tax treatment accorded to private group pensions, Keoghs, and IRAs? If not, how could the Social Security–substitute investments be differentiated from the tax-favored private modes? Do we want to spend funds to monitor tens of millions of Social Security–substitute accounts each year to assure that the funds do not get diverted into the tax-favored kinds? If not, do we want to trust to luck that everyone will play the game straight?

If opting-out accounts receive the same tax treatment as pensions, Keoghs, and IRAs, all of us would pay in one way or another for the hundreds of billions of tax dollars lost in tax advantages, in addition to paying the higher rates a nonuniversal program requires.

Social Security or Going It Alone

Some complain that Social Security is no longer the great deal that it was for their parents or current retirees and that they will not receive back as much as they put in, they will not get their "money's worth." The clincher for those who would scrap Social Security is that, left to invest equal amounts on their own, they believe that their rate of return would be better. This assumes that private investment rates of return, judging from past experience, will produce a larger future return than Social Security promises to pay those now covered and entering the labor market.

It is true that those who came first did get an especially good deal. Social Security did provide benefits that exceeded the actuarial equivalent of contributions made by those who participated at the beginning of the cash system, again when Disability Insurance was added, and yet again in the early days of Medicare. That start-up pattern is inevitable in any retirement and benefit system that does not wait decades before it pays adequate benefits. That has been true of Social Security as it has been of most private defined-benefit plans. The money to pay for those disproportionate benefits almost always comes from later contributors, rather than general revenues. For their part, early participants can properly claim that they built the economy that made possible a system that produces enough to support a retirement program. More than that, those disproportionately generous benefits have already eased our burdens of support for the parents and grandparents of those who think that they will not get a good deal.

For the future, will participants get back what they contribute, including their employers' contributions and interest? Or would participants do better "going it alone"? We discuss these common questions although we do not regard them as the proper questions to ask.

Money's Worth

Usually, the money's worth discussion starts with an analysis of how much various typical participants contribute to the system and how much those prototypes will obtain as benefits. We know in advance the general contours of the results, because the program is *designed* to replace a larger percentage of former pay to low earners. By virtue of the spouse's benefit, we know that a couple composed of a minimum earner with a nonworking spouse will get the biggest return on contributions. The program was built on two principles—social adequacy (which means replacing a large portion of former earnings for the low paid and taking account of family composition), and equity (rewarding greater contributions with larger benefits). Both purposes are served, but because they pull in different directions, neither is served completely.

Money's worth is sometimes expressed as the ratio between the total contributions made by the employee and employer with interest throughout an assumed working life spanning ages twenty-one to sixty-five and the benefits measured at the time of retirement for various categories of retirees: a single man, a single woman, or married couples (separately considering one-earner and two-earner families) at maximum, average, and minimum earning levels.

But, viewing the results *after* the race is run seems inappropriate. The fortunate thirty-year-old with a working wife may feel some misgivings that the contribution/benefit ratio for that couple is less favorable than that for a one-earner couple with equal income. But the projected outcome could change tomorrow if that so-far successful fellow becomes disabled or dies, in which case his children and wife (and he, if he lives) probably will receive far more from the system than they would if he lived and worked to retirement.

To insist that the system yields only what a person's account produces as retirement benefits and to compare that only to the person's contribution ignores the multitude of Social Security protections and underestimates its value. All of us, including those who do not marry, have a stake in the auxiliary benefits and the weighting formula for our parents and grandparents. When we are children, we receive the protection of their coverage for disability and survivor benefits. Even though Dad or Mom does not become disabled or die, the protection is there—for all of us, including the singles of today who were the children of yesterday.

Single men or women may resent the comparatively lower return that either can expect as compared with the one-worker couple with equal earnings, as shown in the usual money's worth analysis. But each may decide to marry; only 8 percent of adults do not. Many singles become one-earner couples, at least for periods of their marriage. Even when past childbearing years, one may marry a person with children and thereafter find the family drawing survivor benefits. Throughout life, as our age, marital, parental, health, and employment status changes, the specific protections afforded each of us by the system probably will change. Very few, indeed, go through working life or even beneficiary status in just one category; often the change is unexpected. We all start with the same package of protection. It does not make sense to see how we fared only after all the cards are turned face up. This stake in the system for ourselves and other family members does not show up in the tables of contribution/benefit ratios.

Moreover, upper-income earners often get a better return than the benefit formula and the money's worth tables suggest. The greater incidence of couples among higher-income groups means that they more frequently obtain the spouse's benefit than do some female-headed families. The family maximum is also more generous for middle- and upper-income earners than for the lowest earners. In consequence, many families of a disabled or deceased person in the middle- and upper-income categories get a better "return" on the disabled or deceased person's contributions than the usual money's worth tables suggest. Because the tables typically limit themselves to the weighting of the primary insurance amount (PIA) benefit formula in favor of the low paid, children's benefits and the more generous yield of auxiliary benefits to the better paid are left out. Moreover, one study concludes that the greater longevity of higher-earning participants offsets the weighting in favor of the low paid, who tend to be shorter lived.[1]

Money's worth tables assume "typical" examples that do not exist in the real world. Former Social Security Administration Chief Actuary Robert Myers and his collaborator Bruce Schobel point out that the usual money's worth discussion and table overstates lifetime income by assuming atypical uninterrupted earnings, by ignoring that part of the benefit formula that allows dropping out the five years of lowest earnings, and by assuming atypically high earnings for the illustrative average and high earner.[2] Most young people do not work uninterruptedly and do not command the average wage. Generally, women earn less than men and their work is more often interrupted, so more fall below the average. In the real world, the average person has lower earnings and contributions than the usual illustrative average but their benefits do not suffer thereby (or at least not commensurately) because actual benefits are figured on average earnings after dropping out the five years of lowest earnings. In their own published table Myers and Schobel suggest that taking account of the drop-out years might improve the benefit ratio by 10 to 20 percent.

The usual money's worth tables illustrate a high earner, one who earns the maximum creditable *nonstop* from age 21 to retirement; that bird is rarer still. In 1986, when $42,000 was the maximum creditable earnings, few individuals under age thirty, or even forty for that matter, pulled down such big bucks; few if any young people will reach the comparable future maximums in their early days of working. Realistically, the usual high earner will be so for no more than half of his or her working life. Myers and Schobel estimate that if maximum earnings begin at age thirty (still a most generous assumption), their contributions/cost ratio would improve significantly; they suggest a possible range of 5 to 10 percent. (We would adjust the Myers-Schobel table by 15 percent because we regard age forty as a more typical point for the beginning of maximum earnings). Hence the first two decades of contributions will be below the maximum, and higher earnings occur later in working life. Tables 10.1 and 10.2 present the Myers-Schobel table with some of the adjustments they justify in their text.

Myers and Schobel properly count *all* contributions (by both employee and employer) because the employer's contribution, most economists agree, is a form of compensation that would be paid the employee in some other form. Their ratios reflect the real interest (nominal interest deflated for inflation) rate.

The adjusted* Myers and Schobel data (tables 10.1 and 10.2) show that practically all participants will get back *directly* their own contributions (including their employer's) *plus* interest. The few exceptions: the single men high earners (starting after the year 2000), and the scarce single women high earners (starting in 2025). All average earners and all below-average earners† will get back all of their contributions, their employer's, and all earnings on both accumulations. Even in narrow money's worth terms, Social Security will pay off advantageously to most participants. The tables do not reflect the greater longevity of upper-income earners (which produces greater total benefits) and the generous family

---

* Obviously, the authors chose not to put the adjustments in their tables. We agree, however, with two other expert commentators who observed, "we would prefer to include a rough adjustment for such an item [the non-steady worker as more typical], and then let the text discuss why the adjustment is rough. . . ." Regrettably no rough estimate exists for the value of inflation proofing. One might say it is priceless, invaluable, unavailable elsewhere at any price.

† Below-average earners are not shown. Their returns would be even greater than those obtained by the average-wage earners.

TABLE 10.1

Present Value of Future Benefits for Average-Wage Earners
Attaining Age Sixty-five in Various Years, as a Percentage of the
Combined Employer-Employee OASI Taxes Accumulated with Interest*

Year of Attaining Age 65	Single Man† (in percentages)	Single Woman† (in percentages)	Married Couple‡ (in percentages)
1985	191	240	345
1990	164	205	293
1995	144	180	256
2000	131	164	232
2005	119	148	210
2010	112	138	195
2015	109	134	190
2020	107	132	186
2025	101	124	175

* Includes COLA but omits the economic value of inflation proofing. (See text for explanation.)
† The average woman will obtain a greater return than the average man due to projected greater longevity.
‡ Assumes only one earner.
Assumptions: Interest rates and wages of II-B assumptions; mortality rates of Actuarial Study No. 87, as they change during retirement; we adjusted the authors' results to include the adjustments they justify in their text: adding 15 percent for lowered early contributions and increasing earnings toward end of working life, thereby reducing interest on the accumulation.
SOURCE: Derived from Robert J. Myers and Bruce D. Schobel, "A Money's Worth Analysis of Social Security Retirement Benefits," Society of Actuaries, *Transactions* 35 (1983): 558, table 2A.

maximums enjoyed by middle-income earners. It also does not show the great value of the cost-of-living guarantee, which has value over and above the COLA payments themselves.

While positive rates of return such as 101 percent (the poorest showing for the average and below-average earners) may seem modest, remember that COLA assures such a return in real dollars and without the variations, uncertainty, and major possibility of loss (a negative return) inherent in other investments.

With the expected increase in two-earner couples, a greater proportion of the population will draw benefits on their own accounts and a progressively smaller group will fall into the one-earner couple category. Hence, the most significant ratios in the next century are those for single earners, both men and women. Admittedly, in the money's-worth exercise, single maximum-income earners would not get a full *direct* return on their contributions, although adding the survivors' benefit and the considerable value of the COLA guarantee would improve their picture substantially. Even so, to quell the dissatisfaction of the higher paid, the replacement rate for the high paid might be improved. That would require a lower rate of return for all other groups. As the group of habitually

TABLE 10.2

Present Value* of Retirement Benefits for Maximum-Wage Earners Attaining Age Sixty-five in Various Years, as a Percentage of the Combined Employer-Employee OASI Taxes Accumulated With Interest

Year of Attaining Age 65	Single Man† (in percentages)	Single Woman† (in percentages)	Married Couple‡ (in percentages)
1985	161	203	293
1990	132	167	239
1995	112	140	201
2000	101	126	179
2005	90	112	159
2010	82	102	144
2015	78	96	136
2020	74	91	129
2025	68	84	118

* Includes COLA but omits the economic value of inflation proofing.
† The average woman will obtain a greater return than the average man due to greater projected longevity. The table does not reflect the better-than-average longevity of upper-income earners; that greater longevity would improve the return of all categories in this table.
‡ Assumes only one earner.
Assumptions: Interest rates and wages of II-B assumptions; mortality rates of Actuarial Study No. 87, as they change during retirement; we adjusted the authors' results to include the adjustment they justify in their text: adding 10 percent to reflect lower than maximum earnings below age thirty.
SOURCE: Derived from Robert J. Myers and Bruce D. Schobel, "A Money's Worth Analysis of Social Security Retirement Benefits," Society of Actuaries, *Transactions* 35 (1983): 558, table 3A.

high earners is relatively small, the actual burden to increase these revenues would not be large.

While few private plans use direct employee contributions, most labor economists regard the employer contribution as employee compensation that otherwise would be paid to employees. Given the fact that only some of the participants achieve benefits, private plan contributions enrich benefit *recipients* but detract from the compensation of those who do not obtain benefits. So it can be said that many private group plan participants get a negative return from their group plans while some get much more than what their "own" contributions would buy. The transfer in these cases goes from the least fortunate (job losers and leavers) to the most fortunate employees, those who hold jobs longest. Social Security has almost all winners and far fewer losers.

A major limitation of the money's-worth analysis* is that it treats OASDI as if it were static whereas it has been dynamic, repeatedly improving. Past improvements were not fully paid for by recipients. So long as the system endures,

---

* Myers and Schobel did not endorse a money's-worth approach. Rather, their presentation said in essence, *if* you are going to do it, here's the way to go about it.

such improvements can be made—and probably will even though, over the last decade, that has been regarded as unthinkable. But, with a reasonably vigorous economy, Social Security improvements will be entertained and, in all likelihood, enacted, thereby improving performance measured by the money's-worth approach.

The Cost and Unavailability of Comparable Coverage

Comparisons purporting to show that an individual fares better by privately investing amounts equivalent to Social Security contributions often assume that the total contribution would be applied to the individual's retirement savings alone. Such comparisons omit the protection offered by Social Security to both young and old workers: income in the event of disablement for one's self, spouse, and dependent children; survivor benefits for spouse and children in the event of death; retirement benefits for a spouse whose own employment record would yield lower benefits; and survivor benefits for a retiree's spouse and minor or severely handicapped children.

Although accident rates are highest for the young, many young people see scant need of disability protection. Two-earner, childless couples see little utility in spouse benefits, but they may underestimate their future interest in having children and the adverse impact of children on current earnings. Certainly, many ignore the value to *themselves* of the weighting of protection for lower-pay people, because they cannot imagine that their jobs, their firm, or their industry may contract or disappear before they are ready to retire.

But the pivotal question is: Would individuals be able to purchase all the protection Social Security provides from the private sector at the same or lower cost? If so, will they? Since many participants do not even know what Social Security provides (income protection for young survivors, disability, and medical care in the event of long-term disability), they will not feel the need to obtain full *substitute* coverage. Experience teaches that many insurers offer unneeded and/or inadequate coverage; witness the mass huckstering of "cancer insurance" and accident insurance that pays benefits only if limbs are severed and not if they become "merely" unusable. Insurers jump into the market with coverage at reasonable prices for low-risk conditions or people. "High-risk" groups and common conditions push premiums beyond affordability.

Many will decide that they do not need insurance for survivors or will believe that their employer already provides it. Life insurance *is* the most pervasive fringe benefit but typically provides payments equal only to one to two years of pay, not enough to sustain family survivors for long and far less than what Social Security offers. Disability insurance and medical coverage for disability or retirement present similar problems. The more remote the hazard in time or imagination, the less likely people will be to purchase substitute coverage. Mean-

241

while, escalating insurance rates have pushed some doctors who say they cannot afford insurance protection to abandon their specialties. This should serve as a warning about the hazards of replacing Social Security with private offerings.

Inflation-Proofed Benefits

One thing is certain. Individuals and even groups will not be able to purchase coverage providing benefits that increase with inflation—the private insurance industry simply has not been able to come up with such a product. No one foresees or foretells the day when such a product will come on the market. Government-issued retirement bonds "indexed against inflation" certainly do not constitute privatization. The unremitting nature of inflation for the past half century makes it reasonable to assume its continuation. Even at low levels, it saps the value of any fixed benefits.

Social Security offers a feature of incalculable value—the indexing of benefits against inflation. While early participants did get a splendid return on their contributions, they did not have the assurance enjoyed by all participants since 1975 that the real value of their benefits will be preserved by automatic COLA. This is no small matter.

The money's worth ratios take no account of the enormous value of Social Security's inflation proofing. That may well be the most significant omission of those analyses.

Intergenerational Fairness

Leaving aside the critical issue of retirement age (see chapter 8), those retiring in the future will obtain benefits that replace the same portion of former comparable pay as now. Moreover, most economists expect real incomes to rise. Annual improvements of only 1 percent would add almost 50 percent to average real income by 2025. In addition, contributions will vary (both up and down) in a quite narrow band as a percentage of gross national product (GNP). That means that proportionally Social Security costs will remain close to constant as a percentage of economic output. Increased real earnings mean that even a higher rate of contribution, should that become necessary, need not impair living standards.

The benefit formula assures that those with comparable earnings and contributions histories and in comparable family status will obtain the same rates of earnings replacement as now enjoyed. As long as the benefit formula stays put (and no change in law impends or even seems likely), each succeeding wave of retirees and other beneficiaries obtain the same percentage of income replacement the system yields now to those with comparable earnings.

Going It Alone: Substitutes for Social Security

The change in normal retirement age from sixty-five to sixty-six during the first decade of the next century and from sixty-six to sixty-seven during the third decade may affect this equation. Proponents of these changes claim that because of future improvements in longevity, these changes produce periods of work and retirement proportional to the current division between them. If that is so, then the contribution/benefit ratio would remain essentially unchanged from what it currently is.

In fact, however, future benefits will improve vis-à-vis current benefits for those who delay their retirement past normal retirement age and earn the higher delayed retirement credit (DRC) (see chapter 8).

Some argue for reducing the payroll tax "burden" on the currently employed. That would result in lower benefits for those taxpayers when they become beneficiaries. That does not sound like any improvement in their lot. On the contribution side, the "best guess" actuarial projections show that the portion of GNP contributed to the cash benefit programs over the next seventy-five years will fluctuate only slightly. For 1987, the cash programs are estimated to cost 4.73 percent of GNP. In 2060, they are estimated to cost 6.12 percent of GNP. The seventy-five-year average is expected to be 5.54 percent.[3] In sum, the OASDI system will impose quite similar burdens and benefits on succeeding generations.

The Claim of Higher Earnings for Private Investment

One key element in the proposition that individuals should be set free of Social Security to "go it alone" is the claim that all or a portion of an individual's FICA/SECA contributions, if privately invested, would provide bigger benefits than Social Security does or can.

Two phenomena fueled the go-it-alone approach that came into vogue in the late 1970s and persists through the 1980s. On the one hand, the media reports that Social Security faced bankruptcy were widely believed and frequently fanned by advertisements for investment opportunities and soaring interest rates of 18 to 20 percent. The results appeared dazzling. Advertisements for IRAs told investors that they could become millionaires—assuming, of course, nominal interest rates of 12 percent throughout a period of twenty years. (By 1987, these rates had dropped down to the 6 percent neighborhood.)

Hidden beneath the hoopla was unprecedented inflation accompanying the bewitching interest rates. True interest rates, the difference between yield and inflation, were more in the range of 1 percent and 2 percent. As Milton Gwirtzman, chair of President Carter's National Commission on Social Security, observed, if the IRA investor did become a millionaire, he would be paying $40 for a hamburger.

Far more dangerous is the assumption that private investment has outperformed Social Security so consistently in the past that individuals can surely do better on their own than they do under Social Security. In fact, Social Security provides a steady, reliable stream of income generated by the economy as a whole. In contrast to the steady 2 percent return so produced, advocates of opting out point to the 6 percent return claimed to be generated by the average of all stocks over a fifty-year period starting in the 1920s.* Of this Alicia Munnell writes:

> The 6 percent real return advanced by [a proponent of going it alone] is the average return on common stocks over the last 50 years. This return has been extraordinarily unstable, however, with a standard deviation of 21 percent. This means that in any given year there is a one-third chance that the return could be as high as 27 percent or as low as −15 percent.[4]

Moreover, the proposals for substituting some mechanisms, such as IRAs, call for tax deductibility and even, in one version, tax credits. Deductibility would mean serious tax revenue losses. Providing tax credits equal to the amounts "invested," as some propose, would mean that the Treasury (read all taxpayers) would pay for the supposed investments; they would cost the investors nothing, but would demolish tax receipts. It is hard to believe that such proposals are serious.

The experience of major pension trust investors indicates that few obtain the smashing investment yields claimed by the advocates of supplanting some or all of Social Security with private investment. Study after study reveals that bank trustees and state and local government trust funds produce earnings below the Dow-Jones or Standard and Poor averages. A study by CDA Investment Technologies of 1,156 money managers handling $333 billion shows that they, in reporter Dan Dorfman's words, "have blown billions so far in 1984,"[5] a year in which the stock market set new highs. Only 12 percent of the mutual funds, 19 percent of the money-managed funds, 20 percent of bank pool funds, and 22 percent of the insurance company–managed equity funds, outperformed the Standard and Poor stock index. The overwhelming majority did less well than the market average!

Nor is this news. Prestigious pension commentators Dan McGill and Don Grubbs wrote of "the unimpressive performance of the investment community over the last decade or so."[6] *Business Week* reported in February 1985 that

---

* This result derives from calculating what $1 invested in 1926 would earn in fifty years if invested in the average of all stocks traded on the stock exchange. If a more realistic pattern of investing $1 every year were used—more realistic because one must constantly invest each year's savings—would produce 10 percent less than that claimed according to calculations made by Joseph Grolnic (then of the Federal Reserve Bank of Boston staff), pursuant to our request.

244

three out of four professional "money managers" used by pension funds failed to match the performance of the Standard and Poor index in 1984. Only 26 percent did better than the index. The article observed: "If a pension fund underperforms the Standard and Poor's 500 by two percentage points a year, that compounds to 10.4% over 5 years and 34.6% over 20."[7] If the pros do so badly, what chance is there for the amateurs?

Some "go it alone" advocates respond that people should sink their money into "passive" indexed funds and avoid all that risk. But if a major portion of institutional investors seek a haven in a fund that simply reproduces the Standard and Poor index, purchasing billions of the stocks comprising the index, they merely bid up the price. Indeed, stocks selected for addition to the index immediately leap in price when named.[8] Increased stock prices reduce earnings. So that bit of conventional wisdom won't work.

This antic management not only produces ludicrous performance, but costs prettily. Again, *Business Week*:

> In a recent study for Harvard University, pension consultant James Meketa estimated basic money-management costs at 1% to 2% of assets each year. That may not sound excessive, but consider this: If a $10 million account grosses 12%,* or $1.2 million (a respectable return), a 2% overhead on assets is $200,000—or nearly 17% of the year's earnings. Where does the money go? Brokerage commissions and related transaction costs eat up ½% to ¾%—and are reflected in the results reported to the various industry data bases. But not included in such results are money managers' fees, which skim an average of ½% off the top. Nor do the results reflect fees paid to consultants, actuaries, or banks that act as custodians for the funds.[9]

Those fees often cost plenty; the more times a security is traded, the higher such costs go. According to Meketa, the *average* manager trades about 70 percent of the portfolio's assets *each year*. Some analysts believe that managers turn over fund assets even more frequently. This activity produces paper profits for some, real losses for others, and management costs for participants.

Even when the stock market performs fabulously, some investors lag behind. For example, as 1986 opened, after the month in which the Dow-Jones average vaulted past 1500, one member of a Gettysburg, Pennsylvania investment club said: "It's been a wonderful year for us. We're nearly back to even."[10] For any particular fund or investor, investments made when the economy is sluggish can act as a drag on the fund even after the economy and earnings turn sprightly. Investments cannot be deferred. Available funds must take the market as they find it. Inevitably it will often offer slight returns or great risks. The prudent

* The nominal, not the real rate (authors' note).

investor balances these factors and seeks earnings that congregate around the average.

Large traders often have superior information that enables them to unload when a stock price is moving down—unload onto the unsuspecting smaller investor. In November 1984, for example, the *New York Times* reported how computer analysis of trading in Helene Curtis stock enabled "big players" to sell while small investors bought and took a shellacking.[11] Insider trading, a major Wall Street concern in 1987, introduces further risk and unfairness both to the small investor and to large funds.

Another as yet uncounted cost is the diversion of talent and energy from other human activities. The office handicapper became a stock movie character in newspaper thrillers. While reporters called in frantically and the people on the rewrite desk scrambled to keep up, the office handicapper mused over the daily racing form. Needless to say, the ponies seldom lived up to the dream. Also, needless to say, this character was not pulling his oar at the office. Now substitute the new character, the office investor, the handicapper of stocks and bonds, the aficionado of interest rates, the IRA buff poring over the *Wall Street Journal* who now has some or all of his or her Social Security contribution to invest. The information will be more conjectural than the tip sheet's morning line of past "outings." What happens if all of America, or some major part, "goes to the races" to seek their retirement income? Wouldn't we all be better off if each person does his or her own thing as engineer, architect, draftsperson, accountant, or programmer, undistracted by attempts to manage a "portfolio" with all the time that takes?

Other nonbenefit expenses of coverage would increase in any substitute private arrangement. In the first place, there are what insurers call acquisition costs—advertising and commissions. Once the billions of dollars now dedicated to Social Security flow directly to earners, the competition among banks, savings and loan associations, brokerage houses, insurers, and many others to obtain those prodigious sums would be formidable. Legitimate investment options will vie with scams to lure as much of those billions as ingenuity, artifice, and, occasionally, dishonesty can concoct. With tens of millions of new prospects, the wooing of investors would become a major industry, which cumulatively would cost billions that must be subtracted from the amounts invested. Nothing in such a scenario assures that any significant portion of those billions would be invested to expand our capacity to produce more goods and services.

Democracy's Solution: Universal and Mandatory Social Security

We are all in the same boat. Most fundamentally, the financial fate of all of us depends on our shared national economy. A shared universal system for social insurance that protects comprehensively serves a national purpose. No other program can do the job as well, or anywhere near as well, as Social Security.

It also makes sense to base an income-maintenance system on work, the chief source of income for almost the entire population. In the broadest sense, the insured-against hazard is loss of earnings. Realistically, only those with current earnings can support the program financially. Those without earnings cannot do so, except for the small group that derives all or most of its income from investments, too small a group on which to base a program. Moreover, the nonearning groups have little or no incentive to support an earnings replacement program. So the participants are bound together by common needs and common interest—more than many realize. If we are to earn credits in an income-maintenance system that reflects *all* of our work, we need a system that provides credits for all of our employment. Similarly, all participants should contribute throughout their working lifetime, otherwise they may be ineligible for benefits or they will unfairly reap benefits without making proportional contributions. In the interests of both effectiveness and fairness, a system providing income protection in the event of disablement, retirement, and death should draw contributions from all substantial employment throughout each individual's working life. To achieve those goals, participation must be both universal and mandatory.

Those who argue for voluntary coverage invoke the hallowed notions of freedom and personal choice—both appealing principles. People differ in both their needs and priorities, particularly at different times of life. Some argue that compulsory coverage smacks of paternalism. Let people look out for themselves, the argument goes, and if they prefer to take risks, let them. Many are persuaded that they can do better if left to dispose of equal sums on their own. Few can accurately calculate their future needs, however, and fewer can calculate their future resources. When an interruption of income occurs, it is too late to make provisions.

As a society we cannot simply ignore the plight of those sturdy American "risk-takers" who do not make it. The losers become society's problem, and it can be an expensive problem. If some do not make adequate provision for their own future and for those who depend on their earnings, they in effect shift

247

burdens to the rest of us. We will not let orphans or the severely disabled starve. Inasmuch as significant groups will fall into those categories, it is only fair to require all of us to make provision for the possibility of our own orphans, widows, widowers, and our disabled selves. That is not paternalism, but prudently preventing the reckless from shifting their burdens to the taxpayer.

As a community we have made similar judgments about providing universal education, a nationwide road system, a universal postal service, a defense program, and public health measures that protect us all. All people pay for education, whether or not they have children. That is not paternalism, but providing basic protections and services which benefit the whole of society. When a majority supports a program for the common benefit, that is the proper function of government. That some may not regard a particular measure as necessary or desirable is unavoidable in democratic decision making. If the congressional decision stems from reasonable evidence and ample debate and majority support, we have the normal democratic process operating in the normal democratic way, which includes compelling participation by some who disagree or have other priorities. The process, moreover, tends to produce better decisions (if evidence and debate are ample) than tens of millions of decisions by many with incomplete information or misinformation. Few can question that any set of issues has been more fully or extensively debated than the issues of Social Security. That the information is not universally precise or complete does not cancel the fact that, as public and private decision-making processes go, those concerning Social Security have been extensive.

A voluntary system also leads to what insurers know as "adverse selection." In Social Security, the higher-pay population would be the ones most likely to opt out (joined by many who prefer current income to future security). They might ask: Why should the better paid pay more to insure the proportionally larger benefits of others? One answer is that, no one knows his or her individual fate. Faced with common risks and common needs, common participation on common terms is fair and effective for the individual and society. Only Social Security meets that formula. It functions effectively and fairly, not least because its costs and benefits are shared universally. Private group plans supplement Social Security and will continue to do so, but they cannot reliably supplant it. When analyzed, the glitter of "going it alone" proves to be fools' gold.

It is all too easy to get diverted by the money's-worth argument, which poses the wrong issue. It is inappropriate to measure the value of a social insurance program after most of the risks are past and all uncertainties about earnings resolved. That measure ignores many protections the program affords throughout life.

OASDI affords protection to family members in the event of a working person's death or disablement. On top of that, it provides a partial income substitute for employees who become disabled. Simultaneously, as children we enjoy those same protections for survivors and family members of the disabled. More than that, children participate in whatever good deal their parents obtain in the early stages of the program or any particular improvement. Similarly, almost all of us enjoy the assurance that parents will receive a secure income, made additionally secure by COLA's protection against inflation. And most of us will draw inflation-proofed retirement benefits with the further assurance that a surviving spouse also will have lifetime protection.

Just what portion of the benefit formula will serve each of us we cannot know at the outset and often even later in our working lives. All may benefit from the weighting in favor of the low paid, although most earn more and get higher benefits, but with a lower replacement rate. Even under the money's-worth tables, most participants get back their own contributions and those of their employer—with interest, and often more. But the value of the protection we receive exceeds the actual dollars we eventually collect.

More than that, by protecting all, Social Security also guards against the costs of caring for those who, left to their own devices, would not or could not save adequately to carry themselves over periods of lost income. And it averts poverty for those large numbers whose own economic fate makes adequate saving impossible; that group may be larger than many of us think because we prefer not to take account of our economic vulnerability.

Not least, this pervasive protection stabilizes society and preserves individual dignity by providing income when death, disability, or retirement occur, with the additional protections—also without needs testing—provided to the disabled and those sixty-five and over when they require medical care.

Going it alone does not serve these many salutary purposes. And while some may get a better deal than Social Security provides, none is assured of it. Although advantages beckon, the downside risks are formidable.

On top of that, going it alone imperils the solvency of the Social Security program, an unacceptable risk.

PART IV

MEDICAL CARE

11 Medicare: Past, Present, and Future

Few, if any, headaches of the elderly exceed worry about the availability of adequate health services and long-term care in the event of serious illness. Worry centers on the financial devastation that even one major medical episode or substantial stint in a nursing home can inflict. Even those with savings cannot feel secure. Rapidly increasing costs of medical care and growth of the elderly population cause concern over the future costs of Medicare and how burdens can be borne.

Medicare was the mid-1960's partial answer to the most urgent medical-care needs of the disabled, the retired, and the relatively small group still at work past age sixty-five, for whom one episode of serious illness could end or curtail their working days. Medicare was meant to assure wide access to medical care for acute illness and, like OASDI, to prevent financial devastation. The proper contours of Medicare are not solidly set. Many pressures are in the process of producing change. This chapter discusses the major issues and suggests possible lines of development for medical care in the future.

The Structure of Medical Care in the United States

Two revolutionary changes in medical care began in the 1930s, one in technology, the other in economics. Antibiotics launched a new era in the successful treatment of infectious diseases; Blue Cross launched a new era in financing health care.

Prior to the discovery of antibiotics, medical care cured few illnesses, though inoculation and hygiene helped many avoid disease. Physicians successfully delivered many babies, treated many injuries, and alleviated some conditions amenable to surgery. Even after the reform of medical school training began with the Flexner Report in 1911, medical treatment often did more harm than good, especially when unscientific fads swept the profession. Medical care was a dubious good, made only modest claims for what it could do, and commanded a minor fraction of national expenditures; most of the population had uncertain access to expensive procedures available only in hospitals.

World War II made multiple contributions on both the technological and economic front. Antibiotics proliferated. Millions of people in the armed services received inoculation against common communicable diseases. The services confronted the problem of treating hundreds of thousands for traumatic wounds, burns, and illness. With new governmental resources available, military doctors devised new means to cope, aided by a revived manufacturing system that focused on supplying whatever the government sought. Furthermore, technological developments unrelated to medical care produced methods and devices that served medical research in the postwar period.

The medical emergency of World War II also produced battalions of new doctors, nurses, and other health professionals. Medical schools that had severely restricted enrollment became relatively high-speed production lines, training as doctors talented people, including many who formerly had been totally excluded for racial, religious, ethnic, or financial reasons. The U.S. Army devised new kinds of health professionals and established courses for the new breed. The armed services invented the medical administrator and the paramedic. The latter was the first step toward providing some initial treatment to large numbers of people by individuals without the full panoply of medical training, an important development in lowering cost.

The GI Bill of Rights added another revolutionary dimension. It brought medical education within the reach of hundreds of thousands who otherwise would not have had the chance of becoming doctors. And later the federal government aided universities in establishing or expanding medical and nursing schools.

Meanwhile, employment-based hospital-care insurance spread throughout U.S. industry, driven by the same forces that encouraged employment-based group pension plans: a tight labor market and governmental limits on cash wages from which group employee insurance plans were exempt. Employers installed group medical-care insurance plans in their competition for employees and the opportunities to produce goods and services for the war effort on an essentially cost-plus basis. Doctors helped launch Blue Cross to insure some hospital stays and services. Blue Cross and doctors helped spawn Blue Shield, which provides payment for their services.

By war's end, medical care was worth having. Wartime deprivation sharpened peoples' appetites and the postwar economic boom raised their expectations, aspirations, and purchasing power. Unions pressed for medical-care insurance. Industry, encouraged by wartime expansion and vast new markets, first at home and later abroad, decided not to haggle over wages and fringes but to concentrate on production. Major industries agreed to increasingly generous health-insurance programs, paid in large measure by employers as part of the compensation package. Nonunion firms frequently followed suit as a means of discouraging unionization and in response to favorable tax treatment for employer contributions to plans. Employment-based group health insurance spread to vast numbers of employees and provided more and more services.

Since public programs like Medicare emulated private health insurance patterns and institutions, their basic design must be understood.

The Basic Structure of Health Insurance

Prepaid health-care arrangements adopted the insurance device: small contributions by many build a fund to meet the costs of illness or injury that all may experience but few in fact do in any given period. When members of the group require health care, costs are met from the common fund. In an employment-based plan, the employer pays all or a portion of the premium, with any remainder paid by the employee. Such plans soon came to provide benefits not only to employees, but to spouses and children as well.

The first plans provided participants with specified hospital services. Later plans indemnified those insured for the cost of services provided by surgeons, anesthesiologists, radiologists, and later, out-of-hospital physicians. Indemnification became the dominant mode used for health care insurance.*

Indemnity now extends not to the full charge, but to the "prevailing, customary, and reasonable" fee for the particular service in the area served. Insurers conduct periodic surveys of provider and physician charges for covered services and set the upper level at, say, 75 or 80 percent of such charges in the locality; that point constitutes the upper limit of what is "reasonable." In this way providers determine prices but need not curtail them. Nor does the formula exercise any discipline over the nature and extent of the services supplied. Quite the contrary, by assuring payment for a major portion of any charge, the provider has an incentive to render services even if some are not strictly needed.

---

* Insurers are known as "third parties." The doctor and patient constitute the first two parties.

Many plans do not provide "first dollar" coverage. But most require the participant to pay for the very first charges up to a specified amount (the deductible). In addition, plans also require beneficiaries to coinsure, that is, pay a portion of covered charges, sometimes with an annual cap. Insurers employ these co-pay devices to keep premiums down, shift costs to participants, and discourage patients from seeking unnecessary care or particular services. However, many health specialists doubt their efficacy because most patients do not have the knowledge to question the need for such services. Deductibles and coinsurance discourage some from seeking timely treatment.

Despite the growing supply of health professionals, changing technology and assured payment from health insurance drove up medical-care prices, including those for physicians' services. These spiraling prices made insurance coverage all the more urgent. The insurance arrangements also enabled providers to charge whatever was necessary to cover expenses, in the case of nonprofit hospitals, and provide comfortable income for physicians and for hospitals operated for profit.

Health insurance concentrated on meeting the costs of the most expensive services—those provided by hospitals and by surgeons, anesthesiologists, or radiologists—because those were the costs with which most people most urgently needed help. But this pattern encouraged physicians to use hospitals to render services that might be performed better or more inexpensively in clinics or offices; hospital use was insured, clinics and office services were not. Rendering insured rather than uninsured services guaranteed providers their payment and helped patients meet their costs.

Other factors also encouraged the use of the most expensive facilities rather than less costly alternatives. The federal government provided financial assistance to build hospitals throughout the country. Physicians found this particular form of federal expenditure an acceptable kind of aid that did not threaten their autonomy. The Hill-Burton program, named after its chief congressional sponsors, carried few strings, requiring only that the recipient hospitals undertake to render some service to indigents. Physicians welcomed Hill-Burton funds and actively sought them for building new hospitals. They did so for reasons of prestige and convenience as well as service. Hospitals permit only a limited number of physicians the right to treat their confined patients. Physicians without such hospital privileges championed new hospitals in which they would be accredited. Hospital building was not limited to demonstrated need for the new institutions. Many other factors contributed to the proliferation of beds, including local pressure groups favoring nearby facilities, tax-favored bonds, and income assured by private insurance and Medicare. More was considered better. But in medical care more, at least more supply, often is decidedly not better.

How Greater Supply Boosts Costs

Once built and equipped, a hospital encounters unavoidable fixed charges—payments due for principal and interest on debt incurred for building and equipment plus irreducible charges for utilities, maintenance, and a basic crew of professionals, such as nurses, equipment technicians, and nonprofessional support staff. The greater the number of patients, the smaller are the per patient costs attributable to these fixed and inevitable charges. The lower the patient population (the utilization rate), the higher must be the charges for any one service. Therefore, to generate the financial capability to purchase up-to-date equipment or even to remain solvent, hospitals must seek the highest possible levels of utilization. Physicians whose hospital privileges depend on the continued existence of their institutions have a vital interest in their perpetuation and, hence, institutional income. The convenience and availability of equipment and supporting personnel also make hospital-based services attractive to physicians.

Hospitals and the physicians who practice in them lack financial incentives to prefer less costly care. The availability of more adequate insurance for hospitalization and hospital-based procedures encourages providers to maximize hospital admissions, the length of hospital stays, and the utilization of hospital-based services, such as tests. Any oversupply of hospital units intensifies pressures on providers with excess capacity to hospitalize patients and to provide unnecessary services. Prescribing tests also aids institutions in meeting economic shortfalls that may result from the purchase of expensive equipment, poor management, rising costs, and the treatment of patients with limited or no insurance.

Many of these problems remained obscure while the economy grew rapidly and private profit margins remained handsome; that is, before the era of oil shock, stern foreign competition, and recession. Then the music changed. But that is getting ahead of the Medicare story.

The Prelude to Medicare

In the bad old days, the desperately ill poor landed in the wards of city hospitals. Most of the mentally ill were dumped in state mental hospitals. The exception was for many veterans, who, regardless of ability to pay, could be treated in Veterans Administration (VA) hospitals throughout the country; veterans' organizations have made support for VA hospitals one of their priorities.

In the late 1940s, Congress legislated federal financial help to states that chose to add health care to their welfare programs. The blind, disabled, elderly, and families with dependent children qualified for aid in needs-tested "cate-

257

gorical" state programs—Aid to the Blind (AB), Aid to Permanently and Totally Disabled (APTD), Old-Age Assistance (OAA), and Aid to Families with Dependent Children (AFDC). The federal government paid a specified portion of the cash benefits and medical-care services provided to people in those categories. The states determined both eligibility and the level of benefits and services and administered the programs. Most states responded to the invitation and provided some forms of medical service to the needy in the covered categories.

But by the end of the 1940s, these arrangements still left about half the population without assurance that their needs for hospitalization would be met and the bulk of the population without assurance that they could obtain surgery, physicians' services, or medications when needed.

Attempts in the late 1940s and early 1950s to meet these needs with some system of national health care or insurance for the entire population foundered, sunk by charges that such a plan would constitute "socialized medicine." Advocates of such measures lowered their sights and began to press for a system of health insurance for the elderly—a group with demonstrably great medical needs, inadequate financial resources, and the loss of employment-based group medical insurance, if any, with the termination or diminution of work. More than that, private health insurers proved reluctant or unable to provide affordable health-insurance coverage to this high-risk group. Pressure for a public program grew. Insurers responded with various "golden" (for golden years) policies, but their premiums proved prohibitive.

The 1960 presidential election provided the first referendum on national health insurance for the elderly. Spurred on by labor unions and the "golden agers" they helped mobilize, Senator John F. Kennedy embraced proposals for a Social Security–based system of health insurance for those sixty-five and over, a non–needs-tested program financed by payroll taxes. Republicans, with an assist from conservative Democrats, responded with proposals for a needs-tested, federal-state grant-in-aid program patterned after the programs for the indigent blind, disabled, and elderly. President Eisenhower called a special session of Congress before the 1960 presidential election to enact a needs-tested health-care program for the elderly. That effort resulted in enactment of the Kerr-Mills program, named after the Democrats who chaired the congressional committees that processed the legislation.

The Kerr-Mills program, also known as the Medical Assistance Act (MAA), employed the pattern of the existing needs-tested federal grant-in-aid programs. It offered states financial assistance if they enacted programs that fit basic federal specifications—in this case, supplying medical care to the elderly. The states determined eligibility (what income and assets were low enough) and the kinds and extent of benefits, in this instance, services. Kerr-Mills used the concept of "medical indigency" rather than destitution to describe need. Recognizing that people who were not poor in the traditional definitions often could not afford the medical care they needed, the new program called for eligibility criteria that reached not only to the poor or near-poor but to the nonpoor who nonetheless could not afford the necessary medical services, the "medically indigent."

The postenactment history of Kerr-Mills made clear that it did not answer the needs of the elderly for health care. As a federal-aid-to-the-states program, dependent on the states for enactment, definition of eligibility and benefits, and partial financing, it was neither effective nor adequate in action. Not all states enacted the requisite state programs; one of the first states to do so, West Virginia, soon reduced its program drastically. Most of all, Kerr-Mills critics argued, the elderly preferred the approach of the Social Security cash programs under which contributions made when working earned benefits "as of right" without needs testing.

Enactment of Kerr-Mills, however, did not settle the matter. Kennedy had gained considerable political mileage from the medical-care issue in 1960. In the 1964 campaign, Lyndon Johnson pressed the issue, and then used his landslide vote for the enactment in 1965 of Medicare, along with a host of other programs.

How Medicare Works

As originally enacted in 1965, Part A of Medicare emulated the Blue Cross pattern; Medicare Part A reimbursed providers for the reasonable cost of hospitalization, most in-hospital services (but not those of physicians), and in-hospital drugs. It became known as Hospital Insurance (HI). All people eligible for Social Security cash benefits and aged sixty-five or older qualify for HI benefits. In addition, a person hospitalized under HI qualifies for skilled nursing institution care for a limited period and for home health, but not custodial, care for longer periods. This combination was designed to move patients into the least costly care arrangements consistent with their needs. By amendment in 1972, those drawing Disability Insurance (DI) qualified after a waiting period of twenty-four months. Spouses and children of the qualified disabled do not qualify for Medicare.

A portion of FICA taxes, 1.45 percent of taxable pay from both the employer and employee, and a comparable amount from SECA, go into the HI trust fund. These contributions constitute almost all of its funding.

Also known as Medicare Part B, Supplementary Medical Insurance (SMI) indemnifies participants for physicians' and surgeons' fees and in-hospital services by anesthesiologists, radiologists, and psychiatrists, and also covers various supportive services such as ambulance transportation. Originally, it also entitled a homebound insured to one hundred home health service visits a year, later extended to an unlimited number, for skilled medical treatment but not for housekeeping assistance. Congress added coverage for some out-of-hospital surgical services such as cataract operations.

These changes were designed to shift services away from the more expensive hospital setting whenever possible. That shift also resulted in trimming HI costs but adding to SMI costs, defrayed by beneficiary premiums and general revenues rather than by payroll tax. Shifting services out of hospitals does not necessarily produce savings equal to the difference between the hospital-based treatment costs and the new out-of-hospital rates if the changes lower the hospitals' utilization rates but do not lower fixed and other irreducible costs. Table 11.1 summarizes the sources of financing and the types of coverage provided by HI and SMI. By the mid-1980s, charges for hospital treatments and services nearly equaled room charges for HI patients.

TABLE 11.1

Medicare Summary for Social Security Recipients Aged Sixty-five and Over and for Social Security Disabled

	Hospital Insurance (HI) (Part A)	*Supplementary Medical Insurance (SMI) (Part B)*
Beneficiary pays:	Deductible Coinsurance	Premium deductible Coinsurance
Other financing:	FICA/SECA	General revenues

Coverage:	Hospitalization
	In-hospital services
	In-hospital drugs
	Skilled nursing
	  facility for acute
	  conditions
	Home health care
	  for acute
	  conditions
		Physicians' Fees
		In-hospital fees for radiologists,
		  psychiatrists,
		  anesthesiologists
		Ambulance
		Home health care

Treatments:		Certain out-of-hospital surgery

Who Is Eligible?

Eligibility for HI turns on eligibility for Social Security or Railroad Retirement benefits. In addition, the individual must be aged sixty-five or older, but need not be actually drawing cash benefits. Disabled persons drawing either DI benefits or the corresponding Railroad Retirement benefits qualify for HI after being on the disability rolls for twenty-four months.

To qualify for SMI, a person sixty-five and over or disabled must elect coverage and pay a monthly premium. The premium covers a quarter of the costs of reimbursements. The remaining three-fourths are paid by the Federal government from general revenues. SMI also features deductibles and coinsurance. It does not cover the costs of medications.

Other amendments require participation by those in the federal civil service, because so many qualified who had paid contributions only on those wages earned sporadically in Social Security–covered employment. Their compulsory inclusion was meant to end a cut-rate deal and to improve Medicare financing.

How HI Provides Benefits

The program pays HI costs directly to the hospital providing the services to the insured. When HI started in 1966, beneficiaries paid the first $40 of billings and HI paid the remainder for the first sixty days of hospitalization for a "benefit period," that is, one spell of illness. By 1987, the initial hospital deductible had become $572.[1] A complicated formula keys the hospital deductible to the average of hospital daily rates. As daily rates have climbed more rapidly than the consumer price index to which cash benefits have been pegged since 1975, HI beneficiary costs have increased more rapidly than cash benefits. Most hospital stays are much shorter than sixty days; hence the deductible often represents a substantial portion of total charges.

In the unusual event of hospitalization for sixty-one to ninety days, the beneficiary must make a *daily* coinsurance payment which grew from $10 in 1966 to $143 by 1987; for each day in excess of ninety, the daily rate doubles. The coinsurance rate also is keyed to the average daily hospital room charge. Despite these complicated provisions, HI meets the bulk of hospital charges for those covered by Medicare.

A person who has spent at least three days in the hospital is eligible for one hundred days in a skilled nursing facility (SNF) which provides skilled medical services. (Relatively few qualify for this benefit.) A person confined to an SNF for twenty days must make a daily coinsurance payment thereafter. In 1967, when such services began, the daily deductible was $5. By 1987, it had become $50. All of the HI deductibles and coinsurance amounts increased tenfold or more during the initial twenty years of the program.

How SMI Pays

The Health Care Financing Administration (HCFA) uses insurance carriers as intermediaries to process claims. The carrier ascertains the approved fees for covered services in accordance with the statutory formula. Any excess over the "approved charge" is the responsibility of the patient.

In 1966, the SMI eligibles paid a $3-a-month premium. By 1987, it had increased to $17.70.* The original $50 annual deductible became $75 by 1985, and coinsurance factor of 20 percent applies to all covered charges. But beneficiaries may end up paying more than the deductible and coinsurance where the fee charges exceed those allowed.

As with the private health insurers, the SMI system pays the customary, prevailing, and reasonable rate for covered services. The provider has the option to take "assignment," that is, to accept as payment the amount that Medicare approves, agreeing to collect the insured portion of that payment from the intermediary (as the administering private agencies are called). The patient remains liable for the deductible and co-pay portion of such bills. Or the provider may insist on payment by the patient of the full charges, leaving it to the patient to obtain reimbursement from Medicare's intermediary. In that way, the patient may end up paying the difference between the billing and what Medicare allows, plus the coinsurance and the deductible. In practice, some providers render their bill and then accept Medicare's 80 percent payment as payment in full. However, more than 30 percent of physicians refuse assignment and their charges run on average 27 percent above carrier-approved billing.[2]

Some providers refuse assignment because Medicare payment is slow. As the intermediaries process millions of claims, the delay factor is all too understandable.

"Medi-Gap": Private Insurance Supplements

An enormous market in private insurance to supplement Medicare has grown up to pay for the deductibles, coinsurance, and partial reimbursement (with its own deductibles and coinsurance) for the cost of uncovered services or supplies, such as private-duty nursing and prescription drugs.

Bearing the generic name of medi-gap, these supplementary policies largely cancel whatever cautionary effect deductibles and coinsurance are supposed to exercise upon beneficiaries and providers. In addition, they eat up a good-sized

* In 1988, the premium will increase by 38 percent, becoming almost $25 a month.

chunk of beneficiary income.* Many may be wasteful because beneficiaries often do not know what Medicare does and does not cover and what constitutes a good medi-gap buy. Mass merchandising of plans with dubious utility indicate that some Medicare participants pay too much for things they do not need. By way of example, one of the authors' mothers, when president of a small business and far from retired, purchased duplicating medi-gap policies and kept them in force after retirement. The waste was compounded in that for these years she made no claims for reimbursement for hundreds of dollars in prescription drugs, because she did not know they were covered. Her oversight came to light at the time of a major operation, when she also learned that neither medi-gap plan paid for desired private nursing care.

Secretary Bowen's task force on catastrophic insurance estimated that some 65 percent of Medicare participants have medi-gap policies; reportedly, "many beneficiaries hold more than one such policy."[3] Although Congress adopted guidelines for medi-gap policies, observance of those limits is problematical.

Health Insurance for Older People at Work

In 1982, Congress, at the administration's prompting, did a curious thing with Medicare. It provided in the Tax Equity and Fiscal Responsibility Act (TEFRA) that employers offering health insurance must give employees aged sixty-five to sixty-nine the option of full participation in the employer's health insurance plan with HI and SMI acting only as "secondary" insurance; that is, the employer's health plan is the first payer; Medicare pays what it normally covers but only to the extent that the employer's plan does not. Obviously, when the employee elects to treat the employer's plan as primary coverage, Medicare's risks and costs are reduced. Then in 1984, Congress, with little discussion, extended that arrangement so that where the working member is below age sixty-five but a spouse is sixty-five or over (that is, eligible for Medicare and very possibly not working) the employee may select the employer's plan as primary for both.[4] Before these amendments, most private health insurance excluded Medicare-covered expenditures. These enactments rendered invalid such exclusionary provisions, thereby increasing private health-insurance costs

* The American Association of Retired Persons offers such coverage under contract with a commercial insurer. Given its role, experience, expertise, and bargaining power, the coverage it negotiates and the price ought to be among the best around. Its monthly charge in 1986 was $14.10 for a retiree and another $14.10 for the spouse. While the annual total of almost $360.00 sounds modest to those of us still employed, it amounts to half of an average couple's Social Security monthly cash benefit—a significant amount. Other policies often are less comprehensive, make a poorer fit with Medicare, and are more expensive, reportedly running as high as $1,500 a year according to the Department of Health and Human Services Report to the President, "Catastrophic Illness Expenses" (1986), p. 30. One estimate in 1987 placed annual premium payments for Medi-gap policies at $6.2 billion. (*New York Times*, [national edition], February 12, 1987, p. 29.)

for those sixty-five and over and employees with spouses sixty-five and over who make the election that the employer must offer.

There has been little discussion of the possibly adverse effects these measures have had on the employment of older people. If, as well might be the case, employers are reluctant to employ older people so as not to incur the costs of expensive coverage for employees, the Medicare savings may prove illusory. These measures may well discourage such employment because group health-insurance rates reflect the age mix of the covered group and plan assumptions assign higher costs for covering older people. Whether or not employees select the employer's plan as primary, the *risk* of these higher costs accompanying employment of those sixty-five and over tends to discourage hiring them in this cost-conscious time. Of course, employment discrimination based on age up to seventy is illegal but exceedingly hard to prove.

These changes in Medicare deserve reexamination in the interests both of program costs and of maximizing employment opportunities for people in their sixties.

How the Medicare Trust Funds Look Ahead*

The HI trust fund employs the demographic and economic assumptions and projections used by the Social Security Administration actuary. These provide the income side of the ledgers and the size of the HI-covered population. In addition, HCFA's actuaries estimate the use and price of the services for which they make reimbursements. Until 1986, the HI trust fund made estimates only for a twenty-five-year period ahead rather than the seventy-five-year period used for OASDI. This brief time frame did not mean that no concern existed over the anticipated higher costs of the program, but the professionals most knowl-edgeable about the programs did not consider the longer-range projections used for OASDI feasible for HI. But then HFCA began making seventy-five-year estimates and projections. In our judgment the extreme volatility of medical-care prices and the rapidity of change in this field make the shorter-term projections more sensible. The SMI program, funded on a yearly basis with three-quarters of its funds derived from general revenues, seeks actuarial soundness only year by year.

---

* For the uninitiated, "How Social Security Looks Ahead" in chapter 2 and the discussion of major program variables in chapter 3 should help. For more detail consult "Actuarial Methodology and Principal Assumptions for the Hospital Insurance Cost Estimates" in *1986 Annual Report of the Board of Trustees of the Federal Hospital Insurance Trust Fund*, H. Doc. 99-190, 99th Cong., 2d sess., 53–70.

Problems Facing Medicare

Concern over the future of Medicare focuses primarily on the growing numbers of the elderly and the escalating prices of hospitalization and medical services. Concern also exists that the availability of Medicare reimbursement may cause overuse of hospitalization, unneeded services, and price inflation. Hospital charges account for about two-thirds of medical care expenditures for the elderly, compared with two-fifths for all health-care expenditures for the entire population. Some differences are to be expected, since older people require more hospital care than younger people. Costs for medical care services have consistently increased more rapidly than the consumer price index (CPI) whether the climb of CPI was modest or dreadful. Such patterns naturally cause grave concern.

It is important to bear in mind that medical care in 1966 (Medicare's first year) differed enormously from medical care two decades later. Medical technology has changed rapidly in that period. The current unit of service is simply not the same as the 1966 unit of service. The daily costs of a semi-private room in a major metropolitan area, $100 in the mid-1960s and $500 in the mid-1980s, are not wholly comparable. Furthermore, today's hospital stays (even before the impact of diagnosis-related groupings [DRGs]) are shorter than they were only two decades ago. Although we pay more, we get more. Often the new and expensive procedures save time, money, and suffering. For example, some costly, debilitating, and dangerous exploratory operations have been displaced to some extent by new, but costly, methods of internal "imaging."

We should try to understand the components of hospital price increases; the HI actuaries have analyzed them in order to predict future costs. Labor costs in hospitals have increased, but not dramatically. Though hospital hourly earnings rose more rapidly than economy-wide labor-cost increases in most years between 1972 and 1983 (the years for which we have data), the differences were slight. The spread of unionization undoubtedly was a factor. Wage rates among unskilled support personnel had been shamefully low, below the poverty level according to the claims of one union vigorously organizing in the New York City metropolitan area. Today the labor-cost surge probably has slowed. Some upgrading of skills among nonprofessional support personnel probably also occurred. The II-B best-guess projections forecast a decided abatement in this cost factor over the next twenty-five years. There is *some* good news.

265

Nonlabor costs also outdistanced CPI boosts due to increases in the quantity and prices of equipment. Some increases represented advances in technology and treatment. But others probably resulted from having assured sources of payment from Medicare and other health insurers. To some degree both purchases and prices were excessive, but providers, intent on their tasks of treatment, and to some extent empire building, had little interest or incentive to seek cost restraint and efficiency. Neither did private third parties. General fiscal concerns forced attention to cost and utilization problems; the visibility of Medicare in the trustees' annual reports made it feasible to isolate and track the main cost components.

Under SMI, physicians' fees account for the major portion of expenditures. Fee charges rose rapidly, only mildly restrained by "fee screens" (as the traditional limitations are called). So Medicare-approved charges steadily increased. In addition, the assurance of reimbursement probably encouraged physicians to order unneeded services. The unscrupulous even charged for services not rendered. Other physicians hold financial interests in laboratories from which they order tests, whose costs were reimbursable under Medicare. Under such circumstances, fees increased rapidly.

The rapid rise of medical malpractice insurance costs drives up medical costs in two ways. First, providers fold the cost of the premium into doctors' charges. Second, the fear of large jury verdicts for some lapse in treatment causes physicians to practice "defensive medicine." Some define that as acting with appropriate care, but the term often connotes overdoing tests and treatment so as to be able to demonstrate that the provider pursued every conceivable route to recovery.

Growth of the eligible population served also has increased Medicare costs.

In sum, the combination of mounting prices, increased and more expensive services, greater numbers of eligibles and users and explosive malpractice insurance charges drove Medicare costs higher. Much the same happened in Medicaid and private health insurance.

Unless costs come under control, the present rate of HI tax and SMI premiums will not suffice to fund the programs. In addition, the general revenue contributions to SMI, already substantial, will increase.

Medicare: How to Fix It

To keep Medicare solvent over the long haul, either costs must be reined in, revenues improved, or services curtailed. Congress, HCFA, and the administration are seeking means to reduce the costs of provider services. Employers, unions, insurers, and federal and state agencies are addressing the problems of rising costs of health care with unprecedented energy and intensity. Efforts to restrain costs should continue to bear some fruit—an outcome greatly to be preferred to reducing services. What are the possibilities for reducing costs? Improving revenues? And if push comes to shove—eventually—how might Medicare be reduced?

Cost Containment

Cost-control efforts have concentrated on stemming price increases, principally for hospital-based stays, and discouraging the provision of unnecessary hospital-based services. Fresh attention also is being extended to out-of-hospital services. These efforts might be called squeezing the providers.

The most dramatic moves consist of the diagnosis-related groupings (DRG) regulations for hospital stays and the fifteen-month price "freeze" in 1984–85 for physicians' services.

The Villains: Cost Reimbursement and Fee-for-Service.   Prior to October 1983, Medicare reimbursed hospitals on a complicated formula for their costs in providing hospital care and in-hospital tests and services. The method did not encourage hospitals, which encountered rising costs in any event, to restrain their costs. With a surplus of capacity in both space and equipment, hospitals found it necessary to place the burden of higher prices on shrinking patient populations, thereby increasing unit costs. Non-hospital providers charge on a fee-for-service basis. Naturally, the more services rendered, the greater the charges. Unfortunately, both such arrangements also encourage physicians and other providers to order marginal or unnecessary services.[5] As reimbursement is keyed to customary charges in the locality, providers have little incentive to restrain fee increases.

Prepayment and Prospective Payment.   Countermeasures instituted by both private and public plan sponsors hold considerable promise. Chief among such measures are "prepayment" and its cousin "prospective payment." Under prepayment, providers undertake to supply needed services (within defined limits) to each group participant for a fixed periodic fee. Under such a plan, supplying services the patient does not need increases the provider's costs but not its income, just the reverse of fee-for-service. The trick is to hold down per capita prices. A knowledgeable group purchaser can do that, by determining the desired package and then putting the package out to bid among providers. The price must be sufficient to encourage an adequate supply of providers.

In effect, Medicare has done something similar by specifying the price it will pay for each hospital admission for specified conditions—DRG-based prospective payment.

How DRG Works.   To help contain Medicare costs, President Carter proposed to limit hospital expenditures, but the majority of Republicans, joined by some Democrats, defeated his proposal. Although HI remained solvent, warnings of impending trouble persuaded Congress to seek some arrangement other than cost as the means of compensating hospitals. In 1982 it directed the Department of Health and Human Services to study "prospective payment" as a means of slowing program costs. In consequence, DRG was born.

Under the DRG regime, Medicare pays the provider a specified amount for each patient according to that individual's diagnosis. The Department of Health and Human Services (HHS) sets the price to meet the average cost of providing the appropriate treatment for the particular diagnosis. In contrast with cost reimbursement this method of reimbursement offers providers incentives to keep hospital stays short and to minimize tests and services. If the hospital stay and treatment cost less than the DRG payment, the provider is ahead. If it costs more, the provider loses money, which it cannot make up by charges for tests and services.

Setting the rates so that they will be adequate, but not overly generous and will fit geographical variations in cost, is a complex process. HHS employs advisory committees of experts to guide its officials in setting DRG prices. One obvious difficulty in setting fees is providing sufficient amounts for especially complex conditions. The regulations promulgating DRG rates make allowance for such cases.

DRGs are designed to curtail program costs by giving providers incentives to confine care to the essentials. Whether it works that way or often leads to inadequate care causes great concern.

Games Providers Can Play with DRG.   Some DRGs will be more "profitable" for some providers than others. This can shape admissions policies or even affect diagnoses. Such patterns may or may not improve medical care. To

268

the extent that expertise with particular conditions reduces cost, such an admission policy will serve patient interests and program goals. But it might defeat program goals if it reduces the supply of facilities needed to serve financially less advantageous DRGs. Such an outcome may result from an agency mistake in DRG pricing; if so, patients bear the brunt of the mistake until it is rectified. Obviously, misclassification can totally undermine the DRG program. With millions of admissions, effective policing against misguided or dishonest classification practices may be very difficult.

Length of stay constitutes a critical factor in setting DRG rates. A rate assumes that some instances will fall above and others below a specified point. However, the mix for particular providers, especially small ones, may not match the experience drawn from larger populations. Providers may respond by discharging people when they reach the limit of the assumed length of stay, whether or not the medical condition warrants discharge; several reports document just such occurrences. Premature discharges can lead to worsened health and even death. The pressure to discharge within assumed time limits also presents skilled nursing facilities with more seriously ill patients without commensurate resources to deal with greater responsibilities. Patients may suffer and some reportedly do.

Humane concern, one expects and hopes, operates to counteract these pressures. But that seems an inadequate lever. We must understand that a major component of prepayment strategy, unaccompanied by more explicit community planning to match facilities with needs, turns into a battle by institutions for survival. The struggle to survive can produce a degree of ferocity even in the most benign. When we put our trust exclusively or primarily in market forces, we cannot reasonably expect them to be ameliorated for long by the milk of human kindness. One consequence of the battle has been widespread resort to provider advertising, thereby increasing costs without improving the quality of care.

Health Maintenance Organizations.　Health Maintenance Organizations (HMOs) constitute a major attempt to avoid the pitfalls of fee-for-service arrangements. In addition, HMOs arguably provide better health care since they have a financial incentive to promote preventive measures in contrast with plans that indemnify for treatment of acute illness and injury but do not cover preventive services, such as physical examinations.

HMOs undertake to provide complete health service for a periodic per capita fee. By covering the whole spectrum of services, an incentive exists for a plan to provide the patient with the least expensive service responsive to the individual's needs. HMOs do not augment income when providing additional services; they only increase their costs. In fee-for-service arrangements, the provider improves its income by providing more services. Similarly, HMO staff

269

physicians, if paid by salary, do not make more money by multiplying their services. Rather, they improve plan income by signing up more people, keeping them healthy, and doing only what must be done for each.

The question naturally arises whether talented physicians will work under such salary limitations and whether such plans, bent on economy, provide adequate services. To attract competent professionals, HMOs must offer adequate salaries. HMO professionals can trade off some loss of income with assurance of sensible and limited tours of duty rather than the grueling hours many private practitioners keep. An organization of sufficient size can offer around-the-clock service with shifts of physicians and other professionals. In addition, HMOs—like any group practice of sufficient scope—enable physicians to work within their own specialties and to refer patients to a wide range of specialists. HMOs, however, often can operate on a scale unavailable to most group practitioners and so achieve economies of scale. Perhaps as important, they enable physicians to take comfort that they and their colleagues can provide all services their patients might need—psychic income that many welcome.

HMOs also provide a good base for rationalizing the scope and composition of services—efforts not available to traditional insurers and traditional providers. With relatively large populations served, they can keep track of the shifts in the demand for services and adjust supply, thereby reducing at least some underutilization. Similarly, they can monitor the performance of individual professionals and have the incentive for doing so. HMOs do not process claims for reimbursement (except possibly for specialists to whom they make referrals on a fee-for-service basis) and so are spared a significant administrative expense.

That is the HMO ideal. The question is whether they work as hoped. Studies of HMO experience in the Minneapolis–St. Paul area provide conflicting reports. One indicates dramatically shorter lengths of hospital stays for HMO patients (48 percent) as compared with Blue Cross–Blue Shield employee groups, which the analysts believe should have had much the same age mix. Another study attributed different experience to differences in age, with greater percentages of older people opting for more traditional forms of coverage. A 1982 study, discounting for age, showed HMO patients with shorter than average lengths of hospital stays—one-quarter below that of patients covered by commercial insurers. Even here, however, the better showing may be attributable to a difference in population, with those who had more favorable medical histories in the HMO group.[6]

Many students of medical care advocate HMOs as a major means of both controlling costs and improving health services. These propositions deserve and are receiving scrutiny. But the jury remains out. Major insurers like Metropolitan Life and Prudential have entered the HMO ranks. Whether for-profit organizations operate HMOs as well as or better than not-for-profit groups bears close attention.

Preferred Provider Organizations.   If excess capacity and competition among providers exist, preferred provider organizations (PPOs) can help curb prices. Employers or other organizations contract with a PPO so that employees/members who use the PPO's services receive a price break. The provider may thereby achieve higher utilization, which makes lower prices possible. PPO competition can lead some providers to shut down with consequent reduction of oversupply, improved utilization, and lower unit prices.

The trick is for employers, especially small employers and user groups, or insurers, or some other organizing entity acting on their behalf, to combine their purchasing power to make PPO arrangements. Groups of retirees can and do combine. In the Minneapolis area, for example, an organization representing about 100,000 Medicare participants deals on their behalf with PPOs; under its contracts, providers agree to accept the Medicare-approved amount as full payment—an advantageous arrangement for patients.

PPOs sound so desirable and logical that one wonders just why they do not develop and spread more rapidly. Perhaps because they challenge the way things have been done, PPOs take some getting used to, but scattered reports indicate they are proliferating.

Co-Payments Also Cost.   Real savings are achieved only if they result in lower total outlays by the combined public program and beneficiaries. Too often claimed "savings" are no more than a shift in costs. Deductibles and co-payments may "save" Medicare money but they cost beneficiaries. That co-payments discourage unnecessary use is questionable. We know with certainty, however, that they increase administrative costs. Medicare intermediaries must calculate and keep records for the required deductibles and co-payments by the millions. Beneficiaries must make applications and secure documentation of their medi-gap policy claims. Then, medi-gap policy insurers must process those claims, by the millions. Mistakes abound when the bureaucratic process is complicated and multilayered. How many elderly people meekly pay improperly high bills? How many of them make inquiries? Do they receive proper credit for their overpayments?

Deductibles and coinsurance do not demonstrably reduce overall program costs by restraining prices or discouraging charges for unneeded services. Timeliness of care is important for both effective treatment and cost containment. Yet many people avoid medical care from fear of the procedure or fear of the

271

deductible and co-pay cost. Such delays can mean that they arrive at the doctor's or hospital's doorstep in worsened condition.

The timing of co-payments and deductibles is especially unfortunate. They become payable when people are ill, a time when income declines and expenses grow, the very time when financial burdens should be eased, not increased.

The public pays a high price for the unproven assumptions of the insurance industry that co-payments curtail overuse, a predilection shared by many economists who keep fashioning new methods of co-payment for the purpose. Eliminating deductibles and coinsurance would remove financial and bureaucratic burdens that many beneficiaries cannot bear. Eliminating them also would lower administrative costs.

Medi-gap policies, held by some 70 percent of Medicare participants, cancel whatever discouragement of overuse co-pay might induce. If the insurance pays for what Medicare does not, the incentive not to overuse Medicare disappears, if it ever existed. Rather, the medi-gap policy holder has an incentive to get his or her money's worth from the private policy. Eliminating medi-gap would eliminate a possibly perverse incentive to overuse and certainly would eliminate another layer of administrative expenses for intermediaries and beneficiaries (and their adult children). Many medi-gap plans pay out as little as 50 or 60 percent of premiums in benefits. Eliminating the need for medi-gap plans should lower the total costs of medical care for the elderly, although, initially at least, some of the costs would be shifted to the public program.

Proposals for Additional Financing

Assuming that Medicare—or some improvement like long-term care—requires additional financing to strengthen its trust funds, sources other than increased FICA and SECA rates warrant investigation. Proposals include expanding the portion of payroll that is taxable (but without increasing net tax burdens), extending mandatory coverage to all state and local government employees, eliminating the special income-tax exemption for the elderly, and imposing what is jocularly dubbed a "sin tax" on alcohol and tobacco.

Expanding Taxable Payroll While Lowering FICA/SECA Rates. The projected shrinkage of taxable payroll projected for the cash programs (see chapter 3) adversely affects the future financial resources of HI as well. If fringe benefits, most of which are not taxable for FICA and SECA, comprise a continually larger portion of compensation, program revenues will be that much smaller than if fringes do not grow as a portion of pay. Changing the FICA/SECA tax base to employees' total compensation would permit lowering the tax rate so that it would continue to yield the same portion as the 1990 rates applicable only to cash pay would yield. Such a measure would stabilize the tax base and avoid the shrinkage in program revenue actuaries forecast, yet would not increase contribution burdens beyond what they are when the last-scheduled rate change is made.

Extending Mandatory Coverage to State and Local Government Employees. Some thirty percent of state and local government employees do not participate in Medicare. Nonetheless most will qualify for Medicare by their own other work or that of spouses, but will pay less for this eligibility than those of us who always work in Social Security–covered jobs. Extending mandatory Medicare coverage to such employees would eliminate their cut-rate participation and add roughly $2 billion a year to HI receipts starting in fiscal year 1989. If instituted in fiscal 1988, the change would add $9.3 billion over its first five years.[7] Both fairness and fiscal considerations recommend such a change. (See chapter 9 for a discussion of coverage, including methods of meeting constitutional questions.) In 1986, Congress required Medicare coverage for newly-hired state and local government employees.

Eliminating the Special Exemption for the Elderly. Tax exemptions often outlive the situations that originally provided their justification. So it was with the double–income tax exemption provided for taxpayers sixty-five and over, which allowed them to exempt twice the amount available to other taxpayers. The double exemption came into being in 1959 when Social Security benefits were even more modest than today and poverty afflicted 35 percent of the elderly. Its inception predated the enactment of Medicare. By 1984, the poverty rate among the elderly had fallen to 14.4 percent. In addition, since then Medicare has helped those sixty-five and over to cope with the costs of hospitalization, surgery, nursing homes, and physician care. In large part, the double exemption has lost its purpose.

The extra exemption, $1,080 in 1986, aided only about half of the sixty-five-and-over group—those fortunate enough to possess income sufficient for taxation. The second exemption would have cost Treasury about $18 billion in uncollected revenue for the period 1987–1991.[8]

With the 1986 Tax Reform Act, Congress raised the personal exemption from $1,080 to $1,900, eliminated the full double exemption, but retained a smaller exemption of $600 for taxpayers sixty-five and over or blind in addition to the $1,900 exemption. That continued preference remains open to the same objections that led to the demise of the second exemption. Eliminating the preferential addition to the exemption would produce billions to add to the funding of SMI, three-quarters of which comes from general tax revenues. This change makes good tax policy (treating all income alike) and does not breach the basic principle that Social Security benefits are not needs-tested. Simultaneously, it trims back the tax package for those among the elderly who enjoy comparatively good incomes. Indeed, it pares away a provision that reduces the progressivity of the income tax, because the exemption is worth more to high-bracket than to low-bracket taxpayers.

Eliminating the Double Exemption for the Blind. Proposals for eliminating the additional exemption for the elderly often come yoked with the same proposal for the blind. The argument goes that neither age nor blindness reliably indicates financial need.

However, blindness does necessitate expenditures, such as care and maintenance of a guide dog, that other taxpayers of equal income do not require. Despite the high achievements of many blind people, coping with everyday life is more laborious and often requires paid help. The extra exemption for the blind is justifiable on that ground. Moreover, the cost of that exemption to the Treasury is minuscule—about one-fiftieth the amount involved in the double exemption for the elderly.[9]

Surcharge on Elderly Taxpayers. In 1986, to bolster the Medicare funds, the Harvard Medicare Project proposed a surcharge of 5 percent on the taxes paid by those sixty-five and over, in addition to eliminating the second exemption.[10] As already noted, among those sixty-five and over, receipt of income in sufficient amounts to warrant taxation indicates better than average income. Hence, a surcharge would tap those in the beneficiary group with ability to pay and yet identify them in an inobtrusive fashion. Moreover, a 5 percent surcharge on their income taxes also calibrates the amount according to the size of their taxable income. In this way, those with small taxable income would pay little. The amounts would become significant only for those with high income.

Such a tax would serve two purposes: it would increase funds available for the elderly, and it would meet the objection that those who do not need help receive it nonetheless for OASDHI. Unlike co-payments, which hit beneficiaries at times of greatest need, the tax would have its greatest impact at times when income is substantial. It has the further virtue that, as an earmarked tax, any increases to meet larger expenditures would generate resistance and so exercise restraint on expenses.

The major misgiving about the surcharge proposal, despite all of the justifications, is that it is open to the charge that it soaks the rich. In contrast, removal of the additional exemption discontinues a preference which has outlived its original justification. Nevertheless, a surcharge and removal of the additional exemption seem preferable to continuation of co-payments that have dubious utility and identifiable adverse effects.

Proposals to Tax Alcohol and Tobacco.   For some time commentators have proposed taxing alcohol and tobacco and contributing their proceeds to defray health-care costs.[11] In 1984, a majority of the Social Security Advisory Council, headed by former Indiana Governor Otis Bowen, later President Reagan's Secretary of Health and Human Services, advocated imposing such taxes and funneling their yield to the Hospital Insurance fund.[12]

Taxes on health-impairing substances serve two major purposes: by increasing the price to the consumer, they provide a financial incentive to reduce use and improve health; and they provide revenue to help offset costs of repairing or ameliorating the damage those substances cause.

It now seems well established that smoking, chewing, or sniffing tobacco constitutes a major cause of chronic lung disease, circulatory problems (including heart disease), and several kinds of cancers. Alcohol also causes diseases, such as cirrhosis of the liver, and is a major factor in automobile accident deaths and serious injury.

In addition to the suffering of the victims and their families, the conditions caused by the use of tobacco and alcohol result in enormous health-care expenditures for the immediate users and their victims (the "passive" smokers and the victim in the car that gets hit) and lost productivity and efficiency on the job because of increased absence rates.

Today the producers and users of alcohol and tobacco pay nothing for the extensive damage that they inflict—estimated in the tens of billions of dollars. If the costs of that damage were added to the purchase price of such goods, market forces would tend to discourage their use. The tax revenue would bolster the HI and SMI funds that foot a large part of the resulting bill. At present, these costs get paid from HI and other sources, such as automobile insurance rates imposed on all drivers. Some studies show that smokers contract lung disease from textile fibers and coal dust at a startlingly greater rate than do nonsmokers, but tobacco producers and users make no contribution to the Black Lung Fund or preventative measures in textile mills.

A 1985 survey and analysis by the congressional Office of Technology Assessment (OTA) found estimates of annual health-care expenditures attributable to tobacco use ranging between $12 and $35 billion; OTA's own middle estimate came in at $22 billion for 1985 alone. Included were estimated Medicare expenditures ranging between $1.7 to $5.4 billion and Medicaid costs of between $0.3 to $1.1 billion that year. OTA's estimated costs to the federal treasury of $0.2 billion equals 14 cents per pack. OTA's estimate of tobacco-caused productivity losses for one year ran from a low of $27 billion to $61 billion. Estimates for combined health-care costs and productivity losses range between $39 and $96 *billion* a year or, OTA says, $2.17 a pack for its middle-range estimate.[13] Nor do the OTA estimates take account of all losses attributable to tobacco use.

Reduced use of these substances would not necessarily result in net gains to OASDHI programs, however, and here the discussion takes a truly cynical turn. The question arises whether the increased mortality at an earlier age caused by tobacco and alcohol use does not in fact save more in benefits and medical services than in damages caused by them. OTA estimated that the tobacco-caused deaths in 1982 resulted in 5.3 million person-years lost—that is, the 186,000 to 398,000 people who died from tobacco-related diseases would have lived that many additional years without tobacco. Of that number, 1.2 million were for years lost before age sixty-five. Many of those deaths (we have seen no estimates) result in Social Security survivor benefit costs. The remaining 4.1 million lost years occurred to people after age sixty-five, most of whom received Social Security benefit payout over a shorter period of time than if they had lived longer. In addition, even if the health-care costs of tobacco deaths had been avoided, longer living people may incur equal or greater medical-care costs later in their lives.

However, as the OTA study points out, the earlier health-care costs and other losses caused by tobacco use must be compared with the delay in expenditures. What we do not pay for health care in any year is available to us for other purposes, including investment for greater productivity. The costs incurred by enterprises for health care for tobacco-caused illness and for increased absence act as a drag on those enterprises. The possibly larger costs of longer life may have a smaller present cost than tobacco-related health-care costs because of the investment factor. Only by using the "present value" of those future costs can we compare the costs of present and future illness. Even with longer life and possibly higher care and longer benefit costs, the economy might come out ahead financially by reducing the use of tobacco and alcohol.

The rationale for imposing higher excise taxes on tobacco and alcoholic beverages depends primarily on the proposition that users should pay for the extra costs that result from their conduct. If, on the other hand, use does not create net costs to the rest of us, then we have less excuse to tax users. It is, some might say, their funeral. But that is not wholly true. Smokers and drinkers impose health losses and cause injury and death to others and, for that additional reason, the rest of us have a right to curb them. Protecting the health and safety of nonusers also provides a powerful justification for a tax designed, in part, to discourage use. The current enthusiasm for healthful activity suggests that support for the tobacco and alcohol tax will grow. Loading the full costs of use upon users will cause some to curtail the extensive use that relatively low current prices permit. One might be willing to pay $1 for a pack of cigarettes but fewer will buy at $3.17 (a price that would include the $2.17 that one OTA estimate said would be the cost of damages caused).

The most practical and politically powerful argument against the "sin" taxes, as they are known, is that many make their bread and butter from smokes, booze, and beer. When on July 18 and 19, 1983, the Social Security Advisory Council held hearings on taxation, business and agricultural interests mustered considerable testimony[14] opposing the sin taxes on the grounds of feared job loss. A representative of cigar manufacturers argued that such a marginal business could be pushed off the edge by a tobacco tax. Tens of thousands of retailers and grocers sell these products and thousands of people are employed in their manufacture. It is little wonder that in the seven to six vote in favor of such a measure, the council members from the U.S. Chamber of Commerce and the National Federation of Independent Business joined with the president of the Retail, Wholesale, and Department Store Employees Union in opposition.[15]

Further, it is argued, such taxes bear most heavily on working people who constitute the bulk of smokers and beer drinkers. This objection might be met partially by imposing the alcohol tax by price rather than volume (the basis of the present federal taxes). In that way, the purchasers of the more expensive products would bear a larger portion of the burden and, even more important, the tax yield would grow apace with price inflation.

A sin tax might be somewhat out of sync with its effects. Although the tax would be collected on a current basis and available to the HI fund immediately, any health effects produced by less use would register in the health of large groups of people at some later time. To some that is not much of an objection because those who saved on purchases and so decreased their own ill health would reap the benefits, while current abusers who pay the tax would make a contribution—for the first time—toward the costs of their future health care.

Not all users are abusers, the argument goes on. While that may be so, use of tobacco and alcohol never improves health. Some argue that small amounts of alcohol have positive effects on heart disease or cholesterol levels, while others contend that even small amounts of alcohol upset the body's and brain's natural balance.

Tax policy considerations also enter the argument. The tobacco and alcohol industries argue that states depend on excise taxes collected from tobacco and alcohol for substantial amounts of their revenues. However, the evidence presented by the Distilled Spirits Council of the United States showed that *all* excise taxes produce on average only 4 percent of state revenues.[16] Given the enormous state expenditures for Medicaid,[17] diminished use of damaging products might reduce medical-care expenditures and so help offset the revenue reduction caused by a federal sin tax. The revenue loss would occur sooner than any Medicaid savings, but if a portion of the federal excise taxes were channeled into the Medicaid program to reduce the states' share, such reductions would offset the revenue loss on a current basis. A fuller Medicaid program also would add jobs in caring for the ill rather than in making people sick.

One traditional argument used against the sin tax claims that excise taxes do not make an assured source of revenue. But then, what does? We have seen that recession plays havoc with even the income tax and the payroll tax. So this traditional argument may have lost some of its traditional force.

Experience with the Greenspan Commission shows that when the need for additional revenue for Social Security becomes sufficiently sharp, the force of arguments against a particular method of raising it diminishes. So it may be with the sin taxes. If and when the need becomes sharp enough, this source of revenue can be tapped for Medicare, Medicaid, and, possibly, long-term care.

Diminishing the Program

Some would respond to cost problems by curtailing the program. Raising the age of eligibility and limiting the program's reach by imposing a needs test are the two major proposals to accomplish that goal. (Of course, much of the apparent "savings" would result in higher costs elsewhere—to patients and other programs.)

Raising the Eligibility Age. Raising the Medicare retirement eligibility age *would* save money for HI and SMI. A proposal to move that age from sixty-five to sixty-seven in two stages starting in the mid-1980s, if implemented, would have saved HI almost $75 billion by 1995 and SMI almost $5 billion through 1989.[18]

Proponents argue that Medicare's age of first eligibility has become less connected with the age of OASI eligibility as more people retire prior to age sixty-five before qualifying for Medicare. To others, that would seem to warrant *lowering* the eligibility age.

Since 1966, longevity has increased by more than three years (which many attribute in large measure to Medicare). This development, the proponents of raising the eligibility age argue, changes the dependency ratio of old to young, the same phenomenon that impelled the 1983 congressional decision to raise the OASI normal retirement age from sixty-five to sixty-seven during the next century. The 1982 Social Security Advisory Council embraced the notion, observing:

> Members did express some concern about alternative sources of health insurance coverage for persons 65 and over. While little hard data exist concerning the types

of health insurance currently purchased by early retirees, the fact that a substantial number do retire before the current age of Medicare eligibility indicates that protection is available in the marketplace. The final decision regarding the age of eligibility increase and its implementation was a function of the fiscal needs of the program balanced against selection of a reasonable length of time for future beneficiaries to adjust to the revised age.[19]

This combination of inadequate data and non sequitur that because people retire before age sixty-five they *can* obtain (not *do* obtain) protection "in the market place" seems inadequate for a policy decision so momentus as changing the eligibility age of Medicare. The recommendation by the council to raise Medicare eligibility to age sixty-seven does not seek to justify such a move as an incentive to delay retirement, a major justification for raising normal retirement age. Rather, the council noted that people do retire despite the unavailability of Medicare before age sixty-five.

Medicare came into being because older people could not obtain health insurance at affordable cost. Since Medicare's enactment, the cost of private coverage has risen—at a rate exceeding the cost of living. Indeed, the sharp increases in everyone's medical-care costs argue that, if anything, retirees need Medicare coverage more keenly than ever. More than that, the framers did not require retirement for eligibility, recognizing that even people still employed have difficulty in obtaining adequate coverage at affordable rates and that illness could quickly cause the loss of job and the health insurance that employment often provides.

The proposal to relate the age of eligibility for Medicare to increasing longevity ignores the adverse impact that putting Medicare out of the reach of millions would have on both personal finances and longevity. Presumably no part of the projected savings derives from higher death rates. But higher death rates at earlier ages would surely result. On this issue of Medicare's age of eligibility, the question of what we can afford is literally a question of life and death.

Conditioning Medicare on Demonstrated Financial Need. Proposals to condition Medicare on some specified low income would reduce the number of participants. Such proposals proceed on the assumption that large groups of people who obtain Medicare benefits can well afford other equivalent health insurance.

Given the extremely modest income of the bulk of OASI beneficiaries, the low rates of employment of people aged sixty-five and over, and the rapidly increasing costs of medical services of all kinds, the basic premise lies somewhere between flawed and wrong. Add the high cost of administering needs-tested programs, and that approach to cost cutting seems misguided.

All of the arguments against needs testing for Social Security retirement benefits (see chapter 9), apply equally to Medicare needs testing. Beyond that, the United States traveled that road with the Kerr-Mills program (MAA) in the 1960s and it worked badly, and proved disastrous for some state budgets.

The 1982 Advisory Council unanimously rejected needs testing for two major reasons: entitlement to benefits is a cornerstone of the program, and Medicare "represents a commitment by the American people to a fundamental social policy to assure that all members, including the elderly and the disabled, have adequate access to health care."[20] Access is the key and needs testing curtails access. Many proud elderly will not submit to the indignities of turning out their pockets for bureaucrats to judge their means. After a lifetime of work, such procedures become especially unacceptable.

Medicare Financing in Perspective

MEDICARE CALLED WORSE OFF THAN BELIEVED

BOARD PREDICTS MEDICARE BANKRUPTCY

Those were the messages in the *St. Louis Post-Dispatch* and the *New York Times* (April 2, 1986) atop stories reporting that the trustees of the Health Insurance trust fund had found some slippage in the financial outlook of Medicare. When put in perspective, the headlines seem absurd. Forecasts made in the 1982 trust fund trustees' report anticipated HI insolvency by 1986 under the II-B "best guess" set of forecasts.[21] By the 1983 report, that forecast had brightened considerably, predicting an exhaustion of funds in 1990.[22] The 1985 report showed a further improvement in fund prospects so that under the II-B estimates, "the HI Trust Fund is expected to remain solvent through calendar year 1998."[23] This dramatic change resulted from a slowing in medical price increases and better-than-predicted increases in employee earnings that produced more ample program payroll tax income. It was in this context that the trustees observed that instead of 1998, calculations in 1986 showed the possibility of running out of reserves by 1996.[24] The causes of this slight relapse occurring in so short a time are hard to isolate. While such a change warrants attention to future developments, the alarms sounded in headlines overstate its significance.

This recovery after the 1982 deathbed scene should tell us two important things: (1) panicky cries of Medicare crisis often exaggerate the case and undervalue the outlook for improvements; and (2) medical-care price increases can be slowed. In addition, the substantial period before the projected onset of HI insolvency means that we have breathing room in which to explore rationalizing the delivery of medical care. Only when we satisfy ourselves that we have done our utmost to limit costs should we choose between curtailing the program or paying more than we currently do for whatever more expensive program we decide we must have.

Before taking drastic steps that limit program services or load more costs on beneficiaries or other programs, we should consider measures to improve the future financial condition of the HI and SMI funds. Prime candidates for consideration are:

- Eliminating the additional exemption for those sixty-five and over;
- Stabilizing the payroll tax base by making all forms of compensation subject to FICA and SECA;
- Expanding the payroll tax base by extending coverage to all state and local employees;
- Taxing the use of health-impairing substances like tobacco and alcohol and channeling those funds to the Medicare and Medicaid programs.

Furthermore, rationalizing medical-care delivery would achieve savings that, combined with suggested improvements in income-producing measures, might make radical measures such as curtailing Medicare coverage or service unnecessary.

Living Longer: Beyond Medical Care

What an irony it is that so many regard lengthening life spans as a crisis rather than an opportunity. Most of us want to live as long as reasonably good health lasts. Now that we do live longer, this marvelous opportunity presents major problems. The longer we live, the greater our exposure to illness and accidents and increased medical-care costs.

Most of us will live longer than our forebears and most of us will spend some substantial portion of those lengthened lives without currently earned income. In addition, many of us will not be able to care for ourselves unaided for some portion of life. Much of the concern for the future centers on the expected growth of the older old; age seventy-five is usually the dividing line. Those eighty-five and over constitute the most rapidly growing group.

We must look for new solutions to meet the new needs of the older elderly. They will differ from the present elderly in at least one significant way—large numbers have enjoyed a lifetime of material comfort or affluence and so have higher expectations and demands than many of the current elderly.

Helping the Elderly Live Independently

Medicare and Medicaid provide assistance to the acutely injured or ill. With lengthening life, the number of elderly with chronic conditions and those with diminishing capacity for independent living will grow.

Not all older people are frail and dependent. Far from it. Most of the younger elderly retain their capacity to live independently and many can work—some perhaps not at full-time, full-year jobs, however. Most can cope with their everyday needs and then some. But with advancing years, one's capacity to do all one formerly did does diminish at some point.

The later years of life ought to be lived as fully and independently as possible. Independence means maximum autonomy consistent with the individual's capacity to cope. These goals have both financial and social dimensions.

The family has been and remains the principal support for helping to cope with life's problems at all ages. Even with increased mobility, families traditionally pitch in with financial help, solace, and practical assistance in times of need. However, new patterns reduce the capacity of young adult families to cope with long-term, perhaps long-distance, needs of their elders. Women have borne the brunt of caring for other family members, but today the increased number of women working for wages reduces their availability and the feasibility of redeploying them to care for older family members even if it were fair to fasten the burden unequally on them. Nonetheless, many do interrupt paid work to do such unpaid work.

Furthermore, the elderly's own children may be retired, another new phenomenon. This does not automatically mean that an eighty-six-year-old widow and her sixty-six-year-old daughter and sixty-nine-year-old son-in-law will want to live together. But we ought to explore how the common needs for care, companionship, and income of the younger and older elderly may be used to encourage cooperative living arrangements for those who might desire them. Numerous ideas have been under study and should generate new patterns to improve the opportunities for independent but cooperative living.

Many families already use the two-family and multi-family house to enable more than one generation of a family to live near but not with one another. But connected apartments, perhaps with some shared facilities, are either unknown or violate zoning laws. Shared facilities offer clear advantages over living alone, at one end of the spectrum, or living in an institution. Even the best institutions are expensive and impose some loss of autonomy.

Without prescribing any particular pattern, we ought to explore new arrangements for cooperative living and new means of encouraging them, in the interest of fuller lives and less expense. Architects and lawyers must be recruited to remove physical and legal barriers. Financial incentives for such new living arrangements also should be considered. Families who undertake care for their elderly must be able to obtain rest and recreation. Funds are probably needed to provide them with "days off," as a 1987 House-passed bill provides. Independent living serves human dignity while reducing the need and expense for institutionalization. All of us have a stake in promoting arrangements that encourage and support independence for the individual and the family.

Dilemmas Posed by the High Cost of Dying

About one-fourth of Medicare expenditures are attributable to illness within the last two years of life.[25] Obviously, large charges often result from final illnesses. Some believe that Medicare makes undue expenditures on heroic efforts during a last illness. Of course, providers cannot always tell whether an illness is terminal until the condition resolves one way or another. Moreover, how can we place a value on any additional period of life that results from heroic treatment?

In 1969, just a few days past his eightieth birthday, the father of one of the authors entered the hospital. Within a few days, he went into the intensive care unit fighting pneumonia. He weathered that immediate crisis with the aid of a pacemaker implant. Although it was clear that his chances for recovery had become zero, no amount of family pleading with the doctors could persuade them that they should not take additional heroic measures to "save" his life. When he actually did die, not quite two weeks after his admission to the hospital and still in intensive care, a doctor was again thumping his chest. For him and for the family, that was no way to die. For Medicare, it was fiercely expensive.

By contrast, in 1983, at age eighty-five, the same author's mother underwent a recommended gall bladder operation. Another attack, her physicians said, would produce a painful death. Although her tolerance for surgery, at that age and with a history of stroke, a heart condition, and high blood pressure, was problematic, there really was only one choice—to have the operation. The operation was performed; she recovered and lived independently another two productive years, during which she made an important difference in the lives of at least four of her seven grandchildren. Without Medicare, her modest savings, on which she needed to live during those years, would have been wiped out. When she did die, it was sudden and at home without doctors, hospitals, or other Medicare costs. Certainly Medicare enabled her to afford the medical care to survive emergencies and live an active life to the end.

These are the human dimensions. One provides an example of costly, painful, and useless efforts to extend life for a few days. The other illustrates costly, painful, and worthwhile efforts to extend life beyond age eighty-five for "only" two useful years.

Without Medicare, most people could not afford this kind of medical care. In its absence, tens of thousands of older people would die sooner rather than later.

A few decades ago, a high official of the British Health Service issued orders that heroic measures were not to be taken for people over eighty. Once known, the order caused a storm of protest and he soon withdrew it. More recently, then Governor Richard Lamm of Colorado asserted that some elderly should die and get out of the way of younger people, that sustaining their lives often was not justifiable. Again, a storm ensued; but some hailed the governor's "courage" in raising a prickly issue.

Most of us do not want government to choose who shall live and who shall die. We must realize that the decision not to provide care often decides between life and death. Yet the programs we adopt, the kinds of eligibility and benefits extended and withheld, have just such an effect. Somehow we are capable of ignoring the moral dimensions of that kind of decision—as when we decide that we cannot "afford" to assure long-term nursing home care or health insurance for the unemployed—a group under great stress and at high risk.

The full resolution of this knot of problems—including how to allocate "extraordinary" medical services and expensive medical technology for the very seriously ill—does not seem imminent. Yet, discussion has begun.

That discussion over who decides the issue of life and death and when it becomes permissible to withhold heroic efforts to continue life already has yielded developments. Some courts have sanctioned the removal of life-sustaining devices when brain death has been established. These decisions have probably emboldened physicians to issue orders not to employ heroic measures should a crisis develop for a patient close to death. Understandably, statistics on the extent of such practices are not available, but we now know that they occur.

In addition, families have been given greater power of decision in such matters. In the absence of health insurance and Medicare, families formerly had to choose whether to authorize efforts to save the severely ill. The entry of health insurance and Medicare often removed the family from such choices. Physicians, practically assured that third parties would pay for life-saving attempts, had no need to consult and obtain authorization. Now families are reentering the decision-making process. In a major development, the American Medical Association declared in 1986 that even if death is not imminent, life-sustaining efforts might properly be withheld from those with no hope of recovery. This sanction will almost surely encourage the withholding of extreme life-saving measures for some patients hopelessly beyond repair.

Several states have enacted legislation providing for living wills—directions by those of sound mind about their treatment in extreme circumstances—a

284

valuable safeguard against abuse, a possibly important element in future life-and-death decisions.

The hospice concept also may constitute a new force in dealing with final illness. A living will or an individual who retains the capacity to decide his or her own treatment can choose a course of care designed to ease pain and the process of dying. This saves the person making such a choice from the imposition of heroic measures that may impose useless suffering. Obviously, such a choice also saves the often substantial expenditures that accompany last-ditch medical measures. For several years, Medicare has been authorized to make payments for hospice care, but at amounts so low that they hardly encourage new institutions to enter the field. Furthermore, the requirement that the patient acknowledge that he or she is dying and agrees to forego all but pain-easing treatment severely limits the hospice alternative. We ought to consider less forbidding conditions.

New forces are at work. We have come to recognize the problems of sustaining life for brief periods at great cost and often much pain. We probably will never "solve" the moral and financial problems of last illnesses. But some progress has been made to provide choices in cases of terminal illness and also to reduce some of the heavy costs that often accompany it.

Medical Care for the Elderly: The Road Ahead

The Social Security cash program "crisis" dominated public debate in the first half of the 1980s. The public and Congress have yet to turn equal attention to the challenges and problems of Medicare. Those who think of them split into two camps. One group sees a specter of rising medical-care costs and an enlarging older population that will overwhelm Medicare. Another growing group of medical-care policy analysts are, figuratively speaking, out in the garage and down in the basement tinkering and thinking. Therein lies our hope. Medical care, Medicare, and Medicaid are only in the horseless carriage stage, sputtering, creating a racket, and scaring bystanders who expect the newfangled contraptions to explode. But better vehicles may be in the making. The provision of adequate medical care, especially for the elderly,* has become an expensive necessity, but, with prudent arrangements, we can afford what we need. There is really no alternative. Just how to achieve that grand goal is, we readily concede, not so clear.

* Providing access to adequate medical care for all age groups remains an urgent need. We are at work on a volume addressing that subject.

The principal culprits of cost inflation, cost reimbursement, and fee-for-service, combined with an oversupply of facilities and equipment make medical care expensive. At every hand we see new evidence of oversupply.

Fresh and determined efforts must be made to bring supply into balance with medical necessity as the principal means for curbing indiscriminate use of hospitalization and expensive equipment. Prescribing precisely how many hospital beds communities should have is not a science. Area served, transportation, density of population, population shifts, local needs due to climate, industry, and a host of other variables affect needs. Furthermore, we have no precise way to determine unnecessary use.

St. Louis might provide an example of the dilemma. In 1985, the city and county closed their hospitals and consolidated services at a formerly private hospital whose utilization had declined. That left a county hospital and an aging city hospital standing vacant. Not far away a vast new wing of a Veterans Administration (VA) hospital is being built. Yet within a decade, the World War II veterans for whom it is presumably being built will be less numerous, composed mostly of men in their seventies and eighties; succeeding groups of Korean and Vietnam War veterans are smaller yet. Before long, we shall have excess VA capacity. Meanwhile, the hospitals clustered around Washington University Medical School and St. Louis University find themselves with excess capacity, much of it of recent vintage. Not far away, other local hospitals, with diminishing populations, tout their services on billboards and television. Clearly, St. Louis has too many hospital beds and building the new VA wing and excess capacity at Children's Hospital seems wasteful and costly.

Surely steps could be taken to rationalize hospital use. Where public and private institutions do not run at or near capacity, it would make sense to make portions of both kinds of facilities available to the populations served by both, and remodel unneeded floors, wings, and whole buildings for different purposes.

After the bulge in the population of older veterans dies out during the next two decades, the need for VA hospital space will contract. Conceivably, we might convert those institutions, especially newer ones, and most particularly those on the drawing boards, to long-term care facilities, in preference to building a whole new set of institutions for that purpose. Where possible, they should be designed so as to be amenable to conversion. Similarly, civilians in currently underserved communities in proximity to VA hospitals should have access to those that have space to spare. Coordinating the services of VA and armed services medical care institutions with those in adjacent communities can achieve economies for both military and civilian care. Of course, not all service hospitals have excess capacity and many are not located where they can do civilian populations much good. But in many urban areas where VA hospitals, service hospitals, and private hospitals operate within hailing distance of one another, coordination should be sought in the interests of all providers and users.

Coordinating the needs and service of these and other health institutions could make available lower-cost service. That is not to say that accomplishing that coordination will be easy. But with such enormous health-care costs already upon us and with more in prospect, the heat is on. Yet, in a misguided fit of economizing, the Reagan administration proposed and Congress approved in 1986 shutting down the health planning councils that issued or withheld certificates of necessity for new health facilities. With the concurrent dismantlement of the federal Office of Health Planning and the National Health Planning Information Center, efforts to bring better balance between medical-care capacity and need suffered a major setback. We must restore or replace these mechanisms if we are to avoid reverting to the chaos that contributes so heavily to the inflation of medical-care prices.

Prepayment, DRGs, PPOs, and HMOs have been marshalled to help deal with the cost problems of fee-for-service and overexpanded/underutilized medical facilities. It remains to be seen whether these and other developments will brake the price juggernaut and at what price to consumers, for whom quality of service may suffer. But as one experienced hospital administrator said, paraphrasing Churchill, we are "just at the end of the beginning"[26] of efforts to control medical-care costs. Providers and employers are cost-conscious as never before. Insurers can hardly remain indifferent, for if they do, they may find that they have totally lost a market they could not serve at reasonable cost. Cost-control studies have become a virtual industry with economists, public health, and public policy specialists and consultants studying mechanisms and methods. These relatively new efforts, reinforced by business, congressional, and public awareness of the urgency of trimming production costs and curbing federal deficits, enhance chances to produce more rational organization, improve efficiency, and reduce abuse in the provision and pricing of health care.

We cannot be certain that such improvements will suffice to bring costs into balance with the funding available under current law and levels of expenditure. Even if it can, that hardly ends the inquiry about the future adequacy of Medicare, for we can hardly regard present costs to beneficiaries as satisfactory. Nor can we be complacent about unmet needs—the costs of catastrophic illness and long-term care that a growing elderly population makes more urgent. Fresh attention must be paid to supporting independent living in the interests of better lives and avoiding the high costs of institutionalization.

In 1985, national medical care expenditures totaled $425 billion, while Medicare expenditures came to $70 billion.[27] Accounting for less than 19 percent of total national health-care outlays, Medicare is not so dominant a factor as some discussions implicitly assume. Yet we must be concerned about the future when the older population will have doubled and many will live longer. Multiplying population growth by the growth rate of medical care cost presents a daunting prospect.

Taming the price tiger will take enormous and concentrated efforts. Many are determined that those efforts will be made. After we reduce costs and recognize the scope of our needs, the odds are that we will be agreeable to paying for what we decide we must have. Perhaps that will mean less fun and games earlier in life. But a growing economy may help improve income so that meeting our needs will not be unduly burdensome. Everyone has a large stake in adequate health care and support for independent living for the last years of life. The odds are that we will choose to arrange our affairs to provide them.

None of us knows his or her fate. Today's good fortune can turn into tomorrow's need. Today's good health can turn into tomorrow's disability. Most of us will gradually move from vigor to diminished capacity, and we will need help. All of us should ensure that such help will be there, just as we should extend help to those who need it today.

The prime method of doing so is called social insurance. And the doing of it is called civilization.

Envoi

While writing this book we have seen our parents, who are in their eighties, weather major health crises—cancer, heart disease, stroke, cataracts—that span the health concerns of most people. We became more aware of the changes in the lives of friends in their sixties and seventies as they contemplated retirement and shifted from full-time work to other enterprises, some involving paid work and some involving service. We became more aware of widows with teenage children and students who had lost parents. We caught some glimpses of the families of disabled adults, people whose predicaments most of us seldom see. Like many others, we have lived in a small laboratory of modern concerns over income and health.

What struck us most forcefully, in addition to the impressive fortitude and resilience of the human species, is that our society does not offer many comforting and fulfilling roles to older people. The exceptionally strong-willed and healthy carve out their own. Others drift or simply "exist" in what some call "God's Waiting Room."

By the time people are in their sixties, most cease full-time work and usually all paid work. Social Security and, to a lesser extent, pension plans and savings provide partial recompense. What is lacking, however, are affirmative patterns and roles for older people.

As we grow older, we experience gradual loss of physical capacity. Although we hardly see the daily changes, we do notice them at intervals. Even joggers slow down, switch to bikes, and eventually settle for walking. After a lifetime of labor, many people start their retirement with obviously diminished capacity, and a small minority with very poor health have to fight day in and day out simply to survive. Only the driven or the lucky keep working—some at jobs they find congenial, manageable, and productive, so that the roles they once performed still exist for them, even if somewhat modified.

But what of the majority of older people? In our society, the end of work, by and large, means the loss of both income and status. Our book addresses the need for income and health services in a society with an aging population. Crucial as those elements are, we also must create new roles for older people that carry status, that do not waste decades of experience, that promote vigor and enjoyment by offering purpose and satisfaction rather than, speaking metaphorically, endless shuffleboard. People differ enormously in their desires, needs, capacities, and potentialities. That is one of the fascinations of life. Clearly, we need a range of opportunities that match this fabulous human diversity.

We must stop looking at the elderly as a nonproductive burden. We mean no condescension to either young or old when we observe that society does not look upon children as unproductive burdens, even though, in strictly economic terms, they are. Nor do we simply value them as future producers of goods and services. No, we value them as human beings; we nurture them out of love and instinct; and we recognize that they are not supposed to support themselves until quite a bit later in life. We delight in their play. We marvel at their concerts, ooh and aah at their dramatic productions, cheer when they are on the field, chuckle at their dinner-table wit. Not infrequently we are caught up short by the moral issues they raise.

The elderly occupy a similar position in life despite the fact that many retain considerable capacity for productive work. Thus the first task of public policy is to promote opportunities, to those who are able and willing, to continue work however best they can. But failure to work does not mean that the elderly or the disabled no longer merit a full bowl. Do we cut the rations—material or emotional—of children before they can earn their own way? We must recognize that, after years of productiveness, human beings merit not only support (which they have earned by their labor) but the opportunity to play, to enjoy, to strive and amuse and guide, even if they do not bring home a paycheck.

We must bury the concept of burden and raise the flag of status. Older people, like their young counterparts, have a full claim to a share of current production. Equally important, they deserve our regard, respect, affection, and recognition for the fact that their years of labor have made possible our education, opportunities, and fuller lives, enabling us in turn to make provision for our children. Each generation owes much to its predecessors.

It is in the realm of opportunity that we need to exercise our imagination and efforts. We waste the capacity of the elderly at our cost. We must devote more attention to fresh roles for our grandparents, parents, and, eventually, for our older selves. We and they are indivisible.

A Short Guide to Social
Security Terms*

Auxiliary Benefits (13) The amounts payable to spouse, children, widow, or widower, calculated as a specified fraction of PIA.

Average Indexed Monthly Earnings (AIME) (10) The average of the amounts of credited earnings in Social Security–covered employment adjusted to the equivalent wage or salary just before retirement.

Bend Points (11) The benefit formula is composed of different rates applicable to the lower, middle, and upper portion of the AIME. The amount at which a different portion of the formula becomes applicable is called a bend point. (See this Guide, Primary Insurance Amount, and chapter 1, appendix A.)

COLA (14) Cost-of-living adjustment to maintain the purchasing power of benefits.

Delayed Retirement Credit (DRC) (17) The factor for additional cash benefits awarded for each period after normal retirement age (currently age sixty-five) during which an eligible person does not draw benefits. Under current law the annual increment is 3 percent. Starting in 1990, it increases slowly, reaching 8 percent after 2008.

Diagnostic-Related Group (DRG) (18) Classifications of illnesses and injuries promulgated by the Department of Health and Human Services designating the amount that HI will pay for a stay in a hospital for each such group. The payment is based upon assumed average stays. (See chapter 11.)

Disability Insurance (DI) (3) In 1956, Congress added Disability Insurance for severely disabled workers. OASI and DI are the two cash benefit programs of Social Security. When referred to in combination, OASI and DI become OASDI. The Social Security Administration manages both programs.

---

* Fuller explanations appear in the body of the book, especially in chapter 1. For more detailed descriptions consult the Index. This guide is arranged alphabetically for quick reference. If you want to read it in logical sequence, follow the numbers after each entry. (1) is Social Security.

Earnings/Retirement Test (15) The formula used to determine whether to reduce benefits for a recipient under age seventy. For each $2 of current earnings above a specified threshhold (in 1987, $6,000 a year for those under sixty-five receiving benefits, an amount that changes in proportion to the national average wage), benefits are reduced by $1. For those sixty-five through sixty-nine, the corresponding amount is $8,160. In 1990, that will become a $1 reduction for each $3 above the threshold for those at or above normal retirement age.

Federal Insurance Contributions Act (FICA) (5) It requires employees to make contributions from their pay and employers to pay equal rates of tax on specified amounts of wages or salary, up to $43,800 in 1987. FICA consists of three segments: 5.2 percent for OASI; 0.50 percent for DI; and 1.45 percent for HI, for a total of 7.15 percent. The employer remits both amounts to the U.S. Treasury.

Health Care Financing Administration (HCFA) (9) It oversees the administration of the Medicare (HI and SMI) programs. The Administrator of HCFA acts as secretary to their boards of trustees.

Medicare (4) Medicare consists of two parts. Part A, **Hospital Insurance (HI)** pays for hospital and skilled nursing facility services to beneficiaries; Part B, **Supplementary Medical Insurance (SMI),** covers costs of physicians' services.

Normal Retirement Age (NRA) (16) The age at which an insured employee becomes eligible for full benefits. The same age, sixty-five, now is used as the first age of eligibility for Medicare. Under current law, Medicare eligibility age will not rise with NRA. (The disabled also become eligible for Medicare.) Normal Retirement Age will go up to sixty-six in the first decade of the next century and to sixty-seven in the third decade. Current law makes no similar change for Medicare.

Old-Age and Survivors Insurance (OASI) (OASDI) (OASDHI) (2) In 1939, when Congress added survivor benefits for widows and children of insured workers the program became OASI. Later, it also provided benefits for widowers. OASDI includes Disability Insurance; OASDHI includes Hospital Insurance as well.

Primary Insurance Amount (PIA) (12) Applying the benefit formula (described in chapter 1 and its appendix A) to the AIME produces the PIA. It is the basis for figuring benefits.

Self-Employed Contributions Act (SECA) (6) It provides for tax collections from the self-employed. SECA's three segments equal the combined employer-employee FICA rates, with an income tax credit until 1990 when half of the total contribution becomes deductible for income tax purposes.

Social Security (1) The original 1935 act provided for benefits for retirees. That part of the act became known as Social Security. But other titles of the law provided for Old-Age Assistance (OAA), a needs-tested program for the elderly; and Aid to Dependent Children (ADC), which became Aid to Families with Dependent Children (AFDC), also known as "welfare." And yet another title established the federal/state Unemployment Insurance (UI) program, which pays Unemployment Compensation (UC).

Social Security Administration (SSA) (8) It administers the OASDI program.

A Short Guide to Social Security Terms

The Commissioner of Social Security is secretary to the Board of Trustees of the OASI and DI trust funds.

Trust Funds (7) Employers remit the FICA contributions to the U.S. Treasury, which credits them to the separate OASI, DI, and HI trust funds. A fourth trust fund for SMI receives premiums paid by Medicare Part B participants and general revenue payments. The premium is set so as to meet about 25 percent of the program's costs, and the remaining 75 percent comes from general revenue Treasury funds. In 1987, the basic monthly premium was $17.90. The secretaries of Treasury, Health and Human Services, and Labor, and two members of the public (from different political parties), serve as trustees for the four trust funds.

Notes

Each year the trustees of the several Social Security programs issue annual reports summarizing program activities, the status of the trust funds, and actuarial projections and the assumptions on which they are based. The reports also announce changes in critical program amounts, such as the "national average wage," and the program changes, such as taxable pay, which vary in tandem with that average wage. Rather than use the long titles of the reports by the trustees of the respective trust funds, we have adopted the following shorthand in these notes for the trustees' reports: Annual OASDI Report; Annual HI Report; Annual SMI Report.

Chapter 1

1. Paul H. Douglas, *Social Security in the United States* (1937; reprint, New York: Da Capo Press, 1971), chap. 4.

2. Paul Light, *Artful Work: The Politics of Social Security Reform* (New York: Random House, 1985) catalogues the repeated Republican attempts to curb Social Security between 1935 and 1982. He summarized the parties' records thus:

> On most of the votes, of course, Republicans were in the minority. Had they been able to win, social security would clearly have been a much smaller program, with lower benefit rates, lower taxes, and fewer covered workers. It would not have grown so generous. Of the 138 votes between 1935 and 1982, Republicans voted for *contraction* 73 times (53 percent) whereas Democrats voted for *expansion* 125 times (91 percent). (P. 100; emphasis in original.)

3. U.S. Senate, Special Committee on Aging, "The Impact of Gramm-Rudman-Hollings on Programs Serving Older Americans: Fiscal Year 1986" (Committee Print, S. Prt. 99-132, 1986), p. 9. SSI outlays totalled $10.97 billion, of which $0.719 billion were administrative expenses.

Chapter 2

1. Paul Light, *Artful Work: The Politics of Social Security Reform* (New York: Random House, 1985), p. 49.

2. Ibid., chap. 6 for a good summary. Although we often disagree with his analysis, Light presents a sprightly account of the commission's work.

3. Ibid., p. 70 for a summary of both polls.

4. Peter G. Peterson, "The Coming Crash of Social Security," *New York Review of Books*, December 2, 1982, p. 34; and December 16, 1982, p. 50.

5. Ibid., p. 50n4. We discuss the impact of immigration in chapter 3.

6. Alicia H. Munnell, "A Calmer Look at Social Security," *New York Review of Books*, March 12, 1983, p. 41.

7. *Report of the National Commission on Social Security Reform*, January 1983, chap. 2, p. 2.

8. Ibid.

Chapter 3

1. *New York Times*, November 30, 1980, editorial page; and April 7, 1981, editorial, p. A18.

2. U.S. General Accounting Office, "Social Security Actuarial Projections" (GAO/HRD-83-92, September 30, 1983), p. 23.

3. John C. Wilkin, Milton P. Glanz, Ronald W. Gresch, and Seung H. An, "Economic Projections for OASDI Cost Estimates, 1983," Office of the Actuary, Social Security Administration, Actuarial Study No. 90 (1984), p. 53. Figures rounded to nearest full percent.

4. Stephen C. Goss, "Long-Range Estimates of the Financial Status of the OASDI Program, 1983," Office of the Actuary, Social Security Administration, Actuarial Study No. 91 (April 1984), p. 6.

5. Stephen C. Goss, Milton P. Glanz, Seung H. An, "Economic Projections for OASDI Cost and Income Estimates, 1984," Office of the Actuary, Social Security Administration, Actuarial Study No. 94 (1985), table 10G for II-B assumptions.

6. U.S. Department of Commerce, Bureau of Census, "Fertility of American Women: June 1985," ser. P-20, no. 406 (June 1986), table 5, p. 26.

7. Vernon M. Briggs, Jr., "Employment Trends and Contemporary Immigration Policy," in Nathan Glazer, ed., *Clamor at the Gates: The New American Immigration* (San Francisco: ICS Press, 1985), p. 136.

8. Goss, "Long-Range Estimates of the Financial Status of the OASDI Program, 1983," p. 24.

9. Economic Policy Council of UNA-USA, *Illegal Immigration: Challenge to the United States* (New York: United Nations Association of the USA, December 1981), p. 2.

10. U.S. General Accounting Office, "Information on the Enforcement of Law Regarding Employment of Aliens in Selected Countries" (GAO/GGD-82-86, August 31, 1982).

11. President's Commission on Pension Policy, *Demographic Shifts and Projections: The Implication for Pension Systems* (Washington, D.C.: GPO, 1979), p. 29.

12. Cynthia M. Taeuber, "America in Transition: An Aging Society," *Current Population Reports*, ser. P-23, no. 128 (December 1983).

Notes

13. This discussion draws upon Edward Denison, *Accounting for Slower Growth* (Washington, D.C.: The Brookings Institution, 1979); Edward Denison, *Trends in American Economic Growth, 1929–1982* (Washington, D.C.: The Brookings Institution, 1985); Zvi Griliches, "R & D and the Productivity Slowdown," *American Economic Review* 70 (May 1980):347; Herbert Stein, "Why Did Consumption Not Reflect the Slackening of the Productivity Trend?" in William Fellner, ed., *Contemporary Economic Problems* (Washington, D.C.: American Enterprise Institute, 1979); William Fellner, "The Declining Growth of American Productivity: An Introductory Note," ibid., pp. 3, 11; John Kendrick, "Productivity Trends and the Recent Slowdown: Historical Perspective, Causal Factors, and Policy Options," ibid., p. 23; and Assar Lindbeck, "The Recent Slowdown in Productivity Growth," *The Economic Journal* 93 (March 1983):13.

14. U.S. Bureau of the Census, *1986 Statistical Abstract of the United States* (Washington, D.C.: GPO, 1986), p. 390: Those working in agriculture in 1984 numbered 3.3 million and constituted 3.1 percent of the labor force. U.S. Bureau of the Census, *Historical Statistics of the United States: Colonial Times to 1970*, H. Doc. 93-78 (1975), 1, 126. The farm working population in 1900 numbered 11 million and constituted 39 percent of the labor force.

15. Karen W. Anderson, "Productivity Study Implies Dim Future," *New York Times*, May 31, 1983, p. D1.

16. U.S. Bureau of the Census, *1985 Statistical Abstract of the United States* (Washington, D.C.: GPO, 1985), table no. 925, p. 542.

17. Annual Reports of the Board of Governors of the Federal Reserve System, 1969–84.

18. Amar Gupta and Hoo-min D. Toong, "Insights into Personal Computers," as quoted in the *New York Times*, July 2, 1985, p. 21.

19. Mark Perlman, "One Man's Baedeker to Productivity Growth Discussions," in William Fellner, ed., *Contemporary Economic Problems*, p. 15.

20. U.S. Congressional Budget Office, "The Economic and Budget Outlook: Fiscal Years 1988–1992," Report to the Senate and House Committees on the Budget (1987), part I, p. 106.
Chapter 3 presents a fine summary of the views reported in several economic analyses of macroeconomic factors. Their variety precludes drawing firm conclusions about either causes or cures.

21. Ibid., p. 20.

22. Lester Thurow, "The Elephant and the Maharajah," a review of Martin Feldstein's *Inflation, Tax Rules and Capital Formation*, in the *New York Review of Books*, December 22, 1983, p. 48.

23. *1986 Economic Report of the President*, table B-5, giving GNP in stable dollars.

24. Seymour Melman, *Profits Without Production* (New York: A. A. Knopf, 1983), p. 88.

25. Ibid., p. 6.

26. Ibid., p. 89.

27. Sar A. Levitan and Diane Werneke, *Productivity: Problems, Prospects and Policies* (Baltimore: The Johns Hopkins University Press, 1984), especially chap. 6.

28. Y. P. Chen, "The Growth of Fringe Benefits," *Monthly Labor Review* (November 1981):4.

29. *Employee Benefit Research Institute News*, February 12, 1985. Some of this change might be ascribed to rapidly rising stock prices.

30. A Congressional Research Service report by Geoffrey Kollman, "Social Security and Tax-Free Fringe Benefits," reports on p. 9 that other analysts share this view.

31. Alicia Munnell, "Social Security and the Budget," *New England Economic Review* (July–August 1985):10.

32. This discussion draws largely upon Alicia H. Munnell and Lynn E. Blais, "Do We Want Large Social Security Surpluses?" *New England Economic Review* (September–October 1984):5. This splendid article lays out with great clarity the arguments for and against accumulating surpluses. Noneconomists can handle this discussion. It kindly segregates a mathematical section that is not central to understanding the many points made in the body of the piece.

33. For a brief description of "crowding out" see James Tobin, "How to Think about the Deficit," *New York Review of Books*, September 25, 1986, pp. 44–45.

34. For a similar analysis see the U.S. General Accounting Office's "Social Security: Past Projections and Future Financing Concerns" (GAO/HRD-86-32, March 1986), pp. 65–66. The report took no position on the desirability of this or other alternative courses.

35. David Koitz, "Favorable Projections Raise Fiscal Policy Questions," *Congressional Research Service Review* 7 (July–August 1986):26.

Chapter 4

1. Murray Webb Latimer, *Industrial Pension Systems in the United States and Canada* (New York: Industrial Relations Counselors Incorporated, 1932).

2. For example, Vallejo v. American R.R. Co. of Porto Rico, 188 F.2d 513 (C.A. 1, 1951); and "Consideration for the Employer's Promise of a Voluntary Pension Plan," *University of Chicago Law Review* 23 (1955):96. This article traces the wearisome road from the gratuity theory to enforceability of plan promises by employees meeting plan-imposed age and length-of-service conditions.

3. For example, Karcz v. Luther Mfg. Co., 338 Mass. 313, 155 N.E. 2d 441 (1959).

4. See Edwin Patterson, *Legal Protections for Private Pension Expectations*, published for the Pension Research Council, Wharton School of Finance and Commerce, University of Pennsylvania (Homewood, IL: R. D. Irwin, 1960), pp. 65–66.

5. IRC sec. 410(b)(1)(A).

6. IRC sec. 401(a)(5). See also Gary Boren, *Qualified Deferred Compensation* § 6:01 (Wilmette, IL: Callaghan, 1983).

7. *Social Security Bulletin, Annual Statistical Supplement* (1971), p. 82.

8. U.S. Bureau of the Census, *1947 Statistical Abstract of the United States* (Washington, D.C.: GPO, 1947), table no. 230, p. 211.

9. See, for example, Merton C. Bernstein, *The Future of Private Pensions* (New York: Free Press/Macmillan, 1964).

10. Ibid., pp. 200–202.

11. Ibid.

12. Robert Metz, "Workers Finding Pensions Empty," *New York Times*, August 16, 1964, sec. 3, p. 11.

13. Harold L. Sheppard, Louis A. Ferman, and Seymour Faber, "Too Old to Work, Too Young to Retire: A Case Study of a Permanent Plant Shutdown," U.S. Senate Special Committee on Unemployment Problems, 86th Cong., 1st sess. (Washington, D.C.: GPO, 1960).

14. Miriam A. Ourin, "Post Layoff Experiences: Republic Aviation Workers" (Washington, D.C.: U.S. Arms Control and Disarmament Agency, 1967).

15. President's Committee on Corporate Pension Funds and Private Retirement and Welfare Programs, *Public Policy and Private Pensions* (Washington, D.C.: GPO, 1965).

16. Summarized in Michael Gordon, "Overview: Why Was ERISA Enacted?" in *The Employee Retirement Income Security Act of 1974: The First Decade* (S. Prt. 98-221, 1984), chap. 1, p. 15.

17. Ibid., p. 17.

Chapter 5

1. 29 U.S.C. § 1001–1461 (1974).

2. 29 U.S.C. § 1052(a)(1)(A)i (1985).

3. 29 U.S.C. § 1052(b)(3) (1985).

4. 29 U.S.C. § 794 (1986).

5. See M. C. Bernstein, "Litigation, Representation and Claimant Protection in Workers Compensation," in *Research of the Interdepartmental Workers Compensation Task Force*, vol. 4 (Washington, D.C.: U.S. Dept. of Labor, Employment Standards Administration, 1979), p. 161.

6. G. Lawrence Atkins, *Spend It or Save It? Pension Lump-Sum Distributions and Tax Reform* (Washington, D.C.: Employee Benefit Research Institute, 1986), chap. 4.

Chapter 6

1. "Since 1969 the share of U.S. employment represented by manufacturing industries has fallen—from 25 percent to 19 percent in 1985. Since 1979 the level of manufacturing employment has fallen as well." Lynne E. Browne, "Taking in Each Other's Laundry— The Service Economy," *New England Economic Review* (July–August 1986):20.

2. *New York Times* (national edition), October 22, 1984, pp. 21–22.

3. Emily S. Andrews, *The Changing Profile of Pensions in America* (Washington, D.C.: Employee Benefit Research Institute, 1985), table I.3, p. 15. This analysis predates the 1984 requirement lowering the mandatory participation age from 25 to 21. Taking account of the change would enlarge the ERISA work force and lower the coverage rates because such a large proportion of young people work in low-pay jobs outside pension coverage.

4. *Wall Street Journal*, November 9, 1984, p. 6.

5. *New York Times*, October 12, 1984, p. 31.

6. "G.M.'s Obsession with Size," *New York Times* (national edition), November 8, 1986, p. 17.

7. Paul O. Flaim and Ellen Sehgal, "Displaced Workers of 1979–83: How Well Have They Fared?" *Monthly Labor Review* (June 1985):3.

8. Letter to the authors from Richard Ippolito, Assistant Administrator, Office of Policy and Research, U.S. Department of Labor, September 27, 1984. He stated that in the 1983 Census Survey, ". . . about five percent of all covered workers reported that they were eligible to receive benefits based on vested service from a prior employer."

9. U.S. General Accounting Office, "Pension Integration: How Large Defined-Benefit

Plans Coordinate Benefits with Social Security" (GAO/HRD-86-118BR, July 1986) summarizes the available studies.

10. G. Lawrence Atkins, *Spend It or Save It? Pension Lump-Sum Distributions and Tax Reform* (Washington, D.C.: Employee Benefit Research Institute, 1986), chap. 4. Based on a household survey census in 1983, it found that 0.043 percent placed their distribution into a "retirement program," and another 0.07 percent purchased an "insurance annuity." Another 0.159 percent invested in some "financial instrument;" 0.098 percent applied the distributed funds to a house purchase. In sum, about one-third (37 percent) used the distribution for some form of saving, with but 0.05 percent applying it directly to retirement purposes (table IV.5).

11. All data from David L. Kennell and John F. Shields, "The Potential Impact of the Senate Finance Committee Tax Reform Proposals on Retirement Incomes in Future Years," ICF, Inc. (processed April 7, 1986), table 6.

12. EBRI's October 1986 "Issue Brief" strongly suggests that these factors will diminish the scope of private plans.

13. U.S. General Accounting Office, "Interim Report" (GAO/HRD-85-82, June 24, 1985).

14. U.S. General Accounting Office, "Pension Plans: Termination of Plans with Excess Assets" (GAO/HRD-86-89BR, 1986), p. 5.

15. U.S. General Accounting Office, "Pension Plans: Plans with Excess Assets" (GAO/HRD-86-100BR, May 1986), p. 2.

16. "Pension Plan Asset Raids," Hearings before House of Representatives Select Committee on Aging, 98th Cong., 1st sess. (Washington, D.C.: GPO, 1983), 12–13 (hereafter, "1983 House Hearings"). Those plans constituted about two-thirds of all large plans.

17. Ibid., p. 82, testimony of UAW actuary Howard Young.

18. A management attorney speaking at a conference on labor law at Duke University Law School, November 1984, attended by a coauthor.

19. U.S. Government Accounting Office, "Funding of State and Local Plans: A National Problem" (HRD-79-66, 1979).

20. "IRAs: Characteristics and Policy Implications," EBRI Issue Brief no. 32, July 5, 1984.

21. U.S. Senate, Special Committee on Aging, *The Employee Retirement Income Security Act of 1974: The First Decade* (Committee Print, S. Prt. 98-221, 1984), pp. 37–38.

Chapter 7

1. For example, a Conference Board official, commenting on a study of discretionary income, referred to "the affluence of the new old." Quoted in an AP story in the *St. Louis Post-Dispatch*, December 17, 1985, pp. 1, 13. The study is discussed in the text to note 11 of this chapter.

2. A *New York Times* report of a Council of Economic Advisers' study on income of the elderly observed that, "the report says that the average elderly couple is wealthier than the rest of the population, receives as much income and pays lower taxes." (February 6, 1985, p. D7.) And a story in the *Washington Post* "Outlook" section declared: "America's elderly are now better off than the population as a whole." (January 5, 1986, p. D1.)

3. Daniel B. Radner, Studies in Income Distribution, no. 14: "Changes in the Money

Notes

Income of the Aged and Nonaged, 1967–1983" (hereafter, "Radner's 1967–1983 Study"), Social Security Administration, Office of Policy and Office of Research, Statistics and International Policy, 1986.

4. Nancy D. Ruggles and Richard Ruggles, "The Anatomy of Earnings Behavior," in F. Thomas Juster, ed., *The Distribution of Economic Well-Being* (Cambridge, Mass.: Ballinger [for the National Bureau of Economic Research], 1977), chap. 4.

5. A 1984 study presents in detail the "Income of the Population 55 and Over" as it stood in 1982, often arranged by age groups. It constitutes the best resource for analyzing the financial situation of older Americans and enables us to consider the quite differing situation of those who draw Social Security (beneficiaries) and those who do not (non-beneficiaries). Susan Grad, "Income of the Population 55 and Over, 1982," Social Security Administration, Office of Retirement and Survivors' Insurance and Office of Policy, SSA Publication No. 13-11871 (Washington, D.C.: GPO, March 1984). Radner's 1967–1983 study (cited in note 3) presents more recent data and very useful analysis. The conclusions reached here on comparisons of the aged and nonaged, written before the publication of the Radner study, are supported fully by it. However, unlike the earlier study, it does not present separate data for Social Security beneficiaries and nonbeneficiaries or a breakdown by age groups within the fifty-five-plus sector. Hence, the Grad material remains more pertinent here.

We did not use a later similar publication by Susan Grad, "Income of the Population 55 and Over, 1984," SSA Publication No. 13-11871 (Revised December 1985) because it lumps "Social Security and public assistance" into one category at crucial places such as table 43. Separately stated data for Social Security are crucial. Moreover, our study of the new tables and consultation with a Social Security Administration expert confirm that the patterns in 1982 and 1984 do not differ in any significant way. Further, the 1982 data show how things stood when the Commission on Social Security Reform was operating.

6. "Economic Goals Cited by Reagan," *New York Times*, February 6, 1985, p. D14.

7. Robert D. Hershey, Jr., "Modern Myths About Elderly," *New York Times*, February 6, 1985, p. D2.

8. *1985 Annual Report of the Council of Economic Advisers* (Washington, D.C.: GPO, 1985), chap. 5.

9. *New York Times*, January 5, 1985, p. D1.

10. "One-Third of Americans Have Money for Extras," *St. Louis Post-Dispatch*, December 17, 1985, pp. 1–13.

11. The Consumer Research Center (The Conference Board and the U.S. Bureau of the Census), "A Marketer's Guide to Discretionary Income" (CRC 8511, n.d., but released in December 1985).

12. The Grad study is based on an extensive household survey. Commentators often question the accuracy of questionnaire data, particularly that concerning money income. Some assert that older respondents tend to understate money received. These critics rely upon a study by Daniel B. Radner entitled "Adjusted Estimates of the Size Distribution of Family Money Income for 1972," Social Security Administration, Office of Research and Statistics, October 1981, Working Paper No. 24, pp. 15–17. Applying cross checks with other data sources, he found understatement of cash income, most significantly among the wealthiest. In the lower-income groups, underreporting was negligible. Still, at median income, those sixty-five and over showed greater underreporting than younger groups.

13. U.S. General Accounting Office, "Benefit Levels of Nonfederal Retirement Programs" (GAO/GGD-85-30, 1985), p. 7, appendix 1.

14. Social Security Administration, Office of Policy and Office of Research, Statistics and International Policy, "The 1982 New Beneficiary Survey" (NBS), published in nine parts starting with the *Social Security Bulletin* of November 1983 and continuing in various issues through July 1985.

15. U.S. Bureau of the Census, "Current Population Survey, March 1983" (American Housing Survey for the Department of Housing and Urban Development, 1983); U.S. Federal Reserve Board, "1983 Survey of Consumer Finances" (1983).

16. Katherine R. Levit et al., "National Health Expenditures, 1984," *Health Care Financing Review* 7 (Fall 1985):10.

17. Daniel R. Waldo and Helen C. Lazenby, "Demographic Characteristics and Health Care Use and Expenditures by the Aged in the United States: 1977–1984," *Health Care Financing Review* 6 (Fall 1984):8.

Chapter 8

1. "The New Definition of Old," *Washington Post* (national weekly edition), June 10, 1985, p. 8.

2. Abraham Epstein, *Insecurity: A Challenge to America* (New York: H. Smith and R. Haas, 1933), chap. 26.

3. U.S. Department of Labor, "Findings from the Survey of Private Pension Benefit Amounts" (1985); U.S. General Accounting Office, "Retirement Age before 65 is a Growing Trend in the Private Sector" (1985); and U.S. General Accounting Office, "Features of Non-federal Retirement Programs" (1984). This last found that most private plans surveyed gave unreduced pensions at age sixty-two.

4. Thomas D. Leavitt, "Early Retirement Incentive Programs," Policy Center on Aging, Brandeis University, December 1983; processed.

5. "Retirement Offer for 4,000 at Xerox," *New York Times* (national edition), October 16, 1986, p. 32.

6. The New Beneficiary Survey (NBS) gathered data on income sources of those who first went on the OASI rolls from mid-1980 through mid-1981. Nine reports summarizing the findings appeared in various issues of *Social Security Bulletin*, November 1983 through 1985. For a sketch see Linda Drazga Maxfield, "The New Beneficiary Survey: An Introduction," *Social Security Bulletin* 46 (November 1983):3.

7. Sally R. Sherman, "Reported Reasons Retired Workers Left Their Last Job: Findings from the New Beneficiary Survey," *Social Security Bulletin* 48 (March 1985):23.

8. For example, see chapter 5 of Henry J. Aaron, *The Economics of Social Security* (Washington, D.C.: the Brookings Institution, 1982); and Mildred Doering, Susan R. Rhodes, and Michael Schuster, *The Aging Worker* (Beverly Hills, CA: Sage Publications, 1983).

9. Henry Aaron, *Economics of Social Security*, p. 57, reports:

> ... most empirical studies have concluded that Social Security reduces labor supply of elderly workers, but the size of the estimated effect varies, and some studies conclude that Social Security has increased labor supply or had no important effect on it. All the studies have been based on household survey data.

10. Philip Rones, "The Retirement Decision: A Question of Opportunity?" *Monthly Labor Review* 103 (November 1980):14.

11. Dena K. Motley, "Availability of Retired Persons for Work: Findings from the Retirement History Study," *Social Security Bulletin* 41 (April 1978):25–26.

12. Howard M. Iams, "Employment of Retired-Worker Women," *Social Security Bulletin* 49 (March 1986):7.

13. Sally R. Sherman, "Reported Reasons Retired Workers Left Their Last Job: Findings From the [1982] New Beneficiary Survey," *Social Security Bulletin* 48 (March 1985):22; Joseph Quinn, "The Microeconomic Determinants of Early Retirement," *Journal of Human Resources*, (Summer 1977):329, found that some with satisfactory health nonetheless gave poor health as the major reason for retiring. Cited and discussed in a fine review of "To Work or Not to Work" in James Schulz, *The Economics of Aging*, 3rd ed. (Belmont, CA: Wadsworth, 1985), p. 57.

Chapter 9

1. For a knowledgeable and detailed discussion of pension problems and proposals, we recommend Phyllis C. Borzi, "A National Retirement Income Policy: Problems and Policy Options," *University of Michigan Journal of Law Reform* 19 (Fall 1985):5ff. In our view, Ms. Borzi, pension counsel to the U.S. House Committee on Labor and Education, overstates the extent of coverage of private plans. Nor does she question private plan performance or potentialities sufficiently. Nonetheless, we recommend the article as a fine and informative contribution to the policy debate.

2. President's Commission on Pension Policy, *Coming of Age: Toward a National Retirement Income Policy* (Washington, D.C.: GPO, 1981).

3. Proposed and discussed in Merton C. Bernstein, *The Future of Private Pensions* (New York: Free Press/Macmillan, 1964), chap. 10.

4. This section is based on Alicia H. Munnell and Joseph H. Grolnic, "Should the U.S. Government Issue Index Bonds?" *New England Economic Review* (September–October 1986):3.

5. William C. Greenough, *A New Approach to Retirement Income* (New York: Teachers Insurance and Annuity Association, 1952).

6. Zvi Bodie, "Purchasing-Power Annuities," Working Paper No. 442 (Cambridge, Mass.: National Bureau of Economic Research, February, 1980), p. 11.

7. See, for example, Emily S. Andrews, *The Changing Profile of Pensions in America* (Washington, D.C.: Employee Benefit Research Institute, 1985). "A number of studies have shown that postretirement increases did not keep up with inflation during the late 1970s, although benefit increases were frequently granted on an ad hoc basis," citing Robert L. Clark et al., *Inflation and the Economic Well-being of the Elderly* (Baltimore and London: The Johns Hopkins University Press, 1984), pp. 28–48.

8. "Estimates of Federal Tax Expenditures for Fiscal Years 1987–1991" (JCS Joint Committee Print 7-86, 1986), table 1. These amounts were based on the tax brackets and rates that applied in 1986.

9. Congressional Budget Office, "Reducing the Deficit: Spending and Revenue Options: A Report to the Senate and House Committees on the Budget—Part II" (Washington, D.C.: GPO, 1987), p. 233.

10. Ibid., pp. 230–231.

11. Ibid., p. 230.

12. Emily S. Andrews, *The Changing Profile of Pensions in America* (Washington, D.C.: Employee Benefit Research Institute, 1985), p. 166.

13. "Poverty Rate Increase," Hearings before the Subcommittee on Oversight and Subcommittee on Public Assistance and Unemployment Compensation of the Committee on Ways and Means of the U.S. House of Representatives, 98th Cong., 1st sess., 1983, 239–240.

14. Congressional Budget Office, "Reducing the Deficit: Spending and Revenue Options, A Report to the Senate and House Committees on the Budget—Part II" (Washington, D.C.: GPO, March 1986), p. 294.

15. Susan Grad, "Income of the Population 55 and Over, 1982," Social Security Administration, Office of Retirement and Survivor's Insurance and Office of Policy, SSA Publication No. 13-11871 (Washington, D.C.: U.S. Government Printing Office, March 1984), p. 31, table 13.

16. A study in Missouri concluded that fewer than half of all eligibles obtained food stamps; fewer than one-quarter asked for surplus commodities; about one-third of the eligibles received benefits under the Women's Infants and Children (WIC) program; and about half the eligible children participated in the school lunch program. A Texas state representative declared that the food stamp program had to be made "available" and "respectable." *New York Times* (national edition), February 8, 1986, p. 8.

17. Derived from U.S. Senate, Special Committee on Aging, "The Impact of Gramm-Rudman-Hollings on Programs Serving Older Americans: Fiscal Year 1986" (Committee Print, S. Prt. 99-132, 1986), p. 9. For another example, see Donald E. Rigby and Charles Scott, "Low-Income Energy Assistance Program," *Social Security Bulletin* 46 (January 1983):11.

18. Recounted in Samuel H. Preston, "Children and the Elderly in the U.S." (hereafter, "Preston's Children"), *Scientific American* 251 (December 1984):48.

19. Barbara A. Lingg, "Social Security Benefits of Female Retired Workers and Two-Worker Couples," *Social Security Bulletin* 45 (February 1982):2.

20. Material in this section derives largely from two excellent volumes: "Report on Earnings Sharing Implementation Study" of the Subcommittee on Social Security of the U.S. House of Representatives' Committee on Ways and Means (Committee Print, 99th Cong., 1st sess., WMCP 99-4, 1985); and Congressional Budget Office, "Earnings Sharings Options for the Social Security System" (Washington, D.C.: GPO, 1986).

21. Congressional Budget Office, "Earnings Sharings Options for the Social Security System," chap. 4.

22. The Supreme Court has vacillated on the question of congressional power to require states to observe federal law in matters pertaining to state and local employees. In 1968, the Court held valid a federal statute requiring states to comply with the hours limitations and overtime pay requirements of the Fair Labor Standards Act (Maryland v. Wirtz, 392 U.S. 183, 1968). But hardly a decade later, the Court overruled that decision, holding that the Tenth Amendment prevented the exercise of such congressional power. (National League of Cities v. Usery, 426 U.S. 833, 1976.) The latest word came in Garcia v. San Antonio Metropolitan Transit Authority, 469 U.S. 258 (1985), overruling National League of Cities. Under the present state of constitutional doctrine, legislative power to require state and local governments to participate in Social Security appears free from doubt.

23. Martin Feldstein, "Social Security Induced Retirement and Aggregate Capital Accumulation," *Journal of Political Economy* 82 (September–October 1974):905–926.

24. Dean R. Leimer and Selig D. Lesnoy, "Social Security and Private Savings: A Reexamination of the Time Series Evidence Using Alternative Social Security Wealth Variables," Office of Research and Statistics, Working Paper, Department of Health, Education and Welfare, 1980.

25. See, for example, Alicia H. Munnell, *The Economics of Private Pensions* (Washington, D.C.: The Brookings Institution, 1982), p. 85.

26. Louis Esposito, "Effect of Social Security Review of Studies Using U.S. Time-Series Data," *Social Security Bulletin* 41 (May 1978):18.

27. Robert B. Avery, Gregory E. Elliehausen, and Thomas Gustafson, "Pensions and Social Security in Household Portfolios: Evidence from the 1983 Survey of Consumer Finances" (hereafter, "1983 Household Portfolio Study"), Research papers in Banking and Financial Economics (Washington, D.C.: Board of Governors of the Federal Reserve System, October 1985), p. 30.

28. Henry Aaron, *The Economic Effects of Social Security* (Washington, D.C.: The Brookings Institution, 1982) pp. 51–52.

29. Both are summarized in Munnell, *The Economics of Private Pensions*, p. 88.

30. Robert Lampman, *Balancing the Books: Social Spending and the American Economy* (Washington, D.C.: National Conference on Social Welfare, 1985), p. 41.

31. Edward Denison, "Interruption of Productivity Growth," *The Economic Journal* (March 1983):720.

32. Munnell, *The Economics of Private Pensions*, p. 90.

33. Aaron, *Economic Effects of Social Security*, p. 10.

Chapter 10

1. Michael D. Hurd and John B. Shoven, "The Distributional Impact of Social Security," in David Wise, ed., *Pensions, Labor and Individual Choice* (Chicago: University of Chicago Press, 1985).

2. Robert J. Myers and Bruce D. Schobel, "A Money's-Worth Analysis of Social Security Retirement Benefits," Society of Actuaries, *Transactions* 35 (1983):533.

3. 1986 OASDI Trustees Report, p. 122.

4. Alicia Munnell, review of Peter J. Ferrara, ed., *Social Security: Prospects for Real Reform* (Washington, D.C.: Cato Institute, 1985), in *Journal of Policy Analysis and Management* (forthcoming, 1987).

5. Dan Dorfman, "Funds Have Lost Bundles This Year," *St. Louis Post-Dispatch*, October 21, 1984, p. 1E.

6. Dan M. McGill with Donald S. Grubbs, Jr., *Fundamentals of Private Pensions*, 5th ed. (Homewood, IL: Richard D. Irwin, 1984), p. 435.

7. "Why Money Managers Don't Do Better," *Business Week* (February 4, 1985): 58.

8. Vartanig G. Vartan, "Picking Stocks for S & P 500," *New York Times* (national edition), May 21, 1986, p. D8.

9. "Why Money Managers Don't Do Better," *Business Week* (February 4, 1985): 58.

10. "Investors Open '86 Confidently," *New York Times* (national edition), January 2, 1986, p. 21.

11. Michael Blumstein, "How the Institutions Rule the Market," *New York Times*, November 25, 1984, p. F21.

Chapter 11

1. As this book goes to press, Congress is considering setting limits on patient out-of-pocket expenses under HI. The House of Representatives passed such a bill; the Senate probably will, too. Whether the outcome will prove acceptable to the president remains to be seen.

2. U.S. House of Representatives, Committee on Ways and Means, Subcommittee on Health, announcement of hearings, June 3, 1982.

3. Department of Health and Human Services, Report to the President, "Catastrophic Illness Expenses" (November 1986), p. 29.

4. Both changes are codified in 29 U.S.C. 623(g) as amendments to the Age Discrimination in Employment Act which applies to employers with at least twenty employees. It would be useful to determine whether, given the election, employment in the age groups changed more in enterprises subject to the provision than in those exempted.

A draft study for HCFA by Joseph M. Anderson, David L. Kennell, and John F. Shields, "Health Plan Costs, Medicare, and Employment of Older Workers," tentatively concluded that the 1982 amendments would have slight "aggregate" effect (n.d., ca. 1986). The memo observed that some employees might be under pressure to refuse coverage so as to increase chances of employment.

5. Arnold Epstein et al., "The Use of Ambulatory Testing in Prepaid and Fee-for-Service Group Practice," *New England Journal of Medicine* 314 (April 24, 1986):1089, found some evidence of greater use in large fee-for-service groups.

6. David Aquilina, "Assessing HMO Performance," *Health Affairs* 3 (Winter 1984): 138–143.

7. Congressional Budget Office, "Reducing the Deficit: Spending and Revenue Options; A Report to the Senate and House Committees on the Budget—Part II" (hereafter, "1987 CBO Options") (Washington, D.C.: GPO, 1987), p. 247.

8. Congressional Budget Office, "Reducing the Deficit: Spending and Revenue Options; A Report to the Senate and House Committees on the Budget—Part II" (Washington, D.C.: GPO, 1986), p. 294.

9. Ibid.

10. Harvard Medicare Project, *Medicare: Coming of Age, a Proposal for Reform* (Cambridge, Mass.: Division of Health Policy Research and Education, Harvard University, 1986). A synopsis appeared as "Special Report: The Future of Medicare," *New England Journal of Medicine* 314 (March 13, 1986):722.

11. See, for example, Merton C. Bernstein, "A Unified System for Compensation and Care of the Disabled," (testimony before the President's Commission on Pension Policy, Washington, D.C., January 12, 1981).

12. "Medicare: Benefits and Financing," Report of the 1982 Advisory Council on Social Security (hereafter, "1982 Advisory Council Medicare Report") (Washington, D.C.: GPO, 1984), pp. 32–34.

13. "Smoking-Related Deaths and Financial Costs," U.S. Congress, Office of Technology Assessment, staff memo (September 1985).

14. 1982 Advisory Council Medicare Report, pp. 214–216.

15. Ibid., p. 299.

16. Ibid., p. 216.

17. In 1984, states expended about $17.5 billion on Medicaid (1986 Statistical Abstract of the United States, table 598, p. 357).

Notes

18. 1982 Advisory Council Medicare Report, pp. 36–38.

19. Ibid., p. 37.

20. Ibid., p. 88.

21. Social Security Administration and Health-Care Financing Administration, "Summary of the 1982 Annual Report of the Social Security Boards of Trustees," processed April 1, 1982, p. 10.

22. 1983 HI Annual Report, p. 40.

23. 1985 HI Annual Report, p. 2.

24. 1986 HI Annual Report, p. 9. Under the pessimistic set of assumptions, the prospects improved; fund exhaustion would occur in 1993 under the 1986 report rather than in 1992 as projected in the 1985 report.

25. James Lubitz and Rhonda Prihoda, "The Use and Costs of Medicare in the Last 2 Years of Life," *Health Care Financing Review* 5 (Spring 1984):117. The data are for 1978, before Medicare provided limited hospice care.

26. Kevin Halpern, "Impact of DRGs on Inner-City Hospitals," 1983 Conference Proceedings, *Diagnosis-Related Groups: The Effect in New Jersey, the Potential for the Nation*, HCFA Pub. No. 03170 (Washington, D.C.: U.S. Department of Health and Human Services, 1984), p. 189.

27. Daniel Waldo, Katherine Levit, and Helen Lazenby, "National Health Expenditures, 1985," *Health Care Financing Review* 8 (Fall 1986):8.

Index

* NOTE: The term Social Security is indicated by S.S.

Index

Fuller, Mary Falvey, 37–38, 48; and COLA, 51

"fully insured" status, 23–24

Future of Private Pensions, The (Bernstein), 103; 298*n*9; 303*n*3

General Accounting Office: on ERISA, 139

GI Bill of Rights: and medical care, 254

Glanz, Milton P., 296*nn*3, 5

GNP: growth expectations for, 76; movements of (table), 78; projections for, 78–79; in recession years, 76–77; and S.S. contributions, 242, 243

Gordon, Michael, 107; 299*nn*16, 17

Goss, Stephen C., *xii*; 296*nn*4, 5, 8

government pensions: of aged sixty-five and over, 166–69

Grad, Susan, 163, 166, 168, 169, 206, 207; 301*nn*5, 12; 304*n*15

Gramm-Rudman: exempts S.S., 83

Great Depression, 94

Greenberg, Edward, *xi*

Greenough, William C., 200; 303*n*5

Greenspan, Alan, 37, 39; and consensus package, 48–49; and National Commission negotiations, 44

Gresch, Ronald W., 296*n*3

Grolnic, Joseph, *xi*, 244; 303*n*4

gross national product, *see* GNP

Grubbs, Donald S., Jr., 244; 305*n*6

Gupta, Amar, 297*n*18

Gustafson, Thomas, 305*n*27

Gwirtzman, Milton, 243

Halpern, Kevin, 307*n*26

Hansen, Lori, 39–40

Harootyan, Linda K., 186

Harris poll: on S.S., 42

Harvard Medicare Project, 306*n*10

health care: basic choice, 152

Health Care Financing Administration (HCFA), 29, 262; defined, 292

health insurance: costs of, 257; as fringe benefit, 80; and Medicaid, 172; for older people at work, 263–64; private, basic structure of, 255–56

Health Maintenance Organizations, *see* HMOs

Heinz, Sen. John, 37, 40, 121, 123

Hershey, Robert D., Jr., 301*n*7

HI, 15–16; beginning of, 259; benefit procedures of, 261; coverage, 260; defined, 292; eligibility for, 260–61; premiums for, 16; provisions of, 259; revenue source of, 16; sources of financing, 260

HI trust fund, 29

higher retirement age, 183–88; and DI, 187; and ill health, 186–88; lower benefits of, 184–86; and similar benefits, 190–91; and S.S., 173; *see also* normal retirement age

Hill-Burton program, 256

Hirshorn, Barbara A., 186

HMOs, 269–71

Hohaus, Reinhard, 10, 214

home ownership: of elderly, 171

"horizontal inequities," 103

hospices, 285

Hospital Insurance (under Medicare), *see* HI

hospitals: coordinating services of, 286–87

housing: and income adequacy, 171–72

H.R. 10s, *see* Keoghs

human dignity: and needs test, 210

Hurd, Michael D., 305*n*1

Hutton, Bill, 39

Iams, Howard M., 183; 303*n*12

ICF projections, 138–39

immigration, 67–70; characteristics of, 67; and dependency ratio, 70; illegal, 68–69; impact of on S.S. assumptions, 67–68; and ineffectiveness of employer sanctions, 69; legislation affecting, 69; and work force, 61

Immigration and Naturalization Service: small work force of, 69

income: of aged fifty-five through sixty-one, 164; of aged sixty-five and over, 165–67;

Index

Waldo, Daniel R., 302*n*17; 307*n*27
war years: birth rate during, 35
Washington Post, 159; and definition of "old," 176
Weaver, Carolyn, 39
"weighting" of benefit formula, 19–21
welfare, 13–14; defined, 292
Welfare and Pension Plan Disclosure Act (1958), 140
Werneke, Diane, 77; 297*n*27
Wheeling Steel-Pittsburgh Steel Corporation: pension plan of, 113–14
White House staff: and consensus package, 49
Wickenden, Elizabeth, 40
widow(ers): disabled (table), 58; divorced (table), 58; and OASDI, 20; *see also* earnings sharing
Wilkin, John C., *xii*, 183; 296*n*3
"windfall" benefits, 52–54; to pension plan participants, 203
Wolff, Edward, 75
women: and care burdens, 282; and "currently insured" status, 24; as displaced employees, 133; as earners, 237–38; and earnings sharing, 218–25; and employment turnover, 98; as heads of households, 162; and incentives to work, 65; income patterns of, 157–58; in labor force, 64; new work/retirement patterns of, 216–24; and pension coverage, 130–31, 138; as pension losers, 125; pension status of (table), 183; and reasons for retirement, 181; and Retirement Equity Act (1984), 109; and second pensions, 182; and S.S. benefits, 4, 12, 217; and S.S. reform, 50; as widows, 139
"Women and Social Security" (Reno), 217
"women's jobs," 216
Woodruff, Thomas C., 148
work ethic, 74
work force: size of, 63–66
World War II: and medical care, 254; and pension plans, 94; and U. S. economy, 11

Young, Howard, 39